The Animation History Bibliography

By Orrin Scott

Scott, Orrin. The Animation History Bibliography.
    Hardcover First Edition. 2022. ISBN-13: 9798419545267.
    Paperback First Edition. 2022. ISBN-13: 9798825657578.
    Also available online at CartoonResearch.com.

Cover Design by Jose De Jesus Salcedo.

The font used throughout this book is Open Sans, designed by Steve Matteson.
It was downloaded through Google Fonts and is licensed under the Apache License, Version 2.0.

Thank You;

To my Parents who've supported my path of animation studies and done so much for me.

To my Sister who has been my editorial rock and my idea wall.

To Jerry Beck whose encouragement, advice, and support made this book so much better.

To every author whose work is contained within.

To my local postal office workers who delivered many, many books for the creation of this bibliography.

And to my friends, especially Alec, Arthur "Irish" T., Chase, Dallas, Dylan, Eric, Heather F., Kari W., Zack, my coworkers and customers at Pitt Stop, and every single person along this journey who put up with my tales of wrestling this book into creation and inspired me with their own stories of creativity and achievements.

Table of Contents

Introduction - Page 7

About the Bibliography - Page 9

The Animation History Bibliography - Page 10
Reference Books - Page 10
Guides - Page 19
Multi-Volume Series - Page 27
Conferences - Page 34
Animation General Studies - Page 39
Genre - Page 47
Computer Generated Animation History - Page 50
Stop-Motion Animation and Puppetry - Page 54
Aesthetics, Abstraction, and Experimental Animation - Page 56
Industry - Page 59
History - Page 63
Culture - Page 66
Saturday Mornings - Page 70
Religion, Spirituality and Ethics - Page 71
Environment - Page 72
Voice Acting, Foley, Music and Sound - Page 73
Storyboarding and Production - Page 77
Individual Studios, Artists, and Figureheads - Page 79
Individual Series and Movies - Page 92
The Art of Individual Artists and Single Topics - Page 104

Disney - Page 108
Walt Disney - Page 108
Notable Artists & Individuals at Disney - Page 114
Industry and the Disney Corporate and Studio Structure - Page 119
Disney Productions - Page 126
The Art of Disney - Page 136
Culture and Disney - Page 144
Disney Music - Page 147
History and Disney - Page 149

Pixar - Page 151
The Art of Pixar - Page 154
The Art of 20th Century Animation and 20th Television Animation - Page 157
The Art of DreamWorks - Page 158
Nickelodeon - Page 161
The Art of Nickelodeon Studios - Page 162
The Art of Frederator Studios - Page 164
Warner Bros. General Studies- Page 165
The Art of Warner Animation Group - Page 167
Hanna-Barbera General Studies – Page 168
The Art of Cartoon Network Studios - Page 170
The Art of Williams Street Productions - Page 172
The Art of Sony Pictures Entertainment - Page 173
The Art of Columbia Pictures - Page 175
The Art of MGM Studios - Page 175
The Art of Netflix - Page 175
The Art of Illumination - Page 176
The Art of Blue Sky Studios - Page 176
The Art of Aardman Animations - Page 177
The Art of Baobab Studios - Page 177
The Art of Cartoon Saloon - Page 178
The Art of LAIKA - Page 179

Anime - Page 180
Guides and Reference Books - Page 180
Industry - Page 185
Individual Movie, Series, Studios, and Notable Artists - Page 188
History - Page 191
Hayao Miyazaki and the Work of Studio Ghibli - Page 192
The Art of Studio Ghibli - Page 197
General Anime Studies - Page 199
The Art of Anime - Page 206

World Animation History - Page 210

Global Perspectives - Page 210
The Arab World - Page 212
Argentina - Page 212
Australia - Page 213
Bulgaria - Page 213
Canada - Page 213
China - Page 214
Czech Republic - Page 216
Czechoslovakia - Page 216
Estonia - Page 216
France - Page 217

Germany - Page 217
Great Britain - Page 217
Italy - Page 219
Malaysia - Page 219
The Middle East - Page 219
New Zealand - Page 219
Russia - Page 220
Singapore - Page 221
South Africa - Page 221
Switzerland - Page 221

Juvenile Literature - Page 222
Non-Fiction Texts - Page 222
Storybooks - Page 235

Comic Books & Manga - Page 239

Periodicals - Page 242
Western Animation - Page 242
Anime - Page 245

Academic Journals - Page 247

Animation History Documentaries - Page 250

Index - Page 262

Introduction

I started this project in March of 2020 when it became apparent that the COVID-19 pandemic would be a part of our lives longer than what was hoped. I needed a project to embrace through the end of the pandemic or, at the very least, until the end of social distancing and isolation.

While a majority of the work for this book was done in the last two years, the idea for a bibliography had been gestating in the back of my head for quite a bit longer. Since I was little, the search for books on animation has been an ongoing pursuit. For the longest time, I didn't think there were many books on the subject because how few I had come across. It wasn't until I put together a list of resources to share at a meeting of ASIFA Central in January of 2020 that I started to seriously entertain compiling a list of animation books.

While my intention for the information in this book is to help as many artists, business people, laymen, and researchers as possible, its origins stem from a personal endeavor. I wanted to know what books were out there about animation. Prior to the completion of this book, I could not find many on my own and, if asked, I would have said there were less than a hundred titles on the subject. In this first edition, the total number of individual titles represented is approaching 1,400!

The books contained here range from topics such as historical non-fiction to the importance of Saturday mornings, from the professional world of the industry to the pioneering world of independents, and the art of everything in between. There are books that look at animation through the lens of dance, architecture, and technological censorship, books that explore the triumphs and setbacks of women and people of color, and books that celebrate the accomplishments of the young and the old.

The reason I decided to call this book *The Animation History Bibliography*, as opposed to anything else, is because of the wide range of topics covered in the following titles. The titles in this book give us a view of what the last century of this art form has accomplished, how it's changed our culture and our society, and what it has allowed ourselves to express to one another. Some of the following titles transcribe how animation has morphed and adapted as technology has evolved. It's all of our history...in animation.

This is not the end-all be-all book about animation books. Even as I put the finishing touches on this book, awesome authors in the world are documenting what's changing and worth noting in animation today. Other books written during the pandemic are also debuting now. This book is already out of date before it has even reached your hands. Plus, while I have attempted to mediate as many factual errors, there will inevitably be an annoying error somewhere therein. However, thanks to Jerry Beck, this bibliography also lives online at CartoonResearch.com where it will continue to evolve. Please join us in that conversation!

Thank you, Reader! Enjoy *The Animation History Bibliography*!

As for me, I've got some cartoons and books to catch-up on....

Orrin Scott

About the Bibliography

In creating this bibliography there is a conscious effort to include any and all publications on the subject of animation; regardless of communal and scholarly reputation. If a title was available in North America and in English, it is included.

Titles are separated into groups of similar topics. These categorizations are but lines in the sand, meant for the reader to peruse easier and they are not meant to be taken as a definitive judgment of a book's contents. Some titles could have been placed in more than one category, but they were only listed once.

In the case of multiple authors, the authors are alphabetized by last name. In the cases of titles that are compendiums of articles by many authors, the editor(s) of the work is listed. In the case of periodicals, either the founder of the publication or the first Editor-in-Chief is listed. Titles without listed authors will be found under "N" for N/A.

An additional book listed under a title indicate a change in book name, but not content.

eBooks, Audiobooks, and Books on Media are included as proof of existence. However, due to the many different digital platforms available for downloading, as well as the creation and dissolution of contractual timed exclusives, additional information made available is limited to release date, publisher, and Narrator (If applicable). It is up to the reader to discover current availability on the platforms and in the formats of your preferred choice.

Publications are written in the following format:

Author's Last Name, First Name. Additional Authors Alphabetically (If present). *Title of Publication*. Type of Binding and Edition. Publisher. Year Published. ISBN-10: XXXXXXXXXX. ISBN-13: XXXXXXXXXXXXX.

> Additional Editions (If Applicable). Publisher. Year Published. ISBN-10: XXXXXXXXXX. ISBN-13: XXXXXXXXXXXXX.

If information is omitted, it is unavailable or non-existent.

Reference Books

Baisley, Sarah. *1997 Animation Industry Directory*. Paperback First Edition. Animation Magazine. 1997. ISBN-10: 189101000X. ISBN-13: 9781891010002.

Baisley, Sarah. *Animation Industry Directory 1998*. Paperback First Edition. Animation Magazine. 1998. ISBN-13: 9789990810325.

Baisley, Sarah. *Animation Industry Directory 1999-2000*. Paperback First Edition. Animation Magazine. 1999. ISBN-10: 1891010018. ISBN-13: 9781891010019.

Baisley, Sarah. *Animation Industry Directory 2001*. Paperback First Edition. Animation Magazine. 2001. ISBN-13: 9781891010026.

Baisley, Sarah. *Animation Industry Directory 2002*. Paperback First Edition. Animation Magazine. 2002. ISBN-10: 1891010042. ISBN-13: 9781891010040.

Beck, Jerry. *The 50 Greatest Cartoons: As Selected by 1,000 Animation Professionals*. Hardcover First Edition. Turner Publishing, Inc. 1994. ISBN-10: 187868549X. ISBN-13: 9781878685490.

Beck, Jerry. *The 100 Greatest Looney Tunes Cartoons*. Hardcover First Edition. Insight Editions. 2010. ISBN-10: 1608870030. ISBN-13: 9781608870035.

> Hardback Second Edition. Insight Editions. 2020. ISBN-10: 1647221374. ISBN-13: 9781647221379.

Beck, Jerry. *The Animated Movie Guide*. Paperback First Edition. Chicago Review Press. 2005. ISBN-10: 1556525915. ISBN-13: 9781556525919.

> eBook. Chicago Review Press. 2005.

Beck, Jerry. Friedwald, Will. *The Warner Bros. Cartoons*. Hardcover First Edition. Scarecrow Press. 1981.

> Hardcover Reprint. Scarecrow Press. 1988. ISBN-10: 0810813963. ISBN-13: 9780810813960.

Looney Tunes and Merrie Melodies: A Complete Illustrated Guide to the Warner Bros. Cartoons. Paperback First Edition. Henry Holt. 1989. ISBN-10: 0805008942. ISBN-13: 9780805008944.

Hardcover Second Edition. Scarecrow Press. 1997.

Davis, Jeffery. *Children's Television, 1947-1990: Over 200 Series, Game and Variety Shows, Cartoons, Educational Programs, and Specials*. Hardcover First Edition. McFarland & Company, Inc. Publishers. 1995. ISBN-10: 0899509118. ISBN-13: 9780899509112.

Paperback Reprint Edition. McFarland & Company, Inc. Publishers. 2011. ISBN-10: 0786467266. ISBN-13: 9780786467266.

Dobson, Nichola. *A to Z of Animation and Cartoons, The A to Z Guide Series*. Paperback First Edition. Scarecrow Press. 2010. ISBN-10: 081087623X. ISBN-13: 9780810876231.

eBook. Scarecrow Press. 2010.

Dobson, Nichola. *Historical Dictionary of Animation and Cartoons (Volume 34)*. Hardcover First Edition. Scarecrow Press. 2009. ISBN-10: 0810858304. ISBN-13: 9780810858305.

Hardcover Second Edition. Rowman & Littlefield Publishers. 2020. ISBN-10: 1538123215. ISBN-13: 9781538123218.

eBook. Rowman & Littlefield Publishers. 2020.

Eatock, James. *He-Man and She-Ra: A Complete Guide to the Classic Animated Adventures*. Hardcover First Edition. Dark Horse Books. 2016. ISBN-10: 1506700640. ISBN-13: 9781506700649.

eBook. Dark Horse Books. 2016.

Edera, Bruno. *Full Length Animated Feature Films*. Hardcover First Edition. Hastings House. 1984. ISBN-10: 803823177. ISBN-13: 9780803823174.

Erickson, Hal. *A Van Beuren Production: A History of the 619 Cartoons, 875 Live Action Shorts, Four Feature Films and One Serial of Amedee Van Beuren*. Paperback First Edition. McFarland & Company, Inc. 2020. ISBN-10: 1476680272. ISBN-13: 9781476680279.

> eBook. McFarland. 2020.

Erickson, Hal. *Television Cartoon Shows: An Illustrated Encyclopedia, 1949 Through 2003*. Hardcover First Edition. McFarland & Company, Inc. Publishers. 1995. ISBN-10: 0786400293. ISBN-13: 9780786400294.

> Two Volume Set. Hardcover Second Edition. McFarland & Company, Inc. Publishers. 2005. ISBN-10: 0786420995. ISBN-13: 9780786420995.

> Two Volume Set. Paperback Second Revised Edition. McFarland & Company, Inc. Publishers. 2016. ISBN-10: 1476665990. ISBN-13: 9781476665993.

Faber, Liz. Walters, Helen. *Animation Unlimited: Innovative Short Films Since 1940*. Paperback First Edition with DVD. Harper Design. 2004. ISBN-10: 1856693465. ISBN-13: 9781856693462.

Farago, Andrew. *Totally Awesome: The Greatest Cartoons of the Eighties*. Hardcover First Edition. Insight Editions. 2017. ISBN-10: 1608877132. ISBN-13: 9781608877133.

Finch, Christopher. Rosenkrantz, Linda. Sotheby's. *Sotheby's Guide to Animation Art*. Paperback First Edition. Henry Holt & Co. 1998. ISBN-10: 0805048545. ISBN-13: 9780805048544.

Frierson, Michael. *Clay Animation: American Highlights 1908 to Present*. Hardcover First Edition. Twayne Publishers. 1994. ISBN-10: 0805793275. ISBN-13: 9780805793277.

> Paperback First Edition. Twayne Publishers. 1994. ISBN-10: 0805793283. ISBN-13: 9780805793284.

Gardner, Ph. D., Garth. *Gardner's Guide to Multimedia & Animation Studios: The Industry Directory*. Paperback First Edition. Garth Gardner Company. 2001. ISBN-10: 0966107586. ISBN-13: 9780966107586.

Paperback Second Edition. Garth Gardner Company. 2003.
ISBN-10: 1589650204. ISBN-13: 9781589650206.

Gifford, Denis. *American Animated Films: The Silent Era, 1897-1929*. Hardcover First Edition. McFarland Publishing. 1990. ISBN-10: 0899504604. ISBN-13: 9780899504605.

Gifford, Denis. *The Great Cartoon Stars: A Who's Who*. Hardcover First Edition. Jupiter Books. 1979. ISBN-10: 0904041344. ISBN-13: 9780904041347.

Gitlin, Martin "Marty". Wos, Joseph. *A Celebration of Animation: The 100 Greatest Cartoon Characters in Television History*. Hardcover First Edition. Lyons Press. 2018. ISBN-10: 1630762784. ISBN-13: 9781630762780.

> eBook. Lyons Press. 2018.

Hilty, Greg. *Watch Me Move: The Animation Show*. Paperback First Edition. Merrell Publishers. 2010. ISBN-10: 1858945585. ISBN-13: 9781858945583.

> Paperback Second Edition. Merrell Publishers Limited. 2011. ISBN-10: 1858946239. ISBN-13: 9781858946238.

Hischak, Thomas S. *100 Greatest American and British Animated Films*. Hardcover First Edition. Rowman & Littlefield Publishers. 2018. ISBN-10: 1538105683. ISBN-13: 9781538105689.

> eBook. Rowman & Littlefield Publishers. 2018.

Horn, Maurice. *The World Encyclopedia of Cartoons (6 Volumes + 1 Index)*. Paperback First Edition. Chelsea House Publishers. 1979. ISBN-10: 0877541213. ISBN-13: 9780877541219.

> Hardcover Second Printing. Chelsea House Publishers. 1980. ISBN-10: 0877540888. ISBN-13: 9780877540885.
>
> Hardcover First Edition. Gale Research Co. 1980. ISBN-10: 0877540977. ISBN-13: 9780877540977.
>
> Revised Hardcover Volume One. Chelsea House Publishers. 1999. ISBN-10: 0791048535. ISBN-13: 9780791048535.

Revised Hardcover Volume Two. Chelsea House Publishers. 1999.
ISBN-10: 0791051854. ISBN-13: 9780791051856.

Revised Hardcover Volume Three. Chelsea House Publishers. 1999.
ISBN-10: 0791051862. ISBN-13: 9780791051863.

Revised Hardcover Volume Four. Chelsea House Publishers. 1999.
ISBN-10: 0791051870. ISBN-13: 9780791051870.

Revised Hardcover Volume Five. Chelsea House Publishers. 1999.
ISBN-10: 0791051889. ISBN-13: 9780791051887.

Revised Hardcover Volume Six. Facts On File, Incorporated 1999.
ISBN-10: 0791051897. ISBN-13: 9780791051894.

Revised Hardcover Volume Seven. Facts On File, Incorporated 1999.
ISBN-10: 0791051900. ISBN-13: 9780791051900.

Kilmer, David. *The Animated Film Collector's Guide: Worldwide Sources for Cartoons on Videotape and Laserdisc*. Paperback First Edition. Indiana University Press. 1998. ISBN-10: 1864620021. ISBN-13: 9781864620023.

Lenburg, Jeff. *The Encyclopedia of Animated Cartoon Series*. Hardcover First Edition. Arlington House Publishers. 1981. ISBN-10: 0870004417. ISBN-13: 9780870004414.

Paperback Second Edition. DaCapo Press. 1983. ISBN-10: 0306801914. ISBN-13: 9780306801914.

Paperback First Edition. Facts on File. 1991. ISBN-10: 0816027757. ISBN-13: 9780816027750.

Lenburg, Jeff. *The Encyclopedia of Animated Cartoons*. Hardcover First Edition. 1999. ISBN-10: 0816022526. ISBN-13: 9780816022526.

Hardcover Second Edition. 1999. Facts on File. ISBN-10: 0816038317. ISBN-13: 9780816022526.

Paperback Second Edition. Checkmark Books. 1999. ISBN-10: 0816038325. ISBN-13: 9780816038329.

Hardcover Third Edition. Facts on File. 2008. ISBN-10: 0816065993. ISBN-13: 9780816065998.

Paperback Third Edition. Checkmark Books. 2008. ISBN-10: 0816066000. ISBN-13: 9780816066001.

Lenburg, Jeff. *Who's Who in Animated Cartoons: An International Guide to Film and Television's Award-Winning and Legendary Animators*. Paperback First Edition. Applause Theatre & Cinema Books. 2006. ISBN-10: 155783671X. ISBN-13: 9781557836717.

eBook. Applause Theatre & Cinema Books. 2006.

Lent, John. *Animation, Caricature, and Gag and Political Cartoons in the United States and Canada: An International Bibliography*. Hardcover First Edition. Greenwood Publishing Group, Inc. 1994. ISBN-10: 0313286817. ISBN-13: 9780313286810.

Levitan, Eli L. *Animation Techniques and Commercial Film Production*. Hardcover First Edition. Reinhold Publishing Corporation. 1962.

Levitan, Eli L. *Electronic Imaging Techniques: A Handbook Of Conventional And Computer-Controlled Animation, Optical, and Editing Processes*. Hardcover First Edition. Simon & Schuster. 1977. ISBN-10: 0442247710. ISBN-13: 9780442247713.

Levitan, Eli L. *Handbook of Animation Techniques*. Hardcover First Edition. Van Nostrand Reinhold. 1979. ISBN-10: 0442261152. ISBN-13: 9780442261153.

Lotman, Jeff. *Animation Art at Auction: Recent Years*. Hardcover First Edition. Schiffer Publishing. 1998. ISBN-10: 0764304119. ISBN-13: 9780764304118.

Lotman, Jeff. *Animation Art: The Early Years, 1911-1954*. Paperback First Edition. Schiffer. 1995. ISBN-10: 0887407633. ISBN-13: 9780887407635.

Lotman, Jeff. Smith, Jonathan. *Animation Art: The Later Years, 1954-1993*. Hardcover First Edition. Schiffer Publishing, Ltd. 1996. ISBN-10: 0887409792. ISBN-13: 9780887409790.

Mangels, Andy. *Animation on DVD: The Ultimate Guide*. Paperback First Edition. Stone Bridge Press. 2003. ISBN-10: 188065668X. ISBN-13: 9781880656686.

McCall, Douglas L. *Film Cartoons: A Guide to 20th Century American Animated Features and Shorts*. Hardcover First Edition. McFarland & Company, Inc., Publishers. 1998. ISBN-10: 0786405848. ISBN-13: 9780786405848.

    Paperback Reprint Edition. McFarland & Company, Inc., Publishers. 2005. ISBN-10: 0786424508. ISBN-13: 9780786424504.

Osmond, Andrew. *100 Animated Feature Films*. Hardcover First Edition. British Film Institute. 2011. ISBN-10: 1844573400. ISBN-13: 9781844573400.

    eBook. British Film Institute. 2019.

    Hardcover Revised Edition. British Film Institute. 2022. ISBN-10: 1893024410. ISBN-13: 9781839024412.

    Paperback Revised Edition. British Film Institute. 2022. ISBN-10: 1839024429. ISBN-13: 9781839024429.

Pallant, Chris. *Animation: Critical and Primary Sources*. Hardcover First Edition. Bloomsbury Academic. 2021. ISBN-10: 1501305751. ISBN-13: 9781501305757.

Perlmutter, David. *The Encyclopedia of American Animated Television Shows*. Hardcover First Edition. Rowman & Littlefield Publishers. 2018. ISBN-10: 1538103737. ISBN-13: 9781538103739.

    eBook. Rowman & Littlefield Publishers. 2018.

Pettigrew, Neil. *The Stop-Motion Filmography: A Critical Guide to 297 Features Using Puppet Animation*. Hardcover First Edition. McFarland & Company, Inc., Publishers. 1999. ISBN-10: 0786404469. ISBN-13: 9780786404469.

    Paperback First Edition - Two Volume Set. McFarland & Company, Inc., Publishers. 2007. ISBN-10: 0786431075. ISBN-13: 9780786431076.

Robinson, Chris. *Animators Unearthed: A Guide to the Best of Contemporary Animation*. Paperback First Edition. Bloomsbury Academic. 2010. ISBN-10: 826429564. ISBN-13: 9780826429568.

Roncarelli, Robi. *The Computer Animation Dictionary: Including Related Terms Used in Computer Graphics, Film and Video, Production, and Desktop Publishing*. Paperback First Edition. Springer. 1989. ISBN-10: 0387970223. ISBN-13: 9780387970226.

    Paperback Reprint. Springer. 2011. ISBN-10: 1461236711. ISBN-13: 9781461236719.

    eBook. Springer. 2012.

Rovin, Jeff. *Illustrated Encyclopedia of Cartoon Animals*. Paperback First Edition. Prentice Hall Direct. 1991. ISBN-10: 0132755610. ISBN-13: 9780132755610.

Scott, Orrin. *The Animation History Bibliography*. Hardcover First Edition. Kindle Direct Publishing. 2022. ISBN-13: 9798419545267.

    Paperback First Edition. Kindle Direct Publishing. 2022. ISBN-13: 9798825657578.

    Available online at CartoonResearch.com.

Stephenson, Ralph. *The Animated Film (The International Film Guide Series)*. Paperback First Edition. The Tantivy Press. A. Zwemmer Ltd. A. S. Barnes & Co. 1967.

    Paperback Later Printing. The Tantivy Press. A. S. Barnes & Co. 1973. ISBN-10: 0900730595. ISBN-13: 9780900730597.

    Paperback Revised. WHSmith. 1973. ISBN-10: 0498012026. ISBN-13: 9780498012020.

Taylor, Richard. *Encyclopedia of Animation Techniques: A Comprehensive, Step-by-Step Directory of Techniques*. Hardcover First Edition. Running Press. 1996. ISBN-10: 156138531X. ISBN-13: 9781561385317.

    Paperback First Edition. Chartwell Books. 2004. ISBN-10: 0785818057. ISBN-13: 9780785818052.

Tumbusch, Thomas E. Welbaum, Bob. *Tomart's Value Guide to Disney Animation Art: An Easy-to-use Compilation of Over 40 Animation Art Auctions Organized by Film, Character and Art Type*. Paperback First Edition. Tomart Publications. 1998. ISBN-10: 0914293419. ISBN-13: 9780914293415.

Webb, Graham. *The Animated Film Encyclopedia: A Complete Guide to American Shorts, Features and Sequences, 1900-1999*. Hardcover First Edition. McFarland & Company, Inc., Publishers. 2000. ISBN-10: 078640728X. ISBN-13: 9780786407286.

> Paperback First Edition, Volume One. McFarland & Company, Inc., Publishers. 2006. ISBN-10: 0786428600. ISBN-13: 9780786428601.
>
> Paperback First Edition, Volume Two. McFarland & Company, Inc., Publishers. 2006. ISBN-10: 0786428619. ISBN-13: 9780786428618.
>
> Paperback Second Edition. McFarland & Company, Inc., Publishers. 2011. ISBN-10: 0786449853. ISBN-13: 9780786449859.
>
> eBook. McFarland & Company, Inc., Publishers. 2011.

Guides

"How to Draw..." books have been omitted from this bibliography. The following "How-to..." guides have been noted for either their historical significance or were authored by a noteworthy member of the animation community.

Bacher, Hans. *Dream Worlds: Production Design for Animation*. Hardcover First Edition. Routledge. 2005. ISBN-10: 0240520939. ISBN-13: 9780240520933.

    eBook. Routledge. 2012.

Baker, Christopher. *How Did They Do It?: Computer Illusion in Film & TV*. Paperback First Edition. Alpha Books. 1994. ISBN-10:1567614221. ISBN-13: 9781567614220.

Blair, Preston. *Advanced Animation*. Paperback First Edition. Walter T. Foster. 1947.

    How to Animate Film Cartoons. Paperback First Edition. Walter T. Foster. 1980.

    Paperback First Edition. Foster Art Service. 1980.

    Paperback First Edition. Walter Foster Publishing. 1989. ISBN-10: 1560100699. ISBN-13: 9781560100690.

    Animation 1: Learn to Animate Cartoons Step by Step. Paperback First Edition. Walter Foster Publishing. 2003. ISBN-10: 0929261518. ISBN-13: 9780929261515.

    Cartooning: Animation 1 With Preston Blair. Paperback First Edition. Walter Foster Publishing. 2019. ISBN-10: 1633227731. ISBN-13: 9781633227736.

Bluth, Don. *Art of Animation Drawing*. Paperback First Edition. Dark Horse Books. 2005. ISBN-10: 1595820086. ISBN-13: 9781595820082.

Boy Scouts of America. *Animation Merit Badge Boy Scouts of America*. Paperback First Edition. Boy Scouts of America. 2015.

Chong, Andrew. *Basics Animation 02: Digital Animation*. Paperback First Edition. AVA Publishing. 2007. ISBN-10: 2940373566. ISBN-13: 9782940373567.

> eBook. Bloomsbury Visual Arts. 2019.

Cook, Benjamin. Thomas, Gary. *The Animate! Book*. Paperback First Edition. Wallflower Press. 2007. ISBN-10: 0954856929. ISBN-13: 9780954856922.

> eBook. Wallflower Press. 2007.

Dale, Alan. *Jr's Fun to Draw*. Paperback First Edition. Knickerbocker Publishing. 1943.

Deitch, Gene. *How to Succeed in Animation: Don't Let a Little Thing Like Failure Stop You!* Digital Book. AWN, Inc. 2013. Available to read at https://www.awn.com/genedeitch.

Edwards, R. Scott. Stobener, Bob. *Cel Magic: The Book on Collecting Animation Art*. Paperback First Edition. Laughs Unlimited. 1991. ISBN-10: 0962479217. ISBN-13: 9780962479212.

Falk, Nat. *How to Make Animated Cartoons*. Paperback First Edition. Foundation Books. 1941.

Fisher, Douglas. Frew, Nancy. *Teaching Visual Literacy: Using Comic Books, Graphic Novels, Anime, Cartoons, and More to Develop Comprehension and Thinking Skills*. Hardcover First Edition. Corwin Press. 2008. ISBN-10: 1412953111. ISBN-13: 9781412953115.

> Paperback First Edition. Corwin Press. 2008. ISBN-10: 141295312X. ISBN-13: 9781412953122.

Gardner, Ph. D., Garth. *Gardner's Guide to Internships at Multimedia and Animation Studios*. Paperback First Edition. Garth Gardner Company. 2001. ISBN-10: 158965000X. ISBN-13: 9781589650008.

Gilliam, Terry. *Animations of Mortality*. Hardcover First Edition. Eyre Methuen. 1978. ISBN-10: 0413393704. ISBN-13: 9780413393708.

> Paperback First Edition. Methuen. 1979. ISBN-10: 0458938106. ISBN-13: 9780458938100.

Godfrey, Bob. Jackson, Anna. *The Do-It-Yourself Film Animation Book*. Paperback First Edition. BBC Publications. 1974. ISBN-10: 0563108290. ISBN-13: 9780563108290.

Goldberg, Eric. *Character Animation Crash Course!* Paperback First Edition. Silman-James Press. 2008. ISBN-10: 1879505975. ISBN-13: 9781879505971.

    eBook. Silman-James Press. 2016.

Graber, Sheila. *Animation: A Handy Guide*. Paperback First Edition with DVD. A&C Black. 2011. ISBN-10: 1408102838. ISBN-13: 9781408102831.

Grandinetti, Fred. *Popeye, the Collectible: Dolls, Coloring Books, Games, Toys, Comic Books, Animation*. Paperback First Edition. Krause Publications Inc. 1990. ISBN-10: 0873411439. ISBN-13: 9780873411431.

Halas, John. Privett, Bob. *How to Cartoon for Amateur Films*. Focal Press. 1951.

    Second Paperback Edition. Focal Press. 1955.

    Third Paperback Edition. Focal Press. 1958.

    Fourth Paperback Edition. Focal Press. 1962.

Halas, John. Manvell, Roger. *The Technique of Film Animation*. Hardcover First Edition. Communication Arts Books. Hastings House. 1959.

    Hardcover First Edition. Hastings House. 1968.

    Hardcover Third Edition. Focal Press. 1971. ISBN-10: 0803870248. ISBN-13: 9780803870246.

    Hardcover Fourth Edition. Focal Press. 1976. ISBN-10: 0240509005. ISBN-13: 9780240509006.

Hamm, Gene. *How To Get A Job In Animation (and Keep It)*. Heinemann Drama. 2006. ISBN-10: 0325008027. ISBN-13: 9780325008028.

Hickner, Steve. *Animating Your Career*. Paperback First Edition. Raphel Marketing, Inc. 2013. ISBN-10: 1938406281. ISBN-13: 9781938406287.

    eBook. Brigantine Media. 2013.

Hoffer, Thomas W. *Animation: A Reference Guide*. Hardcover First Edition. Greenwood. 1981. ISBN-10: 0313210950. ISBN-13: 9780313210952.

Hooks, Ed. *Acting for Animators*. Paperback First Edition. Heinemann Drama. 2001. ISBN-10: 0325002290. ISBN-13: 9780325002293.

    Paperback Revised Edition. Heinemann Drama. 2003. ISBN-10: 032500580X. ISBN-13: 9780325005805.

    Hardcover Third Edition. Routledge. 2011. ISBN-10: 0415580234. ISBN-13: 9780415580236.

    eBook. Taylor & Francis. 2017.

    Hardcover Fourth Edition. Routledge. 2017. ISBN-10: 1138669113. ISBN-13: 9781138669116.

    Paperback Fourth Edition. Routledge. 2017. ISBN-10: 1138669121. ISBN-13: 9781138669123.

Laybourne, Kit. *The Animation Book: A Complete Guide to Animated Filmmaking from Flip-Books to Sound Cartoons*. Hardcover First Edition. Crown Publishers. 1979. ISBN-10: 0517533898. ISBN-13: 9780517533895.

    Revised Paperback Edition. Crown Publishers. 1982. ISBN-10: 0517529467. ISBN-13: 9780517529461.

    Subsequent Paperback Edition. Crown Publishers. 1998. ISBN-10: 0517886022. ISBN-13: 9780517886021.

Lenburg, Jeff. *Career Opportunities in Animation*. Hardcover First Edition. Ferguson Publishing Company. 2011. ISBN-10: 816081824. ISBN-13: 9780816081820.

    Paperback First Edition. Checkmark Books. 2011. ISBN-10: 0816081832. ISBN-13: 9780816081837.

>Audiobook. Narrated by Brian E. Smith. Jeff Lenburg. 2013.

Levy, David B. *Your Career in Animation: How to Survive and Thrive*. Paperback First Edition. Allworth Press. 2006. ISBN-10: 1581154453. ISBN-13: 9781581154450.

>eBook. Allworth Press. 2010.

>Audiobook. Narrated by Richard Allen. Audible Studios. 2013.

>Paperback Second Edition. Allworth Press. 2021.

>eBook Second Edition. Allworth Press. 2021.

McConville, Yasmin. Milic, Lea. *The Animation Producer's Handbook*. Hardcover First Edition. Open University Press. 2006. ISBN-10: 0335220371. ISBN-13: 9780335220373.

>Paperback First Edition. Open University Press. 2006. ISBN-10: 0335220363. ISBN-13: 9780335220366.

McLaughlin Jr., Dan F. *Animation Rules!: Book One: Words*. Paperback First Edition. CreateSpace Independent Publishing Platform. 2017. ISBN-10: 1535194375. ISBN-13: 9781535194372.

McLaughlin Jr., Dan F. *Animation Rules!: Book Two: Art*. Paperback First Edition. CreateSpace Independent Publishing Platform. ISBN-10: 1541104048. 2017. ISBN-13: 9781541104044.

Mitchell, Ben. *Independent Animation: Developing, Producing and Distributing Your Animated Films*. Paperback First Edition. CRC Press. 2016. ISBN-10: 1138855723. ISBN-13: 9781138855724.

>eBook. CRC Press. 2016.

Murray, Joe. *Creating Animated Cartoons with Character: A Guide to Developing and Producing Your Own Series for TV, the Web, and Short Film*. Paperback First Edition. Watson-Guptill. 2010. ISBN-10: 0823033074. ISBN-13: 9780823033072.

Noake, Roger. *Animation: The Guide to Animated Film Techniques*. Hardcover First Edition. Little Brown Company. 1988. ISBN-10: 0356158721. ISBN-13: 9780356158723.

>Hardcover First Edition. Chartwell House. 1989. ISBN-10: 1555213316. ISBN-13: 9781555213312.

Perisic, Zoran. *The Focal Guide to Shooting Animation.* Paperback First Edition. Focal Press. ISBN-10: 0240509730. ISBN-13: 9780240509730.

Pintoff, Ernest. *Animation 101*. Paperback First Edition. Michael Wiese Productions. 1999. ISBN-10: 094118868X. ISBN-13: 9780941188685.

Plympton, Bill. *Making 'Toons That Sell Without Selling Out: The Bill Plympton Guide to Independent Animation Success*. Paperback First Edition. Taylor & Francis. 2012. ISBN-10: 0240817796. ISBN-13: 9780240817798.

>eBook. Routledge. 2012.

Purves, Barry J.C. *Basics Animation 04: Stop-Motion Animation: Frame by Frame Film-Making with Puppets and Models*. Paperback First Edition. Fairchild Books AVA. 2010. ISBN-10: 2940373736. ISBN-13: 9782940373734.

>Paperback Second Edition. Fairchild Books. 2014.
>ISBN-10: 1472521900. ISBN-13: 9781472521903.

>eBook. Fairchild Books. 2015.

>Paperback Second Edition. Bloomsbury Academic. 2019.
>ISBN-10: 1501353799. ISBN-13: 9781501353796

Raugust, Karen. *The Animation Business Handbook*. Hardcover First Edition. St. Martin's Press. 2004. ISBN-10: 0312284284. ISBN-13: 9780312284282.

>eBook. St. Martin's Press. 2004.

Ressel, Steve. *Animation: The Inner Workings*. Paperback First Edition. B*friend. 2010. ISBN-10: 0978748301. ISBN-13: 9780978748302.

Ruddell, Caroline. Ward, Paul. *The Crafty Animator: Handmade, Craft-based Animation and Cultural Value*. Hardcover First Edition. Palgrave Macmillan. 2019. ISBN-10: 3030139425. ISBN-13: 9783030139421.

>Paperback First Edition. Palgrave MacMillan. 2019.
>ISBN-10: 3030139441. ISBN-13: 9783030139445.

>eBook. Palgrave Macmillan. 2019.

Scott, Jameson. *Cartoon Figural Toys*. Paperback First Edition. Schiffer Publishing. 1999. ISBN-10: 0764308327. ISBN-13: 9780764308321.

Turney, Harold Merrill. *Film Guide's Handbook: Cartoon Production*. Paperback First Edition. Film Guide. 1940.

Wells, Paul. *Fundamentals of Animation*. Paperback First Edition. Fairchild Books AVA. 2006. ISBN-10: 2940373027.ISBN-13: 9782940373024.

Moore, Samantha. Wells, Paul. *The Fundamentals of Animation*. eBook First Edition. Bloomsbury Publishing. 2016. ISBN-10: 147257527X. ISBN-13: 9781472575272.

>Paperback Second Edition. Fairchild Books. 2016.
>ISBN-10: 1472575261. ISBN-13: 9781472575265.

>eBook Second Edition. Bloomsbury Visual Arts. 2017.

Webber, Marilyn. *Gardner's Guide to Animation Scriptwriting: The Writer's Road Map*. Garth Gardner Company. 2000. ISBN-10: 0966107594. ISBN-13: 9780966107593.

Wells, Paul. *Basics Animation 01: Scriptwriting*. Paperback First Edition. AVA Publishing. 2007. ISBN-10: 2940373167. ISBN-13: 9782940373161.

>Paperback First Edition. AVA Publishing. 2007. ISBN-10: 2940439826.
>ISBN-13: 9782940439829.

Wells, Paul. *Basics Animation 03: Drawing for Animation*. Paperback First Edition. AVA Publishing. 2008. ISBN-10: 2940373701. ISBN-13: 9782940373703.

>eBook. Bloomsbury Academic. 2019.

Wells, Paul. *Screenwriting For Animation*. Paperback First Edition. Bloomsbury Academic. 2022. ISBN-10: 1350019720. ISBN-13: 9781350019720.

White, Tony. *How to Make Animated Films: Tony White's Complete Masterclass on the Traditional Principles of Animation*. Paperback First Edition. Focal Press. 2009. ISBN-10: 0240810333. ISBN-13: 9780240810331.

    eBook. Routledge. 2013.

    Hardcover First Edition. Routledge. 2018. ISBN-10: 1138403245. ISBN-13: 9781138403246.

Williams, Richard. *The Animator's Survival Kit*. Hardcover First Edition. Faber and Faber. 2000. ISBN-10: 0571205976. ISBN-13: 9780571205974.

    Hardcover Second Edition. Faber & Faber. 2002. ISBN-10: 0571212689. ISBN-13: 9780571212682.

    Paperback Second Edition. Faber & Faber. 2002. ISBN-10: 0571202284. ISBN-13: 9780571202287.

    Hardcover Third Edition. Faber & Faber. 2009. ISBN-10: 0571238335. ISBN-13: 9780571238330.

    Paperback Third Edition. Faber & Faber. 2009. ISBN-10: 0571238343. ISBN-13: 9780571238347.

    Paperback Fourth Revised Edition. Farrar, Straus and Giroux. 2012. ISBN-10: 086547897X. ISBN-13: 9780865478978.

    iPad Application. 2015.

    Paperback Main Edition. Faber & Faber. 2021. ISBN-10: 0571358446. ISBN-13: 9780571358441.

Multi-Volume Series

Ghez, Didier. *They Drew as They Pleased: The Hidden Art of Disney's Golden Age (The 1930s)*. Hardcover First Edition. Chronicle Books, LLC. 2015. ISBN-10: 1452137439. ISBN-13: 9781452137438.

Ghez, Didier. *They Drew As They Pleased Volume Two: The Hidden Art of Disney's Musical Years (The 1940s - Part One)*. Hardcover First Edition. Chronicle Books, LLC. 2016. ISBN-10: 1452137447. ISBN-13: 9781452137445.

Ghez, Didier. *They Drew as They Pleased Volume 3: The Hidden Art of Disney's Late Golden Age (The 1940s - Part Two)*. Hardcover First Edition. Chronicle Books, LLC. 2017. ISBN-10: 1452151938. ISBN-13: 9781452151939.

Ghez, Didier. *They Drew As They Pleased Volume 4: The Hidden Art of Disney's Mid-Century Era*. Hardcover First Edition. Chronicle Books, LLC. 2018. ISBN-10: 1452163855. ISBN-13: 9781452163857.

Ghez, Didier. *They Drew as They Pleased Volume 5: The Hidden Art of Disney's Early Renaissance: The 1970s and 1980s*. Hardcover First Edition. Chronicle Books, LLC. 2019. ISBN-10: 1452178704. ISBN-13: 9781452178707.

Ghez, Didier. *They Drew as They Pleased Volume 6: The Hidden Art of Disney's New Golden Age*. Hardcover First Edition. Chronicle Books, LLC. 2020. ISBN-10: 1797200933. ISBN-13: 9781797200934.

Ghez, Didier. Walt's People: *Volume 1: Talking Disney With The Artists Who Knew Him*. Paperback First Edition. Xilbrus Publishing. 2005. ISBN-10: 1413478670. ISBN-13: 9781413478679.

> Paperback Second Edition. Theme Park Press. 2014. ISBN-10: 1941500013. ISBN-13: 9781941500019.

> eBook. Theme Park Press. 2014.

Ghez, Didier. *Walt's People: Volume 2: Talking Disney With The Artists Who Knew Him*. Paperback First Edition. Xilbrus Publishing. 2005. ISBN-10: 1425700179. ISBN-13: 9781425700171.

> Paperback Second Edition. Theme Park Press. 2015.
> ISBN-10: 1941500285. ISBN-13: 9781941500286.

> eBook. Theme Park Press. 2015.

Ghez, Didier. W*alt's People: Volume 3: Talking Disney With The Artists Who Knew Him*. Paperback First Edition. Xilbrus Publishing. 2006. ISBN-10: 1425713440. ISBN-13: 9781425713447.

> Paperback Second Edition. Theme Park Press. 2015.
> ISBN-10: 1941500455. ISBN-13: 9781941500453.

> eBook. Theme Park Press. 2015.

Ghez, Didier. *Walt's People: Volume 4: Talking Disney With The Artists Who Knew Him*. Paperback First Edition. Xilbrus Publishing. 2007. ISBN-10: 1425746705. ISBN-13: 9781425746704.

> Paperback Second Edition. Theme Park Press. 2015.
> ISBN-10: 1941500595. ISBN-13: 9781941500590.

> eBook. Theme Park Press. 2015.

Ghez, Didier. *Walt's People: Volume 5: Talking Disney With The Artists Who Knew Him*. Paperback First Edition. Xilbrus Publishing. 2007. ISBN-10: 1425783147. ISBN-13: 9781425783143.

> Paperback Second Edition. Theme Park Press. 2016.
> ISBN-10: 1683900111. ISBN-13: 9781683900115.

> eBook. Theme Park Press. 2016.

Ghez, Didier. *Walt's People: Volume 6: Talking Disney With The Artists Who Knew Him*. Paperback First Edition. Xilbrus Publishing. 2008. ISBN-10: 1436318726. ISBN-13: 9781436318723.

Ghez, Didier. *Walt's People: Volume 7: Talking Disney With The Artists Who Knew Him*. Paperback First Edition. Xilbrus Publishing. 2008. ISBN-10: 1436372143. ISBN-13: 9781436372145.

> eBook. Theme Park Press. 2016.

Ghez, Didier. *Walt's People: Volume 8: Talking Disney With The Artists Who Knew Him*. Paperback First Edition. Xilbrus Publishing. 2009. ISBN-10: 1441551832. ISBN-13: 9781441551832.

Ghez, Didier. *Walt's People: Volume 9: Talking Disney With The Artists Who Knew Him*. Paperback First Edition. Xilbrus Publishing. 2010. ISBN-10: 1450087469. ISBN-13: 9781450087469.

Ghez, Didier. *Walt's People: Volume 10: Talking Disney With The Artists Who Knew Him*. Paperback First Edition. Xilbrus Publishing. 2011. ISBN-10: 1456851500. ISBN-13: 9781456851507.

    Paperback First Edition. Theme Park Press. 2017.
    ISBN-10: 1683900863. ISBN-13: 9781683900863.

Ghez, Didier. *Walt's People: Volume 11: Talking Disney With The Artists Who Knew Him*. Paperback First Edition. Xilbrus Publishing. 2011. ISBN-10: 146536840X. ISBN-13: 9781465368409.

Ghez, Didier. *Walt's People: Volume 12: Talking Disney With The Artists Who Knew Him*. Paperback First Edition. Xilbrus Publishing. 2012. ISBN-10: 1477147896. ISBN-13: 9781477147894.

Ghez, Didier. *Walt's People: Volume 13: Talking Disney With The Artists Who Knew Him*. Paperback First Edition. Theme Park Press. 2013. ISBN-10: 098434151X. ISBN-13: 9780984341511.

Ghez, Didier. *Walt's People: Volume 14: Talking Disney With The Artists Who Knew Him*. Paperback First Edition. Theme Park Press. 2014. ISBN-10: 194150003X. ISBN-13: 9781941500033.

Ghez, Didier. *Walt's People: Volume 15: Talking Disney With The Artists Who Knew Him*. Paperback First Edition. Xilbrus Publishing. 2014. ISBN-10: 1941500196. ISBN-13: 9781941500194.

    eBook. Theme Park Press. 2015.

Ghez, Didier. *Walt's People: Volume 16: Talking Disney With The Artists Who Knew Him*. Paperback First Edition. Theme Park Press. 2015. ISBN-10: 1941500501. ISBN-13: 9781941500507.

    eBook. Theme Park Press. 2015.

Ghez, Didier. *Walt's People: Volume 17: Talking Disney With The Artists Who Knew Him*. Paperback First Edition. Theme Park Press. 2015. ISBN-10: 1941500773. ISBN-13: 9781941500774.

    eBook. Theme Park Press. 2015.

Ghez, Didier. *Walt's People: Volume 18: Talking Disney With The Artists Who Knew Him*. Paperback First Edition. Theme Park Press. 2016. ISBN-10: 1683900162. ISBN-13: 9781683900160.

    eBook. Theme Park Press. 2016.

Ghez, Didier. *Walt's People: Volume 19: Talking Disney With The Artists Who Knew Him*. Paperback First Edition. Theme Park Press. 2017. ISBN-10: 1683900448. ISBN-13: 9781683900443.

    eBook. Theme Park Press. 2017.

Ghez, Didier. *Walt's People: Volume 20: Talking Disney With The Artists Who Knew Him*. Paperback First Edition. Theme Park Press. 2017. ISBN-10: 1683901037. ISBN-13: 9781683901037.

    eBook. Theme Park Press. 2017.

Ghez, Didier. *Walt's People: Volume 21: Talking Disney With The Artists Who Knew Him*. Paperback First Edition. Theme Park Press. 2018. ISBN-10: 1683901584. ISBN-13: 9781683901587.

    eBook. Theme Park Press. 2018.

Ghez, Didier. *Walt's People: Volume 22: Talking Disney With The Artists Who Knew Him*. Paperback First Edition. Theme Park Press. 2019. ISBN-10: 1683901851. ISBN-13: 9781683901853.

    eBook. Theme Park Press. 2019.

Ghez, Didier. *Walt's People: Volume 23: Talking Disney With The Artists Who Knew Him*. Paperback First Edition. Theme Park Press. 2019. ISBN-10: 1683902424. ISBN-13: 9781683902423.

    eBook. Theme Park Press. 2019.

Ghez, Didier. *Walt's People: Volume 24: Talking Disney With The Artists Who Knew Him*. Paperback First Edition. Theme Park Press. 2020. ISBN-10: 1683902653. ISBN-13: 9781683902652.

Ghez, Didier. *Walt's People: Volume 25: Talking Disney With The Artists Who Knew Him*. Paperback First Edition. Theme Park Press. 2021. ISBN-10: 1683902998. ISBN-13: 9781683902997.

Hankin, Mike. *Ray Harryhausen - Master of the Majicks Volume 1*. Hardcover First Edition. Archive Editions, LLC. 2013. ISBN-10: 0981782957. ISBN-13: 9780981782959.

Hankin, Mike. *Ray Harryhausen - Master of the Majicks Volume 2*. Hardcover First Edition. Archive Editions, LLC. 2008. ISBN-10: 0981782906. ISBN-13: 9780981782904.

Hankin, Mike. *Ray Harryhausen - Master of the Majicks: The British Films Volume 3*. Hardcover First Edition. Archive Editions, LLC. 2010. ISBN-10: 0981782914. ISBN-13: 9780981782911.

Korkis, Jim. *The Vault of Walt*. Paperback First Edition. Ayefour Publishing. 2010. ISBN-10: 0615402429. ISBN-13: 9780615402420.

Korkis, Jim. Disney Miller, Diane. *The Revised Vault of Walt: Unofficial Disney Stories Never Told*. Paperback First Edition. Theme Park Press. 2012. ISBN-10: 0984341544. ISBN-13: 9780984341542.

    eBook. Theme Park Press. 2012.

Korkis, Jim. *The Vault of Walt: Volume 2: Unofficial, Unauthorized, Uncensored Disney Stories Never Told*. Paperback First Edition. Theme Park Press. 2013. ISBN-10: 0984341579. ISBN-13: 9780984341573.

    eBook. Theme Park Press. 2013.

Korkis, Jim. *The Vault of Walt: Volume 3: Even More Unofficial Disney Stories Never Told*. Paperback First Edition. Theme Park Press. 2014. ISBN-10: 1941500145. ISBN-13: 9781941500149.

    eBook. Theme Park Press. 2014.

Korkis, Jim. *The Vault of Walt: Volume 4: Still More Unofficial Disney Stories Never Told*. Paperback First Edition. Theme Park Press. 2015. ISBN-10: 1941500625. ISBN-13: 9781941500620.

    eBook. Theme Park Press. 2015.

Korkis, Jim. *The Vault of Walt: Volume 5: Additional Unofficial Disney Stories Never Told*. Paperback First Edition. Theme Park Press. 2016. ISBN-10: 168390009X. ISBN-13: 9781683900092.

    eBook. Theme Park Press. 2016.

Korkis, Jim. *The Vault of Walt: Volume 6: Other Unofficial Disney Stories Never Told*. Paperback First Edition. Theme Park Press. 2017. ISBN-10: 1683901088. ISBN-13: 9781683901082.

    eBook. Theme Park Press. 2017.

Korkis, Jim. *The Vault of Walt Volume 7: Christmas Edition: Yuletide Tales of Walt Disney, Disney Theme Parks, Cartoons & More*. Paperback First Edition. Theme Park Press. 2018. ISBN-10: 168390172X. ISBN-13: 9781683901723.

    eBook. Theme Park Press. 2018.

Korkis, Jim. T*he Vault of Walt Volume 8: Outer Space Edition: Out-of-This-World Stories of Walt Disney, Disney Theme Parks, Films & More.* Paperback First Edition. Theme Park Press. 2019. ISBN-10: 1683902270. ISBN-13: 9781683902270.

    eBook. Theme Park Press. 2019.

Korkis, Jim. *Vault of Walt 9: Halloween Edition: Spooky Stories of Disney Films, Theme Parks, and Things That Go Bump In the Night*. Paperback First Edition. Theme Park Press. 2020. ISBN-10: 1683902742. ISBN-13: 9781683902744.

    eBook. Theme Park Press. 2020.

Korkis, Jim. *The Vault of Walt: Volume 10: Final Edition*. Paperback First Edition. Theme Park Press. 2021. ISBN-10: 1683903137. ISBN-13: 9781683903130.

Conferences

Ottawa International Animation Festival

Mumford, Britt. Robinson, Chris. *40 Years of Ottawa: Collected Essays on Award-Winning Animation*. eBook First Edition. Ottawa International Animation Festival. 2017.

Computer Animation and Simulation Conference

Arnaldi, Bruno. Hegron, Gerard. *Computer Animation and Simulation '98*. Paperback First Edition. Springer. 1999. ISBN-10: 3211832572. ISBN-13: 9783211832578.

Boulic Ph. D., Ronan. Hégron Ph. D., Gerard. *Computer Animation and Simulation '96: Proceedings of the Eurographics Workshop in Poitiers, France, August 31–September 1, 1996*. Paperback First Edition. Springer. 1996. ISBN-10: 3211828850. ISBN-13: 9783211828854.

> Paperback Reprint. Springer. 2011. ISBN-10: 3709174872. ISBN-13: 9783709174876.

> eBook. Springer. 2012.

International Conference on Illustration and Animation

Ferreira, Cláudio. *Confia: International Conference on Illustration and Animation 2012*. Paperback First Edition. IPCA. 2012. ISBN-13: 9789899756762.

> eBook. IPCA. 2012.

Ferreira, Cláudio. *Confia: International Conference on Illustration and Animation 2013*. Paperback First Edition. IPCA. 2013. ISBN-13: 9789899756762.

> eBook. IPCA. 2013.

Ferreira, Cláudio. *Confia: International Conference on Illustration and Animation 2015*. Paperback First Edition. IPCA. 2015. ISBN-13: 9789899824195.

    eBook. IPCA. 2015.

Ferreira, Cláudio. *Confia: International Conference on Illustration and Animation 2016*. Paperback First Edition. IPCA. 2016. ISBN-13: 9789899946569.

    eBook. IPCA. 2016.

Ferreira, Cláudio. *Confia: International Conference on Illustration and Animation 2017*. Paperback First Edition. IPCA. 2017. ISBN-13: 9789899986138.

    eBook. IPCA. 2017.

Ferreira, Cláudio. *Confia: International Conference on Illustration and Animation 2018*. Paperback First Edition. IPCA. 2018. ISBN-13: 9789899986169.

    eBook. IPCA. 2018.

Ferreira, Cláudio. *Confia: International Conference on Illustration and Animation 2019*. Paperback First Edition. IPCA. 2019. ISBN-13: 9789895448906.

    eBook. IPCA. 2019.

Ferreira, Cláudio. *Confia: International Conference on Illustration and Animation 2020*. Paperback First Edition. IPCA. 2020. ISBN-13: 9789895493906.

    eBook. IPCA. 2020.

Ferreira, Cláudio. *Confia: International Conference on Illustration and Animation 2020*. Paperback First Edition. IPCA. 2020. ISBN-13: 9789895493906.

    eBook. IPCA. 2021.

Computer Animation Conference

Magnenat-Thalmann, Nadia. Thalmann Ph. D., Daniel. *State-of-the-Art in Computer Animation: Proceedings of Computer Animation '89*. Hardcover First Edition. Springer Publishing. 1989. ISBN-10: 0387700463. ISBN-13: 9780387700465.

> Paperback Reprint. Springer Publishing. 2011. ISBN-10: 4431682953. ISBN-13: 9784431682950.

Magnenat-Thalmann, Nadia. Thalmann Ph. D., Daniel. *Computer Animation '90*. Hardcover First Edition. Springer. 1990. ISBN-10: 3540700617. ISBN-13: 9783540700616.

> Paperback Reprint. Springer. 2011. ISBN-10: 4431682988. ISBN-13: 9784431682981.

Magnenat-Thalmann, Nadia. Thalmann Ph. D., Daniel. *Computer Animation '91*. Hardcover First Edition. Springer-Verlag. 1991. ISBN-10: 0387700773. ISBN-13: 9780387700779.

> Paperback First Edition. Springer. 2012. ISBN-10: 4431668918. ISBN-13: 9784431668916.

Digimedia, Swiss National Research Foundation. *Computer Animation '94: Proceedings: May 25-28, 1994, Geneva, Switzerland*. Paperback First Edition. IEEE Computer Society Press. 1994.

Computer Graphics Society. Digimedia. Swiss National Research Foundation. *Computer Animation '95: Proceedings: April 19-21, 1995, Geneva, Switzerland*. Paperback First Edition. IEEE Computer Society Press. 1995. ISBN-10: 0818670622. ISBN-13: 9780818670626.

Terzopoulos, Demetri. Thalmann Ph. D., Daniel. *Computer Animation and Simulation '95: Proceedings of the Eurographics Workshop in Maastricht, The Netherlands, September 2-3, 1995*. Paperback First Edition. Springer. 1995. ISBN-10: 3211827382. ISBN-13: 9783211827383.

> Paperback Reprint. Springer. 2012.
> ISBN-10: 3709194369. ISBN-13: 9783709194362.

> eBook. Springer. 2012.

Institute of Electrical and Electronics Engineers. *Computer Animation Conference 1996: June 3, 1996 to June 4, 1996, Geneva, Switzerland*. Paperback First Edition. IEEE Computer Society Press. 1996. ISBN-10: 0818675888. ISBN-13: 9780818675881.

Institute of Electrical and Electronics Engineers. *Computer Animation '97: June 5-6, 1997, Geneva, Switzerland*. Paperback First Edition. IEEE Computer Society Press. 1997. ISBN-10: 0818679840. ISBN-13: 9780818679841.

Panne Ph. D., Michiel van de. Thalmann Ph. D., Daniel. *Computer Animation and Simulation '97: Proceedings of the Eurographics Workshop in Budapest, Hungary, September 2-3, 1997*. Paperback First Edition. Springer. 1997. ISBN-10: 3211830480. ISBN-13: 9783211830482.

> Paperback Reprint. Springer. 2011. ISBN-10: 3709168759.
> ISBN-13: 9783709168752.

> eBook. Springer. 2012.

IEEE Computer Society. Institute of Electrical and Electronics Engineers. *Computer Animation '98: Proceedings Philadelphia, University Of Pennsylvania June 8-10, 1998*. Paperback First Edition. IEEE Computer Society Press. 1998. ISBN-10: 0818685417. ISBN-13: 9780818685415.

Magnenat-Thalmann, Nadia. Thalmann Ph. D., Daniel. *Computer Animation and Simulation '99: Proceedings of the Eurographics Workshop in Milano, Italy, September 7-8, 1999*. Paperback First Edition. Springer. 1999. ISBN-10: 3211833927. ISBN-13: 9783211833926.

Paperback Reprint. Springer. 2011. ISBN-10: 3709164249. ISBN-13: 9783709164242.

eBook. Springer. 2012.

Institute of Electrical and Electronics Engineers. *Computer Animation '99: May 26-29, 1999 Geneva, Switzerland*. Paperback First Edition. IEEE Computer Society Press. 1999. ISBN-10: 0769501672. ISBN-13: 9780769501673.

Institute of Electrical and Electronics Engineers. *Computer Animation 2000: May 3, 2000 to May 5, 2000, Philadelphia, Pennsylvania*. Paperback First Edition. IEEE Computer Society Press. 2001. ISBN-10: 0769506836. ISBN-13: 9780769506838.

Institute of Electrical and Electronics Engineers. Ko, Hyeong-Seok. *Computer Animation 2001: The Fourteenth Conference on Computer Animation Seoul, Korea November 7-8, 2001*. Paperback First Edition. IEEE Computer Society Press. 2001. ISBN-10: 0780372379. ISBN-13: 9780780372375.

IEEE Computer Society. *Proceedings Of Computer Animation 2002: 19-21 June 2002 Geneva, Switzerland*. Paperback First Edition. IEEE Computer Society Press. 2002. ISBN-10: 0769515940. ISBN-13: 9780769515946.

Institute of Electrical and Electronics Engineers. *16th International Conference on Computer Animation and Social Agents: 8-9 May 2003, New Brunswick, New Jersey*. Paperback First Edition. IEEE Computer Society Press. 2003. ISBN-10: 0769519342. ISBN-13: 9780769519340.

Chang, Jian. Magnenat-Thalmann, Nadia. Thalmann Ph. D., Daniel. Tian, Feng. Xu, Weiwei. Yang, Xiaosong. Zhang, Jian Jun. *Computer Animation and Social Agents: 33rd International Conference on Computer Animation and Social Agents, CASA 2020, Bournemouth, UK, October 13-15, 2020, Proceedings*. Paperback First Edition. Springer. 2020. ISBN-10: 3030634256. ISBN-13: 9783030634254.

eBook. Springer. 2020.

Animation General Studies

Alys, Francis. Akakce, Haluk. Bendazzi, Giannalberto. Blake, Jeremy. Canemaker, John. Christov-Bakargiev, Carolyn. Galbraith, David. Gillick, Liam. Harries, Larissa. Klein, Norman. Marks, Melissa. Riegel, Karyn. *Animations*. Paperback First Edition. P.S. 1 Contemporary Art Center, Museum of Modern Art. 2003. ISBN-10: 3980426505. ISBN-13: 9783980426503.

Animation World Network. *On Animation - The Director's Perspective*. Paperback First Edition. Cengage Learning PTR. 2010. ISBN-10: 1598634070. ISBN-13: 9781598634075.

Beckerman, Howard. *Animation: The Whole Story*. Paperback First Edition. Allworth Press. 2003. ISBN-10: 1581153015. ISBN-13: 9781581153019.

    eBook. Allworth Press. 2012.

Beckman, Karen Redrobe. *Animating Film Theory*. Hardcover First Edition. Duke University Press Books. 2014. ISBN-10: 0822356406. ISBN-13: 9780822356400.

    Paperback First Edition. Duke University Press Books. 2014. ISBN-10: 082235652X. ISBN-13: 9780822356523.

    eBook. Duke University Press Books. 2014.

Beiman, Nancy. *Animated Performance: Bringing Imaginary Animal, Human and Fantasy Characters to Life*. Paperback First Edition. AVA Publishing. 2010. ISBN-10: 2940373817. ISBN-13: 9782940373819.

    eBook. Bloomsbury Visual Arts. 2017.

    Paperback First Edition. Bloomsbury Academic. 2021. ISBN-10: 1501376675. ISBN-13: 9781501376672.

Binski, Paul. Pointon, Marcia. *Cartoon, Caricature, Animation*. Paperback First Edition. John Wiley & Sons, Inc. 1995. ISBN-10: 0631194878. ISBN-13: 9780631194873.

Bissonnette, Sylvie. *Affect and Embodied Meaning in Animation: Becoming-Animated*. Hardcover First Edition. Routledge. 2019. ISBN-10: 1138483591. ISBN-13: 9781138483590.

>eBook. Routledge. 2019.

>Paperback First Edition. Routledge. 2020. ISBN-10: 0367660377. ISBN-13: 9780367660376.

Blair, Preston. *Cartoon Animation*. Paperback First Edition. Walter Foster Publishing. 1994. ISBN-10: 1633228908. ISBN-13: 9781633228900.

>Paperback Second Edition. Walter Foster Publishing. 2000. ISBN-10: 8983070463. ISBN-13: 9788983070463.

>Revised Paperback Edition. Walter Foster Publishing. 2020. ISBN-10: 1560100842. ISBN-13: 9781560100843.

>eBook. 2021.

Bloodsworth-Lugo, Mary K. King, C. Richard. Lugo-Lugo, Carmen R. *Animating Difference: Race, Gender, and Sexuality in Contemporary Films for Children*. Hardcover First Edition. 2010. ISBN-10: 0742560813. ISBN-13: 742560813.

>Paperback First Edition. Rowman & Littlefield Publishers. 2011. ISBN-10: 0742560821. ISBN-13: 9780742560826.

Buchan, Suzanne. *Pervasive Animation (AFI Film Readers)*. Hardcover First Edition. Routledge. 2013. ISBN-10: 0415807239. ISBN-13: 9780415807234.

>Paperback First Edition. Routledge. 2013. ISBN-10: 0415807247. ISBN-13: 9780415807241.

>eBook. Routledge. 2013.

Canemaker, John. *The Art of the Animated Image. Vol. 1*. Paperback First Edition. The American Film Institute. 1987. ISBN-10: 9991475338. ISBN-13: 9789991475332.

Cawley, John. Korkis, Jim. *Cartoon Confidential*. Paperback First Edition. Malibu Graphics. 1991. ISBN-10: 1563980053. ISBN-13: 9781563980053.

Cholodenko, Alan. *The Illusion of Life: Essays on Animation*. Paperback First Edition. Power Publications. Australian Film Commission. 1991. ISBN-10: 0909952183. ISBN-13: 9780909952181.

Cholodenko, Alan. *The Illusion of Life II: More Essays on Animation*. Paperback First Edition. Power Publications. 2011. ISBN-10: 0909952345. ISBN-13: 9780909952341.

Clifton, Darryl. Hardstaff, Johnny. Wells, Paul. *Re-Imagining Animation: The Changing Face of the Moving Image*. First Edition Paperback. Fairchild Books. 2008. ISBN-10: 2940373698. ISBN-13: 9782940373697.

Crafton, Donald. *Shadow of a Mouse: Performance, Belief, and World-Making in Animation*. Hardcover First Edition. University of California Press. 2012. ISBN-10: 0520261038. ISBN-13: 9780520261037.

    Paperback First Edition. University of California Press. 2012. ISBN-10: 0520261046. ISBN-13: 9780520261044.

Craven, Thomas. *Cartoon Cavalcade*. Hardcover First Edition. Simon & Schuster. 1945.

Curtis, Scott. *Animation (Behind the Silver Screen)*. Hardcover First Edition. Rutgers University Press. 2019. ISBN-10: 0813570263. ISBN-13: 9780813570266.

    eBook. Rutgers University Press. 2019.

    Paperback First Edition. Rutgers University Press. 2019. ISBN-10: 0813570255. ISBN-13: 9780813570259.

Da Silva, Raul. *The World of Animation*. Paperback First Edition. Eastman Kodak Co. 1979. ISBN-10: 879852259. ISBN-13: 9780879852252.

Dobson, Nichola. Ratelle, Amy. Roe, Annabelle Honess. Ruddell, Caroline. *The Animation Studies Reader*. Hardcover First Edition. Bloomsbury Academic. 2018. ISBN-10: 1501332619. ISBN-13: 9781501332616.

Paperback First Edition. Bloomsbury Academic. 2018.
ISBN-10: 1501332600. ISBN-13: 9781501332609.

eBook. Bloomsbury Academic. 2018.

Eastman Kodak Company. Solomon, Charles. Stark, Ron. *The Complete Kodak Animation Book*. Paperback First Edition. Eastman Kodak Company. 1983. ISBN-10: 879853301. ISBN-13: 9780879853303.

Feyersinger, Erwin. *Metalepsis in Animation: Paradoxical Transgressions of Ontological Levels*. Hardcover First Edition. Universitätsverlag Winter. 2015. ISBN-10: 3825364720. ISBN-13: 9783825364724.

Gageldonk, Maarten van. Munteán, László. Shobeiri, Ali. *Animation and Memory*. Hardcover First Edition. Palgrave Macmillan. 2020. ISBN-10: 3030348873. ISBN-13: 9783030348878.

eBook. Palgrave Macmillan. 2020.

Paperback First Edition. Palgrave Macmillan. 2021.
ISBN-10: 3030348903. ISBN-13: 9783030348908.

Gehman, Chris. Reinke, Steve. *The Sharpest Point: Animation at the End of Cinema*. Paperback Canadian First Edition. YYZ Books. 2005. ISBN-10: 0920397328. ISBN-13: 9780920397329.

Giesen, Rolf. Khan, Anna. *Acting and Character Animation: The Art of Animated Films, Acting and Visualizing*. Hardcover First Edition. CRC Press. 2017. ISBN-10: 1138069817. ISBN-13: 9781138069817.

Paperback First Edition. CRC Press. 2017.
ISBN-10: 1498778631. ISBN-13: 9781498778633.

eBook. CRC Press. 2017.

Halas, John. *The Contemporary Animator*. Hardcover First Edition. Focal Press. 1990. ISBN-10: 0240512804. ISBN-13: 9780240512808.

Hodge, James. *Sensations of History: Animation and New Media Art*. Hardcover First Edition. University of Minnesota Press. 2019. ISBN-10: 1517906822. ISBN-13: 9781517906825.

    Paperback First Edition. University of Minnesota Press. 2019. ISBN-10: 1517906830. ISBN-13: 9781517906832.

    eBook. University of Minnesota Press. 2019.

Leslie, Esther. *Hollywood Flatlands: Animation, Critical Theory and the Avant-garde*. Hardcover First Edition. Verso Books. 2002. ISBN-10: 1859846122. ISBN-13: 9781859846124.

    Paperback New Edition. Verso Books. 2004. ISBN-10: 1844675041. ISBN-13: 9781844675043.

Levitt, Deborah. *The Animatic Apparatus: Animation, Vitality, and the Futures of the Image*. Paperback First Edition. Zero Books. 2018. ISBN-10: 1780992696. ISBN-13: 9781780992693.

    eBook. Zero Books. 2018.

Levy, David B. *Directing Animation*. Paperback First Edition. Allworth. 2010. ISBN-10: 1581157460. ISBN-13: 9781581157468.

    eBook. Allworth. 2010.

Lowe, Richard. Schnotz, Wolfgang. *Learning with Animation: Research Implications for Design*. Hardcover First Edition. Cambridge University Press. 2007. ISBN-10: 0521851890. ISBN-13: 9780521851893.

    Paperback First Edition. Cambridge University Press. 2007. ISBN-10: 0521617391. ISBN-13: 9780521617390

Madsen, Roy P. *Animated Film: Concepts, Methods, Uses*. Hardcover First Edition. Interland Publishing Inc. 1969. ISBN-10: 0879890290. ISBN-13: 9780879890292.

    Hardcover Reprint. Amereon Limited. 1976. ISBN-10: 0848808304. ISBN-13: 9780848808303.

Magnenat-Thalmann, Nadia. Thalmann Ph. D., Daniel. *New Trends in Animation and Visualization*. Hardcover First Edition. Wiley. 1991. ISBN-10: 0471930202. ISBN-13: 9780471930204.

Maltin, Leonard. *Leonard Maltin's Movie Crazy*. Paperback First Edition. Dark Horse Comics. 2008. ISBN-10: 1595821198. ISBN-13: 9781595821195.

Peary, Danny. Peary, Gerald. *The American Animated Cartoon: A Critical Anthology*. Paperback First Edition. Plume. 1980. ISBN-10: 0525476393. ISBN-13: 9780525476399.

> Paperback Second Edition. Theme Park Press. 2017. ISBN-10: 1683900510. ISBN-13: 9781683900511.

> eBook. Theme Park Press. 2017.

Pilling, Jayne. *A Reader in Animation Studies*. Paperback First Edition. The Society of Animation Studies. John Libbey Publishing. 1998. ISBN-10: 1864620005. ISBN-13: 9781864620009.

> eBook. John Libbey Publishing. 1998.

Pilling, Jane. *Animating the Unconscious: Desire, Sexuality, and Animation*. Hardcover First Edition. Wallflower Press. 2012. ISBN-10: 0231161980. ISBN-13: 9780231161985.

> Paperback First Edition. Wallflower Press. 2012. ISBN-10: 0231161999. ISBN-13: 9780231161992.

> eBook. Wallflower Press. 2012.

Pilling, Jayne. *Animation: 2D & Beyond*. Paperback First Edition. Diane Publishing Co. 2001. ISBN-10: 0756767245. ISBN-13: 9780756767242.

> Paperback First Edition. Rotovision. 2001. ISBN-10: 2880464455. ISBN-13: 9782880464455.

Rockport Publishers. *Animation*. Paperback First Edition. Quayside. 1998. ISBN-10: 1564964795. ISBN-13: 9781564964793.

Selby, Andrew. *Animation in Process*. Paperback First Edition with DVD. Laurence King Publishing. 2009. ISBN-10: 1856695875. ISBN-13: 9781856695879.

Sito, Tom. *Eat, Drink, Animate: An Animators Cookbook*. Hardcover First Edition. CRC Press. 2019. ISBN-10: 0815399871. ISBN-13: 9780815399872.

    eBook. CRC Press. 2019.

    Paperback First Edition. CRC Press. 2019. ISBN-10: 0815399766. ISBN-13: 9780815399766.

Stephenson, Ralph. *Animation in the Cinema*. Paperback First Edition. Zwemmer Ltd. & A.S. Barnes. 1967. ISBN-10: 9060073363. ISBN-13: 9789060073360.

Street, Rita. *The Best New Animation Design*. Hardcover First Edition. Rockport Publishers. 1996. ISBN-10: 1564961664. ISBN-13: 9781564961662.

Street, Rita. *The Best of New Animation Design 2*. Hardcover First Edition. Rockport Publishers. 1997. ISBN-10: 1564963551. ISBN-13: 9781564963550.

    Paperback Second Edition. Rockport Publishers. 2000. ISBN-10: 1564966836. ISBN-13: 9781564966834.

Torre, Dan. *Animation – Process, Cognition and Actuality*. Hardcover First Edition. Bloomsbury Academic. 2017. ISBN-10: 1501308149. ISBN-13: 9781501308147.

    eBook. Bloomsbury Academic. 2017.

    Paperback First Edition. Bloomsbury Academic. 2019. ISBN-10: 150134966X. ISBN-13: 9781501349669.

Uhrig, Meike. *Emotion in Animated Films*. Hardcover First Edition. Routledge. 2018. ISBN-10: 1138303283. ISBN-13: 9781138303287.

    eBook. Routledge. 2018.

    Paperback First Edition. Routledge. 2020. ISBN-10: 0367584778. ISBN-13: 9780367584771.

Wells, Paul. *Art and Animation*. Paperback First Edition. Academy Group. 1997. ISBN-10: 1854905252. ISBN-13: 9781854905253.

Wells, Paul. *Understanding Animation*. Hardcover First Edition. Routledge. 1998. ISBN-10: 0415115965. ISBN-13: 9780415115964.

> Paperback First Edition. Routledge. 1998. ISBN-10: 0415115973. ISBN-13: 9780415115971.
>
> eBook. Routledge. 2013.
>
> Hardcover Second Edition. Routledge. 2021. ISBN-10: 0415397294. ISBN-13: 9780415397292.

Whitehead, Mark. *Animation*. Paperback First Edition. Pocket Essentials. 2004. ISBN-10: 1903047463. ISBN-13: 9781903047460.

Genre

Ehrlich, Nea. *Animating Truth: Documentary and Visual Culture in the 21st Century*. Hardcover First Edition. 2021. ISBN-10: 1474463363. ISBN-13: 9781474463362.

    eBook available through Edinburg University Press Open Access: https://edinburghuniversitypress.com/book-animating-truth.html

Ehrlich, Nea. Murray, Jonathan. *Drawn from Life: Issues and Themes in Animated Documentary Cinema*. Hardcover First Edition. Edinburgh University Press. 2018. ISBN-10: 0748694110. ISBN-13: 9780748694112.

    Paperback First Edition. Edinburgh University Press. 2020. ISBN-10: 1474431828. ISBN-13: 9781474431828.

Formenti, Christina. *The Classical Animated Documentary and Its Contemporary Evolution*. Hardcover First Edition. Bloomsbury Academic. 2022. ISBN-10: 1501346466. ISBN-13: 9781501346460.

    eBook. Bloomsbury Academic. 2022.

Holliday, Christopher. Sergeant, Alexander. *Fantasy/Animation: Connections Between Media, Mediums and Genres*. Hardcover First Edition. Routledge. 2020. ISBN-10: 1138054372. ISBN-13: 9781138054370.

    Paperback First Edition. Routledge. 2020. ISBN-10: 0367590743. ISBN-13: 9780367590741.

    eBook. Routledge. 2018.

Kriger, Judith. *Animated Realism: A Behind The Scenes Look at the Animated Documentary Genre*. Paperback First Edition. Focal Press. 2011. ISBN-10: 0240814398. ISBN-13: 9780240814391.

    eBook. CRC Press. 2012.

    Hardcover First Edition. Routledge. 2017. ISBN-10: 1138403148. ISBN-13: 9781138403147.

Lyons, Jonathan. *Comedy for Animators*. Hardcover First Edition. Routledge. 2015. ISBN-10: 1138777234. ISBN-13: 9781138777231.

> Paperback First Edition. Routledge. 2015. ISBN-10: 1138777188. ISBN-13: 9781138777187.

> eBook. Routledge. 2015.

Mittell, Jason. *Genre and Television: From Cop Shows to Cartoons in American Culture*. Hardcover First Edition. Routledge. 2004. ISBN-10: 0415969026. ISBN-13: 9780415969024.

> Paperback First Edition. Routledge. 2004. ISBN-10: 0415969034. ISBN-13: 9780415969031.

> eBook. Routledge. 2004.

Patten, Fred. *Furry Tales: A Review of Essential Anthropomorphic Fiction*. Paperback First Edition. McFarland & Company, Inc., Publishers. 2019. ISBN-10: 1476675988. ISBN-13: 9781476675985.

> eBook. McFarland & Company, Inc., Publishers. 2019.

Rall, Hannes. *Adaptation for Animation: Transforming Literature Frame by Frame*. Paperback First Edition. CRC Press. 2019. ISBN-10: 1138886483. ISBN-13: 9781138886483.

> eBook. CRC Press. 2019.

> Hardcover First Edition. CRC Press. 2019. ISBN-10: 1138886475. ISBN-13: 9781138886476.

Roe, Anaabelle Honess. *Animated Documentary*. Hardcover First Edition. Palgrave Macmillan. 2013. ISBN-10: 1137017457. ISBN-13: 9781137017451.

> Paperback First Edition. Palgrave Macmillan. 2013. ISBN-10: 1349437093. ISBN-13: 9781349437092.

> eBook. Palgrave Macmillan. 2013.

Russo, Ron. *Adult Swim and Comedy*. Paperback First Edition. Gai Russo Inc. and Ron Russo. 2005. ISBN-10: 0977137716. ISBN-13: 9780977137718.

    Paperback Second Edition. 2008.

    Paperback Third Edition. Gai Russo. 2012.
    ISBN-10: 0977137740. ISBN-13: 9780977137749.

Telotte, J.P. *Animating the Science Fiction Imagination*. Hardcover First Edition. Oxford University Press. 2017. ISBN-10: 0190695269. ISBN-13: 9780190695262.

    Paperback First Edition. Oxford University Press. 2017.
    ISBN-10: 0190695269. ISBN-13: 9780190695262.

    eBook. Oxford University Press. 2017.

Wells, Paul. *Animation: Genre and Authorship*. Paperback First Edition. Wallflower Press. 2002. ISBN-10: 1903364205. ISBN-13: 9781903364208.

    eBook. Wallflower Press. 2019.

Computer Generated Animation History

Artwick, Bruce. *Microcomputer Displays, Graphics and Animation*. Paperback First Edition. Pearson PTR. 1984. ISBN-10: 0135802261. ISBN-13: 9780135802267.

Badler, Norman. Phillips, Cary B. Webber, Bonnie Lynn. *Simulating Humans: Computer Graphics Animation and Control*. Hardcover First Edition. Oxford University Press. 1993. ISBN-10: 0195073592. ISBN-13: 9780195073591.

Darley, Andrew. *Visual Digital Culture: Surface Play and Spectacle in New Media Genres*. Hardcover First Edition. Routledge. 2000. ISBN-10: 0415165547. ISBN-13: 9780415165549.

> Paperback First Edition. Routledge. 2000. ISBN-10: 0415165555. ISBN-13: 9780415165556.

> eBook. Routledge. 2002.

de Aguiar, Edilson. *Animation And Performance Capture Using Digitized Models*. eBook. Springer. 2009.

> Hardcover First Edition. Springer. 2010. ISBN-10: 3642103154. ISBN-13: 9783642103155.

> Paperback First Edition. Springer. 2010. ISBN-10: 3642103278. ISBN-13: 9783642103278.

Finch, Christopher. *The CG Story: Computer-Generated Animation and Special Effects*. Hardcover First Edition. The Monacelli Press. 2013. ISBN-10: 1580933572. ISBN-13: 9781580933575.

Forchheimer, Robert. Pandzic, Igor. *MPEG-4 Facial Animation: The Standard, Implementation and Applications*. Hardcover First Edition. Wiley. 2002. ISBN-10: 0470844655. ISBN-13: 9780470844656.

Fox, David. Waite, Mitchell. *Computer Animation Primer*. Paperback First Edition. McGraw-Hill Osborne Media. 1984. ISBN-10: 0070217424. ISBN-13: 9780070217423.

Gardner, Ph. D., Garth. *Computer Graphics and Animation: History, Careers, Expert Advice*. Paperback First Edition. Garth Gardner Company. 2001. ISBN-10: 096610756X. ISBN-13: 9780966107562.

Halas, John. *Computer Animation*. Hardcover First Edition. Focal Press. 1974. ISBN-10: 0240507509. ISBN-13: 9780240507507.

Jones, Angie. Oliff, Jamie. *Thinking Animation: Bridging the Gap Between 2D and CG*. Paperback First Edition. Cengage Learning PTR. 2006. ISBN-10: 1598632604. ISBN-13: 9781598632606.

Kelland, Matt. Lloyd, Dave. Morris, Dave. *Machinima*. Paperback First Edition. Cengage Learning PTR. 2005. ISBN-10: 1592006507. ISBN-13: 9781592006502.

Kerlow, Isaac Victor. *The Art of 3-D Computer: Animation and Imaging*. Paperback First Edition. Wiley. 1996. ISBN-10: 0471286494. ISBN-13: 9780471286493.

> Paperback Second Edition. Wiley. 2000. ISBN-10: 047136004X. ISBN-13: 9780471360049.
>
> *The Art of 3-D Computer: Animation and Effects*. Paperback Third Revised Edition. Wiley. 2003. ISBN-10: 0471430366. ISBN-13: 9780471430360.
>
> eBook. Wiley. 2008.
>
> Paperback Fourth Edition. Wiley. 2009. ISBN-10: 0470084901. ISBN-13: 9780470084908.

Lu, Ruqian. Zhang, Songmao. *Automatic Generation of Computer Animation: Using AI for Movie Animation*. Paperback First Edition. Springer. 2002. ISBN-10: 3540431144. ISBN-13: 9783540431145.

> eBook. Springer. 2003.
>
> Paperback Reprint. Springer. 2014. ISBN-10: 3662161583. ISBN-13: 9783662161586.

Magnenat-Thalmann, Nadia. *Communicating With Virtual Worlds*. Hardcover First Edition. Springer-Verlag. 1993. ISBN-10: 0387701257. ISBN-13: 9780387701257.

    Paperback Reprint. Springer. 2012. ISBN-10: 4431684581. ISBN-13: 9784431684589.

Magnenat-Thalmann, Nadia. Thalmann Ph. D., Daniel. *Computer Animation: Theory and Practice*. Hardcover First Edition. Springer-Verlag. 1985. ISBN-10: 0387700056. ISBN-13: 9780387700052.

    Paperback Reprint. Springer. 2012. ISBN-10: 4431681078. ISBN-13: 9784431681076.

Magnenat-Thalmann, Nadia. *Creating and Animating the Virtual World*. Hardcover First Edition. Springer-Verlag. 1992. ISBN-10: 0387700935. ISBN-13: 9780387700939.

    Paperback Reprint. Springer. 2012. ISBN-10: 4431681884. ISBN-13: 9784431681885.

Magnenat Thalmann, Nadia. Thalmann Ph. D., Daniel. *Synthetic Actors in Computer-Generated 3D Films*. Hardcover First Edition. Springer. 1990. ISBN-10: 354052214X. ISBN-13: 9783540522140.

    Paperback Reprint. Springer. 2011. ISBN-10: 3642754554. ISBN-13: 9783642754555.

Menache, Alberto. *Understanding Motion Capture for Computer Animation*. Paperback First Edition. Morgan Kauffman Books. 1999. ISBN-10: 0124906303. ISBN-13: 9780124906303.

    Paperback Second Edition. Morgan Kaufmann Books. 2010. ISBN-10: 0123814960. ISBN-13: 9780123814968.

    eBook. Morgan Kaufmann Books. 2011.

Moody, Juniko. Sawicki, Mark. *Filming the Fantastic with Virtual Technology: Filmmaking on the Digital Backlot*. Hardcover First Edition. Routledge. 2020. ISBN-10: 0367354225. ISBN-13: 9780367354220.

>Paperback First Edition. Routledge. 2020. ISBN-10: 0367354217. ISBN-13: 9780367354213.

>eBook. Routledge. 2020.

Myers, Dale K. *Computer Animation: Expert Advice on Breaking Into the Business*. Paperback First Edition. Oak Cliff Press Inc. 1999. ISBN-10: 0966270967. ISBN-13: 9780966270969.

Russett, Robert. *Hyperanimation: Digital Images and Virtual Worlds*. Hardcover First Edition. John Libbey Publishing. 2009. ISBN-10: 0861966937. ISBN-13: 9780861966936.

>Paperback First Edition. John Libbey Publishing. 2009. ISBN-10: 0861966546. ISBN-13: 9780861966547.

Sito, Tom. *Moving Innovation: A History of Computer Animation*. Hardcover First Edition. MIT Press. 2013. ISBN-10: 0262019094. ISBN-13: 9780262019095.

>Paperback First Edition. MIT Press. 2015. ISBN-10: 0262528401. ISBN-13: 9780262528405.

Tao, Dacheng. Yu, Jun. *Modern Machine Learning Techniques and Their Applications in Cartoon Animation Research*. Hardcover First Edition. Wiley-IEEE Press. 2013. ISBN-10: 1118115147. ISBN-13: 9781118115145.

Valliere, Richard Auzenne. *The Visualization Quest: A History Of Computer Animation*. Hardcover First Edition. Fairleigh Dickinson University Press. 1994. ISBN-10: 0838634400. ISBN-13: 9780838634400.

Vince, John. *Essential Computer Animation Fast: How to Understand the Techniques and Potential of Computer Animation*. Paperback First Edition. Springer. 2000. ISBN-10: 1852331410. ISBN-13: 9781852331412.

>Paperback Reprint. Springer. 2011. ISBN-10: 1447104900. ISBN-13: 9781447104902.

>eBook. Springer. 2012.

Weinstock, Neal. *Computer Animation*. Paperback First Edition. Addison-Wesley. ISBN-10: 020109438X. ISBN-13: 9780201094381.

Stop-Motion Animation and Puppetry

Dalton, Tony. Harryhausen, Ray. *A Century of Model Animation: From Méliès to Aardman*. Hardcover First Edition. Aurum Press. 2008. ISBN-10: 1845133676. ISBN-13: 9781845133672.

Harryhausen, Ray. *A Century of Stop-Motion Animation: From Melies to Aardman*. Hardcover First Edition. Watson-Guptill. 2008. ISBN-10: 0823099806. ISBN-13: 9780823099801.

Holman, L. Bruce. *Puppet Animation In The Cinema: History And Technique*. Hardcover First Edition. A. S. Barnes & Co. 1975. ISBN-10: 0498013855. ISBN-13: 9780563108290.

> Hardcover First Edition. Tanvity Press. 1975. ISBN-10: 0904208605. ISBN-13: 9780904208603.

Kuznets, Lois Rostow. *When Toys Come Alive: Narratives of Animation, Metamorphosis, and Development*. Hardcover First Edition. Yale University Press. 1994. ISBN-10: 0300056451. ISBN-13: 9780300056457.

Lord, Peter. Park, Nick. Sproxton, David. *A Grand Success!: The People and Characters Who Created Aardman*. Hardcover First Edition. Harry N. Abrams. 2019. ISBN-10: 1419729527. ISBN-13: 9781419729522.

> Audiobook. Narrated by Will Watt. Abrams Press. 2019.

> eBook. Abrams Press. 2019.

Lord, Peter. Sproxton, David. *Aardman: An Epic Journey: Taken One Frame At A Time*. Hardcover First Edition. Simon & Schuster. 2018. ISBN-10: 1471164748. ISBN-13: 9781471164743.

> Paperback First Edition. Simon & Schuster. 2018. ISBN-10: 1471164756. ISBN-13: 9781471164750.

Lord, Peter. Sibley, Brian. *Cracking Animation: The Aardman Book of 3-D Animation*. Hardcover First Edition. Thames and Hudson Ltd. 1998. ISBN-10: 0500018812. ISBN-13: 9780500018811.

  Hardcover Second Edition. Gardners Books. 2004.
  ISBN-10: 050051190X. ISBN-13: 9780500511909.

  Hardcover Revised Edition. Harry N. Abrams. 2004.
  ISBN-10: 0810949717. ISBN-13: 9780810949713.

  Paperback Third Revised Edition. Thames and Hudson Ltd. 2010.
  ISBN-10: 0500289069. ISBN-13: 9780500289068.

  Paperback Fourth Edition. Thames and Hudson Ltd. 2015.
  ISBN-10: 0500291993. ISBN-13: 9780500291993.

Mihailova, Mihaela. *Coraline: A Closer Look at Studio LAIKA's Stop-Motion Witchcraft*. Hardcover First Edition. Bloomsbury Academic. 2021. ISBN-13: 9781501347863.

  eBook. Bloomsbury Academic. 2021.

Priebe, Ken A. *The Advanced Art of Stop-Motion Animation*. Paperback First Edition. Cengage Learning PTR. 2010. ISBN-10: 1435456130. ISBN-13: 9781435456136.

  eBook. Course Technology PTR. 2013.

Priebe, Ken. *The Art of Stop-Motion Animation*. Paperback First Edition. Course Technology PTR. 2006. ISBN-10: 1598632442. ISBN-13: 9781598632446.

Roe, Annabelle Honess. *Aardman Animations: Beyond Stop-Motion*. Hardcover First Edition. Bloomsbury Academic. 2020. ISBN-10: 1350114553. ISBN-13: 9781350114555.

  eBook. Bloomsbury Academic. 2020.

  Paperback First Edition. Bloomsbury Academic. 2021.
  ISBN-10: 1350194948. ISBN-13: 9781350194946.

Wilson, S. S. *Puppets and People: Dimensional Animation Combined with Live Action in the Cinema*. Hardcover First Edition. A.S. Barnes & Co. 1980. ISBN-10: 0498023125. ISBN-13: 9780498023125.

Aesthetics, Abstraction, and Experimental Animation

Amidi, Amid. *Cartoon Modern: Style and Design in Fifties Animation*. Hardcover First Edition. Chronicle Books, LLC. 2006. ISBN-10: 0811847314. ISBN-13: 9780811847315.

> eBook available to download at:
> https://animationobsessive.substack.com/p/our-treat-to-you

Bashara, Dan. *Cartoon Vision: UPA Animation and Postwar Aesthetics*. Hardcover First Edition. University of California Press. 2019. ISBN-10: 0520298136. ISBN-13: 9780520298132.

> Paperback First Edition. University of California Press. 2019. ISBN-10: 0520298144. ISBN-13: 9780520298149.

> eBook. University of California Press. 2019.

Francis Parks, Corrie. *Fluid Frames: Experimental Animation with Sand, Clay, Paint, and Pixels*. Hardcover First Edition. 2015. ISBN-10: 1138784907. ISBN-13: 9781138784901.

> Hardcover First Edition. Routledge. 2016 ISBN-10: 1138190624. ISBN-13: 9781138190627.

> Paperback First Edition. Routledge. 2016. ISBN-10: 1138784915. ISBN-13: 9781138784918.

> eBook. Routledge. 2020.

Frank, Hannah. *Frame by Frame: A Materialist Aesthetics of Animated Cartoons*. Paperback First Edition. University of California Press. 2019. ISBN-10: 0520303628. ISBN-13: 9780520303621.

> eBook. University of California Press. 2019.

Furniss, Maureen. *Art in Motion: Animation Aesthetics*. Hardcover First Edition. Indiana University Press. 1998. ISBN-10: 1864620382. ISBN-13: 9781864620382.

　　　　Paperback First Edition. Indiana University Press. 1998.
　　　　ISBN-10: 1864620390. ISBN-13: 9781864620399.

　　　　Paperback Revised Edition. John Libbey Publishing. 2008.
　　　　ISBN-10: 0861966635. ISBN-13: 9780861966639.

　　　　eBook. John Libbey Publishing. 2008.

Hamlyn, Nicky. Smith, Vicky. *Experimental and Expanded Animation: New Perspectives and Practices (Experimental Film and Artists' Moving Image) 2018 Edition*. Hardcover First Edition. Palgrave Macmillan. 2018. ISBN-10: 3319738720. ISBN-13: 9783319738727.

　　　　Paperback First Edition. Springer. ISBN-10: 3030088774.
　　　　ISBN-13: 9783030088774.

　　　　eBook. Palgrave Macmillan. 2018.

Harris, Miriam. Husbands, Lilly. Taberham, Paul. *Experimental Animation: From Analogue to Digital*. Hardcover First Edition. Routledge. 2019. ISBN-10: 113870296X. ISBN-13: 9781138702967.

　　　　Paperback First Edition. Routledge. 2019. ISBN-10: 1138702986.
　　　　ISBN-13: 9781138702981.

　　　　eBook. Routledge. 2019.

Johnston, Andrew R. *Pulses of Abstraction: Episodes from a History of Animation*. Hardcover First Edition. University of Minnesota Press. 2021. ISBN-10: 0816685231. ISBN-13: 9780816685233.

　　　　Paperback First Edition. University of Minnesota Press. 2021.
　　　　ISBN-10: 0816685290. ISBN-13: 9780816685295.

　　　　eBook. University of Minnesota Press. 2021.

Pallant, Chris. *Animated Landscapes: History, Form and Function*. Hardcover First Edition. Bloomsbury Academic. 2015. ISBN-10: 1628923512. ISBN-13: 9781628923513.

eBook. Bloomsbury Academic. 2015.

Paperback Reprint Edition. Bloomsbury Academic. 2017.
ISBN-10: 1501320114. ISBN-13: 9781501320118.

Papapetros, Spyros. *On the Animation of the Inorganic: Art, Architecture, and the Extension of Life*. Hardcover First Edition. University of Chicago Press. 2012. ISBN-10: 0226645681. ISBN-13: 9780226645681.

Paperback Reprint Edition. University of Chicago Press. 2016.
ISBN-10: 022638019X. ISBN-13: 9780226380193.

Pierson, Ryan. *Figure and Force in Animation Aesthetics*. Hardcover First Edition. Oxford University Press. 2019. ISBN-10: 0190949759. ISBN-13: 9780190949754.

Paperback First Edition. Oxford University Press. 2019.
ISBN-10: 0190949767. ISBN-13: 9780190949761.

eBook. Oxford University Press. 2019.

Russet, Robert. Starr, Cecile. *Experimental Animation: Origins of a New Art*. Paperback First Edition. Van Nostrand Reinhold Company. 1976. ISBN-10: 0442271956. ISBN-13: 9780442271954.

Paperback Revised Edition. Da Capo Press 1988. ISBN-10: 0306803143.
ISBN-13: 9780306803147.

Summers, Sam. *DreamWorks Animation: Intertextuality and Aesthetics in Shrek and Beyond*. Hardcover First Edition. Palgrave Macmillan. 2020. ISBN-10: 3030368505. ISBN-13: 9783030368500.

Paperback First Edition. Palgrave Macmillan. 2020.
ISBN-10: 303036853X. ISBN-13: 9783030368531.

eBook. Palgrave Macmillan. 2020.

Industry

Booker, M. Keith. *Drawn to Television: Prime-Time Animation from the Flintstones to Family Guy*. Hardcover First Edition. Praeger Publishing. 2006. ISBN-10: 0275990192. ISBN-13: 9780275990190.

Brasch, Walter M. *Cartoon Monickers: An Insight into the Animation Industry*. Hardcover First Edition. Bowling Green University Popular Press. 1983. ISBN-10: 0879722436. ISBN-13: 9780879722432.

> Paperback First Edition. Bowling Green University Popular Press. 1983. ISBN-10: 0879722444. ISBN-13: 9780879722449.

> Paperback Second Edition. iUniverse. 2000. ISBN-10: 0595145019. ISBN-13: 9780595145010.

Cohen, Karl. *Forbidden Animation: Censored Cartoons and Blacklisted Animators in America*. Hardcover First Edition. McFarland & Company, Inc. Publishers. 1998. ISBN-10: 0786403950. ISBN-13: 9780786403950.

> Paperback Reprint Edition. McFarland & Company, Inc. Publishers. 2004. ISBN-10: 0786420324. ISBN-13: 9780786420322.

> eBook. McFarland & Company, Inc. Publishers. 2013.

Cook, Malcolm. Thompson, Kirsten Moana. *Animation and Advertising*. Hardcover First Edition. Palgrave Macmillan. 2020. ISBN-10: 3030279383. ISBN-13: 9783030279387.

> eBook. Palgrave Macmillan. 2019.

> Paperback First Edition. Palgrave Macmillan. 2019. ISBN-10: 3030279413. ISBN-13: 9783030279417.

Corsaro, Sandro. Parrott, Clifford J. *Hollywood 2D Digital Animation: The New Flash Production Revolution*. Paperback First Edition. Thomson Course Technology. 2004. ISBN-10: 159200170X. ISBN-13: 9781592001705.

Dobbs, G. Michael. *Escape: How Animation Broke into the Mainstream in the 1990s*. BearManor Media. 2007. ISBN-10: 1593931107. ISBN-13: 9781593931100.

    eBook. BearManor Media. 2015.

    Paperback Reprint Edition. BearManor Media. 2016. ISBN-10: 1593931107. ISBN-13: 9781593931100.

Furniss, Maureen. *Animation: Art and Industry*. Paperback First Edition. John Libbey Publishing. 2009. ISBN-10: 0861966805. ISBN-13: 9780861966806.

    eBook. John Libbey Publishing. 2009.

Goldmark, Daniel. Keil, Charlie. *Funny Pictures: Animation and Comedy in Studio-Era Hollywood*. Hardcover First Edition. University of California Press. 2011. ISBN-10: 0520267230. ISBN-13: 9780520267237.

    Paperback First Edition. University of California Press. 2011. ISBN-10: 0520267249. ISBN-13: 9780520267244.

    eBook. University of California Press. 2011.

Herdeg, Walter. *Film and TV Graphics, 2*. Hardcover First Edition. The Graphis Press. 1976. ISBN-10: 0803823223. ISBN-13: 9780803823228.

Hollis, Tim. *Toons in Toyland: The Story of Cartoon Character Merchandise*. Hardcover First Edition. University Press of Mississippi. 2015. ISBN-10: 1628461993. ISBN-13: 9781628461992.

    eBook. University Press of Mississippi. 2015.

Holz, Jo. *Kids' TV Grows Up: The Path from Howdy Doody to SpongeBob*. Paperback First Edition. McFarland & Company, Inc., Publishers. 2017. ISBN-10: 1476668744. ISBN-13: 9781476668741.

    eBook. McFarland & Company, Inc., Publishers. 2017.

Jenkins, Eric. *Special Affects: Cinema, Animation and the Translation of Consumer Culture*. Hardcover First Edition. Edinburgh University Press. 2014. ISBN-10: 0748695478. ISBN-13: 9780748695478.

    Paperback First Edition. Edinburgh University Press. 2016. ISBN-10: 1474414591. IBSN-13: 9781474414593.

    eBook. Edinburgh University Press. 2016.

K, Suresh. Rao, Krishna. *Animation Industry (Industry Analysis Series)*. Paperback First Edition. ICFAI University Press. 2008. ISBN-10: 8131415546. ISBN-13: 9788131415542.

Kanfer, Stefan. *Serious Business: The Art and Commerce of Animation in America from Betty Boop to Toy Story*. Hardcover First Edition. Scribner Books. 1997. ISBN-10: 0684800799. ISBN-13: 9780684800790.

    Paperback First Edition. Da Capo Press. 2000. ISBN-10: 0306809184. ISBN-13: 9780306809187.

Levitan, Eli L. *Animation Art in the Commercial Film*. Paperback First Edition. Reinhold Publishing Corporation. 1960.

    Paperback First Edition. Creative Media Partners, LLC. 2015. ISBN-10: 1297756371. ISBN-13: 9781297756375.

    Paperback Second Edition. Creative Media Partners, LLC. 2018. ISBN-10: 0342588737. ISBN-13: 9780342588732

    Hardcover First Edition. Franklin Classics. 2018. ISBN-10: 0342588745. ISBN-13: 9780342588749.

Neuwirth, Allan. *Makin' Toons: Inside the Most Popular Animated TV Shows and Movies*. Paperback First Edition. Allworth Press. 2002. ISBN-10: 1581152698. ISBN-13: 9781581152692.

    eBook. Allworth Press. 2007.

Robinson, Chris. *The Animation Pimp*. Paperback First Edition. Course Technology PTR. 2007. ISBN-10: 1598634038. ISBN-13: 9781598634037.

Rubin, Susan. *Animation: The Art and the Industry*. Paperback First Edition. Prentice Hall. 1987. ISBN-10: 0130377899. ISBN-13: 9780130377890.

>Hardcover First Edition. Prentice Hall. 1987. ISBN-10: 013037797X. ISBN-13: 9780130377975.

Sammond, Nicholas. *Birth of an Industry: Blackface Minstrelsy and the Rise of American Animation*. Hardcover First Edition. Duke University Press Books. 2015. ISBN-10: 0822358409. ISBN-13: 9780822358404.

>Paperback First Edition. Duke University Press Books. 2015. ISBN-10: 0822358522. ISBN-13: 9780822358527.

>eBook. Duke University Press Books. 2015.

Sito, Tom. *Drawing the Line: The Untold Story of the Animation Unions from Bosko to Bart Simpson*. Hardcover First Edition. University Press of Kentucky. 2006. ISBN-10: 0813124077. ISBN-13: 9780813124070.

>eBook. University Press of Kentucky. 2006.

Tell, Darcy. *Times Square Spectacular: Lighting Up Broadway*. Hardcover First Edition. Smithsonian Books. 2007. ISBN-10: 0060884339. ISBN-13: 9780060884338.

Waguespack, Jason. *Rise and Fall of the 80's Toon Empire: A Behind the Scenes Look at When He-Man, G.I. Joe and Transformers Ruled the Airwaves*. Independent Publisher. 2017. ISBN-10: 1974098605. ISBN-13: 9781974098606.

>eBook. Independent Publisher. 2017.

History

Barrier, Michael. *Hollywood Cartoons: American Animation in Its Golden Age*. Hardcover First Edition. Oxford University Press. 1999. ISBN-10: 0195037596. ISBN-13: 9780195037593.

    Paperback First Edition. Oxford University Press. 2003. ISBN-10: 0195167295. ISBN-13: 9780195167290.

    eBook. Oxford University Press. 2003.

    Hardcover First Edition. Paw Prints. 2008. ISBN-10: 1435298659. ISBN-13: 9781435298651.

Coar, Bob. *A Century of American Animation: Act One: Born on the Silver Screen*. Paperback First Edition. Independently Published. 2022. ISBN-13: 97984484978915.

Crafton, Donald. *Before Mickey: The Animated Film 1898-1928.* Hardcover First Edition. MIT Press. 1982. ISBN-10: 0262030837. ISBN-13: 9780262030830.

    Paperback Reprint. MIT Press. 1984. ISBN-10: 0262530589. ISBN-13: 9780262530583.

    Paperback Reprint. University of Chicago Press. 1993. ISBN-10: 0226116670. ISBN-13: 9780226116679.

    eBook. University of Chicago Press. 2015.

Heraldson, Donald. *Creators of Life: A History of Animation.* Hardcover First Edition. Drake Publishers. 1975. ISBN-10: 0877497338. ISBN-13: 9780877497332.

Korkis, Jim. *Animation Anecdotes: The Hidden History of Classic American Animation*. Paperback First Edition. Theme Park Press. 2014. ISBN-10: 1941500137. ISBN-13: 9781941500132.

    eBook. Theme Park Press. 2014.

Kornhaber, Donna. *Nightmares in the Dream Sanctuary: War and the Animated Film*. Hardcover First Edition. University of Chicago Press. 2019. ISBN-10: 022647268X. ISBN-13: 9780226472683.

Lutz, Edwin George. *Animated Cartoons: How They Are Made, Their Origin and Development*. First Edition. Charles Scribner's Sons. 1920.

> Reprint. Applewood Books. 1998. ISBN-10: 1557094748. ISBN-13: 9781557094742.

> Hardcover Reprint. Horney Press. 2009. ISBN-10: 1444652141. ISBN-13: 9781444652147.

> Paperback Reprint. HardPress Publishing. 2013. ISBN-10: 1313834483. ISBN-13: 9781313834483.

> Paperback Reprint. Applewood Books. 2014. ISBN-10: 1429093633. ISBN-13: 9781429093637.

Maltin, Leonard. *Of Mice and Magic: A History of American Animated Cartoons*. Hardcover First Edition. McGraw-Hill. 1980. ISBN-10: 0070398356. ISBN-13: 9780070398351.

> Paperback First Edition. Plume. 1980. ISBN-10: 0452252407. ISBN-13: 9780452252400.

> Beck, Jerry. Maltin, Leonard. Paperback Revised and Updated Edition. Plume. 1987. ISBN-10: 0452259932. ISBN-13: 9780452259935.

Mitenbuler, Reid. *Wild Minds: The Artists and Rivalries That Inspired the Golden Age of Animation*. Hardcover First Edition. Atlantic Monthly Press. 2020. ISBN-10: 0802129382. ISBN-13: 9780802129383.

> eBook. Atlantic Monthly Press. 2020.

> Audiobook. Narrated by Kevin R. Free. Recorded Books. 2020.

> Paperback First Edition. Grove Press. 2021. ISBN-10: 0802159141. ISBN-13: 9780802159144.

Muller, Jacques. *40 Years of Animated Cartoons*. Paperback First Edition. Partridge Publishing Singapore. 2018. ISBN-10: 1482880873. ISBN-13: 9781482880878.

    eBook. Partridge Publishing Singapore. 2018.

Perlmutter, David. *America Toons In: A History of Television Animation*. Paperback First Edition. McFarland & Company, Inc., Publishers. 2014. ISBN-10: 0786476508. ISBN-13: 9780786476503.

    eBook. McFarland & Company, Inc., Publishers. 2014.

Sampson, Henry T. *That's Enough Folks: Black Images in Animated Cartoons, 1900-1960*. Hardcover First Edition. Scarecrow Press. 1998. ISBN-10: 081083250X. ISBN-13: 9780810832503.

Shull, Michael S. Wilt, David E. *Doing Their Bit: Wartime American Animated Short Films, 1939-1945*. Hardcover First Edition. McFarland & Company, Inc., Publishers. 1987. ISBN-10: 0899502180. ISBN-13: 9780899502182.

    Paperback Second Edition. McFarland & Company, Inc., Publishers. 2004. ISBN-10: 078641555X. ISBN-13: 9780786415557.

Solomon, Charles. *The History of Animation: Enchanted Drawings*. Hardcover First Edition. Alfred A. Knopf. 1989. ISBN-10: 0394546849. ISBN-13: 9780394546841.

    Hardcover Revised Edition. Random House Value Publishing. 1994. ISBN-10: 0517118599. ISBN-13: 9780517118597.

Culture

Arnold, Gordon B. *Animation and the American Imagination: A Brief History*. Hardcover First Edition. Praeger Publishing. 2016. ISBN-10: 1440833591. ISBN-13: 9781440833595.

>eBook. Praeger. 2016.

Dowling, Ryan. *The Animated Heart: A Historical and Cultural Insight Into Animation*. Paperback First Edition. Independently Published. 2019. ISBN-10: 1796472751. ISBN-13: 9781796472752.

>eBook. Kindle Direct Publishing. 2021.

Eury, Michael. *Hero-A-Go-Go: Campy Comic Books, Crimefighters, & Culture of the 1960's*. Paperback First Edition. TwoMorrows Publishing. 2017. ISBN-10: 1605490733. ISBN-13: 9781605490731.

Fink, Moritz. *The Simpsons: A Cultural History*. Hardcover First Edition. Rowman & Littlefield Publishers. 2019. ISBN-10: 1538116162. ISBN-13: 9781538116166.

>eBook. Rowman & Littlefield Publishers. 2019.

Gainer, Darius S. *Black Representation in the World of Animation*. Paperback First Edition. Amatl Comix. 2021. ISBN-10: 1879691981. ISBN-13: 9781879691988.

>eBook. Amatl Comix. 2021. ISBN-10: 1879691981. ISBN-13: 9781879691988.

Grandinetti, Fred. *Popeye: An Illustrated Cultural History*. Paperback First Edition. McFarland & Company, Inc., Publishers. 1994. ISBN-10: 0899509827. ISBN-13: 9780899509822.

>eBook. McFarland. 2003.

>Paperback Second Edition. McFarland & Company, Inc., Publishers. 2004. ISBN-10: 078641605X. ISBN-13: 9780786416059.

Klein, Norman M. *7 Minutes: The Life and Death of the American Animated Cartoon*. Hardcover First Edition. Verso Books. 1993. ISBN-10: 0860913961. ISBN-13: 9780860913962.

>Paperback Revised Edition. Verso Books. ISBN-10: 1859841503. ISBN-13: 9781859841501.

Leab, Daniel. *Orwell Subverted: The CIA and the Filming of Animal Farm*. Hardcover First Edition. The Pennsylvania State University Press. 2007. ISBN-10: 0271029781. ISBN-13: 9780271029788.

>Paperback First Edition. The Pennsylvania State University Press. 2008. ISBN-10: 027102979X. ISBN-13: 9780271029795.

Lehman, Christopher P. *American Animated Cartoons of the Vietnam Era: A Study of Social Commentary in Films and Television Programs, 1961-1973*. Paperback First Edition. McFarland & Company, Inc., Publishers. 2006. ISBN-10: 078642818X. ISBN-13: 9780786428182.

>eBook. McFarland & Company, Inc., Publishers. 2009.

Lehman, Christopher P. *The Colored Cartoon: Black Representation in American Animated Short Films, 1907-1954*. Hardcover First Edition. University of Massachusetts Press. 2007. ISBN-10: 1558496130. ISBN-13: 9781558496132.

>Paperback First Edition. University of Massachusetts Press. 2009. ISBN-10: 155849779X. ISBN-13: 9781558497795.

Mark, Harrison. Stabile, Carol. *Prime Time Animation: Television Animation and American Culture*. Hardcover First Edition. Routledge. 2003. ISBN-10: 0415283256. ISBN-13: 9780415283250.

>Paperback First Edition. Routledge. 2003. ISBN-10: 0415283264. ISBN-13: 9780415283267.

>eBook. Routledge. 2013.

McGowan, David. *Animated Personalities: Cartoon Characters and Stardom in American Theatrical Shorts*. Hardcover First Edition. University of Texas Press. 2019. ISBN-10: 1477317430. ISBN-13: 9781477317433.

Paperback First Edition. University of Texas Press. 2019.
ISBN-10: 1477317449. ISBN-13: 9781477317440.

eBook. University of Texas Press. 2019.

Moen, Kristian. *New York's Animation Culture: Advertising, Art, Design and Film, 1939-1940*. Hardcover First Edition. Palgrave Macmillan. 2019. ISBN-10: 3030279308. ISBN-13: 9783030279301.

eBook. Palgrave Macmillan. 2019.

Paperback First Edition. Palgrave Macmillan. 2020.
ISBN-10: 3030279332. ISBN-13: 9783030279332.

Roeder, Katherine. *Wide Awake in Slumberland: Fantasy, Mass Culture, and Modernism in the Art of Winsor McCay*. Hardcover First Edition. University Press of Mississippi. 2014. ISBN-10: 1617039608. ISBN-13: 9781617039607.

eBook. University Press of Mississippi. 2014.

Smoodin, Eric. *Animating Culture: Hollywood Cartoons from the Sound Era*. Paperback First Edition. Roundhouse Publishing. 1993. ISBN-10: 1857100131. ISBN-13: 9781857100136.

Paperback First Edition. Rutgers University Press. 1993.
ISBN-10: 0813519497. ISBN-13: 9780813519494.

Hardcover First Edition. Rutgers University Press. 1993.
ISBN-10: 0813519489. ISBN-13: 9780813519487.

eBook. Rutgers University Press. 1993.

Wells, Paul. *The Animated Bestiary: Animals, Cartoons, and Culture*. Hardcover First Edition. Rutgers University Press. 2008. ISBN-10: 0813544149. ISBN-13: 9780813544144.

Paperback First Edition. Rutgers University Press. 2008.
ISBN-10: 0813544157. ISBN-13: 9780813544151.

eBook. Rutgers University Press. 2008.

Wells, Paul. *Animation and America*. Paperback First Edition. Rutgers University Press. 2002. ISBN-10: 0813531608. ISBN-13: 9780813531601.

    Hardcover First Edition. Rutgers University Press. 2002. ISBN-10: 0813531594. ISBN-13: 9780813531595.

Wells, Paul. *Animation, Sport and Culture*. Hardcover First Edition. Palgrave Macmillan. 2014. ISBN-10: 1137027622. ISBN-13: 9781137027627.

    Paperback First Edition. Palgrave Macmillan. 2014. ISBN-10: 1349439665. ISBN-13: 9781349439669.

    eBook. Palgrave Macmillan. 2014.

Saturday Mornings

The relationship between Saturday Mornings and animation was, at one point, symbiotic. The following titles document that relationship.

Ashley, Michael. Garner, Joe. *It's Saturday Morning!: Celebrating the Golden Era of Cartoons 1960s-1990s*. Hardcover First Edition. becker&mayer! Books. 2018. ISBN-10: 0760362947. ISBN-13: 9780760362945.

Burke, Kevin. Burke, Timothy. *Saturday Morning Fever: Growing Up with Cartoon Culture*. Paperback First Edition. St. Martin's Griffin. 1998. ISBN-10: 0312169965. ISBN-13: 9780312169961.

Hendershot, Heather. *Saturday Morning Censors: Television Regulation Before the V-Chip*. Hardcover First Edition. Duke University Press Books. 1999. ISBN-10: 0822322110. ISBN-13: 9780822322115.

> Paperback First Edition. Duke University Press Books. 1999. ISBN-10: 0822322404. ISBN-13: 9780822322405.

McCray, Mark. *The Best Saturdays of Our Lives*. Paperback First Edition. iUniverse. 2015. ISBN-10: 1491755083. ISBN-13: 9781491755082.

> eBook. IUniverse. 2015.

Religion, Spirituality and Ethics

Bukatman, Scott. *Poetics of Slumberland: Animated Spirits and the Animating Spirit*. Hardcover First Edition. University of California Press. 2012. ISBN-10: 0520265718. ISBN-13: 9780520265714.

> Paperback First Edition. University of California Press. 2012. ISBN-10: 0520265726. ISBN-13: 9780520265721.

> eBook. University of California Press. 2012.

Feltmate, David. *Drawn to the Gods: Religion and Humor in The Simpsons, South Park & Family Guy*. Hardcover First Edition. New York University Press. 2017. ISBN-10: 1479822183. ISBN-13: 9781479822188.

> Paperback First Edition. New York University Press. 2017. ISBN-10: 9781479890361. ISBN-13: 9781479890361.

> eBook. New York University Press. 2017.

Horvath, Gyongyi. Hu, Tze-yue. Yokota, Masao. *Animating the Spirited: Journeys and Transformations*. Hardcover First Edition. University Press of Mississippi. 2020. ISBN-10: 1496826264. ISBN-13: 9781496826268.

> Paperback First Edition. University Press of Mississippi. 2020. ISBN-10: 1496826256. ISBN-13: 9781496826251.

> eBook. University Press of Mississippi. 2020.

Environment

Murray, Robin L. *That's All Folks?: Ecocritical Readings of American Animated Features*. Hardcover First Edition. University of Nebraska Press. 2011. ISBN-10: 0803235127. ISBN-13: 9780803235120.

    eBook. University of Nebraska Press. 2011.

Pike, Deidre M. *Enviro-Toons: Green Themes in Animated Cinema and Television*. Paperback First Edition. McFarland & Company, Inc., Publishers. 2012. ISBN-10: 0786465921. ISBN-13: 9780786465927.

    eBook. McFarland & Company, Inc., Publishers. 2012.

Voice Acting, Foley, Music and Sound

Altman, Rick. *Sound Theory, Sound Practice.* Paperback First Edition. Routledge. 1992. ISBN-10: 0415904579. ISBN-13: 9780415904575.

    Hardcover First Edition. Routledge. 2015. ISBN-10: 1138129631. ISBN-13: 9781138129634.

Ament, Vanessa Theme. *The Foley Grail: The Art of Performing Sound for Film, Games, and Animation*. Paperback First Edition. Focal Press. 2009. ISBN-10: 0240811259. ISBN-13: 9780240811253.

    Paperback Second Edition. Routledge. 2014. ISBN-10: 0415840856. ISBN-13: 9780415840859.

    eBook. Routledge. 2014

    Hardcover Second Edition. Routledge. 2015. ISBN-10: 1138130141. ISBN-13: 9781138130142.

    Paperback Third Edition. Routledge. 2021. ISBN-10: 0367442248. ISBN-13: 9780367442248.

    Hardcover Third Edition. Routledge. 2021. ISBN-10: 0367442299. ISBN-13: 9780367442293.

Beauchamp, Robin. *Designing Sound for Animation*. Paperback First Edition. A K Peters, Ltd./CRC Press. 2005. ISBN-10: 0240807332. ISBN-13: 9780240807331.

    Paperback Second Edition. Focal Press. 2013. ISBN-10: 0240824989. ISBN-13: 9780240824987.

    Hardcover First Edition. CRC Press. 2017. ISBN-10: 113842854X. ISBN-13: 9781138428546.

    eBook. Routledge. 2013.

Blu, Susan. Mullin, Molly Ann. *Word of Mouth: A Guide to Commercial Voice-Over Excellence*. Paperback First Edition. Pomegranate Press. 1987. ISBN-10: 0938817108. ISBN-13: 9780938817109.

> Paperback Second Edition. Pomegranate Press. 1993.
> ISBN-10: 0938817329. ISBN-13: 9780938817321.

> Paperback Third Edition. Silman-James Press. 2006.
> ISBN-10: 1879505878. ISBN-13: 9781879505872.

Burr, John. *The Voice Over Actor's Handbook: How to Analyze, Interpret, and Deliver Scripts*. Paperback First Edition. CreateSpace Independent Publishing Platform. 2016. ISBN-10: 1533083444. ISBN-13: 9781533083449.

> eBook. CreateSpace Independent Publishing Platform. 2016.

Butler, Daws. *Scenes for Actors and Voices*. Paperback First Edition. BearManor Media. 2015. ISBN-10: 0971457069. ISBN-13: 9780971457065.

> eBooks. BearManor Media. 2010.

> Paperback Reprint Edition. BearManor Media. 2015.
> ISBN-10: 0971457069. ISBN-13: 9780971457065.

Coyle, Rebecca. *Drawn to Sound: Animation Film Music and Sonicity*. Hardcover First Edition. Equinox Publishing. 2009. ISBN-10: 1845533534. ISBN-13: 9781845533533.

> Paperback First Edition. Equinox Publishing. 2010.
> ISBN-10: 1845533526. ISBN-13: 9781845533526.

Goldmark, Daniel. Granata, Charles L. *The Cartoon Music Book.* Paperback First Edition. Chicago Review Press. 2002. ISBN-10: 1556524730 ISBN-13: 9781556524738.

> eBook. Chicago Review Press. 2002.

Goldmark, Daniel Ira. *Tunes for 'Toons: Music and the Hollywood Cartoon*. Hardcover First Edition. University of California Press. 2005. ISBN-10: 0520236173. ISBN-13: 9780520236172.

> eBook. University of California Press. 2005

> Paperback First Edition. University of California Press. 2007.
> ISBN-10: 0520253116. ISBN-13: 9780520253117.

Lawson, Tim. Persons, Alisa. *The Magic Behind the Voices: A Who's Who of Cartoon Voice Actors*. Hardcover First Edition. 2004. ISBN-10: 1578066956. ISBN-13: 9781578066957.

    Paperback First Edition. University Press of Mississippi. 2004. ISBN-10: 1578066964. ISBN-13: 9781578066964.

    eBook. University Press of Mississippi. 2004.

Lallo, M.J. Wright, Jean Ann. *Voice-Over for Animation*. Paperback First Edition. Focal Press. 2009. ISBN-10: 0240810155. ISBN-13: 9780240810157.

    eBook. Routledge. 2013.

Lenburg, Jeff. Owens, Gary. *How to Make a Million Dollars With Your Voice (Or Lose Your Tonsils Trying)*. Paperback First Edition. McGraw-Hill. 2004. ISBN-10: 0071424105. ISBN-13: 9780071424103.

    Paperback Subsequent Edition. Moonwater Press. 2019. ISBN-10: 0990328775. ISBN-13: 9780990328773.

    eBook. Moonwater Press. 2019.

    Hardcover First Edition. Moonwater Press. 2021. ISBN-10: 0996320652. ISBN-13: 9780996320658.

Lowenthal, Yuri. Platt, Tara. *Voice-Over Voice Actor: What It's Like Behind the Mic*. Paperback First Edition. Bug Bot Press. 2010. ISBN-10: 0984074007. ISBN-13: 9780984074006.

Miller, W.R. *The Animated Voice Volume One*. Paperback First Edition. Pulp Hero Press. 2018. ISBN-10: 1683901614. ISBN-13: 9781683901617.

    eBook. Pulp Hero Press. 2018.

Miller, W.R. *The Animated Voice Volume Two*. Paperback First Edition. Pulp Hero Press. 2019. ISBN-10: 1683902300. ISBN-13: 9781683902300.

    eBook. Pulp Hero Press. 2019.

Paulsen, Rob. *Voice Lessons: How a Couple of Ninja Turtles, Pinky, and an Animaniac Saved My Life*. Paperback First Edition. Viva Editions. 2019. ISBN-10: 1632280663. ISBN-13: 9781632280664.

>eBook. Viva Editions. 2019.

>Audiobook. Narrated by Ash Paulsen. 2019.

Scoggin, Lisa. *The Music of Animaniacs: Postmodern Nostalgia in a Cartoon World*. Paperback First Edition. Pendragon Press. 2016. ISBN-10: 1576472426. ISBN-13: 9781576472422.

Wilcox, Janet. *Voiceovers: Techniques and Tactics for Success*. Paperback First Edition. Allworth Press. 2007. ISBN-10: 1581154755. ISBN-13: 9781581154757.

>Paperback Second Edition Allworth Press. 2007. ISBN-10: 1581158114. ISBN-13: 9781581158113.

>eBook. Allworth. 2010.

Storyboarding and Production

Bluth, Don. *The Art of Storyboard*. Paperback First Edition. Dark Horse Books. 2004. ISBN-10: 1595820078. ISBN-13: 9781595820075.

Buchan, Suzanne. *Animated Worlds*. Paperback First Edition. John Libbey Publishing. 2007. ISBN-10: 0861966619. ISBN-13: 9780861966615.

    eBook. John Libbey Publishing. 2007.

Canemaker, John. *Storytelling in Animation Vol. 2: The Art of the Animated Image*. Paperback First Edition. Samuel French Trade. 1988. ISBN-10: 0573606978. ISBN-13: 9780573606977.

Culhane, Shamus. *Animation: From Script to Screen*. Hardcover First Edition. St. Martin's Press. 1990. ISBN-10: 0312021623. ISBN-13: 9780312021627.

    Paperback First Edition. St. Martin's Griffin. 1990.
    ISBN-10: 0312050526. ISBN-13: 9780312050528.

Halas, John. Whitaker, Harold. *Timing for Animation*. Hardcover First Edition. Focal Press. 1981. ISBN-10: 0240508718. ISBN-13: 9780240508719.

    Paperback Second Edition. Focal Press. 2009. ISBN-10: 0240521609. ISBN-13: 9780240521602.

    Hardcover Third Edition. CRC Press. 2021.
    ISBN-10: 0367689359. ISBN-13: 9780367689353.

    Paperback Third Edition. CRC Press. 2021.
    ISBN-10: 9780367527754. ISBN-13: 0367527758.

    eBook. CRC Press. 2021.

Kroyer, Bill. Sito, Tom. *On Animation: The Director's Perspective Volume One*. Hardcover First Edition. CRC Press. 2019. ISBN-10: 1138067075. ISBN-13: 9781138067073.

    Paperback First Edition. CRC Press. 2019. ISBN-10: 1138066532. ISBN-13: 9781138066533.

eBook. CRC Press. 2019.

Kroyer, Bill. Sito, Tom. *On Animation: The Director's Perspective Volume Two*. Hardcover First Edition. CRC Press. 2019. ISBN-10: 1138067091. ISBN-13: 9781138067097.

>Paperback First Edition. CRC Press. 2019. ISBN-10: 1138066567. ISBN-13: 9781138066564.

>eBook. CRC Press. 2019.

MacLean, Fraser. *Setting the Scene: The Art & Evolution of Animation Layout*. Hardcover First Edition. Chronicle Books, LLC. 2011. ISBN-10: 0811869873. ISBN-13: 9780811869874.

Musburger PhD, Robert B. *Animation Production: Documentation and Organization*. Hardcover First Edition. CRC Press. 2017. ISBN-10: 1138080845. ISBN-13: 9781138080843.

>Paperback First Edition. CRC Press. 2017. ISBN-10: 1138032646. ISBN-13: 9781138032644.

>eBook. CRC Press. 2017.

Pallant, Chris. Price, Steven. *Storyboarding: A Critical History*. Hardcover First Edition. Palgrave Macmillan. 2015. ISBN-10: 1137027592. ISBN-13: 9781137027597.

>eBook. Palgrave Macmillan. 2015.

>Paperback First Edition. Palgrave Macmillan. 2018. ISBN-10: 134957323X. ISBN-13: 9781349573233.

Rall, Hannes. *Animation: From Concept to Production*. Hardcover First Edition. CRC Press. 2017. ISBN-10: 1138042226. ISBN-13: 9781138042223.

>Paperback First Edition. CRC Press. 2017. ISBN-10: 113804119X. ISBN-13: 9781138041196.

>eBook. CRC Press. 2017.

Individual Studios, Artists, and Figureheads

Adamson, Joe. *Tex Avery, King of Cartoons*. Paperback First Edition. Big Apple Books. Popular Library. 1975.

> Paperback First Edition. Da Capo Press. 1985. ISBN-10: 0306802481. ISBN-13: 9780306802485.

Adamson, Joe. *The Walter Lantz Story*. Hardcover First Edition. Putnam Adult. 1985. ISBN-10: 0399130969. ISBN-13: 9780399130960.

Alaskey, Joe. *That's Still Not All Folks!* Paperback First Edition. BearManor Media. 2009. ISBN-10: 1593931123. ISBN-13: 9781593931124.

> eBook, BearManor Media. 2012.

> Hardcover First Edition. BearManor Media. 2016.
> ISBN-10: 1593939795. ISBN-13: 9781593939793.

> Paperback Reprint Edition. BearManor Media. 2016.
> ISBN-10: 1593931123. ISBN-13: 9781593931124.

> Audiobook. BearManor Media. Narrated by Joe Bevilacqua. 2021.

Arnold, Mark. *Created and Produced by Total TeleVision Productions*. Paperback First Edition. BearManor Media. 2009. ISBN-10: 1593933452. ISBN-13: 9781593933456.

> eBook. BearManor Media. 2014.

> Audiobook. BearManor Media. Narrated by Jason Sullivan. 2016.

> Hardcover First Edition. BearManor Media. 2019.
> ISBN-10: 1629334871. ISBN-13: 9781629334875.

Arnold, Mark. *Think Pink: The Story of DePatie-Freleng*. Hardcover First Edition. BearManor Media. 2015. ISBN-10: 1593931700. ISBN-13: 9781593931704.

> Paperback First Edition. BearManor Media. 2015.
> ISBN-10: 1593931697. ISBN-13: 9781593931698.

eBook. BearManor Media. 2015.

Bashe, Philip. Blanc, Mel. *That's Not All Folks: My Life in the Golden Age of Cartoons and Radio*. Hardcover First Edition. Grand Central Publishing. 1988. ISBN-10: 0446512443. ISBN-13: 9780446512442.

    Paperback Reprint Edition. Grand Central Publishing. 1989. ISBN-10: 0446390895. ISBN-13: 9780446390897.

Basquin, Kit Smyth. *Mary Ellen Bute: Pioneer Animator*. Paperback First Edition. John Libbey Publishing. 2020. ISBN-10: 0861967445. ISBN-13: 9780861967445.

    eBook. John Libbey Publishing. 2020.

Beck, Jerry. *Outlaw Animation*. Paperback First Edition. Harry N. Abrams. 2003. ISBN-10: 0810991519. ISBN-13: 9780810991514.

Bevilacqua, Joe. Ohmart, Ben. *Daws Butler, Characters Actor*. Paperback First Edition. BearManor Media. 2004. ISBN-10: 1593930151. ISBN-13: 9781593930158.

    eBook. BearManor Media. 2012.

    Audiobook. Narrated by Joe Bevilacqua. BearManor Media. 2016.

    Book on CD. Waterlogg Productions and Blackstone Audio. 2016.

Bluth, Don. *Somewhere Out There: My Animated Life*. Paperback First Edition. Smart Pop. 2022. ISBN-10: 1637740530. ISBN-13: 9781637740538.

Buchan, Suzanne. *The Quay Brothers: Into a Metaphysical Playroom*. Hardcover First Edition. University of Minnesota Press. 2011. ISBN-10: 0816646589. ISBN-13: 9780816646586.

    Paperback First Edition. University of Minnesota Press. 2011. ISBN-10: 0816646597. ISBN-13: 9780816646593.

    eBook. University of Minnesota Press. 2011.

Canemaker, John. *Magic Color Flair: The World of Mary Blair*. Hardcover Annotated First Edition. Weldon Owen. 2014. ISBN-10: 1616287934. ISBN-13: 9781616287931.

Canemaker, John. *Tex Avery: The MGM Years, 1942-1955*. Hardcover First Edition. Turner Publishing. 1996. ISBN-10: 1570362912. ISBN-13: 9781570362910.

Canemaker, John. *The Art and Flair of Mary Blair: An Appreciation*. Hardcover First Edition. Disney Editions. 2003. ISBN-10: 0786853913. ISBN-13: 9780786853915.

> Hardcover Updated Edition. Disney Editions. 2014.
> ISBN-10: 1423127447. ISBN-13: 9781423127444.

Canemaker, John. *Two Guys Named Joe: Master Animation Storytellers Joe Grant & Joe Ranft*. Hardcover First Edition. Disney Editions. 2010. ISBN-10: 1423110676. ISBN-13: 9781423110675.

Canemaker, John. *Winsor McCay: His Life and Art*. Hardcover First Edition. Abbeville Press. 1987. ISBN-10: 5552005791. ISBN-13: 9785552005796.

> Hardcover First Edition. Artabras. 1990. ISBN-10: 0896596877.
> ISBN-13: 9780896596870.

> Hardcover Revised and Expanded Edition. Harry N. Abrams. 2005.
> ISBN-10: 0810959410. ISBN-13: 9780810959415.

> Paperback First Edition. CRC Press. 2018.
> ISBN-10: 113857886X. ISBN-13: 9781138578869.

> eBook. CRC Press. 2018.

Cabarga, Leslie. *The Fleischer Story*. Hardcover First Edition. Crown Publishers, Inc. 1976. ISBN-10: 0517525801. ISBN-13: 9780517525807.

> Paperback Subsequent Edition. Da Capo Press. 1988.
> ISBN-10: 0306803135. ISBN-13: 9780306803130.

Canwell, Bruce. Mullaney, Dean. Toth, Alex. *Genius, Animated: The Cartoon Art of Alex Toth*. Hardcover First Edition. IDW Publishing. 2014. ISBN-10: 161377950X. ISBN-13: 9781613779507.

Cawley, John. *The Animated Films of Don Bluth*. Paperback First Edition. Image Publishing of New York. 1991. ISBN-10: 0685503348. ISBN-13: 9780685503348.

Cech, John. *Imagination and Innovation: The Story of Weston Woods*. Hardcover First Edition. Scholastic Press. 2009. ISBN-10: 0545089220. ISBN-13: 9780545089227.

Clokey, Joe. *Gumby Imagined: The Story of Art Clokey and His Creations*. Hardcover First Edition. Dynamite Entertainment. 2017. ISBN-10: 1524104345. ISBN-13: 9781524104344.

> eBook. Dynamite Entertainment. 2017.

Collier, Kevin Scott. *Chuck and Jack Luchsinger's Cartoon TeleTales*. Paperback First Edition. Independent Publisher. 2018. ISBN-10: 1718944659. ISBN-13: 9781718944657.

Collier, Kevin Scott. Matheson, Tim. *Jonny, Sinbad Jr. & Me*. Paperback First Edition. Independent Publisher. 2017. ISBN-10: 1978414838. ISBN-13: 9781978414839.

Collier, Kevin Scott. *Winsor McCay: Boyhood Dreams: Growing Up In Spring Lake, Michigan 1867-1885*. Paperback First Edition. Independent Publisher. 2017. ISBN-10: 1544922248. ISBN-13: 9781544922249.

Cotte, Olivier. *David Ehrlich: Citizen of the World*. Paperback First Edition. Dreamland. 2002. ISBN-10: 2910027805. ISBN-13: 9782910027803.

Crafton, Donald. *Emile Cohl, Caricature, and Film*. Hardcover First Edition. Princeton University Press. 1990. ISBN-10: 0691055815. ISBN-13: 9780691055817.

> Paperback Reprinting Edition. Princeton University Press. 1992. ISBN-10: 0691008817. ISBN-13: 9780691008813.

> Paperback Reprinting Edition. Princeton University Press. 2014. ISBN-10: 0691609128. ISBN-13: 9780691609126.

> Hardcover Reprinting Edition. Princeton University Press. 2016. ISBN-10: 0691637458. ISBN-13: 9780691637457.

Culhane, Shamus. *Talking Animals and Other People: The Autobiography of a Legendary Animator*. Hardcover First Edition. St. Martin's Press. 1986. ISBN-10: 0312784732. ISBN-13: 9780312784737.

>Paperback First Edition. De Capo Press. 1998.
>ISBN-10: 0306808307. ISBN-13: 9780306808302.

Dalton, Tony. Harryhausen, Ray. *Ray Harryhausen: An Animated Life*. Hardcover First Edition. Aurum Press. 2003. ISBN-10: 1854109405. ISBN-13: 9781854109408.

>Hardcover First Edition. Billboard Books. 2004. ISBN-10: 0823084027. ISBN-13: 9780823084029.

>Paperback Revised Updated Edition. Aurum Press. 2010.
>ISBN-10: 1845135016. ISBN-13: 9781845135010.

De Vries, Tjitte. Mul, Ati. *"They Thought It Was a Marvel": Arthur Melbourne-Cooper (1874-1961), Pioneer of Puppet Animation*. Hardcover First Edition. 2010. ISBN-10: 9085550165. ISBN-13: 9789085550167.

Deitch, Gene. *For the Love of Prague*. Paperback First Edition. Baset Publishers. 1997. ISBN-10: 8072054678. ISBN-13: 9788072054671.

>Paperback New Edition. Pragma Publishers. 1998.
>ISBN-10: 8023827499. ISBN-13: 9788023827491.

>Paperback Reprint. Bay Foreign Language Books. 2002.
>ISBN-10: 8086223094. ISBN-13: 9788086223094.

>eBook. John Caulkins. 2015.

Dobson, Nichola. *Norman McLaren: Between the Frames (Animation: Key Films/Filmmakers)*. Hardcover First Edition. Bloomsbury Academic. 2018. ISBN-10: 1501328816. ISBN-13: 9781501328817.

>eBook. Bloomsbury Academic. 2018.

>Paperback First Edition. Bloomsbury Academic. 2019.
>ISBN-10: 1501354930. ISBN-13: 9781501354939.

Evans, Noell K. Wolfgram. *Animators of Film and Television: Nineteen Artists, Writers, Producers and Others*. Paperback First Edition. McFarland & Company, Inc., Publishers. 2011. ISBN-10: 0786448326. ISBN-13: 9780786448326.

    eBook. McFarland & Company, Inc., Publishers. 2011.

Finch, Christopher. *Jim Henson: The Works - The Art, the Magic, the Imagination*. Hardcover First Edition. Random House. 1993. ISBN-10: 0679412034. ISBN-13: 9780679412038.

Fleischer, Richard. *Out of the Inkwell: Max Fleischer and the Animation Revolution*. Hardcover First Edition. University Press of Kentucky. 2005. ISBN-10: 0813123550. ISBN-13: 9780813123554.

    eBook. The University Press of Kentucky. 2005.

    Paperback Reprint Edition. University Press of Kentucky. 2011. ISBN-10: 0813134641. ISBN-13: 9780813134642.

    Audiobook. Narrated by Gary Galone.
    University Press Audiobooks. 2018.

Foray, June. *Did You Grow Up with Me, Too?: The Autobiography of June Foray*. Hardcover First Edition. BearManor Media. 2009. ISBN-10: 1629330361. ISBN-13: 9781629330365.

    Paperback First Edition. BearManor Media. 2009. ISBN-10: 1593934610. ISBN-13: 9781593934613.

    eBook. BearManor Media. 2015.

Freleng, Friz. Weber, David. *Animation: The Art of Friz Freleng*. Hardcover Limited Edition. Donovan Publishing. 1994. ISBN-10: 1880538067. ISBN-13: 9781880538067.

Garcia, Roger. *Frank Tashlin*. Paperback First Edition. British Film Institute. 1994. ISBN-10: 085170462X. ISBN-13: 9780851704623.

Goldschmidt, Rick. *The Making of Santa Claus Is Comin' To Town and The Daydreamer*. Hardcover First Edition. Miser Bros. Press. 2018. ISBN-10: 0971308187. ISBN-13: 9780971308183.

Grace, Whitney. *Lotte Reiniger: Pioneer of Film Animation*. Paperback First Edition. McFarland & Company, Inc., Publishers. 2017. ISBN-10: 1476662061. ISBN-13: 9781476662060.

    eBook. McFarland & Company, Inc., Publishers. 2017.

Grandinetti, Fred M. *He Am What He Am! Jack Mercer, the Voice of Popeye*. Paperback First Edition. BearManor Media. 2007. ISBN-10: 1593930968. ISBN-13: 9781593930967.

    Paperback Reprint Edition. BearManor Media. 2015. ISBN-10: 1593930968. ISBN-13: 9781593930967.

Grant, John. *Masters of Animation*. Hardcover First Edition. Chrysalis Books. 2001. ISBN-10: 0713486287. ISBN-13: 9780713486285.

    Paperback First Edition. Watson-Guptill. 2001. ISBN-10: 0823030415. ISBN-13: 9780823030415.

Gross, Yoram. *My Animated Life*. Paperback First Edition. ReadHowYouWant. 2014. ISBN-10: 1459677315. ISBN-13: 9781459677319.

    eBook. Brandl & Schlesinger. 2014.

Halas, John. *Masters of Animation*. Hardcover First Edition. BBC Books. 1987. ISBN-10: 0563204176. ISBN-13: 9780563204176.

    Hardcover First Edition. Salem House Publishers. 1987. ISBN-10: 0881623067. ISBN-13: 9780881623062.

Hamonic, Gerald. *Terrytoons: The Story of Paul Terry and His Classic Cartoon Factory*. Hardcover First Edition. John Libbey Publishing. 2018. ISBN-10: 0861967399. ISBN-13: 9780861967391.

    Paperback First Edition. John Libbey Publishing. 2017. ISBN-10: 0861967291. ISBN-13: 9780861967292.

Hand, David Dodd. Hand, David Hale. *Animation Pioneer: David Dodd Hand*. Paperback First Edition. Theme Park Press. 2018. ISBN-10: 1683901355. ISBN-13: 9781683901358.

Hand, David. *Memoirs*. Paperback First Edition. Lighthouse Litho. 1991.

Holt, Nathalia. *The Queens of Animation: The Untold Story of the Women Who Transformed the World of Disney and Made Cinematic History*. Hardcover First Edition. Little, Brown and Company. 2019. ISBN-10: 0316439150. ISBN-13: 9780316439152.

    eBook. Hachette Book Group. 2019.

    Audiobook. Narrated by Saskia Maarleveld.
    Little, Brown & Company. 2019.

    Paperback First Edition. Back Bay Books. 2020. ISBN-10: 0316439142. ISBN-13: 9780316439145.

Jacobs, Chip. *Strange as it Seems: The Impossible Life of Gordon Zahler*. Paperback First Edition. Rare Bird Books. A Vireo Book. 2016. ISBN-10: 1942600240. ISBN-13: 9781942600244.

    eBook. Rare Bird Books. A Vireo Book. 2016.

Katsaridou, Maria. *Sylvain Chomet's Distinctive Animation: From The Triplets of Belleville to The Illusionist*. Hardcover First Edition. Bloomsbury Academic. 2022. ISBN-10: 1501363999. ISBN-13: 9781501363993.

Keefer, Cindy. *Oskar Fischinger (1900-1967): Experiments in Cinematic Abstraction*. Paperback First Edition. Eye Film Museum. The Center For Visual Music. 2013. ISBN-10: 9071338002. ISBN-13: 9789071338007.

Lanpher, Dorse A. *Flyin' Chunks and Other Things to Duck: Memoirs of a Life Spent Doodling for Dollars*. Hardcover First Edition. iUniverse. 2010. ISBN-10: 1450261000. ISBN-13: 9781450261005.

    Paperback First Edition. iUniverse. 2010. ISBN-10: 1450260993. ISBN-13: 9781450260992.

    eBook. iUniverse. 2010.

Lenburg, Jeff. *The Great Cartoon Directors*. Hardcover First Edition. McFarland Publishing. 1983. ISBN-10: 0899500366. ISBN-13: 9780899500362.

Paperback Reprint Edition. De Capo Press. 1993. ISBN-10: 0306805219. ISBN-13: 9780306805219.

Paperback Revised & Expanded Edition. 2021.

Levy, David. *Independently Animated: Bill Plympton: The Life and Art of the King of Indie Animation*. Hardcover First Edition. Universe Publishing. 2011. ISBN-10: 0789322099. ISBN-13: 9780789322098.

Mallory, Michael. Takamoto, Iwao. *Iwao Takamoto: My Life with a Thousand Characters*. Hardcover First Edition. University Press of Mississippi. 2009. ISBN-10: 1604731931. ISBN-13: 9781604731934.

Paperback First Edition. University Press of Mississippi. 2009. ISBN-10: 160473194X. ISBN-13: 9781604731941

eBook. University Press of Mississippi. 2009.

Mangels, Andy. Scheimer, Lou. *Lou Scheimer: Creating the Filmation Generation*. Paperback First Edition. TwoMorrows Publishing. 2012. ISBN-10: 160549044X. ISBN-13: 9781605490441.

Paperback Reprint Edition. TwoMorrows Publishing. 2015. ISBN-10: 1893905969. ISBN-13: 9781893905962.

Manvell, Roger. *Art and Animation: The Story of the Halas and Batchelor Animation Studio*. Hardcover First Edition. Tantivy Press. 1980. ISBN-10: 0904208885. ISBN-13: 9780904208887.

Paperback First Edition. Hastings House Publishers. 1980. ISBN-10: 0803804946. ISBN-13: 9780803804944.

McKibben, Charles H. *Mel Blanc, the Voice of Bugs Bunny...and Me: Inside the Studio with Hollywood's "Man of 1,000 Voices"*. Paperback First Edition. Chronicle Books, LLC. 2017. ISBN-10: 1948339218. ISBN-13: 9781948339216.

eBook. Charles H. McKibben. 2017.

Audiobook. Narrated by Chuck McKibben. 2018.

McKinnon, Robert. *Stepping in the Picture: Cartoon Designer Maurice Noble*. Hardcover First Edition. University Press of Mississippi. 2008. ISBN-10: 1934110434. ISBN-13: 9781934110430.

> Paperback First Edition. University Press of Mississippi. 2008. ISBN-10: 1934110442. ISBN-13: 9781934110447.

McSorley, Tom. *Dark Mirror: The Films of Theodore Ushev*. Paperback First Edition. Canadian Film Institute. 2014. ISBN-10: 0919096506. ISBN-13: 9780919096509.

Merkel, Ulrich. *Dreams of the Rarebit Fiend*. Hardcover First Edition. Fantagraphics Books. 2007. ISBN-10: 3000207511. ISBN-13: 9783000207518.

Moritz, William. *Optical Poetry: The Life and Work of Oskar Fischinger*. Hardcover First Edition. Indiana University Press. 2004. ISBN-10: 086196635X. ISBN-13: 9780861966356.

> Paperback First Edition. Indiana University Press. 2004. ISBN-10: 0253216419. ISBN-13: 9780253216410.

> Hardcover First Edition. John Libbey Publishing. 2004. ISBN-10: 0253343488. ISBN-13: 9780253343482.

> Paperback First Edition. John Libbey Publishing. 2004. ISBN-10: 0861966341. ISBN-13: 9780861966349.

> eBook. John Libbey Publishing. 2004.

Neupert, Richard. *John Lasseter (Contemporary Film Directors)*. Paperback First Edition. University of Illinois Press. 2016. ISBN-10: 0252081641. ISBN-13: 9780252081644.

> Hardcover First Edition. University of Illinois Press. 2016. ISBN-10: 0252040155. ISBN-13: 9780252040153.

> eBook. University of Illinois Press. 2016.

Ohmart, Ben. *Mel Blanc: The Man of a Thousand Voices*. Hardcover First Edition. BearManor Media. 2012. ISBN-10: 1593937881. ISBN-13: 9781593937881.

eBook. BearManor Media. 2012.

Audiobook. Narrated by Fred Frees. BearManor Media. 2013.

Paperback First Edition. BearManor Media. 2014.
ISBN-10: 1593932596. ISBN-13: 9781593932596.

Ohmart, Ben. Reed, Alan. *Yabba Dabba Doo or, Never a Star: The Alan Reed Story*. eBook. BearManor Media. 2010.

Paperback First Edition. BearManor Media. 2015.
ISBN-10: 1593933134. ISBN-13: 9781593933135.

Pilling, Jayne. *The Book of BAA Art- Artists, Animators & Sheep*. Paperback First Edition. British Council. 2007.

Pilling, Jayne. *Women and Animation: A Compendium*. Paperback First Edition. British Film Institute, Exhibition & Distribution Division. 1992. ISBN-10: 0851703771. ISBN-13: 9780851703770.

Place-Verghnes, Floriane. *Tex Avery: A Unique Legacy.* Paperback First Edition. John Libbey Publishing. 2006. ISBN-10: 0861966597. ISBN-13: 9780861966592.

eBook. John Libbey Publishing. 2006.

Pointer, Ray. *(The Art and Inventions of) Max Fleischer: American Animation Pioneer*. Paperback First Edition. McFarland & Company, Inc., Publishers. 2017. ISBN-10: 147666367X. ISBN-13: 9781476663678.

eBook. McFarland & Company, Inc., Publishers. 2017.

Polson, Tod. *The Noble Approach: Maurice Noble and the Zen of Animation Design*. Hardcover First Edition. Chronicle Books, LLC. 2013. ISBN-10: 1452102945. ISBN-13: 9781452102948.

eBook. Chronicle Books, LLC. 2013.

Preston, Greg. *The Artist Within*. Hardcover First Edition. Dark Horse Books. 2007. ISBN-10: 1593075618. ISBN-13: 9781593075613.

Preston, Greg. *The Artist Within: Book 2*. Hardcover First Edition. Sampsel Preston Inc. 2017. ISBN-10: 069291756X. ISBN-13: 9780692917565.

Robinson, Chris. *The Ballad of a Thin Man: In Search of Ryan Larkin*. Paperback First Edition. Course Technology PTR. 2008. ISBN-10: 1598635603. ISBN-13: 9781598635607.

Robinson, Chris. *Unsung Heroes of Animation*. Paperback First Edition. John Libbey Publishing. 2006. ISBN-10: 0861966651. ISBN-13: 9780861966653.

 Paperback First Edition. Indiana University Press. 2006. ISBN-10: 8619666517. ISBN-13: 9788619666510.

Ruzic, Andrijana. *Michael Dudok de Wit: A Life in Animation*. Hardcover First Edition. CRC Press. 2020. ISBN-10: 1138367303. ISBN-13: 9781138367302.

 Paperback First Edition. CRC Press. 2020. ISBN-10: 1138367281. ISBN-13: 9781138367289.

 eBook. CRC Press. 2020.

Schelly, Bill. *John Stanley: Giving Life to Little Lulu*. Hardcover First Edition. Fantagraphics Books. 2017. ISBN-10: 1606999907. ISBN-13: 9781606999905.

 eBook. Fantagraphics Books. 2017.

Sigall, Martha. *Living Life Inside the Lines: Tales from the Golden Age of Animation*. Paperback First Edition. University Press of Mississippi. 2005. ISBN-10: 1578067499. ISBN-13: 9781578067497.

 Hardcover First Edition. University of Mississippi Press. 2005. ISBN-10: 1578067480. ISBN-13: 9781578067480.

Stumpf, Ohart. Stumpf, Charles. *Walter Tetley: For Corn's Sake*. Hardcover First Edition. BearManor Media. 2016. ISBN-10: 1593934459. ISBN-13: 9781593934453.

Paperback First Edition. BearManor Media. 2016.
ISBN-10: 1593934351. ISBN-13: 9781593934354.

Tembo, Kwasu David. *Genndy Tartakovsky: Sincerity in Animation*. Hardcover First Edition. Bloomsbury Academic. 2021. ISBN-10: 1501356291. ISBN-13: 9781501356292.

    eBook. Bloomsbury Academic. 2022.

Turner, Pamela Taylor. *Infinite Animation: The Life and Work of Adam Beckett*. Hardcover First Edition. CRC Press. 2019. ISBN-10: 0815382006. ISBN-13: 9780815382003.

    eBook. CRC Press. 2019.

Vischer, Phil. *Me, Myself & Bob: A True Story About God, Dreams, and Talking Vegetables*. Hardcover First Edition. Thomas Nelson. 2007. ISBN-10: 0785222073. ISBN-13: 9780785222071.

    Paperback First Edition. Thomas Nelson. 2008. ISBN-10: 1595551220. ISBN-13: 9781595551221.

    eBook. Thomas Nelson. 2008.

Walz, Gene. *Cartoon Charlie: The Life and Art of Animation Pioneer Charles Thorson*. Paperback First Edition. Great Plains Publications. 2001. ISBN-10: 0969780494. ISBN-13: 9780969780496.

Wilson, Rowland B. Wilson, Suzanne Lemieux. *Rowland B. Wilson's Trade Secrets: Notes on Cartooning and Animation*. Paperback First Edition. Focal Press. 2012. ISBN-10: 0240817346. ISBN-13: 9780240817347.

    eBook. Routledge. 2012.

Wizig, Enid Denbo. *I Never Asked, Why Me?* Paperback First Edition. CreateSpace Independent Publishing Platform. 2018. ISBN-10: 1986066010. ISBN-13: 9781986066013.

Individual Series and Movies

Abraham, Adam. *When Magoo Flew: The Rise and Fall of Animation Studio UPA*. Hardcover First Edition. Wesleyan University Press. 2012. ISBN-10: 0819569143. ISBN-13: 9780819569141.

    eBook. Wesleyan University Press. 2012.

Adams, T. R. *The Flintstones: A Modern Stone Age Phenomenon*. Hardcover First Edition. Turner Publishing, Inc. 1994. ISBN-10: 157036012X. ISBN-13: 9781570360121.

Adams, T.R. *Tom & Jerry: Fifty Years of Cat and Mouse*. Hardcover First Edition. Crescent Publishing Corp. 1991. ISBN-10: 0517056887. ISBN-13: 9780517056882.

    Hardcover First Edition. Hamlyn. 1991. ISBN-10: 185510086X. ISBN-13: 9781855100862.

Arnold, Mark. *Aaaaalllviiinnn!: The Story of Ross Bagdasarian, Sr., Liberty Records, Format Films and the Alvin Show*. Hardcover First Edition. BearManor Media. 2019. ISBN-10: 1629334332. ISBN-13: 9781629334332.

    Paperback First Edition. BearManor Media. 2019. ISBN-10: 1629334324. ISBN-13: 9781629334325.

    eBook. BearManor Media. 2019.

Arnold, Mark. *The Total Television Scrapboook*. Hardcover First Edition. BearManor Media. 2021. ISBN-10: 1629337781. ISBN-13: 9781629337784.

    Paperback First Edition. BearManor Media. 2021. ISBN-10: 1629337773. ISBN-13: 9781629337777.

Axelrod, Mitchell. *BeatleToons, The Real Story Behind The Cartoon Beatles*. Paperback First Edition. Wynn Publishing. 1999. ISBN-10: 0964280876. ISBN-13: 9780964280878.

Baer, Brian. *How He-Man Mastered the Universe: Toy to Television to the Big Screen*. Paperback First Edition. McFarland & Company, Inc., Publishers. 2017. ISBN-10: 1476665907. ISBN-13: 9781476665900.

    eBook. McFarland & Company, Inc., Publishers. 2017.

Baldwin, Gerard. *From Mister Magoo to Papa Smurf*. Paperback First Edition. Neighborhood Publishers. 2014. ISBN-10: 0990724212. ISBN-13: 9780990724216.

Ballman, J. *The Marvel Super Heroes On TV! A Complete Episode Guide to the 1966 Cartoon Series. Book One: IRON MAN*. Paperback First Edition. Independent Publisher. 2017. ISBN-10: 1545345651. ISBN-13: 9781545345658.

Ballman, J. *Spider-Man on TV! A Full-Color Episode Guide to the Gantray-Lawrence Animation Series. Book One: The 1967 Cartoon*. Paperback First Edition. Independently Published. 2019. ISBN-10: 1795356154. ISBN-13: 9781795356152.

Ballman, J. *The Marvel Super Heroes On TV! A Complete Episode Guide To The 1966 Cartoon Series. Book Two: Thor*. Paperback First Edition. Independently Published. 2021. ISBN-13: 9798724754941.

Barba, Shelley E. Perrin, Joy M. *The Ascendance of Harley Quinn: Essays on DC's Enigmatic Villain*. Paperback First Edition. McFarland & Company, Inc., Publishers. 2017. ISBN-10: 1476665230. ISBN-13: 9781476665238.

    eBook. McFarland & Company, Inc., Publishers. 2017.

Beck, Jerry. Collier, Kevin Scott. Leonardi, Art. *The Animated Administration of James Norcross a.k.a. Super President*. Paperback First Edition. Independent Publisher. 2017. ISBN-10: 1982056495. ISBN-13: 9781982056490.

Beck, Jerry. *The Flintstones: Insight Editions Mini-Classics*. Hardcover First Edition. Insight Editions. ISBN-10: 1933784601. ISBN-13: 9781933784601.

Beck, Jerry. *Pink Panther: The Ultimate Guide*. Hardcover First Edition. Dorling Kindersley Child's H/B. 2005. ISBN-10: 140530930X. ISBN-13: 9781405309301.

>Hardcover Variant Dust Jacket Edition. "The Pink Panther Ultimate Edition" DVD Set. Dorling Kindersley Child's H/B. ISBN-10: 140530930X. ISBN-13: 9781405309301

Beck, Jerry. *Scooby-Doo: Insight Editions Mini-Classics*. Hardcover First Edition. Insight Editions. ISBN-10: 193378461X. ISBN-13: 9781933784618.

Beck, Jerry. *Tom and Jerry: Insight Editions Mini-Classics*. Hardcover First Edition. Insight Editions. 2008. ISBN-10: 1933784628. ISBN-13: 9781933784625.

Bierly, Steve R. *Stronger Than Spinach: The Secret Appeal of the Famous Studios Popeye Cartoons*. Paperback First Edition. BearManor Media. 2009. ISBN-10: 1593935021. ISBN-13: 9781593935023.

>eBook. BearManor Media. 2015.

Biggers, Buck. Stover, Chet. *How Underdog Was Born*. Hardcover First Edition. BearManor Media. 2020. ISBN-10: 1629335487. ISBN-13: 9781629335483.

>Paperback First Edition. BearManor Media. 2020. ISBN-10: 1593930259. ISBN-13: 9781593930257.

>eBook. BearManor Media. 2020.

Brion, Patrick. *Tom & Jerry: The Definitive Guide to Their Animated Adventures*. Hardcover First Edition. Harmony Books. 1990. ISBN-10: 0517573512. ISBN-13: 9780517573518.

Brown, Ph. D., Alan. Logan, Chris. *The Psychology of the Simpsons: D'oh!* Paperback First Edition. Smart Pop. 2006. ISBN-10: 1932100709. ISBN-13: 9781932100709.

>eBook. Smart Pop. 2009.

Burgess, Clare. Sibley, Brian. *Weta Digital*. Hardcover First Edition. HarperCollins Publishers, Inc. 2014. ISBN-10: 006229783X. ISBN-13: 9780062297839.

Canemaker, John. *Felix: The Twisted Tale of the World's Most Famous Cat*. Hardcover First Edition. Pantheon Books. 1991. ISBN-10: 067940127X. ISBN-13: 9780679401278.

> Paperback First Edition. De Capo Press. 1996.
> ISBN-10: 0306807319. ISBN-13: 9780306807312.

Canemaker, John. *The Animated Raggedy Ann & Andy: An Intimate Look at the Art of Animation, Its History, Techniques, and Artists*. Hardcover First Edition. Bobbs-Merrill Company. 1977. ISBN-10: 0672523299. ISBN-13: 9780672523298.

> Paperback First Printing. Bobbs-Merrill Company. 1977.
> ISBN-10: 0672523302. ISBN-13: 9780672523304.

Catalano, Frank. *Rand Unwrapped - Confessions of a Robotech Warrior*. Paperback First Edition. CreateSpace Independent Publishing Platform. 2011. ISBN-10: 1456543652. ISBN-13: 9781456543655.

> Paperback Revised Edition. CreateSpace Independent Publishing Platform. 2013. ISBN-10: 1456543652. ISBN-13: 9781456543655.

Chunovic, Louis. *The Rocky and Bullwinkle Book*. Hardcover First Edition. Bantam Books. 1996. ISBN-10: 0553105035. ISBN-13: 9780553105032.

Citters, Darrell Van. *Mister Magoo's Christmas Carol: The Making of the First Animated Christmas Special*. Hardcover First Edition. Oxberry Press. 2009. ISBN-10: 0692001557. ISBN-13: 9780692001554.

> Paperback First Edition. Published by Darrell Van Citters. 2020.
> ISBN-13: 978-0578778112.

Clarke, James. *Animated Films*. Paperback First Edition. Virgin Books. 2007. ISBN-10: 0753512580. ISBN-13: 9780753512586.

Collier, Kevin Scott. *The Amazing Transformations of Tom Terrific*. Paperback First Edition. Independent Publisher. 2017. ISBN-10: 1974583899. ISBN-13: 9781974583898.

Collier, Kevin Scott. *Calvin and the Colonel: The Reincarnation of Amos 'n' Andy*. Paperback First Edition. Independent Publisher. 2018. ISBN-10: 1986106152. ISBN-13: 9781986106153.

Collier, Kevin Scott. *The Chaplin Animated Silent Cartoons*. Paperback First Edition. Independent Publisher. 2019. ISBN-10: 1098846044. ISBN-13: 9781098846046.

Collier, Kevin Scott. Kerry, Margaret. *Clutch Cargo's Adventure Log Book*. Paperback First Edition. Independent Publisher. 2019. ISBN-10: 1092645543. ISBN-13: 9781092645546.

Collier, Kevin Scott. Stathes, Tommy José. *Dreamy Dud: Wallace A. Carlson's Animation Classic*. Paperback First Edition. Independent Publisher. 2017. ISBN-10: 1973774712. ISBN-13: 9781973774716.

Collier, Kevin Scott. *Happy Hooligan: The Animated Cartoons of 1916-1922*. Paperback First Edition. Independent Publisher. 2018. ISBN-10: 1721211233. ISBN-13: 9781721211234.

Collier, Kevin Scott. *The Hare Raising Tales of Crusader Rabbit*. Paperback First Edition. Independent Publisher. 2018. ISBN-10: 1723388726. ISBN-13: 9781723388729.

Collier, Kevin Scott. *Jay Ward's Animated Cereal Capers*. Paperback First Edition. Independent Publisher. 2017. ISBN-10: 1976576849. ISBN-13: 9781976576843.

Collier, Kevin Scott. *Milton the Monster: Horror Hill Epitaph*. Paperback First Edition. Independent Publisher. 2018. ISBN-10: 1984189808. ISBN-13: 9781984189806.

Collier, Kevin Scott. *Ralph Bakshi's The Mighty Heroes Declassified*. Paperback First Edition. Independent Publisher. 2017. ISBN-10: 1979767041. ISBN-13: 9781979767040.

Collier, Kevin Scott. *Winsor McCay's The Sinking of The Alpena*. Paperback First Edition. Independent Publisher. 2017. ISBN-10: 1975954572. ISBN-13: 9781975954574.

Collier, Kevin Scott. *The Wonderful Animated World of the Wizard of Oz*. Paperback First Edition. Independent Publisher. 2018. ISBN-10: 172632558X. ISBN-13: 9781726325585.

Connelly, Sherilyn. *Ponyville Confidential: The History and Culture of My Little Pony, 1981-2016*. Paperback First Edition. McFarland & Company. 2017. ISBN-10: 1476662096. ISBN-13: 9781476662091.

 eBook. McFarland & Company. 2017.

Cortner, Laura E. Hieronimus, Robert R. *It's All in the Mind: Inside the Beatles' Yellow Submarine, Vol. 2*. Hardcover First Edition. Hieronimus & Company, Incorporated. 2021. ISBN-10: 0967536316. ISBN-13: 9780967536316.

> Paperback First Edition. Hieronimus & Company, Incorporated. 2021. ISBN-10: 0967536308. ISBN-13: 9780967536309.

Cotte, Olivier. *Secrets of Oscar-Winning Animation: Behind the Scenes of 13 Classic Short Animations*. Paperback First Edition. Focal Press. 2007. ISBN-10: 024052070X. ISBN-13: 9780240520704.

Deitch, Gene. *Nudnik Revealed*. Hardcover First Edition. Fantagraphics Books. 2013. ISBN-10: 1606996517. ISBN-13: 9781606996515.

> eBook. Fantagraphics Books. 2016.

Desroches, Ed. *ASIFA 50th Anniversary by The Association Internationale du Film d'Animation*. Hardcover First Edition. ASIFA. The International Animated Film Association. 2011. ISBN-13: 9788989488217.

Dini, Paul. Kidd, Chip. *Batman Animated*. Hardcover First Edition. HarperEntertainment. 1998. ISBN-10: 0067575315. ISBN-13: 9780067575314.

> Paperback First Edition. It Books. 1998. ISBN-10: 006107327X. ISBN-13: 9780061073274.

Dobson, Terence. *Film Work of Norman McLaren*. Hardcover First Edition. John Libbey Publishing. 2007. ISBN-10: 0861966562. ISBN-13: 9780861966561.

> Paperback First Edition. John Libbey Publishing. 2007. ISBN-10: 0861967380. ISBN-13: 9780861967384.

Eatock, James. *He-Man and the Masters of the Universe: A Complete Guide to the Classic Animated Adventures*. Hardcover First Edition. Dark Horse Books. 2016. ISBN-10: 1506700640. ISBN-13: 9781506700649.

> eBook. Dark Horse Books. 2016.

Gibson, Jon M. McDonnell, Chris. *Unfiltered: The Complete Ralph Bakshi*. Hardcover First Edition. Universe Publishing. 2008. ISBN-10: 0789316846. ISBN-13: 9780789316844.

Goldschmidt, Rick. *The Arthur Rankin, Jr. Scrapbook: The Birth of Animagic*. Hardcover First Edition. Miser Bros. Press. 2014. ISBN-10: 0971308152. ISBN-13: 9780971308152.

Goldschmidt, Rick. *The Enchanted World of Rankin/Bass*. Hardcover First Edition. Tiger Mountain Press. 1997. ISBN-10: 0964954273. ISBN-13: 9780964954274.

> Paperback First Edition. Tiger Mountain Press. 1997. ISBN-10: 0964954281. ISBN-13: 9780964954281.
>
> Paperback Second Edition. Miser Bros. Press. 2001. ISBN-10: 097130811X. ISBN-13: 9780971308114.
>
> eBook. Miser Bros. Press. 2011.
>
> *15th Anniversary Edition The Enchanted World Of Rankin/Bass: A Portfolio*. Hardcover First Edition. Miser Bros. Press. 2012. ISBN-10: 0971308144. ISBN-13: 9780971308145.
>
> *20th Anniversary Edition of The Enchanted World of Rankin/Bass: A Portfolio*. Hardcover First Edition. Miser Bros. Press. 2016. ISBN-10: 0971308179 ISBN-13: 9780971308176.

Goldschmidt, Rick. *Rankin/Bass' Frosty the Snowman's 50th Anniversary Scrapbook*. Hardcover First Edition. Miser Bros. Press. 2019. ISBN-10: 0971308195. ISBN-13: 9780971308190.

Goldschmidt, Rick. *Rankin/Bass' Mad Monster Party*. Hardcover First Edition. Miser Bros. Press. 2011. ISBN-10: 0971308136. ISBN-13: 9780971308138.

> Paperback First Edition. Miser Bros. Press. 2011. ISBN-10: 0971308128 ISBN-13: 9780971308121.
>
> eBook. 2021.

Goldschmidt, Rick. *Rudolph The Red-Nosed Reindeer: The Making Of The Rankin/Bass Holiday Classic*. Hardcover First Edition. Miser Bros. Press. 2001. ISBN-10: 0971308101. ISBN-13: 9780971308107.

> eBook. Miser Bros. Press. 2011.

Grandinetti, Fred. *Popeye the Sailor: The 1960s TV Cartoons*. Hardcover First Edition. BearManor Media. 2022. ISBN-10: 1629338516. ISBN-13: 9781629338514.

    eBook. BearManor Media. 2022.

    Paperback First Edition. BearManor Media. 2022. ISBN-10: 1629338508. ISBN-13: 9781629338507.

Grenville, Bruce. *KRAZY!: The Delirious World of Anime + Comics + Video Games + Art*. Paperback First Edition. University of California Press. 2008. ISBN-10: 0520257847. ISBN-13: 9780520257849.

Hahn, Matthew. *The Animated Marx Brothers*. Hardcover First Edition. BearManor Media. 2017. ISBN-10: 1629332259. ISBN-13: 9781629332253.

    eBook. BearManor Media. 2017.

    Audiobook on CD. BearManor Media and Blackstone Audio. 2018.

    Audiobook. Narrated by Nat Segaloff. Blackstone Audio, Inc. 2018.

Hahn, Matthew. *The Animated Peter Lorre*. Hardcover First Edition. BearManor Media. 2020. ISBN-10: 162933460X. ISBN-13: 9781629334608.

    Paperback First Edition. BearManor Media. 2020. ISBN-10: 1629334596. ISBN-13: 9781629334592.

Hieronimus, Robert. *Inside the Yellow Submarine: The Making of the Beatles' Animated Classic*. Paperback First Edition. Krause Publications. 2002. ISBN-10: 0873493605. ISBN-13: 9780873493604.

Hooks, Ed. *Acting in Animation: A Look at 12 Films*. Paperback First Edition. Heinemann Drama. 2005. ISBN-10: 0325007055. ISBN-13: 9780325007052.

Keller, James R. Stratyner, Leslie. *The Deep End of South Park: Critical Essays on Television's Shocking Cartoon Series*. Paperback First Edition. McFarland & Company, Inc., Publishers. 2009. ISBN-10: 0786443073. ISBN-13: 9780786443079.

    eBook. McFarland & Company, Inc., Publishers. 2009.

Keslowitz, Steven. *The World According to The Simpsons: What Our Favorite TV Family Says about Life, Love, and the Pursuit of the Perfect Donut*. Paperback First Edition. Sourcebooks. 2006. ISBN-10: 1402206550. ISBN-13: 9781402206559.

Lane, Andy. *The World of Wallace and Gromit.* Hardcover First Edition. Chrysalis Books. 2002. ISBN-10: 1843470292. ISBN-13: 9781843470298.

> Hardcover First Edition. Pan MacMillan. 2004.
> ISBN-10: 0752215582. ISBN-13: 9780752215587.

Lewald, Eric. *Previously on X-Men: The Making of an Animated Series*. Hardcover First Edition. Jacob Brown Media Group. 2017. ISBN-10: 0998866326. ISBN-13: 9780998866321.

> Paperback First Edition. Jacob Brown Media Group. 2017.
> ISBN-10: 0998866377. ISBN-13: 9780998866376.

> eBook. Jacob Brown Media Group. 2017.

Lollar, Phil. *The Complete Guide To Adventures In Odyssey*. Paperback First Edition. Focus On The Family Publishing. 1997. ISBN-10: 156179466X. ISBN-13: 9781561794669.

McMahan, Alison. *The Films of Tim Burton: Animating Live Action in Contemporary Hollywood*. Hardcover First Edition. Continuum. ISBN-10: 0826415660. ISBN-13: 9780826415660.

> Paperback First Edition. 2005.
> ISBN-10: 0826415679. ISBN-13: 9780826415677.

> eBook. Bloomsbury Academic. 2014.

Murry, Matt. *The World of Smurfs: A Celebration of Tiny Blue Proportions*. Hardcover First Edition. Harry N. Abrams. 2011. ISBN-10: 1419700723. ISBN-13: 9781419700729.

Ortved, John. *The Simpsons: An Uncensored, Unauthorized History*. Hardcover First Edition. Faber and Faber. 2009. ISBN-10: 1616873744. ISBN-13: 9781616873745.

    Hardcover First Edition. Greystone Books. 2009. ISBN-10: 1553655036. ISBN-13: 9781553655039.

    Audiobook on CD. Tantor Audio. 2009. ISBN-10: 1400164486. ISBN-13: 9781400164486.

    Audiobook on CD - Library Edition. Tantor Audio. 2009. ISBN-10: 1400144485. ISBN-13: 9781400144488.

    eBook. Farrar, Straus and Giroux. 2009.

    Audiobook. Narrated by Justine Eyre, John Allen Nelson. Tantor. 2009.

    Paperback First Edition. Faber and Faber. 2010. ISBN-10: 0865479399. ISBN-13: 9780865479395.

Salda, Michael. *Arthurian Animation: A Study of Cartoon Camelots on Film and Television*. Paperback First Edition. McFarland & Company, Inc., Publishers. 2013. ISBN-10: 0786474688. ISBN-13: 9780786474684.

    eBook. McFarland & Company, Inc., Publishers. 2013.

Scott, Keith. *The Moose That Roared: The Story of Jay Ward, Bill Scott, a Flying Squirrel, and a Talking Moose*. Hardcover First Edition. Thomas Dunne Books. 2000. ISBN-10: 0312199228. ISBN-13: 9780312199227.

    Paperback Reprint Edition. Thomas Dunne Books. 2001. ISBN-10: 0312283830. ISBN-13: 9780312283834.

    eBook. Thomas Dunne Books. 2014.

Seitz, Matt Zoller. *The Wes Anderson Collection*. Hardcover First Edition. Harry N. Abrams. 2013. ISBN-10: 081099741X. ISBN-13: 9780810997417.

    eBook. Harry N. Abrams. 2013.

Stevenson, Ryan. Wilford, Lauren. *The Wes Anderson Collection: Isle of Dogs*. Hardcover First Edition. Harry N. Abrams. 2018. ISBN-10: 1419730096. ISBN-13: 9781419730092.

 eBook. Harry N. Abrams. 2018.

Stoffman, Daniel. *The Nelvana Story: Thirty Animated Years*. Paperback First Edition. Kids Can Press. 2001. ISBN-10: 1894786009. ISBN-13: 9781894786003.

Swanigan, Michael. *Animation by Filmation*. Paperback First Edition. Independent Publisher. 2014. ISBN-10: 1481225049. ISBN-13: 9781481225045.

Sweet, Derek R. *Star Wars in the Public Square: The Clone Wars as Political Dialogue*. Paperback First Edition. McFarland. 2015. ISBN-10: 0786477644. ISBN-13: 9780786477647.

 eBook. McFarland. 2015.

Torre, Dan. Torre, Lienors. *Grendel, Grendel, Grendel: Animating Beowulf*. Hardcover First Edition. Bloomsbury Academic. 2021. ISBN-10: 1501337823. ISBN-13: 9781501337826.

Turner, Chris. *Planet Simpson: How a Cartoon Masterpiece Documented an Era and Defined a Generation*. Paperback First Edition. Ebury Publishing. 2004. ISBN-10: 0091897564. ISBN-13: 9780091897567.

 Hardcover First Edition. Da Capo Press. 2004. ISBN-10: 0306813416. ISBN-13: 9780306813412.

 Paperback First Edition. Da Capo Press. 2005. ISBN-10: 030681448X ISBN-13: 9780306814488.

 Paperback First Reprint. Ebury Publishing. 2005. ISBN-10: 009190336X. ISBN-13: 9780091903367.

 eBook. Random House of Canada. 2010.

 Paperback First Reprint Ebook. Ebury Publishing. 2012.

Book on CD. Highbridge Audio and Blackstone Publishing. 2021.

Wallace, Daniel. *The World of RWBY*. Hardcover First Edition. VIZ Media LLC. 2019. ISBN-10: 1974704386. ISBN-13: 9781974704385.

Walsh, John. *Harryhausen: The Lost Movies*. Hardcover First Edition. Titan Books. 2019. ISBN-10: 1789091101. ISBN-13: 9781789091106.

Webber, Roy P. *The Dinosaur Films of Ray Harryhausen: Features, Early 16mm Experiments and Unrealized Projects*. Hardcover First Edition. McFarland & Company, Inc., Publishers. 2004. ISBN-10: 0786416661. ISBN-13: 9780786416660.

    Paperback Reprint Edition. McFarland & Company, Inc., Publishers. 2012. ISBN-10: 0786469366. ISBN-13: 9780786469369.

Zipes, Jack. *The Enchanted Screen: The Unknown History of Fairy-Tale Films*. Hardcover First Edition. Routledge. 2010. ISBN-10: 0415990629. ISBN-13: 9780415990622.

    Paperback First Edition. Routledge. 2010. ISBN-10: 0415990610. ISBN-13: 9780415990615.

    eBook. Routledge. 2011.

The Art of Individual Artists and Single Topics

Animallogic. *The Art of Legend of the Guardians: The Owls of Ga'Hoole*. Hardcover First Edition. Warner Bros. Global Publishing. 2010. ISBN-10: 0646574485. ISBN-13: 9780646574486.

> Hardcover Reprint Edition. Warner Bros. Global Publishing. 2020. ISBN-10: 0646574485. ISBN-13: 9780646574486.

Beck, Jerry. Castiglia, Paul. Evanier, Mark. Gerstein, David. Oriolo, Don. Yoe, Craig. *Felix the Cat Paintings*. Hardcover First Edition. IDW Publishing. 2014. ISBN-10: 1613778392. ISBN-13: 9781613778395.

Begin, Mary Jane. *My Little Pony: The Art of Equestria*. Hardcover First Edition. Harry N. Abrams. 2015. ISBN-10: 1419715771. ISBN-13: 9781419715778.

> eBook. Abrams Books. 2015.

Blair, Gavin. Gibson, Ian. Jackson, Mike. McCarthy, Brendan. Nicholls, Ken. Roberts, David. Su, Jim. *The Art of Reboot*. Hardcover First Edition. Arcana Studio Incorporated. 2007. ISBN-10: 0976309572. ISBN-13: 9780976309574.

> eBook. Arcana Comics. 2007.

Blattner, Evamarie. Reiniger, Lotte. Wiegmann, Karlheinz. *Lotte Reiniger: Born With Enchanting Hands: Three Silhouette Sequels*. Hardcover First Edition. Wasmuth. 2012. ISBN-10: 3803033527. ISBN-13: 9783803033529.

Buchan, Suzanne. Hertz, Betti-Sue. Manovich, Lev. *Animated Painting*. Hardcover First Edition. San Diego Museum of Art. 2007. ISBN-10: 0937108405. ISBN-13: 9780937108406.

> Paperback First Edition. San Diego Museum of Art. 2007. ISBN-10: 0937108375. ISBN-13: 9780937108376.

Citters, Darrell Van. *The Art of Jay Ward Productions*. Hardcover First Edition. Oxberry Press, LLC. 2013. ISBN-10: 0615847862. ISBN-13: 9780615847863.

> Paperback First Edition. Darrell Van Citters. 2021. ISBN-10: 0578845245. ISBN-13: 9780578845241.

Dalton, Tony. Harryhausen, Ray. *The Art of Ray Harryhausen*. Hardcover First Edition. Aurum Press. 2006. ISBN-10: 1845131142. ISBN-13: 9781845131142.

    Hardcover First Edition. Billboard Books. 2006. ISBN-10: 0823084000. ISBN-13: 9780823084005.

    Paperback Reissue. Watson-Guptill. 2008. ISBN-10: 0823084647. ISBN-13: 9780823084647.

    Paperback First Edition. Aurum Press. 2011. ISBN-10: 1845137124. ISBN-13: 9781845137120.

Dart, Rebecca. *The Art of My Little Pony: The Movie*. Hardcover First Edition. VIZ Media LLC. 2017. ISBN-10: 1421596482. ISBN-13: 9781421596488.

    eBook. VIZ Media LLC. 2017.

Farago, Andrew. *Teenage Mutant Ninja Turtles: The Ultimate Visual History*. Hardcover First Edition. Insight Comics. 2014. ISBN-10: 1608871851. ISBN-13: 9781608871858.

Fay, Matha. *Out of Line: The Art of Jules Feiffer*. Hardcover Annotated Edition. Abrams Books. 2015. ISBN-10: 1419700669. ISBN-13: 9781419700668.

    eBook. Abrams Books. 2015.

Graydon, Danny. *The Art of Planet 51*. Hardcover First Edition. Insight Editions. 2009. ISBN-10: 1933784970. ISBN-13: 9781933784977.

Hershenson, Bruce. *Cartoon Movie Posters*. Paperback First Edition. Bruce Hershenson. 1994. ISBN-10: 1887893377. ISBN-13: 9781887893374.

Hershenson, Bruce. *Vintage Hollywood Posters II.* Paperback First Edition. Bruce Hershenson. 1999. ISBN-10: 1887893024. ISBN-13: 9781887893022.

Holliss, Richard. *Harryhausen - The Movie Posters*. Hardcover First Edition. Titan Books. 2018. ISBN-10: 1785656783. ISBN-13: 9781785656781.

Jones, Chuck. *The Animated Art Of Chuck Jones, Volume 1*. 2019. Chuck Jones Gallery.

Jones, Chuck. *The Animated Art Of Chuck Jones, Volume 2*. 2020. Chuck Jones Gallery.

Jones, Chuck. *The Animated Art Of Chuck Jones, Volume 3*. 2022. Chuck Jones Gallery.

Kelts, Roland. *The Art of Blade Runner: Black Lotus*. Hardcover First Edition. Titan Books. 2022. ISBN-10: 1789097142. ISBN-13: 9781789097146.

    eBook. Titan Books. 2022.

Leasher, Ryan. *Wilderness of the Mind: The Art of Joseph Mugnaini*. Art of Fiction. 2009.

Lewald, Eric. Lewald, Julia. *X-Men: The Art and Making of The Animated Series*. Hardcover First Edition. Abrams Books. 2020. ISBN-10: 1419744682. ISBN-13: 9781419744686.

Macek, Carl. *The Art of Heavy Metal, the Movie: Animation for the Eighties*. Paperback First Edition. New York Zoetrope. 1981. ISBN-10: 0918432383. ISBN-13: 9780918432384.

Mattel. *The Art of Masters of the Universe Revelation*. Hardcover First Edition. Dark Horse Books. 2022. ISBN-10: 1506728189. ISBN-13: 9781506728186.

Oriolo, Don. *Another Book of Felix the Cat Paintings: A Second Collection of Paintings from the Prolific Imagination of the Felix the Cat Guy*. Hardcover First Edition. Gugu Press. 2015. ISBN-10: 0692561692. ISBN-13: 9780692561690.

Pearson, Joe. *Pearl Jam: Art of Do The Evolution*. Hardcover First Edition. IDW Publishing. 2020. ISBN-10: 1631407414. ISBN-13: 9781631407413.

    eBook. IDW Publishing. 2020.

Ryder, David. *The Great Movie Cartoon Parade*. Hardcover. First Edition. Bounty Books. 1976. ISBN-10: 0517525852. ISBN-13: 9780517525852.

    Hardcover First Edition. Tribune Books. 1976.
    ISBN-10: 0856740764. ISBN-13: 9780856740763.

Solomon, Charles. *The Art and Making of Peanuts Animation: Celebrating Fifty Years of Television Specials*. Hardcover First Edition. Chronicle Books LLC. 2012. ISBN-10: 1452110913. ISBN-13: 9781452110912.

    eBook. Chronicle Books LLC. 2013.

Studio Colorido. *Penguin Highway Book Set*. Paperback First Edition. ELEVEN ARTS. 2020.

Wallace, Daniel. *The Art of gen:Lock*. Hardcover First Edition. VIZ Media LLC. 2021. ISBN-10: 1974723461. ISBN-13: 9781974723461.

Weta Workshop. *The Art of the Adventures of Tintin*. Hardcover First Edition. Harper Design. 2011. ISBN-10: 0062087495. ISBN-13: 9780062087492.

    Hardcover First Edition. HarperCollins. 2011. ISBN-10: 1869509307. ISBN-13: 9781869509309.

Wrightson, Bernie. *Bernie Wrightson: Art And Designs For The Gang Of Seven Animation Studio*. Hardcover First Edition. Hermes Press. 2017. ISBN-10: 1613451369. ISBN-13: 9781613451366.

Zahed, Ramin. *The Little Prince: The Art of the Movie*. Hardcover First Edition. Titan Books. 2016. ISBN-10: 1783299770. ISBN-13: 9781783299775.

Disney

Walt Disney

Adler, Arthur C. "Buddy". *Walt Disney's Garage of Dreams*. Paperback First Edition. Theme Park Press. 2014. ISBN-10: 194150017X. ISBN-13: 9781941500170.

    eBook. Theme Park Press. 2014.

Barrier, Michael. *The Animated Man: A Life of Walt Disney*. Hardcover First Edition. University of California Press. 2007. ISBN-10: 0520241177. ISBN-13: 9780520241176.

    Paperback First Edition. University of California Press. 2007. ISBN-10: 0520256190. ISBN-13: 9780520256194.

    eBook. University of California Press. 2007.

Burchard, Wolf. *Inspiring Walt Disney: The Animation of French Decorative Arts*. Hardcover First Edition. Metropolitan Museum of Art. 2021. ISBN-10: 1588397416. ISBN-13: 9781588397416.

Burnes, Brian. Butler, Robert W. Viets, Dan. *Walt Disney's Missouri: The Roots of a Creative Genius*. Hardcover First Edition. Kansas City Star Books. 2002. ISBN-10: 0971708061. ISBN-13: 9780971708068.

Captivating History. *Walt Disney: A Captivating Guide to the Life of an American Entrepreneur and Pioneer of Animated Cartoon Films*. Hardcover First Edition. Captivating History. 2020. ISBN-10: 1647485398. ISBN-13: 9781647485399.

    Paperback First Edition. Captivating History. 2020. ISBN-10: 1647486882. ISBN-13: 9781647486884.

    eBook. Captivating History. 2020.

    Audiobook. Narrated by Jason Zenobia. 2020.

Captivating History. *Walt Disney and Salvador Dali: A Captivating Guide to the Individual Lives of an American Animator and a Spanish Surrealist Painter*. Paperback First Edition. Captivating History. 2020. ISBN-10: 1647485010. ISBN-13: 9781647485016.

> Hardcover First Edition. Captivating History. 2020. ISBN-10: 1647486971. ISBN-13: 9781647486976.

> eBook. Captivating History. 2020.

> Audiobook. Narrated by Jason Zenobia. Vicelane LLC. 2020.

Charles River Editors. *Walt Disney and Jim Henson: The Lives and Legacies of the Men Behind America's Favorite Cartoons*. Paperback First Edition. CreateSpace Independent Publishing Platform. 2016. ISBN-10: 1537068938. ISBN-13: 9781537068930.

> eBook. Charles River Editors. 2016.

> Paperback Large Print Edition. CreateSpace Independent Publishing Platform. 2017. ISBN-10: 1979620555. ISBN-13: 9781979620550

Christiansen, A.A. *Walt Disney: The Man Behind the Magic*. Paperback First Edition. Independent Publisher. 2017. ISBN-10: 1522071725. ISBN-13: 9781522071723.

> eBook. Independent Publisher. 2017.

> *The Man Behind the Magic: Walt Disney & Robin Williams - 2 Books in 1*. eBook. Independent Publisher. 2018.

> Hardcover First Edition. Independently Published. 2021. ISBN-10: 9798483661412.

Eliot, Marc. *Walt Disney: Hollywood's Dark Prince*. Hardcover First Edition. Birch Lane Press. 1993. ISBN-10: 155972174X. ISBN-13: 9781559721745.

> Paperback First Edition. Harpercollins. 1994. ISBN-10: 0061007897. ISBN-13: 9780061007897.

> eBook. Carlton Publishing Group. 2003.

Furniss, Maureen. *Walt Disney: Conversations*. Hardcover First Edition. University Press of Mississippi. 2005. ISBN-10: 157806712X. ISBN-13: 9781578067121.

>Paperback First Edition. University Press of Mississippi. 2005. ISBN-10: 1578067138. ISBN-13: 9781578067138.

Gabler, Neal. *Walt Disney: The Biography*. Hardcover First Edition. Aurum Press. 2007. ISBN-10: 1845132777. ISBN-13: 9781845132774.

>Paperback First Edition. Aurum Press. 2011. ISBN-10: 1845136748. ISBN-13: 9781845136741.

Gabler, Neal. *Walt Disney: The Triumph of the American Imagination*. Hardcover First Edition. Knopf Doubleday Publishing Group. 2006. ISBN-10: 067943822X. ISBN-13: 9780679438229.

>eBook. Vintage Books. 2006.

>Abridged Audiobook. Narrated by Leonardo Leoncavallo. Random House Audio. 2006. ISBN-10: 0739340298. ISBN-13: 9780739340295.

>Audiobook. Narrated by Arthur Morey. Books on Tape. 2006.

>Paperback Reprint Edition. Vintage Books. 2007. ISBN-10: 0679757473. ISBN-13: 9780679757474.

>Paperback Reprint Edition. Vintage Books. 2007. ISBN-10: 067943822X. ISBN-13: 9780679438229.

Ghez, Didier. *Disney's Grand Tour: Walt and Roy's European Summer Vacation, Summer 1935*. Hardcover First Edition. Theme Park Press. 2013. ISBN-10: 0984341587. ISBN-13: 9780984341580.

Goldberg, Aaron. *The Disney Story: Chronicling The Man, The Mouse & The Parks*. Paperback First Edition. Quaker Scribe. 2016. ISBN-10: 0692742816. ISBN-13: 9780692742815.

>eBook. Quaker Scribe. 2016.

>Audiobook. Narrated by Susan L. Crawford. Quaker Scribe. 2017.

Green, Amy Boothe. Green, Howard E. *Remembering Walt: Favorite Memories of Walt Disney*. Hardcover First Edition. Disney Editions. 1999. ISBN-10: 078686348X. ISBN-13: 9780786863488.

> Paperback First Edition. Disney Editions. 2002. ISBN-10: 0786853794. ISBN-13: 9780786853793.

Greene, Katherine. Greene, Richard. *Inside the Dream*. Hardcover First Edition. Disney Editions. 2001. ISBN-10: 0786853506. ISBN-13: 9780786853502.

Jackson, Kathy Merlock. *Walt Disney: A Bio-Bibliography*. Hardcover First Edition. Greenwood Publishing Group, Inc. 1993. ISBN-10: 0313258988. ISBN-13: 9780313258985.

Jackson, Kathy Merlock. *Walt Disney: Conversations*. Hardcover First Edition. University Press of Mississippi. 2005. ISBN-10: 157806712X. ISBN-13: 9781578067121.

> Paperback First Edition. University Press of Mississippi. 2005. ISBN-10: 1578067138. ISBN-13: 9781578067138.

Kiste, Andrew Stanley. *The Early Life of Walt Disney*. Hardcover First Edition. White Owl. 2021. ISBN-10: 1526780801. ISBN-13: 9781526780805.

> eBook. White Owl. 2021.

Korkis, Jim. *Call Me Walt: Everything You Never Knew About Walt Disney*. Paperback First Edition. Theme Park Press. 2017. ISBN-10: 1683901010. ISBN-13: 9781683901013.

> eBook. Theme Park Press. 2017.

Korkis, Jim. *Walt's Words*. Paperback First Edition. Theme Park Press. 2016. ISBN-10: 168390026X. ISBN-13: 9781683900269.

> eBook. Theme Park Press. 2016.

Krasniewicz, Louise. *Walt Disney: A Biography*. Hardcover First Edition. Greenwood Publishing Group. 2010. ISBN-10: 0313358303. ISBN-13: 9780313358302.

eBook. Greenwood Publishing Group. 2010.

Lesjak, David. *In the Service of the Red Cross: Walt Disney's Early Adventures: 1918-1919*. Paperback First Edition. Theme Park Press. 2015. ISBN-10: 1941500447. ISBN-13: 9781941500446.

eBook. Theme Park Press. 2015.

Madden, Scott M. *The Mouse and the Mallet: The Story of Walt Disney's Hectic Half-Decade in the Saddle*. Paperback First Edition. Theme Park Press. 2018. ISBN-10: 1683901436. ISBN-13: 978163901433.

eBook. Theme Park Press. 2018.

Martin, Pete. Miller, Diane Disney. *Walt Disney: An Intimate Biography by His Daughter Diane Disney Miller As Told to Pete Martin.* Hardcover First Edition. Odhams Press. 1957.

Mosley, Leonard. *Disney's World: A Biography*. Hardcover First Edition. Stein & Day. 1985. ISBN-10: 0812830733. ISBN-13: 9780812830736.

Paperback First Edition. Madison Books. 1986. ISBN-10: 081288311X. ISBN-13: 9780812883114.

Paperback First Edition. Scarborough House. 1990. ISBN-10: 0812885147. ISBN-13: 9780812885149.

eBook. Scarborough House. 1990.

Robb, Brian J. *A Brief History of Walt Disney*. Paperback First Edition. Robinson. 2014. ISBN-10: 1472110560. ISBN-13: 9781472110565.

eBook. Robinson. 2014.

Paperback First Edition. Running Press. 2014. ISBN-10: 076245475X. ISBN-13: 9780762454754.

Schroeder, Russell. *Walt Disney: His Life in Pictures*. Hardcover First Edition. Disney Press. 1996. ISBN-10: 0786831162. ISBN-13: 9780786831166.

Hardcover Second Edition. Disney Press. 2009. ISBN-10: 1423121058. ISBN-13: 9781423121053.

Sherman, Richard M. Sherman, Robert B. *Walt's Time - From Before to Beyond*. Hardcover First Edition. Camphor Tree Publishers. 1998. ISBN-10: 0964605937. ISBN-13: 9780964605930.

Shows, Charles. *Walt: Backstage Adventures With Walt Disney*. Hardcover First Edition. WIndsong Books International. 1980. ISBN-10: 0934846014. ISBN-13: 9780934846011.

Silvester, William. *The Adventures of Young Walt Disney*. Paperback First Edition. Theme Park Press. 2014. ISBN-10: 1941500188. ISBN-13: 9781941500187.

eBook. Theme Park Press. 2014.

Smith, Dave. *Quotable Walt Disney*. Paperback First Edition. Disney Editions. 2001. ISBN-10: 0786853328. ISBN-13: 9780786853328.

eBook. Disney Editions. 2015.

The Walt Disney Family Museum. *Disney & Dali: Architects of the Imagination*. Paperback First Edition. The Walt Disney Family Museum. 2016.

Thomas, Bob. *Walt Disney: An American Original (Disney Editions Deluxe)*. Paperback First Edition. Disney Editions. 1994. ISBN-10: 0786860278. ISBN-13: 9780786860272.

Thomas, Bob. *Walt Disney Biography*. Hardcover First Edition. New English Library. 1977. ISBN-10: 0450032299. ISBN-13: 9780450032295.

Paperback First Edition. William H. Allen. 1981. ISBN-10: 0352309725. ISBN-13: 9780352309723.

Notable Artists & Individuals at Disney

Anderson, Paul. *Jack of All Trades: Conversations with Disney Legend Ken Anderson*. Paperback First Edition. Theme Park Press. 2017. ISBN-10: 1683900537. ISBN-13: 9781683900535.

>eBook. Theme Park Press. 2017.

Beaudry, Karl. *Disney Destinies: How Passion, Patience, and Determination Can Take Anyone Anywhere*. Paperback First Edition. Theme Park Press. 2014. ISBN-10: 1941500161. ISBN-13: 9781941500163.

>eBook. Theme Park Press. 2014.

Becattini, Alberto. Brightman, Homer. *Life in the Mouse House: Memoir of a Disney Story Artist*. Paperback First Edition. Theme Park Press. 2014. ISBN-10: 0984341528. ISBN-13: 9780984341528.

>eBook. Theme Park Press. 2014.

Bossert, David A. *An Animator's Gallery: Eric Goldberg Draws the Disney Characters*. Hardcover First Edition. Disney Editions. 2015. ISBN-10: 1484723929. ISBN-13: 9781484723920.

Bossert, David A. *Remembering Roy E. Disney: Memories and Photos of a Storied Life*. Hardcover First Edition. Disney Editions. 2013. ISBN-10: 142317805X. ISBN-13: 9781423178057.

Canemaker, John. *Before the Animation Begins: The Art and Lives of Disney's Inspirational Sketch Artists*. Hardcover First Edition. Hyperion. 1996. ISBN-10: 0786861525. ISBN-13: 9780786861521.

Canemaker, John. *Paper Dreams: The Art & Artists of Disney Storyboards*. Hardcover First Edition. Hyperion. 1999. ISBN-10: 0786863072. ISBN-13: 9780786863075.

>Hardcover Second Edition. Disney Editions. 2006. ISBN-10: 0786863072. ISBN-13: 9780786863075.

Canemaker, John. *Walt Disney's Nine Old Men and the Art of Animation*. Hardcover First Edition. Disney Editions. 2001. ISBN-10: 0786864966. ISBN-13: 9780786864966.

Care, Ross. *Disney Legend Wilfred Jackson: A Life in Animation*. Paperback First Edition. Theme Park Press. 2016. ISBN-10: 1683900375. ISBN-13: 9781683900375.

Colvig, Pinto. *It's A Crazy Business: The Goofy Life Of A Disney Legend*. Paperback First Edition. Themer Park Press. 2015. ISBN-10: 1941500498. ISBN-13: 9781941500491.

    eBook. Theme Park Press. 2015.

Deja, Andreas. *The Nine Old Men: Lessons, Techniques, and Inspiration from Disney's Great Animators*. Hardcover First Edition. Routledge. 2015. ISBN-10: 0415843359. ISBN-13: 9780415843355.

    eBook. Routledge. 2015.

Ellenshaw, Peter. *Ellenshaw Under Glass: Going to the Matte for Disney*. Hardcover First Edition. Camphor Tree Publishers. 2003.

Gordon, Bruce. Mumford, David. *A Brush with Disney: An Artist's Journey, Told Through the Words and Works of Herbert Dickens Ryman*. Hardcover First Edition. Camphor Tree Publishers. 2000. ISBN-10: 0964605961. ISBN-13: 9780964605961.

    Leatherbound First Edition. Camphor Tree Publishers. 2000. ISBN-10: 0964605988. ISBN-13: 9780964605985.

Hannah, Jack. *From Donald Duck's Daddy to Disney Legend*. Paperback First Edition. Theme Park Press. 2017. ISBN-10: 168390043X. ISBN-13: 9781683900436.

    eBook. Theme Park Press. 2017.

Hischak, Thomas S. *Disney Voice Actors: A Biographical Dictionary*. Paperback First Edition. McFarland & Company, Inc., Publishers. 2011. ISBN-10: 078646271X. ISBN-13: 9780786462711.

eBook. McFarland & Company, Inc., Publishers. 2011.

Iwerks, Don. *Walt Disney's Ultimate Inventor: The Genius of Ub Iwerks*. Hardcover First Edition. Disney Editions. 2019. ISBN-10: 1484743377. ISBN-13: 9781484743379.

Iwerks, Leslie. Kenworthy, John. *The Hand Behind the Mouse: An Intimate Biography of Ub Iwerks*. Hardcover First Edition. Disney Editions. 2001. ISBN-10: 0786853204. ISBN-13: 9780786853205.

Jeup, Dan. Kaufman, J.B. Larson, Eric. *50 Years in the Mouse House: The Lost Memoir of One of Disney's Nine Old Men*. Paperback First Edition. Theme Park Press. 2015. ISBN-10: 1941500471. ISBN-13: 9781941500477.

Johnson, Jimmy. *Inside the Whimsy Works: My Life with Walt Disney Productions*. Hardcover First Edition. University Press of Mississippi. 2014. ISBN-10: 1617039306. ISBN-13: 9781617039300.

Audiobook. Narrated by Darryl Hughes Kurylo. 2014. University Press Audiobooks.

eBook. University Press of Mississippi. 2014.

Johnson, Mindy. *Ink & Paint: The Women of Walt Disney's Animation*. Hardcover First Edition. Disney Editions. 2017. ISBN-10: 1484727819. ISBN-13: 9781484727812.

Justice, Bill. *Justice for Disney*. Hardcover First Edition. Tomart Publications. 1992. ISBN-10: 0914293133. ISBN-13: 9780914293132.

Mason, Fergus. *Walt Disney's Nine Old Men: A History of the Animators Who Defined Disney Animation*. Paperback First Edition. Independent Publisher. 2014. ISBN-10: 1499307977. ISBN-13: 9781499307979.

Norman, Floyd. *Animated Life: A Lifetime of Tips, Tricks, Techniques and Stories from an Animation Legend*. Paperback First Edition. Routledge. 2013. ISBN-10: 0240818059. ISBN-13: 9780240818054.

Ohmart, Ben. *Welcome Foolish Mortals...The Life and Voices of Paul Frees*. Paperback First Edition. BearManor Media. 2004. ISBN-10: 1593930046. ISBN-13: 9781593930042.

    eBook. BearManor Media. 2014.

    Audiobook. Narrated by Fred Frees. Joe Bevilacqua and Waterlogg Productions. 2015.

    Book on CD. Joe Bevilacqua and Waterlogg Productions. 2015.

    Hardcover Revised Edition. BearManor Media. 2015. ISBN-10: 159393842X. ISBN-13: 9781593938420.

    Paperback Revised Edition. BearManor Media. 2017. ISBN-10: 1593934343. ISBN-13: 9781593934347.

Peri, Don. *Working with Disney: Interviews with Animators, Producers, and Artists*. Hardcover First Edition. University Press of Mississippi. 2011. ISBN-10: 1604739398. ISBN-13: 9781604739398.

    Paperback First Edition. University Press of Mississippi. 2011. ISBN-10: 1604739401. ISBN-13: 9781604739404.

    eBook. University Press of Mississippi. 2011.

Pierce, Todd. *The Life and Times of Ward Kimball: Maverick of Disney Animation*. Hardcover First Edition. University Press of Mississippi. 2019. ISBN-10: 1496820967. ISBN-13: 9781496820969.

    eBook. University Press of Mississippi. 2019.

    Audiobook. Narrated by Al Kessel. Tantor Audio. 2019.

Ryan, Jeff. *A Mouse Divided: How Ub Iwerks Became Forgotten, and Walt Disney Became Uncle Walt*. Hardcover First Edition. Post Hill Press. 2018. ISBN-10: 1682616274. ISBN-13: 9781682616277.

    eBook. Post Hill Press. 2018.

    Audiobook. Narrated by J. D. Jackson. Audible Studios. 2018.

      Paperback Reprint Edition. Post Hill Press. 2019. ISBN-10: 1642930938. ISBN-13: 9781642930931.

Shaw, Mel. *Animator on Horseback: The Autobiography of Disney Artist Mel Shaw*. Paperback First Edition. Theme Park Press. 2016. ISBN-10: 1941500943. ISBN-13: 9781941500941.

Silvester, William. *Saving Disney: The Story of Roy E. Disney*. Paperback First Edition. Theme Park Press. 2015. ISBN-10: 1941500757. ISBN-13: 9781941500750.

      eBook. Theme Park Press. 2015.

Stanchfield, Walt. *Drawn to Life: 20 Golden Years of Disney Master Classes: Volume 1: The Walt Stanchfield Lectures*. Paperback First Edition. Focal Press. 2009. ISBN-10: 0240810961. ISBN-13: 9780240810966.

      eBook. Routledge. 2013. ISBN-10: 1136138331. ISBN-13: 9781136138331.

Stanchfield, Walt. *Drawn to Life: 20 Golden Years of Disney Master Classes: Volume 2: The Walt Stanchfield Lectures*. Paperback First Edition. Focal Press. 2009. ISBN-10: 0240811070. ISBN-13: 9780240811079.

      eBook. CRC Press. 2012.

Szasz, Ioan. *Awaking Beauty: The Art of Eyvind Earle*. Hardcover First Edition. Weldon Owen. 2017. ISBN-10: 168188271X. ISBN-13: 9781681882710.

Tytle, Harry. *One of "Walt's Boys": An Insider's Account of Disney's Golden Years*. Hardcover First Edition. Airtight Seels Allied Production. 1997.

Walt Disney Company. *Marc Davis: Walt Disney's Renaissance Man*. Hardcover First Edition. Disney Editions. 2014. ISBN-10: 1423184181. ISBN-13: 9781423184188.

Industry and the Disney Corporate and Studio Structure

Barrier, Michael. *Building a Better Mouse: Fifty Years of Animation*. Paperback First Edition. Library of Congress. 1978.

Bossert, David A. *Kem Weber: Mid-Century Furniture Designs for the Disney Studios*. Hardcover First Edition. The Old Mill Press. 2018. ISBN-10: 173260200X. ISBN-13: 9781732602007.

    eBook. The Old Mill Press. 2019.

    Paperback First Edition. The Old Mill Press. 2020. ISBN-10: 1732602085. ISBN-13: 9781732602083.

Brode, Douglas. Brode, Shea T. *Debating Disney: Pedagogical Perspectives on Commercial Cinema*. Hardcover First Edition. Rowman & Littlefield Publishers. 2016. ISBN-10: 1442266082. ISBN-13: 9781442266087.

    eBook. Rowman & Littlefield Publishers. 2016.

Budd, Mike. Kirsch, Max H. *Rethinking Disney: Private Control, Public Dimensions*. Hardcover First Edition. 2005. ISBN-10: 0819567892. ISBN-13: 9780819567895.

    Paperback First Edition. Wesleyan University Press. 2005. ISBN-10: 0819567906. ISBN-13: 9780819567901.

Cline, Rebecca. *Walt Disney Studios: A Lot to Remember*. Hardcover First Edition. Disney Editions. 2019. ISBN-10: 1368051782. ISBN-13: 9781368051781.

Cotter, Bill. *The Wonderful World of Disney Television: A Complete History*. Hardcover First Edition. Disney Editions. 1997. ISBN-10: 0786863595. ISBN-13: 9780786863594

    Post-Publishing Supplemental Information available at: https://www.billcotter.com/tvbook/.

Crump, Rolly. Gurr, Bob. Moran, Christian. *Great Big Beautiful Tomorrow: Walt Disney and Technology*. Paperback First Edition. Theme Park Press. 2015. ISBN-10: 1941500404. ISBN-13: 9781941500408.

    eBook. Theme Park Press. 2015.

Eisner, Michael D. Schwartz, Tony. *Work in Progress: Risking Failure, Surviving Success*. Paperback First Edition. Hyperion. 1999. ISBN-10: 786885076. ISBN-13: 9780786885077.

    eBook. Kingswell. 2011.

Flower, Joe. *Prince of the Magic Kingdom: Michael Eisner and the Re-Making of Disney*. Hardcover First Edition. Wiley. 1991. ISBN-10: 0471524654. ISBN-13: 9780471524656.

    Paperback First Edition. Wiley. 1993. ISBN-10: 0471580651. ISBN-13: 9780471580652.

    Paperback Revised Second Edition. Theme Park Press. 2017. ISBN-10: 1683900782. ISBN-13: 9781683900788.

    eBook. Theme Park Press. 2017.

Friedman, Jake S. *The Disney Afternoon: The Making of a Television Renaissance*. Hardcover First Edition. Disney Editions. 2022. ISBN-10: 1368021913. ISBN-13: 9781368021913.

Friedman, Jake S. *The Disney Revolt: The Great Labor War of Animation's Golden Age*. Hardcover First Edition. Chicago Review Press. 2022. ISBN-10: 164160719X. ISBN-13: 9781641607193.

    eBook. Chicago Review Press. 2022.

    Post-Publishing Supplemental Information available at: https://www.thedisneyrevolt.com/.

Girveau, Bruno. *Once Upon a Time: Walt Disney: The Sources of Inspiration for the Disney Studios*. Hardcover First Edition. Prestel Publishing. 2007. ISBN-10: 379133770X. ISBN-13: 9783791337708.

> Paperback First Edition. Prestel Publishing. 2007.
> ISBN-10: 2891923030. ISBN-13: 9782891923033.

Grover, Ron. *The Disney Touch: How a Daring Management Team Revived an Entertainment Empire*. Hardcover First Edition. Business One Irwin. 1991. ISBN-10: 155623385X. ISBN-13: 9781556233852.

> Paperback Revised Subsequent Edition. Irwin Professional Publishing. ISBN-10: 0786310022. ISBN-13: 9780786310029.

Hahn, Don. *The Alchemy of Animation: Making an Animated Film in the Modern Age*. Paperback First Edition. Disney Editions. 2008. ISBN-10: 1423104765. ISBN-13: 9781423104766.

> Paperback Second Edition. Disney Editions. 2008.
> ISBN-10: 1423104765. ISBN-13: 9781423104766.

> Paperback Third Edition. Disney Editions. 2008. ISBN-10: 1423104765. ISBN-13: 9781423104766.

Hahn, Don. Miller-Zarneke, Tracey. *Before Ever After: The Lost Lectures of Walt Disney's Animation Studio*. Hardcover First Edition. Disney Editions. 2015. ISBN-10: 1484710819. ISBN-13: 9781484710814.

Holliss, Richard. *The Disney Studio Story*. Hardcover First Edition. Crown Publishers, Inc. 1988. ISBN-10: 0517570785. ISBN-13: 9780517570784.

> Hardcover First Edition. Random House Value Publishing. 1990.
> ISBN-10: 0517055988. ISBN-13: 9780517055984.

Hulett, Steve. *Mouse in Orbit: An Inside Look at How the Walt Disney Company Took a Neglected, Moribund Art Form and Turned It into a Mainstream Movie Powerhouse*. Paperback First Edition. Theme Park Press. 2018. ISBN-10: 1683901363. ISBN-13: 9781683901365.

> eBook. Theme Park Press. 2018.

Iger, Robert. *The Ride of a Lifetime: Lessons Learned from 15 Years as CEO of the Walt Disney Company*. Hardcover First Edition. Random House. 2019. ISBN-10: 0399592091. ISBN-13: 9780399592096.

eBook. Random House. 2019.

Audiobook. Narrated by Jim Frangione and Robert Iger. Random House Audio. 2019.

Audiobook on CD. Random House Audio. 2019.

Paperback First Edition (Large Print). Random House Large Print. 2019. ISBN-10: 0593170989. ISBN-13: 9780593170984.

Kaufman, J.B. *South of the Border with Disney*. Hardcover First Edition. Disney Editions. 2009. ISBN-10: 1423111931. ISBN-13: 9781423111931.

Kinney, Jack. *Walt Disney and Other Assorted Characters: An Unauthorized Account of the Early Years at Disney's*. Hardcover First Edition. Harmony Books. 1988. ISBN-10: 0517570572. ISBN-13: 9780517570579.

Korkis, Jim. *Who's Afraid of the Song of the South? and Other Forbidden Disney Stories*. Paperback First Edition. Theme Park Press. 2012. ISBN-10: 0984341552. ISBN-13: 9780984341559.

eBook. Theme Park Press. 2012.

Korkis, Jim. *Who's the Leader of the Club? Walt Disney's Leadership Lessons*. Paperback First Edition. Theme Park Press. 2014. ISBN-10: 1941500048. ISBN-13: 9781941500040.

eBook. Theme Park Press. 2014.

Lee, Newton. Madej, Krystina. *Disney Stories: Getting to Digital*. Hardcover First Edition. Springer Publishing Company. 2012. ISBN-10: 1461421004. ISBN-13: 9781461421009.

eBook. Springer Publishing Company. 2012.

Paperback First Edition. Springer Publishing Company. 2014. ISBN-10: 1493901826. ISBN-13: 9781493901821.

Hardcover Second Edition. Springer. 2020. ISBN-10: 3030427374. ISBN-13: 9783030427375.

eBook Second Edition. Springer. 2020.

Paperback First Edition. Springer Publishing Company. 2021.
ISBN-10: 3030427404. ISBN-13: 9783030427405.

Lescher, Mary E. *The Disney Animation Renaissance: Behind the Glass at the Florida Studio*. Hardcover First Edition. University of Illinois Press. 2022. ISBN-10: 0252044770. ISBN-13: 9780252044779.

Paperback First Edition. University of Illinois Press. 2022.
ISBN-10: 0252086864. ISBN-13: 9780252086861.

Masters, Kim. *The Keys to the Kingdom: How Michael Eisner Lost His Grip*. Hardcover First Edition. William Morrow. 2000. ISBN-10: 0688174493. ISBN-13: 9780688174491.

Paperback First Edition. Harper Paperbacks. 2001.
ISBN-10: 0066621097. ISBN-13: 9780066621098.

Meehan, Eileen R. Phillips, Mark. Wasko, Janet. *Dazzled by Disney? The Global Disney Audiences Project*. Hardcover First Edition. Continuum International Publishing Group. 2001. ISBN-10: 0718502612. ISBN-13: 9780718502614.

Paperback First Edition. Continuum International Publishing Group. 2001. ISBN-10: 0718502604. ISBN-13: 9780718502607.

Santoli, Lorraine. *Inside The Disney Marketing Machine: In The Era Of Michael Eisner And Frank Wells*. Paperback First Edition. Theme Park Press. 2015. ISBN-10: 194150048X. ISBN-13: 9781941500484.

eBook. Theme Park Press. 2015.

Schickel, Richard. *The Disney Version: The Life, Times, Art and Commerce of Walt Disney*. Hardcover First Edition. Simon & Schuster. 1968. ISBN-10: 0681217421. ISBN-13: 9780681217423.

Hardcover First Edition. Simon & Schuster. 1972. ISBN-10: 0671213067. ISBN-13: 9780671213060.

Paperback First Edition. Avon Books. 1981. ISBN-10: 0380011425. ISBN-13: 9780380011421.

Paperback Revised & Updated Edition. Touchstone Books. 1985. ISBN-10: 0671547143. ISBN-13: 9780671547141.

Hardcover Revised Edition. Pavilion Books. 1986. ISBN-10: 1851450076. ISBN-13: 9781851450077.

Paperback Third Edition. Ivan R. Dee Publishing. 1997. ISBN-10: 1566631580. ISBN-13: 9781566631587.

Paperback Reissue. Simon & Schuster. 2019. ISBN-10: 198211522X. ISBN-13: 9781982115227.

eBook. Simon & Schuster. 2019.

Smoodin, Eric. *Disney Discourse: Producing the Magic Kingdom*. Hardcover First Edition. Routledge. 1994. ISBN-10: 0415906156. ISBN-13: 9780415906159.

Paperback First Edition. Routledge. 1994. ISBN-10: 0415906164. ISBN-13: 9780415906166.

eBook. Routledge. 2013.

Stewart, James B. *Disney War*. Hardcover First Edition. Simon & Schuster. 2005. ISBN-10: 0684809931. ISBN-13: 9780684809939.

eBook. Simon and Schuster. 2005.

Audiobook. Narrated by Patrick Lawlor. Blackstone Audiobooks. 2005.

Paperback First Edition. Simon & Schuster. 2006. ISBN-10: 0743267095. ISBN-13: 9780743267090.

Taylor, John. *Storming the Magic Kingdom: Wall Street, The Raiders and the Battle for Disney*. Hardcover First Edition. Alfred A. Knopf, Inc. 1987. ISBN-10: 0394546407. ISBN-13: 9780394546407.

Hardcover First Edition. Viking Books. 1988. ISBN-10: 0670820938. ISBN-13: 9780670820931.

Telotte, J. P. *Disney TV*. Paperback First Edition. Wayne State University Press. 2004. ISBN-10: 0814330843. ISBN-13: 9780814330845.

    eBook. Wayne State University Press. 2004.

Telotte, J.P. *The Mouse Machine: Disney and Technology*. Hardcover First Edition. University of Illinois Press. 2008. ISBN-10: 0252033272. ISBN-13: 9780252033278.

    Paperback First Edition. University of Illinois Press. 2008. ISBN-10: 0252075404. ISBN-13: 9780252075407.

    eBook. University of Illinois Press. 2010.

Thomas, Bob. *Building a Company: Roy O. Disney and the Creation of an Entertainment Empire*. Hardcover First Edition. Disney Editions. 1998. ISBN-10: 0786862009. ISBN-13: 9780786862009.

    Paperback First Edition. Disney Editions. 1999. ISBN-10: 0786884169. ISBN-13: 9780786884162.

Wasko, Janet. *Understanding Disney: The Manufacture of Fantasy*. Hardcover First Edition. 2001. ISBN-10: 0745614833. ISBN-13: 9780745614830.

    Paperback First Edition. Polity. 2001. ISBN-10: 0745614841. ISBN-13: 9780745614847.

    Hardcover Second Edition. Polity. 2019. ISBN-10: 0745695639. ISBN-13: 9780745695631.

    Paperback Second Edition. Polity. 2020. ISBN-10: 0745695647. ISBN-13: 9780745695648.

    eBook. Polity. 2020.

Disney Productions

Allan, Robin. Ghez, Didier. Kaufman, J. B. Kothenschulte, Daniel. Lasseter, John. Lüthge, Katja. Merritt, Russell. Sibley, Brian. Solomon, Charles. *The Walt Disney Film Archives: The Animated Movies 1921-1968*. Hardcover First Edition. TASCHEN. 2016. ISBN-10: 3836552914. ISBN-13: 9783836552912.

Allan, Robin. *Walt Disney and Europe: European Influences on the Animated Feature Films of Walt Disney*. Paperback First Edition. Indiana University Press. 1999. ISBN-10: 1864620412. ISBN-13: 9781864620412.

Aloff, Mindy. *Hippo in a Tutu: Dancing in Disney Animation*. Hardcover First Edition. Disney Editions. 2009. ISBN-10: 1423100794. ISBN-13: 9781423100799.

Anderson, Ross. *Pulling a Rabbit Out of a Hat: The Making of Roger Rabbit*. Hardcover First Edition. University Press of Mississippi. 2019. ISBN-10: 1496822285. ISBN-13: 9781496822284.

> Paperback First Edition. University Press of Mississippi. 2019. ISBN-10: 1496822331. ISBN-13: 9781496822338.

> eBook. University Press of Mississippi. 2019.

Apgar, Garry. *A Mickey Mouse Reader*. Hardcover First Edition. University Press of Mississippi. 2014. ISBN-10: 1628461039. ISBN-13: 9781628461039.

Arnold, Mark. *Frozen in Ice: The Story of Walt Disney Productions, 1966-1985*. Paperback First Edition. BearManor Media. 2013. ISBN-10: 1593937512. ISBN-13: 9781593937515.

Bossert, David A. *Oswald the Lucky Rabbit: The Search for the Lost Disney Cartoons*. Hardcover First Edition. Disney Editions. 2017. ISBN-10: 148478037X. ISBN-13: 9781484780374.

> Hardcover Revised Special Edition. Disney Editions. 2019. ISBN-10: 1368042074. ISBN-13: 9781368042079.

Byrne, Eleanor. McQuillan, Martin. *Deconstructing Disney*. Hardcover First Edition. Pluto Press. 2000. ISBN-10: 0745314562. ISBN-13: 9780745314563.

>Paperback First Edition. Pluto Press. 2000. ISBN-10: 0745314511. ISBN-13: 9780745314518.

Canemaker, John. *The Lost Notebook: Herman Schultheis & the Secrets of Walt Disney's Movie Magic*. Hardcover First Annotated Edition. Weldon Owen. 2014. ISBN-10: 1616286326. ISBN-13: 9781616286323.

Clark, Les. Clark, Miriam . *Glimpses into the Golden Age of Disney Animation*. Paperback First Edition. Theme Park Press. 2019. ISBN-10: 1683902262. ISBN-13: 9781683902263.

Culhane, John. *Walt Disney's Fantasia*. Hardcover First Edition. Harry N. Abrams. 1983. ISBN-10: 0810908220. ISBN-13: 9780810908222.

>Hardcover Reissue. Harry N. Abrams. 1987 and 1999. ISBN-10: 0810980789. ISBN-13: 9780810980785.

Davis, Amy M. *Handsome Heroes and Vile Villains: Masculinity in Disney's Feature Films*. Paperback First Edition. John Libbey Publishing. 2014. ISBN-10: 0861967046. ISBN-13: 9780861967049.

>eBook. John Libbey Publishing. 2014.

Deja, Andreas. *Mickey Mouse: From Walt to the World*. Hardcover First Edition. Weldon Owen. 2019. ISBN-10: 1681884682. ISBN-13: 9781681884684.

Deja, Andreas. *The Walt Disney's The Jungle Book: Making a Masterpiece*. Hardcover First Edition. Weldon Owen. 2022. ISBN-10: 1681888939. ISBN-13: 9781681888934.

Field, Robert D. T*he Art of Walt Disney*. Hardcover First Edition. Macmillan Publishers. 1942.

>Hardcover First Edition. Collins. 1944.

>Reprint Hardcover. Collins. 1947.

Finch, Christopher. *The Art of Walt Disney: From Mickey Mouse to the Magic Kingdoms*. Hardcover First Edition. Harry N. Abrams, Inc. 1973. ISBN-10: 0810901226. ISBN-13: 9780810901223.

> Hardcover Concise Edition. Harry N. Abrams, Inc. 1975. ISBN-10: 0810903210. ISBN-13: 9780810990074.
>
> Hardcover New Edition. Brompton Books. 1988. ISBN-10: 0861244915. ISBN-13: 9780861244911.
>
> Hardcover Concise Edition. Portland House. 1988. ISBN-10: 0517664747. ISBN-13: 9780517664742.
>
> Hardcover Concise New Edition. Harry N. Abrams, Inc. 1993. ISBN-10: 0810980525. ISBN-13: 9780810980525.
>
> Hardcover New Edition. Virgin Books. 1995. ISBN-10: 1852275030. ISBN-13: 9781852275037.
>
> Hardcover Revised Edition. Harry N. Abrams. 1995. ISBN-10: 0810919621. ISBN-13: 9780810919624.
>
> Hardcover Revised. Virgin Books. 2004. ISBN-10: 1852272309. ISBN-13: 9781852272302.
>
> Hardcover Revised and Expanded Edition. Harry N. Abrams. 2004. ISBN-10: 0810949644. ISBN-13: 9780810949645.
>
> Hardcover New Reprinting. Harry N. Abrams. 2011. ISBN-10: 0810998149. ISBN-13: 9780810998148.

Gerstein, David. Kaufman, J.B. *Walt Disney's Mickey Mouse: The Ultimate History*. Hardcover First Edition. TASCHEN. 2018. ISBN-10: 3836552841. ISBN-13: 9783836552844.

> Hardcover Anniversary Edition. TASCHEN. 2020. ISBN-10: 3836580993. ISBN-13: 9783836580991.

Grant, John. *Encyclopedia of Walt Disney's Animated Characters: From Mickey Mouse to Hercules*. Hardcover First Edition. Harper & Row. 1987. ISBN-10: 0060157771. ISBN-13: 9780060157777.

>Hardcover First Edition. Random House Value Publishing. 1989. ISBN-10: 0517649594. ISBN-13: 9780517649596.

>Hardcover First Edition. Hyperion. 1993. ISBN-10: 1562829041. ISBN-13: 9781562829049.

>Hardcover Revised Edition. Hyperion. 1998. ISBN-10: 0786863366. ISBN-13: 9780786863365.

Holliday, Christopher. Pallant, Chris. *Snow White and the Seven Dwarfs: New Perspectives on Production, Reception, Legacy*. Hardcover First Edition. Bloomsbury Academic. 2021. ISBN-10: 1501351222. ISBN-13: 9781501351228.

Holliss, Richard. Sibley, Brian. *Walt Disney's Snow White and the Seven Dwarfs & the Making of the Classic Film*. Hardcover First Edition. Simon & Schuster. 1987. ISBN-10: 1570822328. ISBN-13: 9781570822322.

>Hardcover First Edition. Carlton Books Limited. 1987. ISBN-10: 0233981802. ISBN-13: 9780233981802.

>Hardcover First Edition. Disney Editions. 1994. ISBN-10: 0786861339. ISBN-13: 9780786861330.

Hulett, Steve. *Mouse in Transition: An Insider's Look at Disney Feature Animation*. Paperback First Edition. Theme Park Press. 2014. ISBN-10: 1941500242. ISBN-13: 9781941500248.

>eBook. Theme Park Press. 2014.

Jackson, Kathy Merlock. West, Mark I. *Walt Disney, from Reader to Storyteller: Essays on the Literary Inspirations*. Paperback First Edition. McFarland & Company, Inc., Publishers. 2014. ISBN-10: 0786472324. ISBN-13: 9780786472321.

>eBook. McFarland & Company, Inc., Publishers. 2014.

Jeffery, S. B. *The History of Walt Disney Animation*. Paperback First Edition. Independent Publisher. 2011. ISBN-10: 1466386207. ISBN-13: 9781466386204.

Johnson, David. *Snow White's People: An Oral History of the Disney Film Snow White and the Seven Dwarfs (Volume 1)*. Paperback First Edition. Theme Park Press. 2017. ISBN-10: 1683900545. ISBN-13: 9781683900542.

    eBook. Theme Park Press. 2017.

Johnson, David. *Snow White's People: An Oral History of the Disney Film Snow White and the Seven Dwarfs (Volume 2)*. Paperback First Edition. Theme Park Press. 2018. ISBN-10: 1683901207. ISBN-13: 9781683901204.

    eBook. Theme Park Press. 2018.

Johnson, Mindy. *Tinker Bell: An Evolution*. Hardcover First Edition. Disney Editions. 2013. ISBN-10: 1423172019. ISBN-13: 9781423172017.

Johnston, Ollie. Thomas, Frank. *The Disney Villain*. Hardcover First Edition. Disney Editions. 1993. ISBN-10: 1562827928. ISBN-13: 9781562827922.

Johnston, Ollie. Thomas, Frank. *The Illusion of Life: Disney Animation*. Hardcover First Edition. Disney Editions. 1981. ISBN-10: 0896592324. ISBN-13: 9780896592322.

    Hardcover Revised and Subsequent Edition. Disney Editions. 1995. ISBN-10: 0786860707. ISBN-13: 9780786860708.

Johnston, Ollie. Thomas, Frank. *Too Funny for Words: Disney's Greatest Sight Gags*. Hardcover First Edition. Abbeville Press. 1987. ISBN-10: 0896597474. ISBN-13: 9780896597471.

Kallay, William. *The Making of Tron: How Tron Changed Visual Effects and Disney Forever*. Paperback First Edition. William Kallay. 2011. ISBN-10: 0615494501. ISBN-13: 9780615494500.

Kaufman, J.B. *Pinocchio - The Making of an Epic*. Hardcover First Edition. Weldon Owen. 2015. ISBN-10: 1616288094. ISBN-13: 9781616288099.

Kaufman, J.B. *The Fairest One of All: The Making of Snow White and the Seven Dwarfs*. Hardcover First Edition. 2012. ISBN-10: 1616284382. ISBN-13: 9781616284381.

Kaufman, J.B. *The Making of Walt Disney's Fun and Fancy Free*. Hardcover First Edition. Hyperion Historical Alliance Press. 2019. ISBN-10: 0578527448. ISBN-13: 9780578527444.

Kaufman, J. B. Merritt, Russell. *Walt Disney's Silly Symphonies: A Companion to the Classic Cartoon Series*. Hardcover First Edition. La Cineteca del Friuli. 2006. ISBN-10: 8886155271. ISBN-13: 9788886155274.

    Hardcover Revised Updated Edition. Disney Editions. 2016. ISBN-10: 1484751329. ISBN-13: 9781484751329.

Kaufman, J. B. Merritt, Russell. *Walt in Wonderland: The Silent Films of Walt Disney*. Paperback First Edition. John Hopkins University Press. 1993. ISBN-10: 8886155026. ISBN-13: 9788886155021.

    Hardcover Revised Edition. Johns Hopkins University Press. 1994. ISBN-10: 0801849071. ISBN-13: 9780801849077.

    Paperback Second Edition. Johns Hopkins University Press. 2000. ISBN-10: 0801864291. ISBN-13: 9780801864292

Koenig, David. *Mouse Under Glass: Secrets of Disney Animation and Theme Parks*. Hardcover First Edition. Bonaventure Press. 1997. ISBN-10: 964060507. ISBN-13: 9780964060500.

    eBook. Bonaventure Press. 2011.

    Paperback First Edition. Bonaventure Press. 2015. ISBN-10: 0964060515. ISBN-13: 9780964060517.

Korkis, Jim. *Everything I Know I Learned from Disney Animated Feature Films: Advice for Living Happily After*. Paperback First Edition. Theme Park Press. 2015. ISBN-10: 1941500528. ISBN-13: 9781941500521.

    eBook. Theme Park Press. 2015.

Korkis, Jim. *Gremlin Trouble! The Cursed Roald Dahl Film Disney Never Made*. Paperback First Edition. Theme Park Press. 2017. ISBN-10: 1683900502. ISBN-13: 9781683900504.

>eBook. Theme Park Press. 2017.

Korkis, Jim. *Secret Stories of Mickey Mouse*. Paperback First Edition. Theme Park Press. 2018. ISBN-10: 1683901622. ISBN-13: 9781683901624.

>eBook. Theme Park Press. 2018.

Korkis, Jim. Williams, Don. *The Book of Mouse: A Celebration of Walt Disney's Mickey Mouse*. Paperback First Edition. Theme Park Press. 2013. ISBN-10: 0984341501. ISBN-13: 9780984341504.

>eBook. Theme Park Press. 2014.

Kurtti, Jeff. *Walt Disney's Sleeping Beauty: The Storybook and the Making of a Masterpiece*. Hardcover First Edition. Disney Editions. 2008. ISBN-10: 1423119177. ISBN-13: 9781423119173.

Lambert, Pierre. *Mickey Mouse*. Hardcover First Edition. Disney Editions. 1998. ISBN-10: 0786864532. ISBN-13: 9780786864539.

Lambert, Pierre. *Pinocchio*. Hardcover First Edition. Disney Editions. 1997. ISBN-10: 0786862475. ISBN-13: 9780786862474.

Lyons, Michael. *Drawn to Greatness: Disney's Animation Renaissance*. Paperback First Edition. Theme Park Press. 2022. ISBN-10: 168390317X. ISBN-13: 9781683903178.

Maltin, Leonard. *The Disney Films*. Hardcover First Edition. Crown Publishers, Inc. 1973. ISBN-10: 0517500469. ISBN-13: 9780517500460.

>Hardcover Second Edition. Bonanza Books. 1973.
>ISBN-10: 0517177412. ISBN-13: 9780517177419.

>Paperback First Edition. Popular Library. 1978.
>ISBN-10: 0445042761. ISBN-13: 9780445042766.

Hardcover Updated and Revised Edition. Crown Publishers, Inc. 1987.
ISBN-10: 0517554070. ISBN-13: 9780517554074.

Paperback Third Edition. Hyperion Books. 1995. ISBN-10: 0786881372.
ISBN-13: 9780786881376.

Paperback Fourth Edition. Disney Editions. 2000.
ISBN-10: 0786885270. ISBN-13: 9780786885275.

Montini, Barbara. Scollon, Bill. *Disney The Lion King: The Full Film Script.* Hardcover First Edition. Canterbury Classics. 2022. ISBN-10: 168412879X. ISBN-13: 9781684128792.

Montini, Barbara. Scollon, Bill. *Disney The Little Mermaid: The Full Film Script.* Hardcover First Edition. Canterbury Classics. 2022. ISBN-10: 1645171523. ISBN-13: 9781645171522.

Pallant, Chris. *Demystifying Disney: A History of Disney Feature Animation.* Hardcover First Edition. Continuum International Publishing Group. 2011. ISBN-10: 1441174214. ISBN-13: 9781441174215.

eBook. Continuum International Publishing Group. 2011.
Paperback Reprint Edition. Bloomsbury Academic. 2013.
ISBN-10: 1623567440. ISBN-13: 9781623567446.

Renault, Christian. *The Best of Disney's Animated Features: Volume One.* Paperback First Edition. Theme Park Press. 2020. ISBN-10: 1683902882. ISBN-13: 9781683902881.

Smith, Dave. *Disney A to Z: The Official Encyclopedia.* Hardcover First Edition. Disney Editions. 1996. ISBN-10: 0786862238. ISBN-13: 9780786862238.

Hardcover Second Edition. Disney Editions. 1998.
ISBN-10: 0786863919. ISBN-13: 9780786863914.

Hardcover Third Editions. Disney Editions. 2006. ISBN-10: 0786849193. ISBN-13: 9780786849192.

Smoodin, Eric. *Snow White and the Seven Dwarfs (BFI Film Classics).* Paperback First Edition. British Film Institute. 2012. ISBN-10: 184457475X. ISBN-13: 9781844574759.

   eBook. British Film Institute. 2019.

Solomon, Charles. *Once Upon a Dream: From Perrault's Sleeping Beauty to Disney's Maleficent*. Hardcover First Edition. Disney Editions. 2014. ISBN-10: 1423199022. ISBN-13: 9781423199021.

Spain, Steve. *The Art of Disney's 'Golden Age' Films and the Animation Process That Brought Them to Life: The Steve Spain Disney Art Collection*. Paperback First Edition. 2016.

Sperb, Jason. *Disney's Most Notorious Film: Race, Convergence, and the Hidden Histories of Song of the South*. Hardcover First Edition. University of Texas Press. 2012. ISBN-10: 0292739745. ISBN-13: 9780292739741.

   eBook. University of Texas Press. 2012.

   Paperback First Edition. University of Texas Press. 2013. ISBN-10: 0292756771. ISBN-13: 9780292756779.

Telotte, J.P. *Animating Space: From Mickey to WALL-E*. Hardcover First Edition. University Press of Kentucky. 2010. ISBN-10: 0813125863. ISBN-13: 9780813125862.

   eBook. The University Press of Kentucky. 2010.

   Audiobook. Narrated by Robert A. K. Gonyo. 2019.

Van Riper, A. Bowdoin. *Learning from Mickey, Donald and Walt: Essays on Disney's Edutainment Films*. Paperback First Edition. McFarland & Company, Inc., Publishers. 2011. ISBN-10: 0786459573. ISBN-13: 9780786459575.

   eBook. McFarland & Company, Inc., Publishers. 2011.

Wakabayashi, Hiro Clark. *Lilo & Stitch: Collected Stories from the Film's Creators*. Paperback First Edition. Disney Editions. 2002. ISBN-10: 0786853824. ISBN-13: 9780786853823.

Ward, Annalee R. *Mouse Morality: The Rhetoric of Disney Animated Films*. Hardcover First Edition. University of Texas Press. 2002. ISBN-10: 0292791526. ISBN-13: 9780292791527.

Paperback First Edition. University of Texas Press. 2002. ISBN-10: 0292791534. ISBN-13: 9780292791534.

eBook. University of Texas Press. 2010.

Whitley, David. *The Idea of Nature in Disney Animation (Studies in Childhood, 1700 to the Present)*. Hardcover First Edition. Routledge. 2008. ISBN-10: 0754660850. ISBN-13: 9780754660859.

Paperback Second Edition. Routledge. 2012. ISBN-10: 1409437493. ISBN-13: 9781409437499.

eBook. Routledge. 2013.

The Art of Disney

Bailey, Adrian. *Walt Disney's World of Fantasy*. Paperback First Edition. Everest House. 1984. ISBN-10: 0896961176. ISBN-13: 9780896961173.

Bancroft, Tom. *The Art of Disney's Dragons*. Hardcover First Edition Disney Editions. 2016. ISBN-10: 148474716X. ISBN-13: 9781484747162.

Bossert, David A. *Dali and Disney: Destino: The Story, Artwork, and Friendship Behind the Legendary Film*. Hardcover First Edition. Disney Editions. 2015. ISBN-10: 1484707133. ISBN-13: 9781484707135.

>Hardcover Limited Edition. Disney Editions. 2017. ISBN-10: 1484781899. ISBN-13: 9781484781890.

Bossert, David A. *The Art of Tennessee Loveless: The Mickey Mouse TEN x TEN x TEN Contemporary Pop Art Series*. Hardcover First Edition. Disney Editions. 2017. ISBN-10: 1484746899. ISBN-13: 9781484746899.

Culhane, John. *Disney's Aladdin: The Making of an Animated Film*. Hardcover First Edition. Disney Editions. 1992. ISBN-10: 1562828924. ISBN-13: 9781562828929.

>Paperback First Edition. Disney Editions. 1993. ISBN-10: 156282757X. ISBN-13: 9781562827571.

Culhane, John. *Fantasia 2000: Visions of Hope*. Hardcover First Edition. Disney Editions. 1999. ISBN-10: 0786861983. ISBN-13: 9780786861989.

Disney. *The Art of Encanto*. Hardcover First Edition. Chronicle Books. 2021. ISBN-10: 1797200860. ISBN-13: 9781797200866.

Disney Book Group. *Disney's Dogs*. Hardcover First Edition. Disney Editions. 2008. ISBN-10: 1423109201. ISBN-13: 9781423109204.

Disney Book Group. *The Disney Poster: The Animated Film Classics from Mickey Mouse to Aladdin*. Hardcover First Edition. Disney Editions. 1993. ISBN-10: 1562829246. ISBN-13: 9781562829247.

>Hardcover Second Edition. Disney Editions. 1995. ISBN-10: 0786861851. ISBN-13: 9780786861859.

Disney Book Group. *The Art of Minnie Mouse*. Hardcover First Edition. Disney Editions. 2016. ISBN-10: 148476773X. ISBN-13: 9781484767733.

Disney Book Group. Ward, Jessica. *The Art of Walt Disney's Mickey Mouse and Minnie Mouse*. Hardcover First Edition. Disney Editions. 2018. ISBN-10: 1368028756. ISBN-13: 9781368028752.

Disney Book Group. *Walt Disney's Bambi: The Sketchbook Series*. Hardcover First Edition. Disney Editions. 1997. ISBN-10: 0786863021. ISBN-13: 9780786863020

    Hardcover First Edition. Applewood Books. 1997. ISBN-10: 1557093423. ISBN-13: 9781557093424.

Finch, Christopher. *The Art of The Lion King*. Hardcover First Edition. Hyperion Press. 1994. ISBN-10: 0786860286. ISBN-13: 9780786860289.

    Hardcover First Edition. Hyperion Books. 1994. ISBN-10: 0786860316. ISBN-13: 9780786860319.

Goldman, Michael. *The Art and Making of the Lion King*. Hardcover First Edition. Disney Editions. 2019. ISBN-10: 1368023436. ISBN-13: 9781368023436.

Green, Howard E. *Tarzan Chronicles*. Hardcover First Edition. Disney Editions. 1999. ISBN-10: 0786864036. ISBN-13: 9780786864034.

Handke, Daniel. Hunt, Vanessa. *Poster Art of the Disney Parks (A Disney Parks Souvenir Book)*. Hardcover First Edition. Disney Editions. 2012. ISBN-10: 1423124111. ISBN-13: 9781423124115.

Hurter, Albert. *He Drew As He Pleased*. Simon and Schuster. 1948.

Ison, Stephen H. Krause, Martin. Witowski, Linda. *Walt Disney's Snow White and the Seven Dwarfs: An Art in Its Making*. Hardcover First Edition. Disney Editions. 1994. ISBN-10: 0786861444. ISBN-13: 9780786861446.

    Hardcover Second Edition. Disney Editions. ISBN-10: 0786861878. ISBN-13: 9780786861873.

Johnston, Ollie. Thomas, Frank. *Disney's Lady and the Tramp: The Sketchbook Series*. Hardcover First Edition. Applewoods. 1998. ISBN-10: 1557093466. ISBN-13: 9781557093462.

Johnston, Ollie. Thomas, Frank. *Disney's Peter Pan: The Sketchbook Series*. Hardcover First Edition. Applewoods. 1998. ISBN-10: 1557093458. ISBN-13: 9781557093455.

Johnston, Ollie. Thomas, Frank. *Walt Disney's Bambi: The Story and the Film*. Hardcover First Edition. Stewart Tabori & Chang. 1990. ISBN-10: 1556701608. ISBN-13: 9781556701603.

Julius, Jessica. *The Art of Big Hero 6*. Hardcover First Edition. Chronicle Books, LLC. 2014. ISBN-10: 1452122210. ISBN-13: 9781452122212.

Julius, Jessica. *The Art of Frozen 2*. Hardcover First Edition. Chronicle Books, LLC. 2019. ISBN-10: 1452169497. ISBN-13: 9781452169491.

Julius, Jessica. Malone, Maggie. *The Art of Moana*. Hardcover First Edition. Chronicle Books, LLC. 2016. ISBN-10: 1452155364. ISBN-13: 9781452155364.

Julius, Jessica. *The Art of Wreck-It Ralph 2*. Hardcover First Edition. Chronicle Books, LLC. 2018. ISBN-10: 1452163685. ISBN-13: 9781452163680.

Julius, Jessica. *The Art of Zootopia*. Hardcover First Edition. Chronicle Books, LLC. 2016. ISBN-10: 1452122237. ISBN-13: 9781452122236.

Kaufman, J.B. *Snow White and the Seven Dwarfs: The Art and Creation of Walt Disney's Classic Animated Film*. Hardcover First Edition. Weldon Owen. 2012. ISBN-10: 1616284374. ISBN-13: 9781616284374.

Kurtti, Jeff. *Atlantis: The Lost Empire: The Illustrated Script*. Hardcover First Edition. Disney Editions. 2001. ISBN-10: 0786853271. ISBN-13: 9780786853274.

Kurtti, Jeff. *Dinosaur: The Evolution of an Animated Feature*. Paperback First Edition. Disney Editions. 2000. ISBN-10: 0786851058. ISBN-13: 9780786851058.

Kurtti, Jeff. *From All of Us to All of You The Disney Christmas Card*. Hardcover First Edition. Disney Editions. 2018. ISBN-10: 1368018718. ISBN-13: 9781368018715.

Kurtti, Jeff. *The Art of Mulan*. Hardcover First Edition. Hyperion Books. 1998. ISBN-10: 0786863889. ISBN-13: 9780786863884.

    Hardcover Deluxe Edition. Disney Editions. 2020. ISBN-10: 1368018734. ISBN-13: 9781368018739.

Kurtti, Jeff. *The Art of The Little Mermaid*. Hardcover First Edition. Hyperion Books. 1997. ISBN-10: 0786863358. ISBN-13: 9780786863358.

Kurtti, Jeff. *The Art of The Princess and the Frog*. Hardcover First Edition. Chronicle Books. 2009. ISBN-10: 0811866351. ISBN-13: 9780811866354.

Kurtti, Jeff. *The Art of Tangled*. Hardcover First Edition. Chronicle Books, LLC. 2010. ISBN-10: 0811875555. ISBN-13: 9780811875554.

Kurtti, Jeff. Revenson, Jody. *Treasure Planet: A Voyage of Discovery*. Paperback First Edition. Disney Editions. 2001. ISBN-10: 0786853662. ISBN-13: 9780786853663.

Lambert, Pierre. *Bambi*. Hardcover First Edition. Huginn & Muninn. 2017. ISBN-10: 2364805511. ISBN-13: 9782364805514.

    English Translation Booklet. Stuart Ng Books. 2017.

Lambert, Pierre. *La Belle au Bois Dormant*. Hardcover First Edition. Les Editions de l'Ecole Georges Méliès. 2013. ISBN-10: 2954208309. ISBN-13: 9782954208305.

    English Translation Booklet. Stuart Ng Books. 2013.

Lee, Jennifer. Malone, Maggie. *The Art of Wreck-It Ralph*. Hardcover First Edition. Chronicle Books, LLC. 2012. ISBN-10: 1452111014. ISBN-13: 9781452111018.

Miller-Zarneke, Tracey. *The Art of Meet the Robinsons*. Hardcover First Edition. Disney Editions. 2007. ISBN-10: 1423102657. ISBN-13: 9781423102656.

Miller-Zarneke, Tracey. *The Art of Planes*. Hardcover First Edition. Chronicle Books, LLC. 2014. ISBN-10: 1452127999. ISBN-13: 9781452127996.

Musker, John. *Walt Disney Animation Studios: Studio Caricatures 1989-2006*. Hardcover First Edition. Walt Disney Animation Studios. 2008.

Disney's The Little Mermaid: The Sketchbook Series. Hardcover First Edition. Applewood. 1997. ISBN-10: 155709344X. ISBN-13: 9781557093448.

Norman, Floyd. *Son Of Faster Cheaper A Sharp Look Inside The Animation Business*. Paperback First Edition. Vignette Multimedia. 2004. ISBN-10: 1881368378. ISBN-13: 9781881368373.

    Paperback First Edition. Theme Park Press. 2015. ISBN-10: 1941500374. ISBN-13: 9781941500378.

Peterson, Monique. Revenson, Jody. *Home on the Range: The Adventures of a Bovine Goddess.* Paperback First Edition. Disney Editions. 2004. ISBN-10: 0786854081. ISBN-13: 9780786854080.

Rebello, Stephen. *The Art of Hercules: The Chaos of Creation*. Hardcover First Edition. Hyperion Books. 1997. ISBN-10: 0786862904. ISBN-13: 9780786862900.

    Hardcover Limited Edition. Disney Editions. 1997. ISBN-10: 0786862904. ISBN-13: 9780786862900.

Rebello, Stephen. *The Art of The Hunchback of Notre Dame*. Hardcover First Edition. Hyperion Books. 1996. ISBN-10: 0786862084. ISBN-13: 9780786862085.

    Hardcover Limited Edition. Disney Editions. 1996. ISBN-10: 0786862149. ISBN-13: 9780786862146.

    Hardcover First Edition. Disney Editions. 1997. ISBN-10: 078686334X. ISBN-13: 9780786863341.

Rebello, Stephen. *The Art of Pocahontas*. Hardcover First Edition. Hyperion Books. 1995. ISBN-10: 0786861584. ISBN-13: 9780786861583.

    Hardcover Limited Edition. Disney Editions. 1995. ISBN-10: 0786861746. ISBN-13: 9780786861743.

    Hardcover Reprint Edition. Disney Editions. 1996. ISBN-10: 0786862114. ISBN-13: 9780786862115.

Salisbury, Mark. *Frankenweenie: The Visual Companion*. Hardcover First Edition. Disney Editions. 2013. ISBN-10: 1423141865. ISBN-13: 9781423141860.

Shue, Ken. *A Disney Sketchbook*. Hardcover First Edition. Disney Editions. 2012. ISBN-10: 1423165691. ISBN-13: 9781423165699.

Smith, Lella F. *New Orleans Museum of Art: Dreams Come True*. Paperback First Edition. Disney Editions. 2009. ISBN-10: 1423121503. ISBN-13: 9781423121503.

Solomon, Charles. *Disney Lost and Found: Exploring the Hidden Artwork from Never-Produced Animation*. Hardcover First Edition. Disney Editions. 2008. ISBN-10: 1423116011. ISBN-13: 9781423116011.

Solomon, Charles. *Tale as Old as Time: The Art and Making of Beauty and the Beast*. Hardcover First Edition. Disney Editions. 2010. ISBN-10: 1423124812. ISBN-13: 9781423124818.

>Hardcover Second Edition. Disney Editions. 2017. ISBN-10: 1484758374. ISBN-13: 9781484758373.

Solomon, Charles. *The Art of Frozen*. Hardcover First Edition. Chronicle Books LLC. 2013. ISBN-10: 1452117160. ISBN-13: 9781452117164.

Solomon, Charles. *The Disney That Never Was: The Stories and Art from Five Decades of Unproduced Animation*. Hardcover First Edition. Hyperion Books. 1995. ISBN-10: 0786860375. ISBN-13: 9780786860371.

Springer, Justin. *The Art of Tron: Legacy*. Hardcover First Edition. Disney Editions. 2010. ISBN-10: 1423131495. ISBN-13: 9781423131496.

Thomas, Bob. *The Art of Animation: The Story of the Disney Studio Contribution to a New Art*. Hardcover First Edition. Golden Press and Walt Disney Productions. 1958.

Thomas, Bob. *Walt Disney: The Art of Animation*. Hardcover First Edition. Simon & Schuster. 1958.

>Hardcover First Edition. Golden Press and Walt Disney Productions. 1958.

>Revised Edition. Disney-Hyperion. 1992. ISBN-10: 1562829971. ISBN-13: 9781562829971.

>*Disney's Art of Animation: From Mickey Mouse to Beauty and the Beast*. Paperback First Edition. Disney Editions. 1991. ISBN-10: 1562828991. ISBN-13: 9781562828998.

Hardcover Revised Edition. Hyperion Book. ISBN-10: 1562829971.
ISBN-13: 9781562829971.

Disney's Art of Animation #2: From Mickey Mouse, To Hercules. Hardcover
First Edition. Disney Editions. 1997. ISBN-10: 0786862416.
ISBN-13: 9780786862412.

Hardcover Subsequent Editions. Disney Editions. 2017.
ISBN-10: 0786862416. ISBN-13: 9780786862412.

Thompson, Frank. *Tim Burton's Nightmare Before Christmas: The Film - The Art - The Vision*. 2001. Hardcover First Edition. Hyperion. 1993. ISBN-10: 156282774X. ISBN-13: 9781562827748.

Paperback First Edition. Disney Editions. 2009. ISBN-10: 142312541X.
ISBN-13: 9781423125419.

Vaz, Mark Cotta. *The Art of Bolt*. Hardcover First Edition. Chronicle Books, LLC. 2008. ISBN-10: 0811865312. ISBN-13: 9780811865319.

Wallace, Daniel. *The Art of Star Wars Rebels*. Hardcover First Edition. Dark Horse Books. 2020. ISBN-10: 1506710913. ISBN-13: 9781506710914.

Solomon, Charles. *The Disney Princess: A Celebration of Art and Creativity*. Hardcover First Edition. Chronicle Books. 2020. ISBN-10: 1452159114. ISBN-13: 9781452159119.

Wakabayashi, Hiro Clark. *Brother Bear: A Transformation Tale*. Hardcover First Edition. Chronicle Books, LLC. 2003. ISBN-10: 0786854200. ISBN-13: 9780811839754.

Walt Disney Animation Research Library. *Animation*. Hardcover First Edition. Disney Editions. 2009. ISBN-10: 1423117166. ISBN-13: 9781423117162.

Walt Disney Animation Research Library. *The Archive Series: Design*. Hardcover First Edition. Disney Editions. 2010. ISBN-10: 1423134206. ISBN-13: 9781423134206.

Walt Disney Animation Research Library. *The Archive Series: Layout & Background*. Hardcover First Edition. Disney Editions. 2011. ISBN-10: 142313866X. ISBN-13: 9781423138662.

Walt Disney Animation Research Library. *The Archive Series: Story*. Hardcover First Edition. Disney Editions. 2008. ISBN-10: 1423107233. ISBN-13: 9781423107231.

Walt Disney Company. *Disney's Neglected Prince: The Art of Disney's Knights in Shining Armor (and Loincloth)*. Hardcover First Edition. Disney Editions. 2009. ISBN-10: 1423113942. ISBN-13: 9781423113942.

Ward, Jessica. *The Art of Walt Disney's Mickey Mouse*. Hardcover First Edition. Disney Editions. 2018. ISBN-10: 1368011241. ISBN-13: 9781368011242.

White, Mark Andrew. *A Century Of Magic: The Animation Of The Walt Disney Studio*. Paperback First Edition. Fred Jones Jr. Museum Of Art. 2011. ISBN-10: 0971718792. ISBN-13: 9780971718791.

Culture and Disney

Apgar, Garry. *Mickey Mouse: Emblem of the American Spirit*. Hardcover First Edition. Weldon Owen. 2015. ISBN-10: 1616286725. ISBN-13: 9781616286729.

Bell, Elizabeth. Haas, Lynda. Sells, Laura. *From Mouse to Mermaid: The Politics of Film, Gender, and Culture*. Hardcover First Edition. Indiana University Press. 1995. ISBN-10: 253329051. ISBN-13: 9780253329059.

>Paperback First Edition. Indiana University Press. 1995. ISBN-10: 0253209781. ISBN-13: 9780253209788.

>eBook. Indiana University Press. 1995.

Brode, Douglas. *From Walt to Woodstock: How Disney Created the Counterculture*. Hardcover First Edition. University of Texas Press. 2004. ISBN-10: 0292709242. ISBN-13: 9780292709249.

>Paperback First Edition. University of Texas Press. 2004. ISBN-10: 0292702736. ISBN-13: 9780292702738.

>eBook. University of Texas Press. 2014.

Brode, Douglas. *Multiculturalism and the Mouse: Race and Sex in Disney Entertainment*. Paperback First Edition. University of Texas Press. 2006. ISBN-10: 0292709609. ISBN-13: 9780292709607.

>eBook. University of Texas Press. 2009.

Cheu, Johnson. *Diversity in Disney Films: Critical Essays on Race, Ethnicity, Gender, Sexuality and Disability*. Paperback First Edition. McFarland & Company, Inc., Publishers. 2013. ISBN-10: 0786446013. ISBN-13: 9780786446018.

>eBook. McFarland & Company, Inc., Publishers. 2013.

Davis, Amy M. *Good Girls and Wicked Witches: Changing Representations of Women in Disney's Feature Animation, 1937-2001*. Paperback First Edition. John Libbey Publishing. 2006. ISBN-10: 0861966732. ISBN-13: 9780861966738.

>eBook. John Libbey Publishing. 2018.

Giroux, Henry A. *The Mouse that Roared: Disney and the End of Innocence*. Hardcover First Edition. Rowman & Littlefield Publishers. 1999. ISBN-10: 742509834. ISBN-13: 9780742509832.

    Paperback First Edition. Rowman & Littlefield Publishers. 2001. ISBN-10: 0847691101. ISBN-13: 9780847691104.

    Paperback Updated and Expanded Edition. Rowman & Littlefield Publishers. 2010. ISBN-10: 1442201436. ISBN-13: 9781442201439.

    eBook. Rowman & Littlefield Publishers. 2010.

    Paperback Second Edition. Rowman & Littlefield Publishers. 2010. ISBN-10: 1442203293. ISBN-13: 9781442203297.

Harrington, Seán J. *The Disney Fetish*. Paperback First Edition. John Libbey Publishing. 2015. ISBN-10: 0861967135. ISBN-13: 9780861967131.

    Audiobook. Narrated by Emil Nicholas Gallina. University Press Audiobooks. 2015.

    eBook. John Libbey Publishing. 2015.

Hiaasen, Carl. *Team Rodent: How Disney Devours the World*. Paperback First Edition. Ballantine Books. 1998. ISBN-10: 0345422805. ISBN-13: 9780345422804.

    Unabridged Audiobook. Dove Entertainment Inc. 1998. ISBN-10: 0787117900. ISBN-13: 9780787117900.

    Audiobook. Narrated by Richard Gilliland. Phoenix Books. 1999.

    eBook. Ballantine Books. 2010.

Mollet, Tracey L. *A Cultural History of the Disney Fairy Tale: Once Upon an American Dream*. Hardcover First Edition. Palgrave Macmillan. 2020. ISBN-10: 3030501485. ISBN-13: 9783030501488.

    eBook. Palgrave Macmillan. 2020.

       Paperback First Edition. Palgrave Macmillan. 2021.
       ISBN-10: 3030501515. ISBN-13: 9783030501518.

Pinsky, Mark I. *The Gospel According to Disney: Faith, Trust, and Pixie Dust*. Paperback First Edition. Westminster John Knox Press. 2004. ISBN-10: 0664225918. ISBN-13: 9780664225919.

       eBook. Westminster John Knox Press. 2004.

Rothrock, Richard. *Sunday Nights With Walt: Everything I Know I Learned From The Wonderful World Of Disney*. Paperback First Edition. Theme Park Press. 2017. ISBN-10: 1683900871. ISBN-13: 9781683900870.

       eBook. Theme Park Press. 2017.

Sammond, Nicholas. *Babes in Tomorrowland: Walt Disney and the Making of the American Child, 1930-1960*. Hardcover First Edition. Duke University Press Books. 2005. ISBN-10: 0822334518. ISBN-13: 9780822334514.

       Paperback First Edition. Duke University Press Books. 2005. ISBN-10: 0822334631. ISBN-13: 9780822334637.

       eBook. Duke University Press Books. 2005.

Spiegel, Josh. *Walt's Original Sins: Disney and Racism*. Paperback First Edition. Theme Park Press. 2018. ISBN-10: 1683901371. ISBN-13: 9781683901372.

       eBook. Theme Park Press. 2018.

Watts, Steven. *The Magic Kingdom: Walt Disney and the American Way of Life*. Hardcover First Edition. Houghton Mifflin Harcourt. 1998. ISBN-10: 0395835879. ISBN-13: 9780395835876.

       Paperback First Edition. University of Missouri Press. 2001. ISBN-10: 0826213790. ISBN-13: 9780826213792.

       eBook. University of Missouri Press. 2013.

Disney Music

Beaudry, Karl. *Disney Melodies: The Magic of Disney Music*. Paperback First Edition. Theme Park Press. 2015. ISBN-10: 1941500358. ISBN-13: 9781941500354.

    eBook. Theme Park Press. 2015.

Bohn, James. *Music in Disney's Animated Features: Snow White and the Seven Dwarfs to the Jungle Book*. Hardcover First Edition. University Press of Mississippi. 2017. ISBN-10: 149681214X. ISBN-13: 9781496812148.

    eBook. University Press of Mississippi. 2017.

    Paperback Reprint Edition. University Press of Mississippi. 2018. ISBN-10: 1496818334. ISBN-13: 9781496818331.

Ehrbar, Greg. Hollis, Tim. *Mouse Tracks: The Story of Walt Disney Records*. Hardcover First Edition. University Press of Mississippi. 2006. ISBN-10: 1578068487. ISBN-13: 9781578068487.

    Paperback First Edition. University Press of Mississippi. 2006. ISBN-10: 1578068495. ISBN-13: 9781578068494.

Hischak, Thomas S. Robinson, Mark A. *The Disney Song Encyclopedia*. Hardcover First Edition. Scarecrow Press. 2009. ISBN-10: 0810869373. ISBN-13: 9780810869370.

    eBook. Scarecrow Press. 2009.

    Paperback Updated Edition. Scarecrow Press. 2012. ISBN-10: 1589797132. ISBN-13: 9781589797130.

Hodge, Matthew. *Cool Cats and a Hot Mouse: A History of Jazz and Disney*. Paperback First Edition. Theme Park Press. 2020. ISBN-10: 1683902688. ISBN-13: 9781683902683.

    eBook. Theme Park Press. 2020.

Ohmart, Ben. *Buddy Baker: Big Band Arranger, Disney Legend & Musical Genius*. Hardcover First Edition. BearManor Media. 2016. ISBN-10: 1593931964. ISBN-13: 9781593931964.

>Paperback First Edition. BearManor Media. 2016. ISBN-10: 1593931956. ISBN-13: 9781593931957.

>Audiobook on CD. BearManor Media. Blackstone Audio. 2016.

>Audiobook. Narrated by David Zarbock. BearManor Media. 2016.

>eBook. BearManor Media. 2016.

Price, Kathryn M. *Walt Disney's Melody Makers: A Biography of the Sherman Brothers*. Paperback First Edition. Theme Park Press. 2018. ISBN-10: 1683901142. ISBN-13: 9781683901143.

>eBook. Theme Park Press. 2018.

Rodosthenous, George. *The Disney Musical on Stage and Screen: Critical Approaches from 'Snow White' to 'Frozen'*. Hardcover First Edition. Methuen Drama. 2017. ISBN-10: 1474234178. ISBN-13: 9781474234177.

>Paperback First Edition. Methuen Drama. 2017. ISBN-10: 147423416X. ISBN-13: 9781474234160.

>eBook. Methuen Drama. 2017.

Schroeder, Russell. *Disney's Lost Chords*. Hardcover First Edition. Voigt Publications. 2007. ISBN-10: 0615134513. ISBN-13: 9780615134512.

Schroeder, Russell. *Disney's Lost Chords: Volume Two*. Hardcover First Edition. Voigt Publications. 2008. ISBN-10: 0615206336. ISBN-13: 9780615206332.

History and Disney

Apgar, Garry. Bossert, David. Ghez, Didier. Hollifield, Jim. Pierce, Todd James. Seastrom, Lucas. *2019 Hyperion Historical Society Alliance Annual Report*. Paperback First Edition. Hyperion Historical Alliance Press. 2019. ISBN-10: 1793898421. ISBN-13: 9781793898425.

Baxter, John. *Disney During World War II: How the Walt Disney Studio Contributed to Victory in the War*. Hardcover First Edition. Disney Editions. 2014. ISBN-10: 1423180275. ISBN-13: 9781423180272.

Beck, Jerry. Ehrbar, Greg. Fanning, Jim. Ghez, Didier. Jurtti, Jeff. Kaufman, J.B. Korkis, Jim. Lowery, Paula Sigman. *How to Be a Disney Historian: Tips from the Top Professionals*. Paperback First Edition. Theme Park Press. 2016. ISBN-10: 1941500927. ISBN-13: 9781941500927

    eBook. Theme Park Press. 2016.

Clark, Steven. Smith, David. *Disney: The First 100 Years*. Hardcover First Edition. Disney Editions. 1999. ISBN-10: 0786864427. ISBN-13: 9780786864423.

    Paperback Revised Edition. Disney Editions. 2003. ISBN-10: 0786853808. ISBN-13: 9780786853809.

Ghez, Didier. Johnson, Mindy. Kaufman, J.B. Kern, Kevin M. Moryc, Matt. *2020 Hyperion Historical Society Alliance Annual Report*. Paperback First Edition. Hyperion Historical Alliance Press. 2020. ISBN-13: 9798623207241.

Hahn, Don. *Yesterday's Tomorrow: Disney's Magical Mid-Century*. Hardcover First Edition. Disney Editions. 2017. ISBN-10: 1484737644. ISBN-13: 9781484737644.

Lesjak, David. *Service with Character: The Disney Studio & World War II*. Paperback First Edition. Theme Park Press. 2014. ISBN-10: 1941500056. ISBN-13: 9781941500057.

Mollet, Tracey. *Cartoons in Hard Times: The Animated Shorts of Disney and Warner Brothers in Depression and War 1932-1945*. Hardcover First Edition. Bloomsbury Academic. 2017. ISBN-10: 1501328778. ISBN-13: 9781501328770.

    eBook. Bloomsbury Academic. 2017.

Paperback First Edition. Bloomsbury Academic. 2019. ISBN-10: 1501351966. ISBN-13: 9781501351969.

Rawls, Walton H. *Disney Dons Dogtags: The Best of Disney Military Insignia from World War II*. Hardcover First Edition. Abbeville Publishing Group. 1992. ISBN-10: 1558594019. ISBN-13: 9781558594012.

Shale, Richard. *Donald Duck Joins Up: The Walt Disney Studio During World War II*. Hardcover First Edition. UMI Research Press. 1982. ISBN-10: 0835713105. ISBN-13: 9780835713108.

Susanin, Timothy S. *Walt Before Mickey: Disney's Early Years, 1919-1928*. Hardcover First Edition. University Press of Mississippi. 2011. ISBN-10: 1604739606. ISBN-13: 9781604739602.

eBook. University Press of Mississippi. 2011.

Paperback Illustrated Edition. University Press of Mississippi. 2014. ISBN-10: 1628461632. ISBN-13: 9781628461633.

Audiobook. Narrated by Al Kessel. 2017.

The Walt Disney Family Museum. *The Walt Disney Studios and WWII*. Paperback First Edition. The Walt Disney Family Museum. 2021.

Pixar

Brown, Noel. Smith, Susan. Summers, Sam. *Toy Story: How Pixar Reinvented the Animated Feature (Animation: Key Films/Filmmakers)*. Hardcover First Edition. Bloomsbury Academic. 2018. ISBN-10: 1501324918. ISBN-13: 9781501324918.

    eBook. Bloomsbury Academic. 2018.

    Paperback First Edition. Bloomsbury Academic. 2019. ISBN-10: 1501354914. ISBN-13: 9781501354915.

Catmull, Ed. *Creativity, Inc.* Hardcover First Edition. Random House Books. 2014. ISBN-10: 0812993012. ISBN-13: 9780812993011.

    Paperback First Edition. Transworld Publishers Limited. 2014. ISBN-10: 0593070100. ISBN-13: 9780593070109.

    Hardcover First Edition. Random House Books Canada. 2014. ISBN-10: 0307361179. ISBN-13: 9780307361172.

    Audio CD. Random House Audio. 2014.

    eBook. Random House Books. 2014.

    Audiobook. Narrated by Peter Altschuler. Random House Audio. 2014.

Clarke, James. *The Films of Pixar Animation Studio*. Paperback First Edition. Kamera Books. 2013. ISBN-10: 1842439375. ISBN-13: 9781842439371.

    eBook. Oldcastle Books. 2013.

Gillam, Ken. Wooden, Shannon R. *Pixar's Boy Stories: Masculinity in a Postmodern Age*. Hardcover First Edition. Rowman & Littlefield Publishers. 2016. ISBN-10: 1442233583. ISBN-13: 9781442233584.

    eBook. Rowman & Littlefield Publishers. 2014.

    Paperback First Edition. Rowman & Littlefield Publishers. 2016. ISBN-10: 1442275650. ISBN-13: 9781442275652.

Herhuth, Eric. *Pixar and the Aesthetic Imagination: Animation, Storytelling, and Digital Culture*. Hardcover First Edition. University of California Press. 2017. ISBN-10: 0520292553. ISBN-13: 9780520292550.

>Paperback First Edition. University of California Press. 2017. ISBN-10: 0520292561. ISBN-13: 9780520292567.

>eBook. University of California Press. 2017.

Kemper, Tom. *Toy Story: A Critical Reading (BFI Film Classics)*. Paperback First Edition. British Film Institute. 2015. ISBN-10: 1844576671. ISBN-13: 9781844576678.

>eBook. British Film Institute. 2019.

Kinder, Bill. O'Steen, Bobbie. *Making the Cut at Pixar: The Art of Editing Animation*. Hardcover First Edition. Routledge. 2022. ISBN-10: 0367766582. ISBN-13: 9780367766580.

>Paperback First Edition. Routledge. 2022. ISBN-10: 0367766140. ISBN-13: 9780367766146.

Meinel, Dietmar. *Pixar's America: The Re-Animation of American Myths and Symbols*. Hardcover First Edition. Palgrave Macmillan. 2018. ISBN-10: 3319316338. ISBN-13: 9783319316338.

>eBook. Palgrave Macmillan. 2016.

>Paperback First Edition. Palgrave Macmillan. 2018. ISBN-10: 3319810839. ISBN-13: 9783319810836.

Paik, Karen. *To Infinity and Beyond!: The Story of Pixar Animation Studios*. Hardcover First Edition. Chronicle Books, LLC. 2007. ISBN-10: 0811850129. ISBN-13: 9780811850124.

>Hardcover First Edition. Virgin Books. 2007. ISBN-10: 1905264216. ISBN-13: 9781905264216.

Price, David A. *The Pixar Touch: The Making of a Company*. Hardcover First Edition. Alfred A. Knopf. 2008. ISBN-10: 0307265757. ISBN-13: 9780307265753.

    Audiobook. Narrated by David Drummond. Tantor Audio. 2008.

    Audiobook on CD. Tantor Audio. 2008.

    Audioplayer - Library Edition. Tantor Audio. 2008.

    eBook. Vintage. 2008.

    Paperback First Edition. Vintage Books. 2009. ISBN-10: 0307278298. ISBN-13: 9780307278296.

Rösing, Lilian Munk. *Pixar with Lacan: The Hysteric's Guide to Animation*. Hardcover First Edition. Bloomsbury Academic. 2015. ISBN-10: 1628920599. ISBN-13: 9781628920598.

    eBook. Bloomsbury Academic. 2015.

    Paperback Reprint Edition. Bloomsbury Academic. 2017. ISBN-10: 1501320173. ISBN-13: 9781501320170.

Solomon, Charles. *The Toy Story Films: An Animated Journey*. Hardcover First Edition. Disney Editions. 2012. ISBN-10: 1423144945. ISBN-13: 9781423144946.

Spiegel, Josh. *Pixar and the Infinite Past: Nostalgia and Pixar Animation*. Paperback First Edition. Theme Park Press. 2018. ISBN-10: 1683901177. ISBN-13: 9781683901174.

    eBook. Theme Park Press. 2018.

Spiegel, Josh. *Yesterday is Forever: Nostalgia and Pixar Animation Studios*. Paperback First Edition. The Critical Press. 2015. ISBN-10: 1941629237. ISBN-13: 9781941629239.

Walt Disney Company. *Pixar: 25 Years Of Animation*. Paperback First Edition. Chronicle Books, LLC. 2010. ISBN-10: 0811876721. ISBN-13: 9780811876728.

The Art of Pixar

Amidi, Amid. *The Art of Pixar: 25th Anniversary: The Complete Color Scripts and Select Art from 25 Years of Animation*. Hardcover First Edition. Chronicle Books, LLC. 2011. ISBN-10: 0811879631. ISBN-13: 9780811879637.

    Hardcover Revised and Expanded Edition. Chronicle Books. 2020. ISBN-10: 1452182787. ISBN-13: 9781452182780.

Amidi, Amid. *The Art of Pixar Short Films*. Hardcover First Edition. Chronicle Books, LLC. 2009. ISBN-10: 0811866068. ISBN-13: 9780811866064.

Beecroft, Simon. *Walt Disney Company Ltd. Pixar Museum: Stories and Art from the Animation Studio*. Hardcover First Edition. Studio Press. 2021. ISBN-10: 1787416577. ISBN-13: 9781787416574.

Cooley, Josh. *The Art of Toy Story 4*. Hardcover First Edition. Chronicle Books, LLC. 2019. ISBN-10: 1452163820. ISBN-13: 9781452163826.

Daly, Steve. Lasseter, John. *Toy Story The Art and Making of the Animated Film*. Hardcover First Edition. Disney Editions. 1995. ISBN-10: 0786861800. ISBN-13: 9780786861804.

    Hardcover Gift Edition. Disney Editions. 1996. ISBN-10: 0786862548. ISBN-13: 9780786862542.

    Hardcover Reprint Edition. Disney Editions. 2009. ISBN-10: 1423129679. ISBN-13: 9781423129677.

Disney - Pixar. *Funny!: Twenty-Five Years of Laughter from the Pixar Story Room*. Hardcover First Edition. Chronicle Books. 2015. ISBN-10: 1452122288. ISBN-13: 9781452122281.

Disney - Pixar. *The Art of Luca*. Hardcover First Edition. Chronicle Books. 2021. ISBN-10: 1797207253. ISBN-13: 9781797207254.

Disney - Pixar. *Toy Story: The Sketchbook Series*. Hardcover First Edition. Applewood Books. 2000. ISBN-10: 1557093407. ISBN-13: 9781557093400.

Disney and Pixar. *The Art of Turning Red*. Hardcover First Edition. Chronicle Books. 2022. ISBN-10: 1797200852. ISBN-13: 9781797200859.

Docter, Pete. *The Art of Inside Out*. Hardcover First Edition. Chronicle Books, LLC. 2015. ISBN-10: 1452135185. ISBN-13: 9781452135182.

Docter, Pete. Lasseter, John. *The Art of Monsters, Inc*. Hardcover First Edition. Chronicle Books. 2001. ISBN-10: 0811833887. ISBN-13: 9780811833882.

Hauser, Tim. *The Art of Up*. Hardcover First Edition. Chronicle Books, LLC. 2009. ISBN-10: 0811866025. ISBN-13: 9780811866026.

Hauser, Tim. *The Art of WALL-E*. Hardcover First Edition. Chronicle Books, LLC. 2008. ISBN-10: 0811862356. ISBN-13: 9780811862356.

Higgins, Steven. Magliozzi, Ronald S. *Pixar: At the Museum of Modern Art*. Hardcover First Edition. Chronicle Books, LLC. 2006. ISBN-10: 0811852164. ISBN-13: 9780811852166.

> Paperback First Edition. Chronicle Books, LLC. 2006. ISBN-10: 0811852164. ISBN-13: 9780811852166.

> Hosted Online at https://www.moma.org/calendar/exhibitions/91.

Kratter, Tia. *The Color of Pixar*. Hardcover First Edition. Chronicle Books, LLC. 2017. ISBN-10: 1452159203. ISBN-13: 9781452159201.

Kurtti, Jeff. *A Bug's Life: The Art and Making of an Epic of Miniature Proportions*. Hardcover First Edition. Disney Editions. 1998. ISBN-10: 0786864419. ISBN-13: 9780786864416.

> Hardcover Collector's Edition. Disney Editions. 1998. ISBN-10: 0786865164. ISBN-13: 9780786865161.

Lasseter, John. *The Art of Cars 3*. Hardcover First Edition. Chronicle Books, LLC. 2017. ISBN-10: 1452156425. ISBN-13: 9781452156422.

Lasseter, John. *The Art of Coco*. Hardcover First Edition. Chronicle Books, LLC. 2017. ISBN-10: 1452156433. ISBN-13: 9781452156439.

Lasseter, John. *The Art of Finding Dory*. Hardcover First Edition. Chronicle Books, LLC. 2016. ISBN-10: 1452122245. ISBN-13: 9781452122243.

Lerew, Jenny. *The Art of Brave*. Hardcover First Edition. Chronicle Books, LLC. 2012. ISBN-10: 1452101426. ISBN-13: 9781452101422.

Paik, Karen. Queen, Ben. *The Art of Cars 2*. Hardcover First Edition. Chronicle Books, LLC. 2011. ISBN-10: 0811878910. ISBN-13: 9780811878913.

Paik, Karen. *The Art of Incredibles 2*. Hardcover First Edition. Chronicle Books, LLC. 2018. ISBN-10: 1452163847. ISBN-13: 9781452163840.

Paik, Karen. *The Art of Monsters University*. Hardcover First Edition. Chronicle Books, LLC. 2013. ISBN-10: 145211207X. ISBN-13: 9781452112077.

Paik, Karen M. *Art of Ratatouille*. Hardcover First Edition. Chronicle Books, LLC. 2007. ISBN-10: 0811858340. ISBN-13: 9780811858342.

Patel, Sanjay. *The Art of Sanjay's Super Team*. Hardcover First Edition. Chronicle Books. 2015. ISBN-10: 1452152063. ISBN-13: 9781452152066.

Pixar. *The Art of Soul*. Hardcover First Edition. Chronicle Books. 2020. ISBN-10: 1452179816. ISBN-13: 9781452179810.

Sohn, Peter. *The Art of The Good Dinosaur*. Hardcover First Edition. Chronicle Books, LLC. 2015. ISBN-10: 1452122202. ISBN-13: 9781452122205.

Solomon, Charles. *The Art of Toy Story 3*. Hardcover First Edition. Chronicle Books, LLC. 2010. ISBN-10: 0811874346. ISBN-13: 9780811874342.

Taylor, Drew. *The Art of Onward*. Hardcover First Edition. Chronicle Books, LLC. 2020. ISBN-10: 1452179808. ISBN-13: 9781452179803.

Vaz, Mark Cotta. *The Art of Finding Nemo*. Hardcover First Edition. Chronicle Books, LLC. 2003. ISBN-10: 0811839753. ISBN-13: 9780811839754.

Vaz, Mark Cotta. *The Art of The Incredibles*. Hardcover First Edition. Chronicle Books, LLC. 2004. ISBN-10: 0811844331. ISBN-13: 9780811844338.

Wallis, Michael. Wallis, Suzanne Fitgerald. *The Art of Cars*. Hardcover First Edition. Chronicle Books, LLC. 2006. ISBN-10: 0811849007. ISBN-13: 9780811849005.

The Art of 20th Century Animation and 20th Television Animation

Anderson, Wes. *The Making of Fantastic Mr. Fox*. Hardcover First Edition. Rizzoli International Publishing. 2009. ISBN-10: 0847833542. ISBN-13: 9780847833542.

Deneroff, Harvey. *The Art of Anastasia: A Twentieth Century Fox Presentation*. Hardcover First Edition. Harper Collins. 1997. ISBN-10: 0067575307. ISBN-13: 9780067575307.

Gutierrez, Jorge. *The Art of the Book of Life*. Hardcover First Edition. Dark Horse Books. 2014. ISBN-10: 1616555335. ISBN-13: 9781616555337.

    eBook. Hardcover First Edition. Dark Horse Books.

Moore, Frazier. *Inside Family Guy: An Illustrated History*. Hardcover First Edition. Dey Street Books. 2019. ISBN-10: 006211252X. ISBN-13: 9780062112521.

The Art of DreamWorks

Abele, Robert. *The Art of DreamWorks Turbo*. Hardcover First Edition. Insight Editions. 2013. ISBN-10: 1608872122. ISBN-13: 9781608872121.

Beck, Jerry. *The Art of the Bee Movie*. Hardcover First Edition. Chronicle Books, LLC. 2007. ISBN-10: 0811859517. ISBN-13: 9780811859516.

Beck, Jerry. *The Art of DreamWorks Madagascar: Escape 2 Africa*. Hardcover First Edition. Insight Editions. 2008. ISBN-10: 1933784709. ISBN-13: 9781933784700.

Beck, Jerry. *The Art of DreamWorks Mr. Peabody & Sherman*. Hardcover First Edition. Pocket Books. 2014. ISBN-10: 1608872580. ISBN-13: 9781608872589.

Burton, Bonnie. *The Art of Abominable*. Hardcover First Edition. Cameron+Company. 2019. ISBN-10: 1944903917. ISBN-13: 9781944903916.

Hopkins, John. *Shrek: From the Swamp to the Screen*. Hardcover First Edition. Harry N. Abrams. 2004. ISBN-10: 0810943093. ISBN-13: 9780810943094.

Hueso, Noela. *The Art of DreamWorks The Croods*. Hardcover First Edition. Titan Books. 2013. ISBN-10: 1781164118. ISBN-13: 9781781164112.

Jones, Kathleen. *Shrek: The Art of the Quest*. Hardcover First Edition. Insight Editions. 2007. ISBN-10: 1933784180. ISBN-13: 9781933784182.

Miller-Zarneke, Tracey. *The Art of How to Train Your Dragon*. Hardcover First Edition. Titan Books. Ltd. 2010. ISBN-10: 1848566654. ISBN-13: 9781848566651.

Miller-Zarneke, Tracey. *The Art of DreamWorks Kung Fu Panda*. Hardcover First Edition. Insight Editions. 2008. ISBN-10: 1933784571. ISBN-13: 9781933784571.

Miller-Zarneke, Tracey. *The Art of Kung Fu Panda 2*. Hardcover First Edition. Insight Editions. 2011. ISBN-10: 1608870189. ISBN-13: 9781608870189.

Miller-Zarneke, Tracey. *The Art of Kung Fu Panda 3*. Hardcover First Edition. Titan Books. 2015. ISBN-10: 1783298359. ISBN-13: 9781783298358.

Hardcover First Edition. Insight Editions. 2016. ISBN-10: 160887494X. ISBN-13: 9781608874941.

Robertson, Barbara. *The Art of DreamWorks Madagascar 3*. Hardcover First Edition. Insight Editions. 2012. ISBN-10: 1608870758. ISBN-13: 9781608870752.

Robertson, Barbara. *The Art of DreamWorks Penguins of Madagascar*. Hardcover First Edition. Insight Editions. 2014. ISBN-10: 1608874923. ISBN-13: 9781608874927.

Schmitz, Jerry. *The Art of Shrek Forever After*. Hardcover First Edition. Insight Editions. 2010. ISBN-10: 1608870022. ISBN-13: 9781608870028.

Schmitz, Jerry. *The Art of Trolls*. Hardcover First Edition. Cameron Books. 2016. ISBN-10: 1937359956. ISBN-13: 9781937359959.

Soloman, Charles. *The Prince of Egypt: A New Vision in Animation*. Hardcover First Edition. Harry N. Abrams. 1998. ISBN-10: 0500019134. ISBN-13: 9780500019139.

Sunshine, Linda. *The Art of DreamWorks How to Train Your Dragon 2*. Hardcover First Edition. Dey Street Books. 2014. ISBN-10: 0062323350. ISBN-13: 9780062323354.

Sunshine, Linda. *The Art of How to Train Your Dragon: The Hidden World*. Hardcover First Edition. Dark Horse Books. 2019. ISBN-10: 150670977X. ISBN-13: 9781506709772.

    eBook. Dark Horse Books. 2019.

Sunshine, Linda. *The Art of Monsters vs. Aliens*. Hardcover First Edition. Newmarket Press. 2009. ISBN-10: 155704824X. ISBN-13: 9781557048240.

von Busack, Richard. *The Art of DreamWorks Megamind: Bad, Brilliant, Blue*. Hardcover First Edition. Insight Editions. 2010. ISBN-10: 1608870022. ISBN-13: 9781608870028.

Zahed, Ramin. *The Art of The Boss Baby*. Hardcover First Edition. Insight Editions. 2017. ISBN-10: 1608876829. ISBN-13: 9781608876822.

Zahed, Ramin. *The Art of Captain Underpants: The First Epic Movie*. Hardcover First Edition. Titan Books. 2017. ISBN-10: 1785652907. ISBN-13: 9781785652905.

Zahed, Ramin. *The Art of DreamWorks Animation: Celebrating 20 Years of Art*. Hardcover First Edition. Harry N. Abrams. 2014. ISBN-10: 1419711660. ISBN-13: 9781419711664.

Zahed, Ramin. *The Art of DreamWorks Puss in Boots*. Hardcover First Edition. Insight Editions. 2011. ISBN-10: 1608870340. ISBN-13: 9781608870349.

> Hardcover First Edition. Titan Publishing Company. 2011. ISBN-10: 0857689355. ISBN-13: 9780857689351.

Zahed, Ramin. *The Art of DreamWorks Rise of the Guardians*. Hardcover First Edition. Insight Editions. 2012. ISBN-10: 1608871088. ISBN-13: 9781608871087.

Zahed, Ramin. *The Art of Home*. Hardcover First Edition. Insight Edition. 2015. ISBN-10: 1608873846. ISBN-13: 9781608873845.

Nickelodeon

Beck, Jerry. *Not Just Cartoons: Nicktoons!* Hardcover First Edition. DK ADULT. 2007. ISBN-10: 1595910433. ISBN-13: 9781595910431.

Beck, Jerry. *You Can't Do That on Television: The Rebellious History of Nickelodeon*. Hardcover First Edition. Struck. 2015.

Hendershot, Heather. *Nickelodeon Nation: The History, Politics, and Economics of America's Only TV Channel for Kids*. Hardcover First Edition. New York University Press. 2004. ISBN-10: 0814736513. ISBN-13: 9780814736517.

>Paperback First Edition. New York University Press. 2004. ISBN-10: 0814736521. ISBN-13: 9780814736524.

Komorowski, Thad. *Sick Little Monkeys: The Unauthorized Ren & Stimpy Story*. Paperback First Edition. BearManor Media. 2013. ISBN-10: 1593932340. ISBN-13: 9781593932343.

>Hardcover Second Edition. BearManor Media. 2017. ISBN-10: 162933183X. ISBN-13: 9781629331836.

>Paperback Second Edition. BearManor Media. 2017. ISBN-10: 1629331821. ISBN-13: 9781629331829.

>eBook. BearManor Media. 2017.

>Paperback Abridged Reprint Edition. BearManor Media. 2018. ISBN-10: 1629332682. ISBN-13: 9781629332680.

Trueheart, Eric. *The Medium-Sized Book of Zem Scripts Vol. 1: Pigs 'n' Waffles: The Stories and the Stories Behind the Stories of Your Favorite Invader*. Paperback First Edition. BookBaby. 2020. ISBN-10: 1734692502. ISBN-13: 9781734692501.

>eBook. BookBaby. 2020.

The Art of Nickelodeon Studios

Cohen, David S. *The Ballad of Rango: The Art and Making of an Outlaw Film*. Hardcover First Edition. Insight Editions. 2011. ISBN-10: 1608870170. ISBN-13: 9781608870172.

DiMartino, Michael. Konietzko, Bryan. *Avatar: The Last Airbender (The Art of the Animated Series)*. Hardcover First Edition. Dark Horse Books. 2010. ISBN-10: 1595825045. ISBN-13: 9781595825049.

    eBook. Dark Horse Books. 2013.

    Hardcover Second Edition. Dark Horse Books. 2020. ISBN-10: 1506721699. ISBN-13: 9781506721699.

    Hardcover Second Deluxe Edition. Dark Horse Books. 2020. ISBN-10: 1506721702. ISBN-13: 9781506721705.

DiMartino, Michael Dante. Konietzko, Bryan. Santos, Joaquim Dos. *Legend of Korra: The Art of the Animated Series Book One: Air*. Hardcover First Edition. Dark Horse Books. 2013. ISBN-10: 1616551682. ISBN-13: 9781616551681.

    eBook. Dark Horse Books. 2013.

    Hardcover Second Edition. Dark Horse Books. 2021. ISBN-10: 1506721893. ISBN-13: 9781506721897.

    Hardcover Special Edition. Dark Horse Books. 2021. ISBN-10: 1506721907. ISBN-13: 9781506721903.

DiMartino, Michael Dante. Konietzko, Bryan. Santos, Joaquim Dos. *Legend of Korra: The Art of the Animated Series Book Two: Spirits*. Hardcover First Edition. Dark Horse Books. 2014. ISBN-10: 1616554622. ISBN-13: 9781616554620.

    eBook. Dark Horse Books. 2014.

    Hardcover Second Edition. Dark Horse Books. 2021. ISBN-10: 1506721931. ISBN-13: 9781506721934.

Hardcover Special Edition. Dark Horse Books. 2021.
ISBN-13: 150672194X. ISBN-13: 9781506721941.

DiMartino, Michael Dante. Konietzko, Bryan. Santos, Joaquim Dos. *The Legend of Korra: The Art of the Animated Series Book Three: Change*. Hardcover First Edition. Dark Horse Books. 2015. ISBN-10: 1616555653. ISBN-13: 9781616555658.

eBook. Dark Horse Books. 2015.

Hardcover Second Edition. Dark Horse Books. 2022.
ISBN-10: 1506721915. ISBN-13: 9781506721910.

Hardcover Special Edition. Dark Horse Books. 2022.
ISBN-10: 1506721923. ISBN-13: 9781506721927.

DiMartino, Michael Dante. Konietzko, Bryan. Santos, Joaquim Dos. *The Legend of Korra: The Art of the Animated Series Book Four: Balance*. Hardcover First Edition. Dark Horse Books. 2015. ISBN-10: 1616556870. ISBN-13: 9781616556877.

eBook. Dark Horse Books. 2015.

McDonnell, Chris. *The Art of Invader Zim*. Hardcover First Edition. Abrams Books. 2020. ISBN-10: 1419734601. ISBN-13: 9781419734601.

The Art of Frederator Studios

Calaitges, Kelsey. *The Art of Bravest Warriors*. Hardcover First Edition. Dark Horse Books. 2019. ISBN-10: 1506712339. ISBN-13: 9781506712338.

Frederator Studios. *Castlevania: The Art of the Animated Series*. Hardcover First Edition. Dark Horse Books. 2021. ISBN-10: 1506715702. ISBN-13: 9781506715704.

    eBook. Dark Horse Books. 2021.

Goldman, Michael. Homan, Eric. Seibert, Fred. *Original Cartoons, Volume 2: The Frederator Studios Postcards 2006-2010*. Paperback First Edition. Frederator Books. 2010. ISBN-10: 1451586132. ISBN-13: 9781451586138.

Homan, Eric. *Original Cartoon Posters: From Frederator Studios*. Paperback First Edition. Frederator Books. 2010. ISBN-10: 1451559992. ISBN-13: 9781451559996.

Homan, Eric. Seibert, Fred. *Original Cartoons: The Frederator Studio Postcards 1998-2005*. Paperback First Edition. Easton Studio Press. 2005. ISBN-10: 0974380636. ISBN-13: 9780974380636.

Warner Bros. General Studies

Adamson, Joe. *Bugs Bunny: Fifty Years and Only One Grey Hare*. Hardcover First Edition. Henry Holt & Co. 1990. ISBN-10: 0805011900. ISBN-13: 9780805011906.

>Paperback Reprint Edition. Henry Holt & Co. 1991. ISBN-10: 0805018557. ISBN-13: 9780805018554.

Auslander, Shalom. Beck, Jerry. *"I Tawt I Taw a Puddy Tat": Fifty Years of Sylvester and Tweety*. Hardcover First Edition. Henry Holt & Co. 1991. ISBN-10: 0805016449. ISBN-13: 9780805016444.

>Paperback First Edition. Henry Holt & Co. 1994. ISBN-10: 0805035907. ISBN-13: 9780805035902.

Beck, Jerry. Friedwald, Will. *Warner Bros. Animation Art: The Characters, the Creators, the Limited Editions*. Hardcover First Edition. Warner Brothers Publication. 1997. ISBN-10: 0883633604. ISBN-13: 9780883633601.

>Hardcover First Edition. Virgin Publishing. 1998. ISBN-10: 1852277726. ISBN-13: 9781852277727.

Findlay, Kurtis. Mulaney, Dean. *Chuck Jones: The Dream that Never Was*. Hardcover First Edition. IDW Publishing. 2011. ISBN-10: 1613770308. ISBN-13: 9781613770306.

Furniss, Maureen. *Chuck Jones: Conversations*. Hardcover First Edition. University Press of Mississippi. 2005. ISBN-10: 1578067286. ISBN-13: 9781578067282.

>Paperback First Edition. University Press of Mississippi. 2005. ISBN-10: 1578067294. ISBN-13: 9781578067299.

Jones, Chuck. *Chuck Amuck: The Life and Times of an Animated Cartoonist*. Hardcover First Edition. Farrar, Straus and Giroux. 1989. ISBN-10: 0374123489. ISBN-13: 9780374123482.

>Paperback Reprint Edition. Avon Books. 1990. ISBN-10: 0380712148. ISBN-13: 9780380712144.

>Paperback Second Edition. Farrar, Straus and Giroux. 1999.
>ISBN-10: 0374526206. ISBN-13: 9780374526207.

>eBook. Farrar, Straus and Giroux. 1999.

Jones, Chuck. *Chuck Reducks: Drawing from the Fun Side of Life*. Hardcover First Edition. Grand Central Publishing. 1996. ISBN-10: 044651893X. ISBN-13: 9780446518932.

Kenner, Hugh. *Chuck Jones: A Flurry of Drawings (Portraits of American Genius #3)*. Hardcover First Edition. University of California Press. 1994. ISBN-10: 0520087976. ISBN-13: 9780520087972.

McKimson Jr., Robert. *"I Say, I Say . . . Son!": A Tribute to Legendary Animators Bob, Chuck, and Tom McKimson*. Hardcover First Edition. Santa Monica Press. 2012. ISBN-10: 1595800697. ISBN-13: 9781595800695.

>eBook. Santa Monica Press. 2012.

Sandler, Kevin S. *Reading the Rabbit: Explorations in Warner Bros. Animation*. Hardcover First Edition. Rutgers University Press. 1998. ISBN-10: 0813525373. ISBN-13: 9780813525372.

>Paperback First Edition. Rutgers University Press.
>ISBN-10: 0813525381. ISBN-13: 9780813525389.

>eBook. Rutgers University Press. 1998.

Schneider, Steve. *That's All Folks!: Art of Warner Bros. Animation*. Hardcover First Edition. Henry Holt & Co. 1988. ISBN-10: 0805008896. ISBN-13: 9780805008890.

>Paperback Reprint Edition. Henry Holt & Co. 1990.
>ISBN-10: 0805014853. ISBN-13: 9780805014853.

>Hardcover First Edition. Barnes & Noble Press. 1999.
>ISBN-10: 0760712158. ISBN-13: 9780760712153.

Weinman, Jaime. *Anvils, Mallets & Dynamite: The Unauthorized Biography of Looney Tunes*. Hardcover First Edition. Sutherland House. 2021. ISBN-10: 1989555462. ISBN-13: 9781989555460.

    eBook. The Sutherland House Inc. 2021.

The Art of Warner Animation Group

Miller-Zarneke, Tracey. *The LEGO® Batman Movie: The Making of the Movie*. Hardcover First Edition. DK Children. 2017. ISBN-10: 1465456619. ISBN-13: 9781465456618.

Zahed, Ramin. *The Art of The Iron Giant*. Hardcover First Edition. Insight Editions. 2016. ISBN-10: 1608878880. ISBN-13: 9781608878888.

Hanna-Barbera General Studies

Barbera, Joseph. *My Life in Toons: From Flatbush to Bedrock in Under a Century*. Hardcover First Edition. Turner Publishing, Inc. ISBN-10: 1570360421. ISBN-13: 9781570360428.

Beck, Jerry. Kowalski, Jesse. Mallory, Michael. *Hanna-Barbera: The Architects of Saturday Morning*. Paperback First Edition. Norman Rockwell Museum. ISBN-10: 961527390. ISBN-13: 9780961527396.

Beck, Jerry. *The Flintstones: A Retro Guide to the Hanna-Barbera Classic*. Hardcover First Edition. Insight Editions. 2009. ISBN-10: 1933784989. ISBN-13: 9781933784984.

Beck, Jerry. *The Hanna-Barbera Treasury: Rare Art and Mementos from Your Favorite Cartoon Classics*. Hardcover First Edition. Insight Editions. ISBN-10: 1933784288. ISBN-13: 9781933784281.

Browsh, Jared Bahir. *Hanna-Barbera: A History*. Hardcover First Edition. McFarland. ISBN-10: 1476675791. ISBN-13: 9781476675794.

Fischer, Stuart. *The Hanna-Barbera Story: The Life and Times of TV's Greatest Animation Studio*. Paperback First Edition. America Star Books. ISBN-10: 1462633544. ISBN-13: 9781462633548.

Hanna, William. *A Cast of Friends*. Hardcover First Edition. Taylor Publishing. ISBN-10: 0878339167. ISBN-13: 9780878339167.

> Paperback First Edition. Da Capo Press. 2000.
> ISBN-10: 0306809176. ISBN-13: 9780306809170.

Mallory, Michael. *Hanna-Barbera Cartoons*. Paperback First Edition. Universe Publishing. ISBN-10: 0883631083. ISBN-13: 9780883631089.

Mariotti, Brian. *Classic Hanna-Barbera Collectibles: An Authorized Guide*. Hardcover First Edition. Funko Print. 2007.

The Museum of Television & Radio. *The World of Hanna-Barbera Cartoons*. Paperback First Edition. The Museum of Television & Radio. 1995.

Sennett, Ted. *The Art of Hanna-Barbera: Fifty Years of Creativity*. Hardcover First Edition. Studio. 1989. ISBN-10: 0670829781. ISBN-13: 9780670829781.

Stern, Leslie. *Living with a Legend: A Personal Look at Animation Legend Iwao Takamoto, Designer of Scooby-Doo*. Hardcover First Edition. TotalRecall Publications. ISBN-10: 159095095X. ISBN-13: 9781590950951.

> Paperback First Edition. TotalRecall Publications. 2012. ISBN-10: 1590950968. ISBN-13: 9781590950968.

> eBook. TotalRecall Publications. 2012.

Valinoti, Jr., Raymond. *Hanna-Barbera's Prime Time Cartoons*. Hardcover First Edition. BearManor Media. 2020. ISBN-10: 1629335894. ISBN-13: 9781629335896.

> Paperback First Edition. BearManor Media. 2020. ISBN-10: 1629335886. ISBN-13: 9781629335889.

The Art of Cartoon Network Studios

Cartoon Network: 20th Anniversary Book. Hardcover First Edition. Mark Murphy Design. 2012.

Dilworth, John R. *The Art of Courage the Cowardly Dog*. Paperback First Edition. Independent Publisher. 2019.

Edgar, Sean. McHale, Patrick. *The Art of Over the Garden Wall*. Hardcover First Edition. Dark Horse Books. 2017. ISBN-10: 1506703763. ISBN-13: 9781506703763.

    eBook. Dark Horse Books. 2017.

McDonnell, Chris. *Adventure Time: The Art of Ooo*. Hardcover First Edition. Harry N. Abrams. 2014. ISBN-10: 1419704508. ISBN-13: 9781419704505.

McDonnell, Chris. *Steven Universe: Art & Origins*. Hardcover First Edition. Harry N. Abrams. 2017. ISBN-10: 1419724436. ISBN-13: 9781419724435.

    eBook. Harry N. Abrams. 2017.

McDonnell, Chris. *Steven Universe: End of an Era*. Hardcover First Edition. Abrams Books. 2020. ISBN-10: 1419742841. ISBN-13: 9781419742842.

    eBook. Abrams Books. 2020.

O'Leary, Shannon. *The Art of Regular Show*. Hardcover First Edition. Titan Books. 2015. ISBN-10: 1783295996. ISBN-13: 9781783295999.

Sands, Ryan. Sugar, Rebecca. *The Art of Steven Universe: The Movie*. Paperback First Edition. Dark Horse Books. 2019. ISBN-10: 1506715079. ISBN-13: 9781506715070.

    eBook. Dark Horse Books. 2019.

Ward, Pendleton. *Adventure Time: The Original Title Cards (Volume 1) The Original Cartoon Title Cards Season 1 & 2*. Hardcover First Edition. Titan Books. 2014. ISBN-10: 1783292873. ISBN-13: 9781783292875.

Ward, Pendleton. *Adventure Time: The Original Title Cards (Vol 2) The Original Cartoon Title Cards Season 3 & 4*. Hardcover First Edition. Titan Books. 2014. ISBN-10: 1783298960. ISBN-13: 9781783298969.

>Hardcover Reprint Edition. Titan Books. 2015. ISBN-10: 1783295112. ISBN-13: 9781783295111.

The Art of Williams Street Productions

Gallery 1988. *Rick and Morty: Show Me What You Got - The Gallery 1988 Artwork*. Hardcover First Edition. Titan Books. 2019. ISBN-10: 1789092078. ISBN-13: 9781789092073.

Gilfor, Jeremy. *The Art of Rick and Morty Volume 2*. Hardcover First Edition. Dark Horse Books. 2021. ISBN-10: 1506720463. ISBN-13: 9781506720463.

The Art of Rick and Morty Volume 2 Deluxe Edition. Hardcover First Edition. Dark Horse Books. ISBN-10: 1506722288. ISBN-13: 9781506722283.

eBook. Dark Horse Books. 2021.

Hammer, Doc. Plume, Ken. Publick, Jackson. *Go Team Venture!: The Art and Making of The Venture Bros*. Hardcover First Edition. Dark Horse Books. 2018. ISBN-10: 1506704875. ISBN-13: 9781506704876.

eBook. Dark Horse Books. 2018.

Siciliano, James. *The Art of Rick and Morty*. Hardcover First Edition. Dark Horse Books. 2017. ISBN-10: 1506702694. ISBN-13: 9781506702698.

The Art of Sony Pictures Entertainment

Miller-Zarneke, Tracey. *Surf's Up: The Art and Making of a True Story*. Hardcover First Edition. Insight Editions. 2007. ISBN-10: 1933784156. ISBN-13: 9781933784151.

Miller-Zarneke, Tracey. *The Art and Making of Cloudy with a Chance of Meatballs*. Hardcover First Edition. Insight Editions. 2009. ISBN-10: 193378489X. ISBN-13: 9781933784892.

Miller-Zarneke, Tracey. *The Art of Cloudy with a Chance of Meatballs 2: Revenge of the Leftovers*. Hardcover First Edition. Cameron Books. 2013. ISBN-10: 1937359492. ISBN-13: 9781937359492.

Miller-Zarneke, Tracey. *The Art and Making of Hotel Transylvania*. Hardcover First Edition. Titan Publishing. 2012. ISBN-10: 1781164177. ISBN-13: 9781781164174.

    Hardcover First Edition. Titan Books. 2012. ISBN-10: 1781164150. ISBN-13: 9781781164150.

Rector, Brett. *The Art and Making of Hotel Transylvania 2*. Hardcover First Edition. Titan Books. ISBN-10: 1783298812. 2015. ISBN-13: 9781783298815.

    Hardcover First Edition. Cameron Books. 2015. ISBN-10: 1937359808. ISBN-13: 9781937359805.

Sony Pictures. *The Art of Hotel Transylvania 3*. Digital Book. 2018. Available to read at: https://www.artofhoteltransylvania3.com/.

Sunshine, Linda. *The Art of Open Season*. Paperback First Edition. Insight Editions. 2006. ISBN-10: 1933784040. ISBN-13: 9781933784045.

Zahed, Ramin. *Spider-Man: Into the Spider-Verse - The Art of the Movie*. Hardcover First Edition. Titan Books. 2018. ISBN-10: 1785659464. ISBN-13: 9781785659461.

Zahed, Ramin. *The Art of The Mitchells vs. The Machines*. Hardcover First Edition. Abrams Books. 2021. ISBN-10: 1419747495. ISBN-13: 9781419747496.

    eBook. Abrams Books. 2021.

Zahed, Ramin. *The Art of VIVO*. Hardcover First Edition. Abrams Books. 2021. ISBN-10: 1417947509. ISBN-13: 9781419747502.

    eBook. Abrams Books. 2021.

The Art of Columbia Pictures

Sorenson, Jim. *The Art of the Angry Birds Movie*. Hardcover First Edition. IDW Publishing. 2016. ISBN-10: 1631406043. ISBN-13: 9781631406041.

    eBook. IDW Publishing. 2016.

The Art of MGM Studios

Zahed, Ramin. *The Art of The Addams Family*. Hardcover First Edition. Titan Books. 2019. ISBN-10: 1789092752. ISBN-13: 9781789092752.

The Art of Netflix

Ehasz, Aaron. Richmond, Justin. *The Art of the Dragon Prince*. Hardcover First Edition. Dark Horse Books. 2020. ISBN-10: 1506717780. ISBN-13: 9781506717784.

    eBook. Dark Horse Books. 2020.

Gutierrez, Jorge. *The Art of Maya and the Three*. Hardcover First Edition. Dark Horse Books. 2021. ISBN-10: 1506725953. ISBN-13: 9781506725956.

Maltin, Leonard. *Over the Moon: Illuminating the Journey*. Hardcover First Edition. Titan Books. 2020. ISBN-10 : 1789096510. ISBN-13: 9781789096514.

McDonnell, Chris. *BoJack Horseman: The Art Before the Horse*. Hardcover First Edition. Harry N. Abrams. 2018. ISBN-10: 1419727737. ISBN-13: 9781419727733.

    eBook. Harry N. Abrams. 2018.

Sava, Scott Christian. *The Art of Animal Crackers*. Hardcover First Edition. Stuart Ng Books. 2021. ISBN-10: 0998562602. ISBN-13: 9780998562605.

Zahed, Ramin. *Klaus: Art of the Movie*. Hardcover First Edition. Titan Books. 2019. ISBN-10: 1789093120. ISBN-13: 9781789093124.

The Art of Illumination

Croll, Ben. *The Art of Eric Guillon: From the Making of Despicable Me to Minions, The Secret Life of Pets, and More*. Hardcover First Edition. Insight Editions. 2021. ISBN-10: 1683836812. ISBN-13: 9781683836810.

The Art of Blue Sky Studios

Amidi, Amid. *The Art of Robots*. Hardcover First Edition. Chronicle Books, LLC. 2004. ISBN-10: 0811845494. ISBN-13: 9780811845496.

Bennett, Tara. *The Art of Epic*. Hardcover First Edition. Titan Books. 2013. ISBN-10: 1781166978. ISBN-13: 9781781166970.

Bennett, Tara. *The Art of Ferdinand*. Hardcover First Edition. Titan Books. 2017. ISBN-10: 1785654187. ISBN-13: 9781785654183.

Bennett, Tara. *The Art of Ice Age*. Hardcover First Edition. Titan Books. 2016. ISBN-10: 1785651064. ISBN-13: 9781785651069.

Bennett, Tara. *The Art of Rio: Featuring a Carnival of Art From Rio and Rio 2*. Hardcover First Edition. Titan Books. 2014. ISBN-10: 1781169780. ISBN-13: 9781781169780.

Friedman, Jake S. *The Art of Blue Sky Studios*. Hardcover First Edition. Titan Books. 2001. ISBN-10: 1783293543. ISBN-13: 9781783293544.

    Hardcover First Edition. Insight Editions. 2014. ISBN-10: 160887317X. ISBN-13: 9781608873173.

Schmitz, Jerry. *The Art and Making of The Peanuts Movie*. Hardcover First Edition. Titan Books. 2015. ISBN-10: 1783293241. ISBN-13: 9781783293247.

    Hardcover Limited Edition. Titan Books. 2005.

Weishar, Peter. *Blue Sky: The Art of Computer Animation*. Paperback First Edition. Harry N. Abrams. 2002. ISBN-10: 810990695. ISBN-13: 9780810990692.

The Art of Aardman Animations

Aardman Animations. Sony Pictures Animation, Inc. Sunshine, Linda. *The Art & Making of Arthur Christmas: An Inside Look at Behind-the-Scenes Artwork with Filmmaker Commentary*. Hardcover First Edition. Newmarket Press. 2011. ISBN-10: 1557049971. ISBN-13: 9781557049971.

Aardman Animations. *The Art of Aardman: The Makers of Wallace & Gromit, Chicken Run, and More*. Hardcover First Edition. Chronicle Books, LLC. 2017. ISBN-10: 145216651X. ISBN-13: 9781452166513.

  eBook. Chronicle Books, LLC. 2017.

Lane, Andy. Simpson, Paul. *The Art of Wallace & Gromit: The Curse of the Were-Rabbit*. Hardcover First Edition. Titan Books. 2005. ISBN-10: 1845761367. ISBN-13: 9781845761363.

  Paperback First Edition. Titan Books. 2005.
  ISBN-10: 1845762150. ISBN-13: 9781845762155.

Sibley, Brian. *Chicken Run: Hatching the Movie*. Hardcover First Edition. Harry N. Abrams. 2000. ISBN-10: 0810941244. ISBN-13: 9780810941243.

Sibley, Brian. *Wallace and Gromit - "The Wrong Trousers": Storyboard Collection*. Hardcover First Edition. BBC Consumer Publishing. 1998. ISBN-10: 0563380845. ISBN-13: 9780563380849.

The Art of Baobab Studios

Johnston, Jacob. *The Art of Baobab: The Beginning*. Hardcover First Edition. Baobab Studios. 2020.

  eBook. Baobab Studios. 2020.

Miller-Zarneke, Tracey. *The Art of Baba Yaga*. Hardcover First Edition. Baobab Studios. 2021.

  eBook. Baobab Studios. 2021.

The Art of Cartoon Saloon

Moore, Tomm. Stewart, Ross. *Designing the Secret of Kells*. Hardcover First Edition. Cartoon Saloon. 2021. ISBN-10: 0992916305. ISBN-13: 9780992916305.

Moore, Tomm. *Song of the Sea Artbook*. Hardcover First Edition. Cartoon Saloon. 2015. ISBN-10: 099291633X. ISBN-13: 9780992916336.

Solomon, Charles. *The Art of Wolfwalkers*. Hardcover First Edition. Abrams Books. 2020. ISBN-10: 141974805X. ISBN-13: 9781419748059.

eBook. Abrams Books. 2020.

The Art of LAIKA

Alger, Jed. *The Art and Making of ParaNorman*. Hardcover First Edition. Chronicle Books, LLC. 2012. ISBN-10: 1452110921. ISBN-13: 9781452110929.

Brotherton, Phil. *The Art of The Boxtrolls*. Hardcover First Edition. Chronicle Books, LLC. 2014. ISBN-10: 1452128359. ISBN-13: 9781452128351.

Haynes, Emily. *The Art of Kubo and the Two Strings*. Hardcover First Edition. Chronicle Books, LLC. 2016. ISBN-10: 1452153159. ISBN-13: 9781452153155.

    eBook. Chronicle Books, LLC. 2016.

Jones, Stephen. *Coraline: A Visual Companion*. Hardcover First Edition. It Books. 2009. ISBN-10: 0061704229. ISBN-13: 9780061704222.

Salisbury, Mark. *Tim Burton's Corpse Bride: An Invitation to the Wedding*. Hardcover First Edition. Newmarket. 2005. ISBN-10: 1557046980. ISBN-13: 9781557046987.

    Hardcover First Edition. Titan Books Ltd. 2005. ISBN-10: 1845762223. ISBN-13: 9781845762223.

    Paperback First Edition. Newmarket. 2005. ISBN-10: 1557046999. ISBN-13: 9781557046994.

    Paperback First Edition. Titan Books Ltd. 2005. ISBN-10: 1845762843. ISBN-13: 9781845762841.

Zahed, Ramin. *The Art of Missing Link*. Hardcover First Edition. Insight Editions. 2019. ISBN-10: 1683836863. ISBN-13: 9781683836865.

Anime

Guides and Reference Books

Azuma, Hiroki. *Otaku: Japan's Database Animals*. Hardcover First Edition. University of Minnesota Press. 2009. ISBN-10: 0816653518. ISBN-13: 9780816653515.

>Paperback First Edition. University of Minnesota Press. 2009. ISBN-10: 0816653526. ISBN-13: 9780816653522.

>eBook. University of Minnesota Press. 2009.

Baricordi, Andrea. De Giovanni, Massimiliano. Pietroni, Andrea. Rossi, Barbara. Tunesi, Sabrina. *Anime: A Guide to Japanese Animation (1958-1988)*. Paperback First Edition. Protoculture Inc. 2000. ISBN-10: 2980575909. ISBN-13: 9782980575907.

Brophy, Philip. *100 Anime (Screen Guides)*. Hardcover First Edition. British Film Institute. 2005. ISBN-10: 1844570835. ISBN-13: 9781844570836.

>Paperback First Edition. British Film Institute. 2006. ISBN-10: 1844570843. ISBN-13: 9781844570843.

>eBook. British Film Institute. 2019.

Camp, Brian. Davis, Julie. *Anime Classics Zettai!: 100 Must-See Japanese Animation Masterpieces*. Paperback First Edition. Stone Bridge Press. 2007. ISBN-10: 1933330228. ISBN-13: 9781933330228.

Clements, Jonathan. McCarthy, Helen. *The Erotic Anime Movie Guide*. Paperback First Edition. Overlook Books. 1999. ISBN-10: 0879517050. ISBN-13: 9780879517052.

Clements, Jonathan. McCarthy, Helen. *The Anime Encyclopedia: A Century of Japanese Animation*. Paperback First Edition. Stone Bridge Press. 2001. ISBN-10: 1880656647. ISBN-13: 9781880656648.

>Paperback Revised and Expanded Second Edition. Stone Bridge Press. 2006. ISBN-10: 1933330104. ISBN-13: 9781933330105.

Hardcover Revised Third Edition. Stone Bridge Press. 2015.
ISBN-10: 1611720184. ISBN-13: 9781611720181.

eBook. Third Edition. Stone Bridge Press. 2015.

Drazen, Patrick. *Anime Explosion!: The What? Why? and Wow! of Japanese Animation*. Paperback First Edition. Stone Bridge Press. 2002. ISBN-10: 1880656728. ISBN-13: 9781880656723.

Paperback Second Edition. Stone Bridge Press. 2014.
ISBN-10: 1611720133. ISBN-13: 9781611720136.

eBook. Stone Bridge Press. 2014.

Ebihara, Isao. *All the World Is Anime*. Paperback First Edition. Global Educational Advance, Inc. 2010. ISBN-10: 1935434055. ISBN-13: 9781935434054.

Galbraith, Patrick. *The Moe Manifesto: An Insider's Look at the Worlds of Manga, Anime, and Gaming*. Paperback First Edition. Tuttle Publishing. 2017. ISBN-10: 0804848882. ISBN-13: 9780804848886.

eBook. Tuttle Publishing. 2014.

Galbraith, Patrick. *The Otaku Encyclopedia: An Insider's Guide to the Subculture of Cool Japan*. Paperback First Edition. Kodansha USA Publishing, LLC. 2009. ISBN-10: 4770031017. ISBN-13: 9784770031013.

Paperback First Edition. Kodansha International Publishing, LLC. 2014.

Garcia, Hector. *A Geek in Japan: Discovering the Land of Manga, Anime, Zen, and the Tea Ceremony*. Paperback First Edition. Tuttle Publishing. 2011. ISBN-10: 4805311290. ISBN-13: 9784805311295.

Paperback Second Edition. Tuttle Publishing. 2019.
ISBN-10: 4805313919. ISBN-13: 9784805313916.

eBook. Tuttle Publishing. 2019.

Graham, Miyako. Smith, Toren. *A Viewer's Guide to Japanese Animation*. Paperback First Edition. Books Nippan. 1985.

Kalen, Elizabeth. *Mostly Manga: A Genre Guide to Popular Manga, Manhwa, Manhua, and Anime*. Hardcover First Edition. Libraries Unlimited. 2012. ISBN-10: 1598849387. ISBN-13: 9781598849387.

Lamarre, Thomas. *The Anime Ecology: A Genealogy of Television, Animation, and Game Media*. Hardcover First Edition. University of Minnesota Press. 2018. ISBN-10: 1517904498. ISBN-13: 9781517904494.

> Paperback First Edition. University of Minnesota Press. 2018. ISBN-10: 1517904501. ISBN-13: 9781517904500.

> eBook. University of Minnesota Press. 2018.

Le Blanc, Michelle. Odell, Colin. *Anime*. Paperback First Edition. Kamera Books. 2014. ISBN-10: 1842435868. ISBN-13: 9781842435861.

> eBook. Oldcastle Books. 2014.

Ledoux, Trish. Ranney, Doug. *The Complete Anime Guide: Japanese Animation Film Directory & Resource Guide*. Paperback First Edition. Tiger Mountain Press. 1996. ISBN-10: 0964954230. ISBN-13: 9780964954236.

> Paperback Second Edition. Tiger Mountain Press. 1997. ISBN-10: 0964954257. ISBN-13: 9780964954250.

Macias, Patrick. Sattin, Samuel. *Crunchyroll Essential Anime: Fan Favorites, Memorable Masterpieces, and Cult Classics*. Paperback First Edition. Running Press Adult. 2022. ISBN-10: 076247243X. ISBN-13: 9780762472437.

> eBook. Running Press Adult. 2022.

Marshall, Dallas. *Anime Adrenaline!* Paperback First Edition. Independently Published. 2020. ISBN-13: 9798561869440.

> eBook. Dark Moon Press. 2020.

McCarthy, Helen. *500 Essential Anime Movies: The Ultimate Guide*. Paperback First Edition. Harper Design. 2009. ISBN-10: 0061474509. ISBN-13: 9780061474507.

McCarthy, Helen. *Anime! A Beginner's Guide to Japanese Animation*. Paperback First Edition. Titan Books. 1993. ISBN-10: 1852864923. ISBN-13: 9781852864927.

McCarthy, Helen. *The Anime Movie Guide: Movie-by-Movie Guide to Japanese Animation since 1983*. Paperback First Edition. Overlook Books. 1997. ISBN-10: 0879517816. ISBN-13: 9780879517816.

Napier, Susan J. *Anime: from Akira to Princess Mononoke, Experiencing Contemporary Japanese Animation*. Paperback First Edition. Palgrave Macmillan. 2001. ISBN-10: 0312238630. ISBN-13: 9780312238636.

> Hardcover First Edition. Palgrave Macmillan. 2003. ISBN-10: 0312238622. ISBN-13: 9780312238629.

> Paperback Revised Second Edition. St. Martin's Griffin. 2005. ISBN-10: 1403970521. ISBN-13: 9781403970527.

> eBook. Macmillan. 2016.

Patten, Fred. *Funny Animals and More: From Anime to Zoomorphics*. Paperback First Edition. Theme Park Press. ISBN-10: 1941500005. ISBN-13: 9781941500002.

> eBook. Theme Park Press. 2014.

Poitras, Gilles. *The Anime Companion: What's Japanese in Japanese Animation*. Paperback First Edition. Stone Bridge Press. 1999. ISBN-10: 1880656329. ISBN-13: 9781880656327.

Poitras, Gilles. *The Anime Companion 2: More What's Japanese in Japanese Animation*. Stone Bridge Press. 2000. ISBN-10: 1880656965. ISBN-13: 9781880656969.

Poitras, Gilles. *Anime Essentials: Every Thing a Fan Needs to Know*. Paperback First edition. Stone Bridge Press. 2005. ISBN-10: 1880656531. ISBN-13: 9781880656532.

Pope, Nathan R. *The Anime Encyclopedia*. Paperback First Edition. CreateSpace Independent Publishing. 2015. ISBN-10: 1518836755. ISBN-13: 9781518836756.

Richmond, Simon. *The Rough Guide to Anime*. Paperback First Edition. Rough Guides. 2009. ISBN-10: 1858282055. ISBN-13: 9781858282053.

Stuckmann, Chris. *Anime Impact: The Movies and Shows that Changed the World of Japanese Animation*. Hardcover First Edition. Mango Publishing. 2018. ISBN-10: 1633537323. ISBN-13: 9781633537323.

    eBook. Mango Publishing. 2018.

Tezuka Productions. *Tezuka School of Animation Vol. 1: Learning the Basics*. Paperback First Edition. Watson-Guptill. 2003. ISBN-10: 1569709955. ISBN-13: 9781569709955.

Tezuka Productions. *Tezuka School of Animation Vol. 2: Animals in Motion*. Paperback First Edition. Watson-Guptill. 2003. ISBN-10: 1569709947. ISBN-13: 9781569709948.

Industry

Allison, Anne. *Millennial Monsters: Japanese Toys and the Global Imagination*. Hardcover First Edition. University of California Press. 2006. ISBN-10: 0520221486. ISBN-13: 9780520221482.

    Paperback First Edition. University of California Press. 2006. ISBN-10: 0520245652. ISBN-13: 9780520245655.

    eBook. University of California Press. 2006.

Cavallaro, Dani. *Kyoto Animation: A Critical Study and Filmography*. Paperback First Edition. McFarland & Company, Inc., Publishers. 2012. ISBN-10: 0786470682. ISBN-13: 9780786470686.

    eBook. McFarland & Company, Inc., Publishers. 2012.

Clements, Jonathan. *Schoolgirl Milky Crisis: Adventures in the Anime and Manga Trade*. Paperback First Edition. Titan Books. 2009. ISBN-10: 1848560834. ISBN-13: 9781848560833.

    eBook. A-Net Digital LLC. 2009.

Condry, Ian. *The Soul of Anime: Collaborative Creativity and Japan's Media Success Story*. Hardcover First Edition. 2013. ISBN-10: 0822353806. ISBN-13: 9780822353805.

    Paperback First Edition. Duke University Press Books. 2013. ISBN-10: 0822353946. ISBN-13: 9780822353942.

    eBook. Duke University Press Books. 2013.

Daliot-Bul, Michal. Otmazgin, Nissim. *The Anime Boom in the United States: Lessons for Global Creative Industries*. Hardcover First Edition. Harvard University Asia Center. 2017. ISBN-10: 0674976991. ISBN-13: 9780674976993.

    Paperback Reprint Edition. Harvard University Asia Center. 2019. ISBN-10: 0674241193. ISBN-13: 9780674241190.

Davis, Northrop. *Manga and Anime Go to Hollywood*. Hardcover First Edition. Bloomsbury Academic. 2015. ISBN-10: 1623562481. ISBN-13: 9781623562489.

    Paperback First Edition. Bloomsbury Academic. 2015. ISBN-10: 1623561442. ISBN-13: 9781623561444.

    eBook. Bloomsbury Academic. 2015.

Deneroff, Harvey. Ladd, Fred. *Astro Boy and Anime Come to the Americas: An Insider's View of the Birth of a Pop Culture Phenomenon*. Paperback First Edition. McFarland & Company, Inc., Publishers. 2008. ISBN-10: 0786438665. ISBN-13: 9780786438662.

    eBook. McFarland & Company, Inc., Publishers. 2009.

Hernández-Pérez, Manuel. *Japanese Media Cultures in Japan and Abroad: Transnational Consumption of Manga, Anime, and Media-Mixes*. Paperback First Edition. MDPI. 2019. ISBN-10: 3039210084. ISBN-13: 9783039210084.

Kelts, Roland. *Japanamerica: How Japanese Pop Culture Has Invaded the U.S.* Hardcover First Edition. Palgrave Macmillan. 2006. ISBN-10: 1403974756. ISBN-13: 9781403974754.

    eBook. St. Martin's Press. 2006.

    Paperback First Edition. St. Martin's Griffin. 2007. ISBN-10: 140398476X. ISBN-13: 9781403984760.

Pellitteri, Marco. Wong, Heung-wah. *Japanese Animation in Asia: Transnational Industry, Audiences, and Success*. Hardcover First Edition. Routledge. 2021. ISBN-10: 1138566462. ISBN-13: 9781138566460.

Steinberg, Marc. *Anime's Media Mix: Franchising Toys and Characters in Japan*. Hardcover First Edition. University of Minnesota Press. 2012. ISBN-10: 081667549X. ISBN-13: 9780816675494.

    Paperback First Edition. University of Minnesota Press. 2012. ISBN-10: 0816675503. ISBN-13: 9780816675500.

    eBook. University of Minnesota Press. 2012.

Whaley, Deborah Elizabeth. *Black Women in Sequence: Re-Inking Comics, Graphic Novels, and Anime*. Hardcover First Edition. University of Washington Press. 2015. ISBN-10: 0295994959. ISBN-13: 9780295994956.

    Paperback First Edition. University of Washington Press. 2015. ISBN-10: 0295994967. ISBN-13: 9780295994963.

    eBook. University of Washington Press. 2015.

Individual Movies, Series, Studios, and Notable Artists

Baena, Ana Soler. Iglesias, José Andrés Santiago. *Anime Studies: Media-Specific Approaches to Neon Genesis Evangelion*. Paperback First Edition. Stockholm University Press. 2021. ISBN-10: 917635167X. ISBN-13: 9789176351673.

    eBook available through Stockholm University Press Open Access: https://www.stockholmuniversitypress.se/site/books/e/10.16993/bbp/

Blanc, Michelle Le. *Akira (BFI Film Classics)*. Paperback First Edition. British Film Institute. 2014. ISBN-10: 1844578089. ISBN-13: 9781844578085.

    eBook. British Film Institute. 2019.

Blue, Jed A. *The Very Soil: An Unauthorized Critical Study of Puella Magi Madoka Magica*. eBook. 2015.

    Paperback First Edition. CreateSpace Independent Publishing. 2021. ISBN-10: 1508800421. ISBN-13: 9781508800422.

Cavallaro, Dani. *The Art of Studio Gainax: Experimentation, Style, and Innovation at the Leading Edge of Anime*. Paperback First Edition. McFarland & Company, Inc., Publishers. 2008. ISBN-10: 0786433760. ISBN-13: 9780786433766.

    eBook. McFarland & Company, Inc., Publishers. 2015.

de Wit, Alex Dudok. *Grave of the Fireflies (BFI Film Classics)*. Paperback First Edition. British Film Institute. 2021. ISBN-13: 9781838719258.

    eBook. British Film Institute. 2021.

Fleming, Jeff. Lubowsky Talbott, Susan. Murakami, Takashi. *My Reality: Contemporary Art And The Culture Of Japanese Animation*. Paperback First Edition. Independent Curators International, New York. 2001. ISBN-10: 1879003333. ISBN-13: 9781879003330.

Hara, Kunio. *Joe Hisaishi's Soundtrack for My Neighbor Totoro (33 1/3 Japan)*. Hardcover First Edition. Bloomsbury Academic. 2020. ISBN-10: 1501345117. ISBN-13: 9781517911300.

Paperback First Edition. Bloomsbury Academic. 2020.
ISBN-10: 1501345125. ISBN-13: 9781501345128.

eBook. Bloomsbury Academic. 2020.

Hayashibara, Megumi. *The Characters Taught Me Everything: Living Life One Episode at a Time*. eBook. Yen Press. 2021. ISBN-10: 1975333683. ISBN-13: 9781975333683.

Paperback First Edition. Yen On. 2021.
ISBN-10: 1975333675. 9781975333676.

Masamune, Shirow. *Ghost in the Shell README: 1995-2017*. Hardcover First Edition. Kodansha Comics. 2017. ISBN-10: 1632365316. ISBN-13: 9781632365316.

Nelson, Reed. *50 Animated Years of LUPIN THE 3rd*. Hardcover First Edition. Magnetic Press. 2022. ISBN-10: 1951719441. ISBN-13: 9781951719449.

Okada, Mari. *From Truant to Anime Screenwriter: My Path to "Anohana" and "The Anthem of the Heart"*. eBook. J-Novel Club. 2018.

Owada, Hideki. *The Men Who Created Gundam*. Paperback First Edition. Denpa Books. 2022. ISBN-10: 1634429745. ISBN-13: 9781634429740.

Robinson, Jeremy Mark. *The Akira Book: Katsuhiro Otomo: The Movie and the Manga*. Hardcover First Edition. Crescent Moon Publishing. 2017. ISBN-10: 1861716869. ISBN-13: 9781861716866.

Hardcover Revised Edition. Crescent Moon Publishing. 2018.
ISBN-10: 1861717598. ISBN-13: 9781861717597.

Robinson, Jeremy Mark. *The Art of Masamune Shirow: Volume 2: Anime*. Hardcover First Edition. Crescent Moon Publishing. 2021. ISBN-10: 1861717962. ISBN-13: 9781861717962.

Robinson, Jeremy Mark. *Berserk: Kentaro Miura: The Manga and the Anime*. Hardcover First Edition. Crescent Moon Publishing. 2021. ISBN-10: 1861718217. ISBN-13: 9781861718211.

> Hardcover First Revised Edition. Crescent Moon Publishing. 2021. ISBN-10: 1861718365. ISBN-13: 9781861718365.

Robinson, Jeremy Mark. *Cowboy Bebop: The Anime TV Series and Movie*. Hardcover First Edition. Crescent Moon Publishing. 2016. ISBN-10: 1861715676. ISBN-13: 9781861715678.

> Paperback First Edition. Crescent Moon Publishing. 2015. ISBN-10: 1861714963. ISBN-13: 9781861714961.

Ruh, Brian. *Stray Dog of Anime: The Films of Mamoru Oshii*. Hardcover First Edition. Palgrave Macmillan. 2004. ISBN-10: 1403963290. 2004. ISBN-13: 9781403963291.

> Paperback First Edition. Springer Publishing Company. 2004. ISBN-10: 1403963347. ISBN-13: 9781403963345.

> Paperback Second Edition. Palgrave Macmillan. 2014. ISBN-10: 1137355670. ISBN-13: 9781137355676.

> eBook. Palgrave Macmillan. 2016.

Schodt, Frederik L. *The Astro Boy Essays: Osamu Tezuka, Mighty Atom, and the Manga/Anime Revolution*. Paperback First Edition. Stone Bridge Press. 2007. ISBN-10: 1933330546. ISBN-13: 9781933330549.

> eBook. Stone Bridge Press. 2007.

Takeda, Yasuhiro. *The Notenki Memoirs: Studio Gainax and the Men Who Created Evangelion*. Paperback First Edition. ADV Manga. 2005. ISBN-10: 1413902340. ISBN-13: 9781413902341.

History

Clements, Jonathan. *Anime: A History*. Paperback First Edition. British Film Institute. 2013. ISBN-10: 1844573907. ISBN-13: 9781844573905.

Koyama-Richard, Brigitte. *Japanese Animation: From Painted Scrolls to Pokémon*. Hardcover First Edition. Flammarion. 2010. ISBN-10: 2080301535. ISBN-13: 9782080301536.

>Hardcover Reprint Edition. Flammarion. 2015. ISBN-10: 2080202421. ISBN-13: 9782080202420.

Litten, Frederick. *Animated Film in Japan Until 1919: Western Animation and the Beginnings of Anime*. Paperback First Edition. Books on Demand. 2017. ISBN-10: 3744830527. ISBN-13: 9783744830522.

Novielli, Maria Roberta. *Floating Worlds: A Short History of Japanese Animation*. Hardcover First Edition. CRC Press. 2018. ISBN-10: 1138571288. ISBN-13: 9781138571280.

>eBook. CRC Press. 2018.

Papp, Zilia. *Anime and Its Roots in Early Japanese Monster Art*. Hardcover First Edition. Brill. Global Oriental. 2010. ISBN-10: 1906876185. ISBN-13: 9781906876180.

>eBook. Brill. 2010.

Hayao Miyazaki and the Work of Studio Ghibli

Alpert, Steve. *Sharing a House with the Never Ending Man*. Hardcover First Edition. Stone Bridge Press. 2020. ISBN-10: 1611720605. ISBN-13: 9781611720600.

> Paperback First Edition. Stone Bridge Press. 2020. ISBN-10: 1611720575. ISBN-13: 9781611720570.

> eBook. Stone Bridge Press. 2020.

Berton, Gael. *The Works of Hayao Miyazaki: The Master of Japanese Animation*. Hardcover First Edition. Third Editions. 2021. ISBN-10: 237784278X. ISBN-13: 9782377842780.

Cavallaro, Dani. *The Anime Art of Hayao Miyazaki*. Paperback First Edition. McFarland & Company, Inc., Publishers. 2006. ISBN-10: 0786423692. ISBN-13: 9780786423699.

> eBook. McFarland & Company, Inc., Publishers. 2015.

Cavallaro, Dani. *Hayao Miyazaki's World Picture*. Paperback First Edition. McFarland & Company, Inc., Publisher. 2015. ISBN-10: 0786496479. ISBN-13: 9780786496471.

> eBook. McFarland & Company, Inc., Publishers. 2015.

Cavallaro, Dani. *The Late Works of Hayao Miyazaki: A Critical Study 2004-2013*. Paperback First Edition. McFarland & Company, Inc., Publishers. 2014. ISBN-10: 0786495189. ISBN-13: 9780786495184.

> eBook. McFarland & Company, Inc., Publishers. 2014.

Denison, Rayna. *Princess Mononoke: Understanding Studio Ghibli's Monster Princess (Animation: Key Films/Filmmakers)*. Hardcover First Edition. Bloomsbury Academic. 2018. ISBN-10: 1501329766. ISBN-13: 9781501329760.

> eBook. Bloomsbury Academic. 2018.

　　　　Paperback First Edition. Bloomsbury Academic. 2019.
　　　　ISBN-10: 1501354876. ISBN-13: 9781501354878.

Docter, Pete. Kothenschulte, Daniel. Niebel, Jessica. *Hayao Miyazaki.* Hardcover First Edition. DelMonico Books/Academy Museum of Motion Pictures. 2021. ISBN-10: 1942884818. ISBN-13: 9781942884811.

Greenberg, Raz. *Hayao Miyazaki: Exploring the Early Work of Japan's Greatest Animator (Animation: Key Films/Filmmakers)*. Hardcover First Edition. Bloomsbury Academic. 2018. ISBN-10: 1501335944. ISBN-13: 9781501335945.

　　　　eBook. Bloomsbury Academic. 2018.

　　　　Paperback First Edition. Bloomsbury Academic. 2020.
　　　　ISBN-10: 1501361643. ISBN-13: 9781501361647.

McCarthy, Helen. *Hayao Miyazaki: Master of Japanese Animation*. Paperback First Edition. Stone Bridge Press. 1999. ISBN-10: 1880656418. ISBN-13: 9781880656419.

　　　　Audiobook. Narrated by James Yaegashi. Recorded Books, Inc. 2008.

　　　　Audiobook on CD. Recorded Books, Inc. 2008.

Napier, Susan. *Miyazakiworld: A Life in Art*. Hardcover First Edition. Yale University Press. 2018. ISBN-10: 0300226853. ISBN-13: 9780300226850.

　　　　eBook. Yale University Press. 2018.

　　　　Paperback Reprint Edition. Yale University Press. 2019.
　　　　ISBN-10: 0300248598. ISBN-13: 9780300248593.

　　　　Audiobook on CD. Brilliance Audio. 2019.

　　　　Audiobook. Narrated by Susan Napier. Brilliance Audio. 2019.

Osmond, Andrew. *The BFI Film Classics Study of Spirited Away*. Paperback First Edition. British Film Institute. 2008. ISBN-10: 1844572307. ISBN-13: 9781844572304.

>Paperback Second Edition. British Film Institute. 2020. ISBN-10: 1838719520. ISBN-13: 9781838719524.

>eBook. British Film Institute. 2020.

Le Blanc, Michelle. Odell, Colin. *Studio Ghibli: The Films of Hayao Miyazaki and Isao Takahata*. Paperback First Edition. Kamera Books. 2009. ISBN-10: 1842432796. ISBN-13: 9781842432792.

>eBook Oldcastle Books. 2009.

>Paperback Second Edition. Kamera Books. 2015. ISBN-10: 1843444887. ISBN-13: 9781843444886.

>Paperback Third Edition. Kamera Books. 2020. ISBN-10: 0857303562. ISBN-13: 9780857303561.

Miyazaki, Hayao. *Starting Point: 1979-1996*. Hardcover First Edition. VIZ Media LLC. 2009. ISBN-10: 1421505940. ISBN-13: 9781421505947.

>Paperback First Edition. VIZ Media LLC. 2014. ISBN-10: 1421561042. ISBN-13: 9781421561042.

>eBook. Viz Media LLC. Studio Ghibli Library. 2021.

Miyazaki, Hayao. *Turning Point: 1997-2008*. Hardcover First Edition. VIZ Media LLC. 2014. ISBN-10: 1421560909. ISBN-13: 9781421560908.

>Paperback First Edition. VIZ Media LLC. 2021. ISBN-10: 1974724506. ISBN-13: 9781974724505.

>eBook. VIZ Media. 2021.

Ogihara-Schuck, Eriko. *Miyazaki's Animism Abroad: The Reception of Japanese Religious Themes by American and German Audiences*. Paperback First Edition. McFarland & Company, Inc., Publishers. 2014. ISBN-10: 0786472626. ISBN-13: 9780786472628.

    eBook. McFarland & Company, Inc., Publishers. 2014.

Robinson, Jeremy Mark. *The Cinema of Hayao Miyazaki*. Paperback First Edition. Crescent Moon Publishing. 2011. ISBN-10: 1861713053. ISBN-13: 9781861713056.

    Paperback Second Edition. Crescent Moon Publishing. 2012. ISBN-10: 1861713908. ISBN-13: 9781861713902.

    Hardcover Revised and Updated Edition. Crescent Moon Publishing. 2015. ISBN-10: 1861713363. ISBN-13: 9781861713360.

    Paperback Third Edition. Crescent Moon Publishing. 2015. ISBN-10: 1861714416. ISBN-13: 9781861714411.

    Paperback Second Edition. Crescent Moon Publishing. 2016. ISBN-10: 1861715536. ISBN-13: 9781861715531.

Robinson, Jeremy Mark. *Hayao Miyazaki: Pocket Guide.* Hardcover First Edition. Crescent Moon Publishing. 2015. ISBN-10: 1861715161. ISBN-13: 9781861715166.

    Paperback First Edition. Crescent Moon Publishing. 2015. ISBN-10: 186171517X. ISBN-13: 9781861715173.

    eBook. Crescent Moon Publishing. 2015.

Robinson, Jeremy Mark. *Princess Mononoke: Pocket Movie Guide*. Paperback First Edition. Crescent Moon Publishing. 2012. ISBN-10: 1861713711. ISBN-13: 9781861713711.

    Paperback Second Edition. Crescent Moon Publishing. 2015. ISBN-10: 1861715188. ISBN-13: 9781861715180.

    Hardcover Second Edition. Crescent Moon Publishing. 2016. ISBN-10: 1861715250. ISBN-13: 9781861715258.

Robinson, Jeremy Mark. *Spirited Away: Hayao Miyazaki: Pocket Movie Guide*. Paperback First Edition. Crescent Moon Publishing. 2012. ISBN-10: 1861713479. ISBN-13: 9781861713476.

> Paperback Second Edition. Crescent Moon Publishing. 2015. ISBN-10: 1861713479. ISBN-13: 9781861713476.

The Art of Studio Ghibli

Miramax. *Princess Mononoke: The Art and Making of Japan's Most Popular Film of All Time*. Hardcover First Edition. Miramax Books. 1999. ISBN-10: 0786866098. ISBN-13: 9780786866090.

Miyazaki, Hayao. *Nausicaä of the Valley of the Wind: Watercolor Impressions*. Hardcover First Edition. VIZ Media LLC. 2007. ISBN-10: 1421514990. ISBN-13: 9781421514994.

Miyazaki, Hayao. *Princess Mononoke: The First Story*. Hardcover First Edition. VIZ Media LLC. 2014. ISBN-10: 1421575868. ISBN-13: 9781421575865.

Miyazaki, Hayao. *The Art of Castle in the Sky*. Hardcover First Edition. VIZ Media LLC. 2016. ISBN-10: 1421582724. ISBN-13: 9781421582726.

Miyazaki, Hayao. *The Art of Howl's Moving Castle*. Hardcover First Edition. VIZ Media LLC. 2005. ISBN-10: 1421500493. ISBN-13: 9781421500492.

Miyazaki, Hayao. *The Art of Kiki's Delivery Service*. Hardcover First Edition. VIZ Media LLC. 2006. ISBN-10: 1421505932. ISBN-13: 9781421505930.

Miyazaki, Hayao. *The Art of My Neighbor Totoro*. Hardcover First Edition. VIZ Media LLC. 2005. ISBN-10: 1591166985. ISBN-13: 9781591166986.

Miyazaki, Hayao. *The Art of Ponyo*. Paperback First Edition. VIZ Media LLC. 2009. ISBN-10: 1421530643. ISBN-13: 9781421530642.

    Hardcover Reprint Edition. VIZ Media LLC. 2013. ISBN-10: 1421566028. ISBN-13: 9781421566023.

Miyazaki, Hayao. *The Art of Porco Rosso*. Hardcover First Edition. VIZ Media LLC. 2005. ISBN-10: 1591167043. ISBN-13: 9781591167044.

Miyazaki, Hayao. *The Art of Princess Mononoke*. Hardcover First Edition. VIZ Media LLC. 2014. ISBN-10: 1421565978. ISBN-13: 9781421565972.

Miyazaki, Hayao. *The Art of Spirited Away*. Hardcover First Edition. VIZ Media LLC. 2002. ISBN-10: 1569317771. ISBN-13: 9781569317778.

Miyazaki, Hayao. *The Art of The Wind Rises*. Hardcover First Edition. VIZ Media LLC. 2014. ISBN-10: 1421571757. ISBN-13: 9781421571751.

My Neighbor Hayao: Art Inspired by the Films of Miyazaki. Hardcover First Edition. Cernunnos. 2020. ISBN-10: 2374951359. ISBN-13: 9782374951355.

Studio Ghibli. *Hayao Miyazaki and the Ghibli Museum.* Two-Volume Hardcover First Edition. Iwanami Shoten, Publishers. 2021. ISBN-10: 4000248936. ISBN-13: 9784000248938.

Takahata, Isao. *The Art of the Tale of the Princess Kaguya*. Hardcover First Edition. VIZ Media LLC. 2022. ISBN-10: 1974727831. ISBN-13: 9781974727834.

Yonebayashi, Hiromasa. *The Art of The Secret World of Arrietty.* Paperback First Edition. VIZ Media LLC. 2012. ISBN-10: 1421541181. ISBN-13: 9781421541181.

>Hardcover Reprint Edition. VIZ Media LLC. 2018. ISBN-10: 197470033X. ISBN-13: 9781974700332.

General Anime Studies

Ashmore, Darren-Jon. McCarthy, Helen. *Leiji Matsumoto: Essays on the Manga and Anime Legend*. Paperback First Edition. McFarland & Company, Inc., Publishers. 2021. ISBN-10: 1476679967. ISBN-13: 9781476679969.

    eBook. McFarland. 2021.

Azuma, Hiroki. Lawson, Dawn. Saitō, Tamaki. Vincent, J. Keith. *Beautiful Fighting Girl*. Paperback First Edition. University of Minnesota Press. 2011. ISBN-10: 0816654514. ISBN-13: 9780816654512.

    Hardcover Reprint Edition. University of Minnesota Press. 2011. ISBN-10: 0816654506. ISBN-13: 9780816654505.

    eBook. University of Minnesota Press. 2011.

Bolton, Christopher. *Interpreting Anime*. Hardcover First Edition. University of Minnesota Press. 2018. ISBN-10: 1517904021. ISBN-13: 9781517904029.

    Paperback First Edition. University of Minnesota Press. 2018. ISBN-10: 151790403X. ISBN-13: 9781517904036.

    eBook. University of Minnesota Press. 2018.

Bolton, Christopher. *Robot Ghosts and Wired Dreams: Japanese Science Fiction from Origins to Anime*. Hardcover First Edition. University of Minnesota Press. 2007. ISBN-10: 0816649731. ISBN-13: 9780816649730.

    Paperback First Edition. University of Minnesota Press. 2007. ISBN-10: 081664974X. ISBN-13: 9780816649747.

    eBook. University of Minnesota Press. 2007.

Brenner, Robin E. *Understanding Manga and Anime*. Paperback Annotated Edition. Libraries Unlimited. 2007. ISBN-10: 1591583322. ISBN-13: 9781591583325.

    eBook. Libraries Unlimited. 2007.

Brophy, Philip. Chatfield, Carl. Clements, Jonathan. Costa, Jordi. Della Casa, Luca. Delorme, Stéphane. Di Giorgio, Davide. Dottorini, Daniele. Gariglio, Stefano. Gravett, Paul. Higuinen, Erwan. Liberti, Fabrizio. McCarthy, Helen. Modina, Fabrizio. Nazzaro, Giona A. Paganelli, Grazia. Roberta, Maria. Rondolino, Gianni. Roudevitch, Michel. Rumor, Mario A. Sarrazin, Stephen. Surman, David. *Manga Impact: The World of Japanese Animation*. Paperback First Edition. Phaidon Press. 2010. ISBN-10: 0714857416. ISBN-13: 9780714857411.

Brown, Steven T. *Cinema Anime*. Hardcover First Edition. Palgrave Macmillan. 2006. ISBN-10: 1403970602. ISBN-13: 9781403970602.

> Paperback First Edition. Palgrave Macmillan. 2008.
> ISBN-10: 0230606210. ISBN-13: 9780230606210.

Brown, Steven T. *Tokyo Cyberpunk: Posthumanism In Japanese Visual Culture*. Hardcover First Edition. Palgrave Macmillan. 2010. ISBN-10: 0230103596. ISBN-13: 9780230103597.

> Paperback First Edition. Palgrave Macmillan. 2010.
> ISBN-10: 023010360X. ISBN-13: 9780230103603.

> eBook. Palgrave Macmillan. 2016.

Cavallaro, Dani. *Anime and the Art of Adaptation*. Paperback First Edition. McFarland & Company, Inc., Publishers. 2010. ISBN-10: 0786458607. ISBN-13: 9780786458608.

> eBook. McFarland & Company, Inc., Publishers. 2010.

Cavallaro, Dani. *Anime Intersections: Tradition and Innovation in Theme and Technique.* Paperback First Edition. McFarland & Company, Inc. 2007. ISBN-10: 0786432349. ISBN-13: 9780786432349.

Cavallaro, Dani. *Anime and Memory: Aesthetic, Cultural and Thematic Perspectives*. Paperback First Edition. McFarland & Company, Inc., Publishers. 2009. ISBN-10: 0786441127. ISBN-13: 9780786441129.

> eBook. McFarland & Company, Inc., Publishers. 2011.

Cavallaro, Dani. *Anime and the Visual Novel: Narrative Structure, Design and Play at Crossroads of Animation and Computer Games*. Paperback First Edition. McFarland & Company, Inc., Publishers. 2009. ISBN-10: 0786444274.ISBN-13: 9780786444274.

  eBook. McFarland & Company, Inc., Publishers. 2009.

Cavallaro, Dani. *Art in Anime: The Creative Quest as Theme and Metaphor*. Paperback First Edition. McFarland & Company, Inc., Publishers. 2011. ISBN-10: 0786465611. ISBN-13: 9780786465613.

Cavallaro, Dani. *The Cinema of Mamoru Oshii: Fantasy, Technology and Politics*. Paperback First Edition. McFarland & Company, Inc., Publishers. 2006. ISBN-10: 0786427647. ISBN-13: 9780786427642.

  eBook. McFarland & Company, Inc., Publishers. 2014.

Cavallaro, Dani. *CLAMP in Context.* Paperback First Edition. McFarland & Company, Inc., Publishers. 2012. ISBN-10: 0786469544. ISBN-13: 9780786469543.

  eBook. McFarland & Company, Inc., Publishers. 2012.

Cavallaro, Dani. *The Fairy Tale and Anime: Traditional Themes, Images and Symbols at Play on Screen*. Paperback First Edition. McFarland & Company, Inc., Publishers. 2011. ISBN-10: 0786459468. ISBN-13: 9780786459469.

  eBook. McFarland & Company, Inc., Publishers. 2011.

Cavallaro, Dani. *Japanese Aesthetics and Anime: The Influence of Tradition*. Paperback First Edition. McFarland & Company, Inc., Publishers. 2013. ISBN-10: 0786471514. ISBN-13: 9780786471515.

  eBook. McFarland & Company, Inc., Publishers. First Edition. 2012.

Cavallaro, Dani. *Magic as Metaphor in Anime: A Critical Study*. Paperback First Edition. McFarland & Company, Inc., Publishers. 2009. ISBN-10: 0786447443. ISBN-13: 9780786447442.

  eBook. McFarland & Company, Inc., Publishers. 2010.

Cornog, Martha. *Mangatopia: Essays on Manga and Anime in the Modern World*. Paperback First Edition. Libraries Unlimited. 2011. ISBN-10: 1591589088. ISBN-13: 9781591589082.

    eBook Libraries Unlimited. 2011.

Denison, Rayna. *Anime: A Critical Introduction*. Hardcover Annotated Edition. Bloomsbury Academic. 2015. ISBN-10: 1847884806. ISBN-13: 9781847884800.

    Paperback Annotated Edition. Bloomsbury Academic. 2015. ISBN-10: 1847884792. ISBN-13: 9781847884794.

    eBook. Bloomsbury Academic. 2015.

Drazen, Patrick. *A Gathering of Spirits: Japan's Ghost Story Tradition: From Folklore and Kabuki to Anime and Manga*. Paperback First Edition. iUniverse Publishing. 2007. IISBN-10: 1462029426. ISBN-13: 9781462029426.

    eBook. iUniverse Publishing. 2011.

Drazen, Patrick. *Holy Anime!: Japan's View of Christianity*. Paperback First Edition. Hamilton Books. 2017. ISBN-10: 0761869077. ISBN-13: 9780761869078.

    eBook. Hamilton Books. 2017.

Hu, Tze-yue. *Frames of Anime: Culture and Image-Building*. Hardcover First Edition. Hong Kong University Press. 2010. ISBN-10: 9622090974. ISBN-13: 9789622090972.

    Paperback First Edition. Hong Kong University Press. 2010. ISBN-10: 9622090982. ISBN-13: 9789622090989.

    eBook. 2010. Hong Kong University Press.

Lamarre, Thomas. *The Anime Machine: A Media Theory of Animation*. Hardcover First Edition. University of Minnesota Press. 2009. ISBN-10: 081665154X. ISBN-13: 9780816651542.

    Paperback First Edition. University of Minnesota Press. 2009. ISBN-10: 0816651558. ISBN-13: 9780816651559.

eBook. University of Minnesota Press. 2013.

Levi, Antonia. *Samurai from Outer Space: Understanding Japanese Animation*. Open Court Publishing Company. 1998. ISBN-10: 0812693329. ISBN-13: 9780812693324.

MacWilliams, Mark W. *Japanese Visual Culture: Explorations in the World of Manga and Anime*. Hardcover First Edition. Routledge. 2008. ISBN-10: 0765616017. ISBN-13: 9780765616012.

> Paperback First Edition. Routledge. 2008. ISBN-10: 0765616025. ISBN-13: 9780765616029.

> eBook. Routledge. 2014.

Napier, Susan J. *From Impressionism to Anime: Japan as Fantasy and Fan Cult in the Mind of the West*. Hardcover First Edition. Palgrave Macmillan. 2008. ISBN-10: 1403962138. ISBN-13: 9781403962133.

> Paperback First Edition. Palgrave Macmillan. 2008. ISBN-10: 1403962146. ISBN-13: 9781403962140.

Ng, Andrew Hock Soon. *Asian Gothic: Essays on Literature, Film and Anime*. Paperback First Edition. McFarland & Company, Inc. 2008. ISBN-10: 0786433353. ISBN-13: 9780786433353.

Okuyama, Yoshiko. *Japanese Mythology in Film: A Semiotic Approach to Reading Japanese Film and Anime*. Hardcover First Edition. Lexington Books. 2015. ISBN-10: 073919092X. ISBN-13: 9780739190920.

> eBook. Lexington Books. 2015.

> Paperback First Edition. Lexington Books. 2016. ISBN-10: 1498514332. ISBN-13: 9781498514330.

Patten, Fred. *Watching Anime, Reading Manga: 25 Years of Essays and Reviews*. Stone Bridge Press. 2004. ISBN-10: 1880656922. ISBN-13: 9781880656921.

> eBook. Stone Bridge Press. 2004.

Robinson, Chris. *Japanese Animation: Time Out of Mind*. Paperback First Edition. John Libbey Publishing. 2010. ISBN-10: 861966929. ISBN-13: 9780861966929.

Steiff, Josef. Tamplin, Tristan D. *Anime and Philosophy: Wide Eyed Wonder*. Paperback First Edition. Open Court. 2010. ISBN-10: 0812696700. ISBN-13: 9780812696707.

    eBook. Open Court. 2010.

Suan, Stevie. *Anime's Identity: Performativity and Form Beyond Japan*. Hardcover First Edition. University of Minnesota Press. 2021. ISBN-10: 151791177X. ISBN-13: 9781517911775.

    Paperback First Edition. University of Minnesota Press. 2021. ISBN-10: 1517911788. ISBN-13: 9781517911782.

    eBook. University of Minnesota Press. 2021.

Suan, Stevie. *The Anime Paradox: Patterns and Practices Through the Lens of Traditional Japanese Theatre*. Hardcover First Edition. Global Oriental. 2013. ISBN-10: 9004222146. ISBN-13: 9789004222144.

Swale, Alistair. *Anime Aesthetics: Japanese Animation and the 'Post-Cinematic' Imagination*. Hardcover First Edition. Palgrave Macmillan. 2015. ISBN-10: 1137463341. ISBN-13: 9781137463340.

    Paperback First Edition. Palgrave Macmillan. 2016. ISBN-10: 1349553573. ISBN-13: 9781349553570.

    eBook. Palgrave Macmillan. 2015.

Thomas, Jolyon Baraka. *Drawing on Tradition: Manga, Anime, and Religion in Contemporary Japan*. eBook. University of Hawaii Press. 2012.

    Paperback First Edition. University of Hawaii Press. 2012. ISBN-10: 0824836545. ISBN-13: 9780824836542.

    Hardcover First Edition. University of Hawaii Press. 2012. ISBN-10: 0824835891. ISBN-13: 9780824835897.

West, Mark I. *The Japanification of Children's Popular Culture: From Godzilla to Miyazaki*. Paperback First Edition. Scarecrow Press. 2008. ISBN-10: 0810851210. ISBN-13: 9780810851214.

    eBook. Scarecrow Press. 2008.

Yokota, Masao. *Japanese Animation: East Asian Perspectives*. Hardcover First Edition. University Press of Mississippi. 2013. ISBN-10: 1617038091. ISBN-13: 9781617038099.

    Paperback First Edition. University Press of Mississippi. 2014. ISBN-10: 1628461799. ISBN-13: 9781628461794.

    eBook. University Press of Mississippi. 2013.

The Art of Anime

Aoyama, Takako. *Anime Poster Art: Japan's Movie House Masterpieces*. Paperback First Edition. DH Publishing, Inc. 2003. ISBN-10: 0972312447. ISBN-13: 9780972312448.

Carlton, Ardith. Reynolds, Kay. *Robotech Art I*. Hardcover First Edition. Donning Company Publishers. 1986. ISBN-10: 089865503X. ISBN-13: 9780898655032.

  Paperback First Edition. Walsworth Publishing Company. 1986. ISBN-10: 0898654122. ISBN-13: 9780898654127.

Davisson, Zack. Kon, Satoshi. *The Art of Satoshi Kon*. Hardcover First Edition. Dark Horse Books. 2015. ISBN-10: 1616557419. ISBN-13: 9781616557416.

GAINAX. *The FLCL Archives*. Paperback First Edition. UDON Entertainment. 2019. ISBN-10: 1772940917. ISBN-13: 9781772940916.

Harmony Gold. *Robotech Visual Archive: The Macross Saga*. Hardcover First Edition. UDON Entertainment Corporation. 2017. ISBN-10: 1772940232. ISBN-13: 9781772940237.

  Hardcover Second Edition. UDON Entertainment Corporation. 2018. ISBN-10: 1772940771. ISBN-13: 9781772940770.

Hellige, Hendrik. Hillmen, Jan-Rikus. Klanten, Robert. Meyer, Birga. Tielgekamp, Vicky. *Anime!* Paperback First Edition. Die Gestalten Verlag. 2001. ISBN-10: 3931126722. ISBN-13: 9783931126728.

Hobby Book Editorial Department. *Overlord: The Complete Anime Artbook II III*. Paperback First Edition. Yen Press. 2022. ISBN-10: 1975314352. ISBN-13: 9781975314354.

  eBook. Yen Press. 2022.

Hosoda, Mamoru. *Summer Wars: Material Book*. Paperback First Edition. UDON Entertainment. 2021. ISBN-10: 1926778685. ISBN-13: 9781926778686.

Itou, Naoyuki. *Overlord: The Complete Anime Artbook*. Paperback First Edition. Yen Press. 2020. ISBN-10: 1975314328. ISBN-13: 9781975314323.

khara, Inc. *Evangelion Illustrations 2007-2017*. Paperback First Edition. VIZ Media LLC. 2019. ISBN-10: 1974707032. ISBN-13: 9781974707034.

Kurata, Hideyuki. Masunari, Koji. *Read or Die: R.O.D. Official Archive*. Paperback First Edition. UDON Entertainment. 2013. ISBN-10: 1926778626. ISBN-13: 9781926778624.

Macek, Carl. *Robotech Art 3: The Sentinels*. Hardcover First Edition. Donning Company Publishers. 1988. ISBN-10: 0898655765. ISBN-13: 9780898655766.

> Paperback First Edition. Walsworth Publishing Company. 1988. ISBN-10: 0898655757. ISBN-13: 9780898655759.

Mori, Haruji. *Osamu Tezuka: Anime Character Illustrations*. Hardcover First Edition. UDON Entertainment. 2015. ISBN-10: 192792538X. ISBN-13: 9781927925386.

Osamu Tezuka: Anime & Manga Character Sketchbook. Hardcover First Edition. UDON Entertainment. 2015. ISBN-10: 1927925398. ISBN-13: 9781927925393.

Murase, Shūkō. *Art of Gundam Wing*. Paperback First Edition. VIZ Media LLC. 2001. ISBN-10: 1569315736. ISBN-13: 9781569315736.

Neon Genesis Evangelion: TV Animation Production Art Collection. Hardcover First Edition. UDON Entertainment. 2019. ISBN-10: 1772940429. ISBN-13: 9781772940428.

Otomo, Katsuhiro. *OTOMO: A Global Tribute to the Mind Behind Akira*. Hardcover First Edition. Kodansha Comics. 2017. ISBN-10: 1632365227. ISBN-13: 9781632365224.

PIE International. *Everyday Scenes from a Parallel World*. Paperback First Edition. PIE International. 2018. ISBN-10: 4756249582. ISBN-13: 9784756249586.

Reynolds, Kay. *Robotech Art 2: New Illustrations & Original Art from The Robotech Universe*. Hardcover First Edition. Donning Company Publishers. 1987. ISBN-10: 0898655277. ISBN-13: 9780898655278.

> Paperback First Edition. Walsworth Publishing Company. 1987. ISBN-10: 0898655277. ISBN-13: 9780898655278.

Riekeles, Stefan. *Anime Architecture: Imagined Worlds and Endless Megacities*. Hardcover First Edition. Thames & Hudson. 2020. ISBN-10: 0500294526. ISBN-13: 9780500294529.

Riekeles, Stefan. *Proto Anime Cut: Archive*. Hardcover First Edition. Caja Madrid, Obra Social. 2012. ISBN-10: 846153557X. ISBN-13: 9788461535576.

Robinson, Jeremy Mark. *The Art of Katsuhiro Otomo*. Hardcover First Edition. Crescent Moon Publishing. 2017. ISBN-10: 1861716877. ISBN-13: 9781861716873.

    Hardcover Second Edition. Crescent Moon Publishing. 2018. ISBN-10: 1861717555. ISBN-13: 9781861717559.

Sadamoto, Yoshiyuki. *Der Mond: The Art of Neon Genesis Evangelion*. Hardcover First Edition. VIZ Media LLC. 2006. ISBN-10: 1421507676. ISBN-13: 9781421507675.

Shinkai, Makoto. *your name. The Official Visual Guide.* Paperback First Edition. Yen Press. 2022. ISBN-10: 1975358716. ISBN-13: 9781975358716.

Solomon, Charles. *The Man Who Leapt Through Film: The Art of Mamoru Hosoda*. Hardcover First Edition. Abrams. 2022. ISBN-10: 141975372X. ISBN-13: 9781419753725.

    eBook. Abrams. 2022.

Sorenson, Jim. *Transformers: A Visual History.* Hardcover First Edition. VIZ Media LLC. 2019. ISBN-10: 1974710580. ISBN-13: 9781974710584.

    Hardcover Limited Edition. VIZ Media LLC. 2019. ISBN-10: 1974710572. ISBN-13: 9781974710577.

Tatsunoko Production. *Samurai Pizza Cats: Official Fan Book*. Paperback First Edition. UDON Entertainment. 2019. ISBN-10: 1772940380. ISBN-13: 9781772940381.

UDON. *Robotech Visual Archive: Genesis Climber MOSPEADA.* Hardcover First Edition. UDON Entertainment. 2021. ISBN-10: 1772940259. ISBN-13: 9781772940251.

UDON. *Robotech Visual Archive: The Southern Cross.* Hardcover First Edition. UDON Entertainment. 2021. ISBN-10: 1772940240. ISBN-13: 9781772940244.

Yune, Tommy. *The Art of Robotech: The Shadow Chronicles.* Paperback First Edition. Stone Bridge Press. 2007. ISBN-10: 1933330295. ISBN-13: 9781933330297.

World Animation History

Global Perspectives

Beck, Jerry. *Animation Art: From Pencil to Pixel, the World of Cartoon, Anime, & CGI*. Paperback First Edition. Ted Smart. 2004. ISBN-10: 1844512347. ISBN-13: 9781844512348.

>Paperback First Edition. Flame Tree Publishing. 2004. ISBN-10: 1844511405. ISBN-13: 9781844511402.

>Paperback First Edition. Harper Design. 2004. ISBN-10: 0060737131. ISBN-13: 9780060737139.

>eBook. Flame Tree Publishing. 2015.

Bendazzi, Giannalberto. *Animation: A World History: Volume 1: Foundations - The Golden Age*. Hardcover First Edition. Routledge. 2015. ISBN-10: 1138854522. ISBN-13: 9781138854529.

>eBook. Routledge. 2015.

>Paperback First Edition. Routledge. 2016. ISBN-10: 1138035319. ISBN-13: 9781138035317.

Bendazzi, Giannalberto. *Animation: A World History: Volume 2: The Birth of Style - The Three Markets*. Hardcover First Edition. Routledge. 2015. ISBN-10: 1138854816. ISBN-13: 9781138854819.

>eBook. Routledge. 2015.

>Paperback First Edition. Routledge. 2016. ISBN-10: 1138035327. ISBN-13: 9781138035324.

Bendazzi, Giannalberto. *Animation: A World History: Volume 3: Contemporary Times*. Hardcover First Edition. Routledge. 2015. ISBN-10: 1138854824. ISBN-13: 9781138854826.

>eBook. Routledge. 2015.

       Paperback First Edition. Routledge. 2016. ISBN-10: 1138035335.
       ISBN-13: 9781138035331.

Bendazzi, Giannalberto. *Cartoons: One Hundred Years of Cinema Animation*. Paperback First Edition. John Libbey Publishing. 1994. ISBN-10: 0861964454. ISBN-13: 9780861964451.

       Paperback Reprint Edition. Indiana University Press. 1995.
       ISBN-10: 0253209374. ISBN-13: 9780253209375.

Bradley, Joff P. N. Ju-yu Cheng, Catherine. *Thinking with Animation*. Hardcover First Edition. Cambridge Scholars Publishing. 2021. ISBN-10: 1527571661. ISBN-13: 9781527571662.

Bruckner, Franziska. Gilic, Nikica. Lang, Holger. Šuljic, Daniel. Turkovic, Hrvoje. *Global Animation Theory: International Perspectives at Animafest Zagreb*. Hardcover First Edition. 2018. ISBN-10: 1501337130. ISBN-13: 9781501337130.

       eBook. Bloomsbury Academic. 2018.

       Paperback Reprint Edition. Bloomsbury Academic. 2020.
       ISBN-10: 9781501365010. ISBN-13: 9781501365010.

Cavalier, Stephen. *The World History of Animation*. Hardcover First Edition. University of California Press. 2011. ISBN-10: 0520261127. ISBN-13: 9780520261129.

       Hardcover First Edition. Aurum Press. 2011. ISBN-10: 1845137140.
       ISBN-13: 9781845137144.

Cranfield, Bill. *Flips 7: Animation*. Paperback First Edition. Systems Design Ltd. 2003. ISBN-10: 9889706563. ISBN-13: 9789889706562.

Furniss, Maureen. *A New History of Animation*. Paperback First Edition. Thames & Hudson Ltd. 2016. 2016. ISBN-10: 0500292094. ISBN-13: 9780500292099.

       eBook. Thames & Hudson. 2016

Furniss, Maureen. *Animation: The Global History*. Paperback First Edition. Thames & Hudson Ltd. 2017. ISBN-10: 0500252173. ISBN-13: 9780500252178.

Lent, John. *Animation in Asian and the Pacific*. Hardback First Edition. John Libbey. 2000. ISBN-10: 1864620366. ISBN-13: 9781864620368.

    Hardcover First Edition. Indiana University Press. 2001. ISBN-10: 0253340357. ISBN-13: 9780253340351.

Tobin, Joseph. *Pikachu's Global Adventure: The Rise and Fall of Pokémon*. Hardcover First Edition. Duke University Press Books. 2004. ISBN-10: 0822332507. ISBN-13: 9780822332503.

    Paperback First Edition. Duke University Press Books. 2004. ISBN-10: 0822332876. ISBN-13: 9780822332879.

    eBook. Duke University Press Books. 2004.

Wiedemann, Julius. *Animation Now!* Paperback First Edition. TASCHEN. 2007. ISBN-10: 3822825883. ISBN-13: 9783822837894.

The Arab World

Ghazala, Mohamed. *Animation in The Arab World: A Glance on the Arabian Animated Films Since 1936*. Paperback First Edition. LAP Lambert Academic Publishing. 2011. ISBN-10: 3844385487. ISBN-13: 9783844385489.

Sayfo, Omar. *Arab Animation: Images of Identity*. Hardcover First Edition. Edinburgh University Press. 2021. ISBN-10: 1474479480. ISBN-13: 9781474479486.

Argentina

Bendazzi, Giannalberto. *Twice the First: Quirino Christiani and the Animated Feature Film*. Hardcover First Edition. CRC Press. 2017. ISBN-10: 1138554464. ISBN-13: 9781138554467.

    eBook. CRC Press. 2017.

Australia

Torre, Dan. Torre, Lienors. *Australian Animation: An International History*. Hardcover First Edition. Palgrave Macmillan. 2018. ISBN-10: 3319954911. ISBN-13: 9783319954912.

> eBook. Palgrave Macmillan. 2018.

> Paperback First Edition. Palgrave Macmillan. 2019. ISBN-10: 3030405346. ISBN-13: 9783030405342.

Bulgaria

Hristova, Svetla. Minaeva, Oksana. *The Animation World of Ivan Vesselinov*. Paperback First Edition. New Bulgarian University. 2015. ISBN-10: 9545358424. ISBN-13: 9789545358425.

Canada

Mazurkewich, Karen. *Cartoon Capers: The History of Canadian Animators*. Paperback First Edition. Mcarthur & Company. 1999. ISBN-10: 1552780937. ISBN-13: 9781552780930.

Melnyk, George. *One Hundred Years of Canadian Cinema*. Hardcover First Edition. University of Toronto Press. Scholarly Publishing Division. 2004. ISBN-10: 080203568X. ISBN-13: 9780802035684.

> Paperback Second Edition. University of Toronto Press. Scholarly Publishing Division. 2004. ISBN-10: 0802084443. ISBN-13: 9780802084446.

Robinson, Chris. *Canadian Animation: Looking for a Place to Happen*. Paperback First Edition. John Libbey Publishing. 2008. ISBN-10: 0861966880. ISBN-13: 9780861966882.

China

Chen, Shaopeng. *The New Generation in Chinese Animation*. Hardcover First Edition. Bloomsbury Academic. 2021. ISBN-10: 1350118958. ISBN-13: 9781350118959.

    eBook. Bloomsbury Academic. 2021

Du, Daisy Yan. *Animated Encounters: Transnational Movements of Chinese Animation, 1940s-1970s*. Hardcover First Edition. University of Hawaii Press. 2019. ISBN-10: 082487210X. ISBN-13: 9780824872106.

    Paperback First Edition. University of Hawaii Press. 2019. ISBN-10: 0824877640. ISBN-13: 9780824877644.

    eBook. University of Hawaii Press. 2019.

Du, Daisy Yan. *Chinese Animation and Socialism: From Animators Perspectives*. Hardcover First Edition. Brill Academic Publishers. 2021. ISBN-10: 9004499598. ISBN-13: 9789004499591.

    eBook. Brill Academic Publishers. 2021.

Gieson, Rolf. *Chinese Animation: A History and Filmography, 1922-2012*. Paperback First Edition. McFarland & Company, Inc., Publishers. 2014. ISBN-10: 786459778. ISBN-13: 9780786459773.

    eBook. McFarland & Company, Inc., Publishers. 2014.

Macdonald, Sean. *Animation in China: History, Aesthetics, Media*. Hardcover First Edition. Routledge. 2017. ISBN-10: 1138938807. ISBN-13: 9781138938809

    Paperback First Edition. Routledge. 2017. ISBN-10: 036786780X. ISBN-13: 9780367867805.

    eBook. Routledge. 2015.

Sun, Lijun. *The History of Chinese Animation Volume I*. Hardcover First Edition. Routledge. 2020. ISBN-10: 0367427516. ISBN-13: 9780367427511.

    eBook. Routledge. 2020.

    Paperback First Edition. Routledge. 2022.
    ISBN-10: 1032235721. ISBN-13: 9781032235721.

Sun, Lijun. *The History of Chinese Animation Volume II*. Hardcover First Edition. Routledge. 2020. ISBN-10: 0367427753. ISBN-13: 9780367427757.

    eBook. Routledge. 2020.

    Paperback First Edition. Routledge. 2022.
    ISBN-10: 103223573X. ISBN-13: 9781032235738.

Wu, Weihua. *Chinese Animation, Creative Industries and Digital Culture*. Hardcover First Edition. Routledge. 2017. ISBN-10: 0415810353. ISBN-13: 9780415810357.

    eBook. Routledge. 2017.

    Paperback First Edition. Routledge. 2019. ISBN-10: 036786780X.
    ISBN-13: 9780367867805.

Zhou, Wenhai. *Chinese Independent Animation: Renegotiating Identity in Modern China*. Hardcover First Edition. Palgrave Macmillan. 2020. ISBN-10: 3030406962. ISBN-13: 9783030406967.

    eBook. Palgrave Macmillan. 2020.

    Paperback First Edition. Palgrave Macmillan. 2021.
    ISBN-10: 3030406997. ISBN-13: 9783030406998.

Czech Republic

Schmitt, Bertrand. *Jan Švankmajer: Dimensions of Dialogue: Between Film and Fine Art*. Paperback First Edition. Arbor Vitae. 2013. ISBN-10: 8074670163. ISBN-13: 9788074670169.

Struskova, Eva. *The Dodals: Pioneers of Czech Animated Film*. Paperback First Edition with DVD. Academy of Performing Arts in Prague and National Film Archive Prague. 2014. ISBN-10: 8073312719. ISBN-13: 9788073312718.

Whybray, Adam. *The Art of Czech Animation: A History of Political Dissent and Allegory*. Bloomsbury Academic. 2020. ISBN-10: 1350104590. ISBN-13: 9781350104594.

> eBook. Bloomsbury Academic. 2020.

> Paperback First Edition. Bloomsbury Academic. 2022. ISBN-10: 1350194980. ISBN-13: 9781350194984.

Czechoslovakia

Beckerman, Howard. Poš, Jan. Wechsler, Jeffrey. *Krátký Film: The Art of Czechoslovak Animation*. Paperback First Edition. Jane Voorhees Zimmerli Art Museum, Rutgers. 1991.

> Hardcover First Edition. Bloomsbury Academic. 2020. ISBN-10: 1350104590. ISBN-13: 9781350104594.

> eBook. Bloomsbury Academic. 2020.

Estonia

Robinson, Chris. *Estonian Animation: Between Genius and Utter Illiteracy*. Paperback First Edition. John Libbey Publishing. 2007. ISBN-10: 0861966678. ISBN-13: 9780861966677.

> eBook. John Libbey Publishing. 2007.

France

Neupert, Richard. *French Animation History*. Hardcover First Edition. Wiley-Blackwell. 2011. ISBN-10: 1444338366. ISBN-13: 9781444338362.

>eBook. Wiley-Blackwell. 2011.

>Paperback First Edition. Wiley-Blackwell. 2014. ISBN-10: 1118798767. ISBN-13: 9781118798768.

Germany

Giesen, Rolf. *Animation Under the Swastika: A History of Trickfilm in Nazi Germany, 1933-1945*. Paperback First Edition. McFarland & Company, Inc., Publishers. 2012. ISBN-10: 0786446404. ISBN-13: 9780786446407.

>eBook. McFarland & Company, Inc., Publishers. 2012.

Great Britain

Cook, Malcolm. *Early British Animation: From Page to Stage to Cinema Screens*. Hardcover First Edition. Palgrave Macmillan. 2018. ISBN-10: 3319734288. ISBN-13: 9783319734286.

>eBook. Palgrave Macmillan. 2018.

>Paperback Reprint Edition. Palgrave Macmillan. 2019. ISBN-10: 3030087875. ISBN-13: 9783030087876.

Gifford, Denis. *British Animated Films, 1895-1985: A Filmography*. Hardcover First Edition. McFarland & Company, Inc., Publishers. 1987. ISBN-10: 0899502415. ISBN-13: 9780899502410.

Halas, Vivien. Wells, Paul. *Halas & Batchelor Cartoons: An Animated History*. Turtleback Paperback First Edition with DVD. Southbank Publishing. 2007. ISBN-10: 1904915175. ISBN-13: 9781904915171.

Holloway, Ronald. *Z is for Zagreb*. Hardcover First Edition. A. S. Barnes. 1972. ISBN-10: 0498011232. ISBN-13: 9780498011238.

Kitson, Clare. *British Animation: The Channel 4 Factor*. Paperback First Edition. Indiana University Press. 2009. ISBN-10: 0253220963. ISBN-13: 9780253220967.

    Audiobook on CD. John Libbey. ISBN-10: 0861966775. ISBN-13: 9780861966776.

Manvell, Roger. *Art and Animation: The Story of the Halas and Batchelor Animation Studio*. Hardcover First Edition. Tantivy Press. 1980. ISBN-10: 0904208885. ISBN-13: 9780904208887.

    Paperback First Edition. Hastings House Publishers. 1980. ISBN-10: 0803804946. ISBN-13: 9780803804944.

Moseley, Rachel. *Hand-Made Television: Stop-Frame Animation for Children in Britain, 1961-1974*. Hardcover First Edition. Palgrave Pivot. 2015. ISBN-10: 1137551623. ISBN-13: 9781137551627.

    eBook. Palgrave Pivot. 2016.

Norris, Van. *British Television Animation 1997-2010: Drawing Comic Tradition*. Hardcover First Edition. Palgrave Macmillan. 2014. ISBN-10: 1137330937. ISBN-13: 9781137330932.

    Paperback First Edition. Palgrave Macmillan. 2014. ISBN-10: 1137330937. ISBN-13: 9781137330932.

    eBook. Palgrave Macmillan. 2014.

Stewart, Jez. *The Story of British Animation*. Hardcover First Edition. British Film Institute. 2021. ISBN-10: 1911239732. ISBN-13: 9781911239734.

    Paperback First Edition. British Film Institute. 2021. ISBN-10: 1911239732. ISBN-13: 9781911239734.

    eBook. British Film Institute. 2021.

Italy

Bellano, Marco. Pallant, Chris. *Allegro Non Troppo: Bruno Bozzetto's Animated Music*. Hardcover First Edition. Bloomsbury Academic. 2021. ISBN-10: 1501350862. ISBN-13: 9781501350863.

>eBook available through Bloomsbury Open Access: http://dx.doi.org/10.5040/9781501350894.

>Paperback First Edition. Bloomsbury Academic. 2022. ISBN-10: 1501376284. ISBN-13: 9781501376283.

Malaysia

Muthalib, Hassan Abdul. *From Mouse Deer To Mouse – 70 Years of Malaysian Animation*. Paperback First Edition. Akademi Seni Budaya dan Warisan Kebangsaan (ASWARA - National Arts, Culture & Heritage Academy). 2016. ISBN-10: 9832538335. ISBN-13: 9789832538332.

The Middle East

Van de Peer, Stefanie. *Animation in the Middle East: Practice and Aesthetics from Baghdad to Casablanca*. Hardcover First Edition. I.B. Tauris. 2017. ISBN-10: 1784533262. ISBN-13: 9781784533267.

>eBook. I.B. Tauris. 2017.

>Paperback First Edition. Bloomsbury Academic. 2021. ISBN-10: 1350243906. ISBN-13: 9781350243903.

New Zealand

Horrocks, Roger. *Len Lye: A Biography*. Paperback First Edition. Auckland University Press. 2001. ISBN-10: 1869402472. ISBN-13: 9781869402471.

>eBook. Auckland University Press. 2013.

Russia

Alley, Maria. Merrill, Jason. Mikhailova, Julia. *Animation for Russian Conversation*. Paperback First Edition. Focus Press. 2008. ISBN-10: 1585103101. ISBN-13: 9781585103102.

Collier, Kevin Scott. *Russia's Winnie-the-Pooh: Fyodor Khitruk's Vinni-Pukh*. Paperback First Edition. Independent Publisher. 2018. ISBN-10: 1731277113. ISBN-13: 9781731277114.

Katz, Maya Balakirsky. *Drawing the Iron Curtain: Jews and the Golden Age of Soviet Animation*. Hardcover First Edition. Rutgers University Press. 2016. ISBN-10: 0813577012. ISBN-13: 9780813577012.

> Paperback First Edition. Rutgers University Press. 2016. ISBN-10: 0813576628. ISBN-13: 9780813576626.

> eBook. Rutgers University Press. 2016.

Kitson, Clare. *Yuri Norstein and Tale of Tales: An Animator's Journey*. Paperback First Edition. Indiana University Press. 2005. ISBN-10: 0253218381. ISBN-13: 9780253218384.

Leigh, Michele. Mjolsness, Lora. *She Animates: Gendered Soviet and Russian Animation*. Paperback First Edition. Academic Studies Press. 2020. ISBN-10: 1644690667. ISBN-13: 9781644690666.

> Hardcover First Edition. Academic Studies Press. 2020. ISBN-10: 1644690349. ISBN-13: 9781644690345.

> eBook. Academic Studies Press. 2021.

MacFadyen, David. *Yellow Crocodiles and Blue Oranges: Russian Animated Film since World War II*. Hardcover First Edition. McGill-Queen's University Press. 2005. ISBN-10: 0773528717. ISBN-13: 9780773528710.

> eBook. McGill-Queen's University Press. 2005.

Pontieri, Laura. *Soviet Animation and the Thaw of The 1960s: Not Only for Children*. Paperback First Edition. John Libbey Publishing. 2012. ISBN-10: 861967054. ISBN-13: 9780861967056.

Singapore

Rall, Hans-Martin. *Tradigital Mythmaking: Singaporean Animation for the 21st Century*. Paperback First Edition. LAP - Lambert Academic Publishing. 2012. ISBN-10: 384337323X. ISBN-13: 9783843373234.

South Africa

Shapurjee, Shanaz. *South African Animation: A Historical Enquiry into the South African Broadcasting Corporation's Animation Unit: 1976-88*. Paperback First Edition. VDM Verlag Dr. Müller. 2009. ISBN-10: 3639216830. ISBN-13: 9783639216837.

Switzerland

Andersson, Lars Gustaf. Sundholm, John. Widding, Astrid Söderbergh. *A History of Swedish Experimental Film Culture: From Early Animation to Video Art*. Paperback First Edition. John Libbey Publishing. 2010. ISBN-10: 0861966996. ISBN-13: 9780861966998.

Juvenile Literature

Non-Fiction Texts

1966

Thomas, Bob. *Walt Disney: Magician of the Movies*. Hardcover First Edition. Rutledge Books/Grosset & Dunlap. ISBN-10: 1131331095. ISBN-13: 9781131331096.

    Paperback First Edition. Theme Park Press. 2016. ISBN-10: 1941500994. ISBN-13: 9781941500996.

    eBook. Theme Park Press. 2016.

1973

Young Filmakers Foundation. *Young Animators And Their Discoveries: A Report From Young Filmakers Foundation*. Hardcover First Edition. Harcourt Incorporated College. ISBN-10: 0275257509. ISBN-13: 9780275257507.

    Hardcover First Edition. Encore Editions. 1976. ISBN-10: 0684147173. ISBN-13: 9780684147178.

1989

Amos, Janine. Lane, Kim. *Animation*. Hardcover First Edition. HarperCollins Publishers. ISBN-10: 0001900757. ISBN-13: 9780001900752.

    Paperback First Edition. HarperCollins Publishers. 1990. ISBN-10: 0001900757. ISBN-13: 9780001900752.

Ford, Barbara. *Walt Disney: A Biography*. Hardcover First Edition. Walker & Co. ISBN-10: 0802768644. ISBN-13: 9780802768643.

Selden, Bernice. *The Story of Walt Disney: Maker of Magical Worlds*. Paperback First Edition. Yearling. ISBN-10: 0440402409. ISBN-13: 9780440402404.

    Hardcover First Edition. Gareth Stevens Publishing. 1996. ISBN-10: 0836814681. ISBN-13: 9780836814682.

eBook. Yearling. 2009.

1991

Greene, Katherine. Greene, Richard. *The Man Behind the Magic: The Story of Walt Disney*. Hardcover First Edition. Viking Books for Young Readers. ISBN-10: 0670822590. ISBN-13: 9780670822591.

> Hardcover Second Edition. Bt Bound. 1998. ISBN-10: 0613892232. ISBN-13: 9780613892230.

> Paperback First Edition. Viking Books for Young Readers. 1998. ISBN-10: 0670884766. ISBN-13: 9780670884766.

1992

Nardo, Don. *Animation: Drawings Spring to Life*. Hardcover First Edition. Lucent Books. ISBN-10: 1560062185. ISBN-13: 9781560062189.

Schultz, Ron. *Looking Inside Cartoon Animation*. Hardcover First Edition. Turtleback Books Publishing, Ltd. ISBN-10: 1417600667. ISBN-13: 9781417600663.

> Paperback First Edition. John Muir Publications. 1992. ISBN-10: 156261066X. ISBN-13: 9781562610661.

1993

Viska, Peter. *The Animation Book.* Hardcover First Edition. Ashton Scholastic. ISBN-10: 0868969583. ISBN-13: 9780868969589.

> Hardcover First Edition. Scholastic. 1994. ISBN-10: 0590475738. ISBN-13: 9780590475730.

1995

Keenan, Sheila. *The History of Moviemaking: Animation and Live-Action, from Silent to Sound, Black-And-White to Color*. Hardcover First Edition. Scholastic Inc. ISBN-10: 0590476459. ISBN-13: 9780590476454.

1997

Hammontree, Marie. *Walt Disney: Young Movie Maker*. Paperback First Edition. Aladdin Books. ISBN-10: 0689813244. ISBN-13: 9780689813245.

> Hardcover First Edition. Turtleback Books Publishing, Ltd. 1997. ISBN-10: 0613021681. ISBN-13: 9780613021685.

1998

Graham, Jefferson. *Ultimate Rugrats Fan Book*. Paperback First Edition. Scholastic Book Services. ISBN-10: 0590128388. ISBN-13: 9780590128384.

> Hardcover First Edition. San Val Inc. 1998. ISBN-10: 0613732618. ISBN-13: 9780613732611.

> Paperback First Edition. Simon Spotlight/Nickelodeon. 1998. ISBN-10: 0689816782. ISBN-13: 9780689816789.

1999

Simon, Charnan. *Walt Disney: Creator of Magical Worlds*. Hardcover First Edition. Hardcover First Edition. Children's Press. ISBN-10: 0516211986. ISBN-13: 9780516211985.

> Paperback First Edition. Children's Press. 2000. ISBN-10: 0516265156. ISBN-13: 9780516265155.

2000

Lockman, Darcy. *Computer Animation*. Hardcover First Edition. Cavendish Square Publishing. ISBN-10: 0761410481. ISBN-13: 9780761410485.

National Geographic Learning. *I Make Pictures Move: Inside Theme Book*. Paperback First Edition. National Geographic School Publishing. ISBN-10: 0736209530. ISBN-13: 9780736209533.

Sacks, Terence J. *Opportunities in Animation and Cartooning Careers*. Hardcover First Edition. VGM Career Horizons. ISBN-10: 0658001825. ISBN-13: 9780658001826.

Paperback First Edition. McGraw-Hill. 2000. ISBN-10: 0658001833. ISBN-13: 9780658001833.

Woods, Samuel G. *Made in the USA - Computer Animation*. Hardcover First Edition. Blackbirch Press. ISBN-10: 1567113966. ISBN-13: 9781567113969.

<u>2001</u>

Dowen, Elizabeth. *What's it Like to be a... Animator?* Paperback First Edition. A&C Black Childrens. ISBN-10: 1408105128. ISBN-13: 9781408105122.

Gilman, John. Heide, Robert. *Mickey Mouse: The Evolution, The Legend, The Phenomenon!* Hardcover First Edition. Disney Editions. ISBN-10: 0786853530. ISBN-13: 9780786853533.

Paperback First Edition. Disney Editions. 2003. ISBN-10: 0786854073. ISBN-13: 9780786854073.

Isbouts, Jean-Pierre. *Discovering Walt: The Magical Life of Walt Disney*. Hardcover First Edition. Disney Editions. ISBN-10: 0786853549. ISBN-13: 9780786853540.

Otfinoski, Steven. *Book Treks: Clay Magic: The Art of Clay Animation*. Paperback First Edition. Celebration Press. ISBN-10: 0673617475. ISBN-13: 9780673617477.

<u>2002</u>

Cullimore, Stan. *Behind the Scenes: Animation*. Paperback First Edition. Pearson Schools. ISBN-10: 058249768X. ISBN-13: 9780582497689.

<u>2003</u>

Fingeroth, Danny. *Backstage at an Animated Series*. Hardcover First Edition. Turtleback Books. ISBN-10: 0613595815. ISBN-13: 9780613595810.

Paperback First Edition. Children's Press. 2003. ISBN-10: 0516243853. ISBN-13: 9780516243856.

Ford, Carin T. *Walt Disney: Meet the Cartoonist*. Hardcover First Edition. Enslow Publishers, Inc. ISBN-10: 0766018571. ISBN-13: 9780766018570.

Preszler, June. *Walt Disney: A Photo-Illustrated Biography*. Paperback First Edition. Capstone Press. ISBN-10: 0736834427. ISBN-13: 9780736834421.

> Hardcover First Edition. Capstone Press. 2003. ISBN-10: 0736822267. ISBN-13: 9780736822268.

Tieman, Robert. *The Disney Treasures*. Hardcover First Edition with CD. Disney Editions. ISBN-10: 0786853905. ISBN-13: 9780786853908.

2004

Cohen, Judith Love. *You Can Be A Woman Animator*. Hardcover First Edition. Cascade Pass. ISBN-10: 1880599708. ISBN-13: 9781880599709.

> Paperback First Edition. Cascade Pass. 2004. ISBN-10: 1880599694. ISBN-13: 9781880599693.

2005

Brown, Jonatha A. *Walt Disney (People We Should Know)*. Paperback First Edition. Weekly Reader Publishing. Gareth Stevens Publishing. ISBN-10: 0836847539. ISBN-13: 9780836847536.

> Hardcover First Edition. Weekly Reader Publishing. Gareth Stevens Publishing. 2005. ISBN-10: 0836847466. ISBN-13: 9780836847468.

> Paperback First Edition. Weekly Reader Publishing. Gareth Stevens Publishing. 2005. ISBN-10: 0836847539. ISBN-13: 9780836847536.

Feinstein, Stephen. Walt Disney Company. *Read About Walt Disney*. Hardcover First Edition. Enslow Publishers, Inc. ISBN-10: 0766025950. ISBN-13: 9780766025950.

Gresh, Lois H. Weinberg, Robert. *The Science of Anime: Mecha-Noids and AI-Super-Bots*. Paperback First Edition. Thunder's Mouth Press. ISBN-10: 1560257687. ISBN-13: 9781560257684.

2006

Glass, Sherri. Wentzel, Jim. *Cool Careers Without College for People Who Love Manga, Comics, and Animation*. Hardcover First Edition. ISBN-10: 1404207546. ISBN-13: 9781404207547.

Horn, Geoffrey M. *Movie Animation (The Magic of Movies)*. Hardcover First Edition. Gareth Stevens Publishing Hi-Lo Must Reads. ISBN-10: 0836868374. ISBN-13: 9780836868371.

Josephson, Judith Pinkerton. *Walt Disney: Genius of Entertainment*. Hardcover First Edition. Enslow Publishers, Inc. ISBN-10: 0766026248. ISBN-13: 9780766026247.

Kolk, Melinda. *Teaching with Clay Animation*. Paperback First Edition. Tech4Learning, Inc. ISBN-10: 1930870906. ISBN-13: 9781930870901.

Spilsbury, Richard. *Cartoons and Animation (Art Off the Wall)*. Hardcover First Edition. Heinemann. ISBN-10: 0431014736. ISBN-13: 9780431014739.

> Paperback First Edition. Heinemann. 2008. ISBN-10: 0431014795. ISBN-13: 9780431014791.

2007

Marcovitz, Hal. *Computer Animation (Eye on Art)*. Hardcover First Edition. Lucent Books. ISBN-10: 142050004X. ISBN-13: 9781420500042.

> Hardcover Rerelease (Cover Change). Lucent Books. 2008. ISBN-10: 142050004X. ISBN-13: 9781420500042.

Svitil, Torene. *So You Want to Work in Animation & Special Effects?* Hardcover First Edition. Enslow Publishers, Inc. ISBN-10: 0766027376. ISBN-13: 9780766027374.

> Paperback First Edition. Enslow Publishers, Inc. 2008. ISBN-10: 0766032590. ISBN-13: 9780766032590.

2008

Rauf, Don. Vescia, Monique. *Virtual Apprentice: Cartoon Animator*. Hardcover First Edition. Ferguson Publishing Company. ISBN-10: 0816067600. ISBN-13: 9780816067602.

    eBook. Ferguson Publishing Company. 2008.

    Paperback First Edition. Checkmark Books. 2009. ISBN-10: 0816078920. ISBN-13: 9780816078929.

Saddleback Educational Publishing. *Walt Disney, Graphic Biography*. Paperback First Edition. ISBN-10: 159905230X. ISBN-13: 9781599052304.

    eBook. Saddleback Educational Publishing. 2019.

Woog, Adam. *John Lasseter: Pixar Animator*. Hardcover First Edition. KidHaven Publishing. ISBN-10: 0737740809. ISBN-13: 9780737740806.

2009

Cohn, Jessica. *Animator (Cool Careers: Cutting Edge)*. Hardcover First Edition. Gareth Stevens Publishing. ISBN-10: 1433919532. ISBN-13: 9781433919534.

    Paperback First Edition. Gareth Stevens Publishing. 2009. ISBN-10: 1433921529. ISBN-13: 9781433921520.

Stewart, Whitney. *Who Was Walt Disney?* Paperback First Edition. Penguin Workshop. ISBN-10: 0448450526. ISBN-13: 9780448450520.

    eBook. Penguin Workshop. 2009.

    Hardcover First Edition. Turtleback Books Publishing, Ltd. 2009. ISBN-10: 0606041605. ISBN-13: 9780606041607.

    Audiobook. Narrated by Dan Woren. Listening Library. 2016.

    Book on CD. Listening Library. 2016.

2010

Bliss, John. *Art That Moves: Animation Around the World (Culture in Action)*. Hardcover First Edition. Raintree. ISBN-10: 1410939227. ISBN-13: 9781410939227.

Ferguson Publishing. *Animation (Ferguson's Careers in Focus)*. Hardcover First Edition. Ferguson Publishing Company. ISBN-10: 0816080151. ISBN-13: 9780816080151.

> Second Edition eBook. Ferguson. 2019.

Ferguson Publishing. *What Can I Do Now? Animation*. Hardcover First Edition. Ferguson Publishing. ISBN-10: 0816080771. ISBN-13: 9780816080779.

Mullins, Matt. *Multimedia Artist and Animator (Cool Careers)*. Hardcover First Edition. Cherry Lake Publishing Group. ISBN-10: 1602799423. ISBN-13: 9781602799424.

> eBook. Cherry Lake Publishing. 2014.

2011

Lenburg, Jeff. *Tex Avery: Hollywood's Master of Screwball Cartoons*. Hardcover First Edition. Chelsea House Publishers. ISBN-10: 1604138351. ISBN-13: 9781604138351.

> Audiobook. Narrated by Scott O'Neill. Jeff Lenburg. 2013.

> eBook. Chelsea House Publishers. 2014.

Lenburg, Jeff. *Matt Groening: From Spitballs to Springfield*. Hardcover First Edition. Chelsea House Publishers. ISBN-10: 1604138386. ISBN-13: 9781604138382.

> Audiobook. Narrated by Charlie James. Jeff Lenburg. 2013.

> eBook. Chelsea House Publishers. 2014.

Lenburg, Jeff. *Walt Disney: The Mouse That Roared*. Hardcover First Edition. Chelsea House Publishers. ISBN-10: 160413836X. ISBN-13: 9781604138368.

    Audiobook. Narrated by Al Kessel. Jeff Lenburg. 2013.

    eBook. Chelsea House Publishers. 2014.

Lenburg, Jeff. *William Hanna and Joseph Barbera: The Sultans of Saturday Morning*. Hardcover First Edition. Chelsea House Publishers. ISBN-10: 1604138378. ISBN-13: 9781604138375.

    Audiobook. Narrated by Barry Abrams. Jeff Lenburg. 2013.

    eBook. Chelsea House Publishers. 2014.

2012

Connor, Samuel. *Making it Move: A Short History of Animation*. Paperback First Edition. Collins. ISBN-10: 0007489064. ISBN-13: 9780007489060.

Lenburg, Jeff. *Genndy Tartakovsky: From Russia to Coming-of-Age Animator*. Hardcover First Edition. Chelsea House Publishers. ISBN-10: 1604138424. ISBN-13: 9781604138429.

    eBook. Chelsea House Publishers. 2014.

    Audiobook. Narrated by Amanda Thorp. 2014.

Lenburg, Jeff. *Hayao Miyazaki: Japan's Premier Anime Storyteller*. Hardcover First Edition. Chelsea House Publishers. ISBN-10: 1604138416. ISBN-13: 9781604138412.

    Audiobook. Narrated by Mark Douglas Nelson. Jeff Lenburg. 2013.

    eBook. Chelsea House Publishers. 2014.

Lenburg, Jeff. *John Lasseter: The Whiz Who Made Pixar King*. Hardcover First Edition. Chelsea House Publishers. ISBN-10: 1604138408. ISBN-13: 9781604138405.

    Audiobook. Narrated by Stan Jenson. Jeff Lenburg. 2013.

eBook. Chelsea House Publishers. 2014.

Lenburg, Jeff. *Walter Lantz: Made Famous by a Woodpecker*. Hardcover First Edition. Chelsea House Publishers. ISBN-10: 1604138394. ISBN-13: 9781604138399.

    Audiobook. Narrated by Scott R. Pollak. Jeff Lenburg. 2013.

    eBook. Chelsea House Publishers. 2014.

<u>2013</u>

Apodaca, Blanca. Serwich, Michael. *All in a Day's Work: Animator*. Hardcover First Edition. Teacher Created Materials. ISBN-10: 1433374307. ISBN-13: 9781433374302.

    eBook. Teacher Created Materials. 2013.

    Paperback Second Edition. Teacher Created Materials. 2013. ISBN-10: 1433349078. ISBN-13: 9781433349072.

Levete, Sarah. *Make an Animation!* Paperback First Edition. Arcturus Publishing. ISBN-10: 1848585748. ISBN-13: 9781848585744.

    Hardcover First Edition. Franklin Watts. 2012.
    ISBN-10: 1445110121. ISBN-13: 9781445110127.

Monnin, Katie. *Get Animated! Teaching 21st Century Early Readers and Young Adult Cartoons in Language Arts*. Paperback First Edition. Kendall Hunt Publishing. ISBN-10: 1465231978. ISBN-13: 9781465231970.

    Paperback Reprint. Kendall Hunt Publishing. 2021.
    ISBN-10: 1524927465. ISBN-13: 9781524927462.

Selby, Andrew. *Animation*. Paperback First Edition. Laurence King Publishing. ISBN-10: 1780670974. ISBN-13: 9781780670973.

    eBook. Laurence King Publishing. 2013.

2014

Allen, John. *Anime and Manga (Discovering Art)*. Hardcover First Edition. ReferencePoint Press. ISBN-10: 1601526962. ISBN-13: 9781601526960.

Bancroft, Tom. Hunter, Nick. *Animator: The Coolest Jobs on the Planet*. Hardcover First Edition. Raintree. ISBN-10: 1410966402. ISBN-13: 9781410966407.

>Paperback First Edition. Raintree. 2014. ISBN-10: 1410966461. ISBN-13: 9781410966469.

>eBook. Raintree. 2015.

Gregory, Josh. *Animation: From Concept to Consumer*. Hardcover First Edition. Children's Press. ISBN-10: 0531206130. ISBN-13: 9780531206133.

>Paperback First Edition. Children's Press. 2014. ISBN-10: 0531210723. ISBN-13: 9780531210727.

Scollon, Bill. *Walt Disney: Drawn from Imagination*. Hardcover First Edition. Disney Press. ISBN-10: 1423196473. ISBN-13: 9781423196471.

>Paperback First Edition. Disney Press. 2018. ISBN-10: 1368027571. ISBN-13: 9781368027571.

2015

Hammelef, Danielle S. *Eye-Popping CGI: Computer-Generated Special Effects*. Hardcover First Edition. Capstone Press. ISBN-10: 1491420014. ISBN-13: 9781491420010.

Hansen, Grace. *Walt Disney: Animator & Founder*. Paperback First Edition. Abdo Kids. 2015. ISBN-10: 1629707066. ISBN-13: 9781629707068.

>Hardcover First Edition. Capstone Classroom. 2017. ISBN-10: 1496612299. ISBN-13: 9781496612298.

2016

Blohm, Craig E. *Great Cartoonists (Collective Biographies)*. Hardcover First Edition. Referencepoint Press. ISBN-10: 1601529961. ISBN-13: 9781601529961.

2017

Bartolotta, Kenneth L. *Anime: Japanese Animation Comes to America*. Hardcover First Edition. Lucent Press. ISBN-10: 1534561021. ISBN-13: 9781534561021.

Dellaccio, Tanya. *Computer Animation: Telling Stories with Digital Art*. Hardcover First Edition. Lucent Press. ISBN-10: 1534560971. ISBN-13: 9781534560970.

Kramer, Barbara. N*ational Geographic Readers: Walt Disney*. Hardcover First Edition. National Geographic Kids. ISBN-10: 1426326742. ISBN-13: 9781426326745.

> Paperback First Edition. National Geographic Kids. 2017. ISBN-10: 1426326734. ISBN-13: 9781426326738.

> eBook. National Geographic Kids. 2017.

Hamalainen, Karina. *Animation*. Hardcover First Edition. Children's Press. ISBN-10: 0531235041. ISBN-13: 9780531235041.

> Paperback First Edition. Children's Press. 2017. ISBN-10: 0531241475. ISBN-13: 9780531241479.

2018

Centore, Michael. *Pixar, Disney, DreamWorks and Digital Animation*. Hardcover First Edition. Mason Crest Publishers. ISBN-10: 1422240576. ISBN-13: 9781422240571.

2019

Blohm, Craig E. Marcovitz, Hal. *The Art of Animation*. Hardcover First Edition. Referencepoint Press. ISBN-10: 1682825779. ISBN-13: 9781682825778.

Green, Sara. *Animation*. Hardcover First Edition. Bellwether Media. ISBN-10: 1644870428. ISBN-13: 9781644870426.

2020

Hinote Lanier, Wendy. *Making an Animated Movie (How It's Done)*. Hardcover First Edition. Focus Readers. ISBN-10: 1644930390. ISBN-13: 9781644930397.

>Paperback First Edition. Focus Readers. 2020. ISBN-10: 1644931184. ISBN-13: 9781644931189.

Jacobs, Brendan. *Explanatory Animations in the Classroom: Student-Authored Animations as Digital Pedagogy*. Paperback First Edition. Springer. ISBN-10: 9811535248. ISBN-13: 9789811535246.

>eBook. Springer. 2020.

Owen, Ruth. Willis, John. *CGI Artists*. Hardcover First Edition. Av2. ISBN-10: 1791121837. ISBN-13: 9781791121839.

>Paperback First Edition. Av2. 2020. ISBN-10: 1791121845. ISBN-13: 9781791121846.

2021

Otfinoski, Steven. *Tim Burton*. eBook. Chelsea House Publishers. ISBN-13: 9781646937752.

Storybooks

1994

Peet, Bill. *Bill Peet: An Autobiography*. Paperback First Edition. Houghton Mifflin Harcourt Books for Young Readers. ISBN-10: 0395689821. ISBN-13: 9780395689820.

> Hardcover First Edition. San Val. 1994.
> ISBN-10: 0780739671. ISBN-13: 9780780739673.

1997

Schroeder, Russell. *Mickey Mouse: My Life in Pictures*. Hardcover First Edition. Disney Press. ISBN-10: 0786850590. ISBN-13: 9780786850594.

> Hardcover First Edition. Disney Press. 1997.
> ISBN-10: 0786831502. ISBN-13: 9780786831500.

2014

LaReau, Kara. *No Slurping, No Burping! A Tale of Table Manners: Walt Disney Animation Studios Artist Showcase Book*. Hardcover First Edition. Disney-Hyperion. ISBN-10: 1423157338. ISBN-13: 9781423157335.

> eBook. Disney Publishing. 2015.

Pilcher, Steve. *Over There: Pixar Animation Studios Artist Showcase Book*. Hardcover First Edition. Disney Press. ISBN-10: 1423147936. ISBN-13: 9781423147930.

> eBook. Disney Press. 2014.

2015

Becker, Bonny. Klocek, Noah. *Cloud Country: Pixar Animation Studios Artist Showcase*. Hardcover First Edition. Disney Press. ISBN-10: 142315732X. ISBN-13: 9781423157328.

> eBook. Disney Press. 2015.

2017

Briggs, Paul. *Catch My Breath: Walt Disney Animation Studios Artist Showcase*. Hardcover First Edition. Disney-Hyperion. ISBN-10: 1484728378. ISBN-13: 9781484728376.

    eBook. Disney-Hyperion. 2017.

Guglielmo, Amy. Tourville, Jacqueline. *Pocket Full of Colors: The Magical World of Mary Blair, Disney Artist Extraordinaire*. Hardcover First Edition. Atheneum Books for Young Readers. ISBN-10: 1481461311. ISBN-13: 9781481461313.

    eBook. Atheneum Books for Young Readers. 2017.

Rubiano, Brittany. Sherman, Richard. *A Kiss Goodnight*. Hardcover First Edition. Disney Editions. ISBN-10: 1484782283. ISBN-13: 9781484782286.

    eBook. Disney Editions. 2020.

Shum, Benson. *Holly's Day at the Pool: Walt Disney Animation Studios Artist Showcase*. Hardcover First Edition. Disney-Hyperion. ISBN-10: 1484709381. ISBN-13: 9781484709382.

    eBook. Disney-Hyperion. 2017.

2018

Hartline, Aaron. *Box Meets Circle: Pixar Animation Studios Artist Showcase*. Hardcover First Edition. Disney Press. ISBN-10: 1368015875. ISBN-13: 9781368015875.

    eBook. Disney Press. 2018.

Wu, Mike. *Henri's Hats: Pixar Animation Studios Artist Showcase*. Hardcover First Edition. Disney Press. ISBN-10: 1484709039. ISBN-13: 9781484709030.

    eBook. Disney Press. 2018.

<u>2019</u>

Johnson, Mindy. *Pencils, Pens & Brushes: A Great Girls' Guide to Disney Animation*. Hardcover First Edition. Disney Press. ISBN-10: 1368028683. ISBN-13: 9781368028684.

    eBook. Disney Press. 2019.

Novesky, Amy. *Mary Blair's Unique Flair: The Girl Who Became One of the Disney Legends*. Hardcover First Edition. Disney Press. ISBN-10: 1484757203. ISBN-13: 9781484757208.

    eBook. Disney Press. 2019.

Sastrawinata-Lemay, Griselda. *Blue Spot: Walt Disney Animation Studios Artist Showcase*. Hardcover First Edition. Disney Press. ISBN-10: 1368024599. ISBN-13: 9781368024594.

    eBook. Disney Press. 2019.

Sullivan, Rosana. *Mommy Sayang: Pixar Animation Studios Artist Showcase*. Hardcover First Edition. Disney Press. ISBN-10: 1368015905. ISBN-13: 9781368015905.

    eBook. Disney Press. 2019.

<u>2020</u>

Radivoeva, Svetla. *Malina's Jam: Walt Disney Animation Studios Artist Showcase*. Hardcover First Edition. Disney Press. ISBN-10: 1368024580. ISBN-13: 9781368024587.

    eBook. Disney Press. 2020.

<u>2021</u>

Sussman, Elissa. *Drawn That Way*. Hardcover First Edition. Simon & Schuster Books for Young Readers. ISBN-10: 1534492976. ISBN-13: 9781534492974.

    eBook. Simon & Schuster Books for Young Readers. 2021.

Paperback First Edition. Simon & Schuster for Young Readers. 2022. ISBN-10: 1534492984. ISBN-13: 9781534492981.

Kaiser, Lisbeth. *Who Was Walt Disney?: A Who Was? Board Book*. Board Book First Edition. Rise x Penguin Workshop. ISBN-10: 0593223608. ISBN-13: 9780593223604.

eBook. Rise x Penguin Workshop. 2021.

2022

Robinson, Fiona. *Out of the Shadows: How Lotte Reiniger Made the First Animated Fairytale Movie*. Hardcover First Edition. Harry N. Abrams. ISBN-10: 1419740857. ISBN-13: 9781419740855.

eBook. Abrams Books for Young Readers. 2022.

Audiobook. Narrated by Natasha Soudek.
Dreamscape Media, LLC. 2022.

Audio CD. Dreamscape Media, LLC. 2022.

Comic Books & Manga

Ban, Toshio. Tezuka Productions. *The Osamu Tezuka Story: A Life in Manga and Anime*. Paperback First Edition. Stone Bridge Press. 2016. ISBN-10: 1611720257. ISBN-13: 9781611720259.

Delisle, Guy. *Pyongyang: A Journey in North Korea*. Hardcover First Edition. Drawn and Quarterly. 2005. ISBN-10: 1896597890. ISBN-13: 9781896597898.

> Paperback First Edition. Drawn and Quarterly. 2007. ISBN-10: 1897299214. ISBN-13: 9781897299210.

> eBook. Random House. 2017.

> Paperback Second Edition. Drawn and Quarterly. 2018. ISBN-10: 1770463372. ISBN-13: 9781770463370.

Dunlavey, Ryan. Van Lente, Fred. *"Silent...But Deadly."* Comic Books History of Animation. Volume 1, Issue 1. One Variant. IDW Publishing. 2020.

> eBook. IDW. 2020.

Dunlavey, Ryan. Van Lente, Fred. *"Looney Studios!"* Comic Books History of Animation. Volume 1, Issue 2. One Variant. IDW Publishing. 2020.

> eBook. IDW. 2020.

Dunlavey, Ryan. Van Lente, Fred. *"Cartoon Cool."* Comic Books History of Animation. Volume 1, Issue 3. One Variant. IDW Publishing. 2021.

> eBook. IDW. 2021.

Dunlavey, Ryan. Van Lente, Fred. *"Saturday Morning Funhouse."* Comic Books History of Animation. Volume 1, Issue 4. One Variant. IDW Publishing. 2021.

> eBook. IDW. 2021.

Dunlavey, Ryan. Van Lente, Fred. *"Anime Conquers the World!"* Comic Books History of Animation. Volume 1, Issue 5. One Variant. IDW Publishing. 2021.

    eBook. IDW. 2021.

Dunlavey, Ryan. Van Lente, Fred. *The Comic Book History of Animation: True Toon Tales of the Most Iconic Characters, Artists and Styles!* Trade Paperback First Edition. Idea & Design Works. 2021. ISBN-10: 1684058295. ISBN-13: 9781684058297.

Findlay, Kurtis. Mulaney, Dean. *Chuck Jones: The Dream that Never Was*. Hardcover First Edition. IDW Publishing. 2011. ISBN-10: 1613770308. ISBN-13: 9781613770306.

Floyd, Norman. *Disk Drive: Animated Humor in the Digital Age*. Paperback First Edition. Blurb Self Publishing. 2010.

Hoena, Blake. McClintock Miller, Shannon. *A Stop-Motion Animation Mission*. Hardcover First Edition. Capstone Press. 2019. ISBN-10: 1496579518. ISBN-13: 9781496579515.

    Paperback First Edition. Capstone Press. 2019. ISBN-10: 1496579550. ISBN-13: 978-1496579553.

    eBook. Stone Arch Books. 2020.

Merkel, Ulrich. *Dreams of the Rarebit Fiend*. Hardcover First Edition. Fantagraphics Books. 2007. ISBN-10: 3000207511. ISBN-13: 9783000207518.

"Bubblegum Crisis." Settei: The Anime Reference Guide. Volume 1, Issue 1. Antarctic Press. 1993.

"Gundam 0080: War in the Pocket." Settei: The Anime Reference Guide. Volume 1, Issue 2. Antarctic Press. 1993.

"Project A-Ko." Settei Super Special. Volume 1, Issue 1. Antarctic Press. 1994.

Norman, Floyd. *How The Grinch Stole Disney*. Paperback First Edition. Leo Sullivan Multimedia. 2005. ISBN-10: 1881368386. ISBN-13: 9781881368380.

    Paperback First Edition. Lancer Creative Services. 2020. ISBN-10: 173523480X. ISBN-13: 9781735234809.

Norman, Floyd. *Suspended Animation: The Art Form That Refuses To Die*. Paperback First Edition. Blurb Self Publishing. 2012.

Norman, Floyd. *Faster! Cheaper!: The Flip Side to the Art of Animation*. Paperback First Edition. Get Animated. 1992. ISBN-10: 094290902X. ISBN-13: 9780942909029.

    Paperback First Edition. Lancer Creative Services. 2020. ISBN-10: 1735234818. ISBN-13: 9781735234816.

Nourigat, Natalie. *I Moved to Los Angeles to Work in Animation*. eBook. BOOM! Box. 2018.

    Paperback First Edition. BOOM! Box. 2019. ISBN-10: 1684152917. ISBN-13: 9781684152919.

Periodicals

Western Animation

1959

Gutterman, Leon. *"Walt Disney."* Wisdom: The Magazine of Knowledge for Lifetime Learning and Education. December, 1959.

1963

Grosvenor, Gilbert Melville. *National Geographic*. Volume 124, Number 2. August, 1963.

1966

Barrier, Michael. *Funnyworld*. 16 Issues. 1966-1975. ISSN: 0071-9943.

    Lilien, Mark. *Funnyworld*. Six Issues.

1975

ASIFA. *AnimaFilm*.

    ASIFA Magazine. 31 Volumes. 1975-Present.

Corliss, Richard. "*The Hollywood Cartoon*." Film Comment. January-February, 1975.

1976

Mruz, David. *Mindrot*. 19 Issues. 1976-1981. Note: Magazine changes name to *Animania* (1981).

1977

Computer Graphics World. Eight Issues. 1977-Present.

1981

Mruz, David. *Animania*. Eight Issues. 1981-1983.

Markstein, Don. Dane, Gigi. *Apatoons*. 150 Issues. 1981-2008?

1983

Ventrella, Michael A. *Animato!* 40 Issues. 1983-1999.

Hartt, Reg. *Animazine*. 1983-1985.

Walt Disney Productions. *Disney Channel Magazine*. 106 Issues. 1983-1997.

1984

Cawley, John. *Get Animated*. Seven Issues. 1984-1998.

1986

Thoren, Terry. *Animation News*. Five Issues. 1986-1988.

Van Hise. James. *Cartoon File Magazine Spotlight On The Jonny Quest Files*. One Issue. Psi Fi Movie Press. ISBN-10: 0809580853. ISBN-13: 9780809580859.

1987

Jefferson, David. *Animator Magazine*. 33 Issues. 1987-1995.

Thoren, Terry. *Animation Magazine*. 308 Issues as of March 2021. 1987-Present.

> Animation Magazine. *Animation Magazine: 20-Year Collection*. Hardcover First Edition. Animation Magazine. 2007. ISBN-10: 1424338514. ISBN-13: 9781424338511.

1990

The Walt Disney Company. *The Storyboard: The Art of Laughter: The Journal of Animation Art*. 22 Issues. 1990-1995.

1990

In Toon: The Magazine of Animation Art Collecting. 18 Issues. 1991-1996.

1991

Townsend, Emru. *FPS Magazine*. 1992-2010.

1992

Anderson, Paul F. *Persistence of Vision*. 46 Issues. Est. 1992.

1993

Gore, Chris. *Wild Cartoon Kingdom*. Larry Flynt Publications. Five Issues. 1993-1994.

Swanigan, Michael. *TOON Magazine*. Three Volumes, Two Issues. Est. 1993.

1997

Animation World Network. *Animation World Magazine*. eMagazine. 1996-Present.

1997

Dobbs, G. Michael. *Animation Planet*. Three Issues. 1997-1998.

1998

Animated Life. Two Issues. Est. 1998.

2000

Bluth, Don. *Don Bluth's Toon Talk*. At least eight Issues. 2000-2001.

Graves, Wayne. *MavCore 3D Animation Magazine*. Four Issues. 2016-2017.

2018

Animation Guild. *Keyframe Animation Magazine*. Ten Issues. 2018- Present.

Anime

1986

Fenelon, Robert. *Anime-zine*. Three Issues. 1986-1988.

1987

Anacleto, Matthew. Fong, Dana. Schubert, Ann. *Animag: The Magazine of Japanese Animation*. 15 Issues. 1987-1993.

Dubreuil, Alain. Gareau, Michel. Pelletier, Claude J. *Protoculture Addicts*. 103 Issues. 1987-2008.

1990

Thompson, Jeff. *Animenominous!* Five Issues. 1990-1993.

1991

Anacleto, Matthew. *V.Max*. 17 Issues. 1991-1996.

IANVS Publication. *Mecha Press*. 18 Issues. 1991-1995.

Goll, Peter. Kyte, Steve. McCarthy, Helen. Overton, Wil. *Anime UK*.

Tatsugawa, Mike. *The Anime Reference Guide*. Four Issues. 1991-1995.

1992

VIZ Media. *Animerica*. 162 Issues. 1992-2005.

Karahashi, Takayuki. *Anime Interviews: The First Five Years of Animerica, Anime & Manga Monthly*. Paperback First Edition. VIZ Media LLC. ISBN-10: 1569312206. ISBN-13: 9781569312209.

Viz Media. *The Best Of Animerica: 2003 Edition*. Paperback First Edition. VIZ Media LLC. 2004. ISBN-10: 1569318999. ISBN-13: 9781569318997.

> Hardcover First Edition. San Val. ISBN-10: 0613790448. ISBN-13: 9780613790444.

1995

Japanese Animation Society of Hawai'i. *Animeco*. 10 Issues. 1995-1998.

1997

Scovil Jr., Ronald. *Mixx Zine*. 12 Issues. 1997-1999.

1999

Persons, Dan. *Animefantastique!* 4 Issues. 1999. ISSN: 1521-7205

Beckett Anime. 1999-2007.

2001

Wizard Entertainment. *Anime Insider*. 68 Issues. 2001-2009.

2002

A.D. Vision. *Newtype USA*. 65 Issues. 2002-2008.

2004

Taylor, Stu. Trent, Claire. *NEO*. 2004-Present.

2007

Macias, Patrick. *Otaku USA*. 2007-Present.

2008

Gifford, Kevin. *PiQ*. Four Issues. 2008. ISSN: 1941-0522.

2015

Luster, Joseph. *Anime USA*. 11 Issues. 2015-Spring 2020. ISSN: 1939-3318.

Academic Journals

1991

Tatsugawa, Mike. *ä-ni-mé: The Berkeley Journal of Japanese Animation.* One Volume, Two Issues. 1991.

2006

Bolton, Christopher. Lamarre, Thomas. Lunning, Frenchy. *Mechademia: An Annual Forum for Anime, Manga, and the Fan Arts.* 13 Volumes, 15 Issues. 2006-Present. ISSN: 1934-2489.

Lunning, Frenchy. *Mechademia 1: Emerging Worlds of Anime and Manga.* Paperback First Edition. University of Minnesota Press. 2006. ISBN-10: 0816649456. ISBN-13: 9780816649457.

    eBook. University of Minnesota Press. 2006.

Lunning, Frenchy. *Mechademia 2: Networks of Desire.* Paperback First Edition. University of Minnesota Press. 2007. ISBN-10: 081665266X. ISBN-13: 9780816652662.

    eBook. University of Minnesota Press. 2007.

Lunning, Frenchy. *Mechademia 3: Limits of the Human.* Paperback First Edition. University of Minnesota Press. 2008. ISBN-10: 0816654824. ISBN-13: 9780816654826.

    eBook. University of Minnesota Press. 2008.

Lunning, Frenchy. *Mechademia 4: War/Time.* Paperback First Edition. University of Minnesota Press. 2009. ISBN-10: 0816667497. ISBN-13: 9780816667499.

    eBook. University of Minnesota Press. 2009.

Lunning, Frenchy. *Mechademia 5: Fanthropologies*. Paperback First Edition. University of Minnesota Press. 2010. ISBN-10: 081667387X. ISBN-13: 9780816673872.

    eBook. University of Minnesota Press. 2010.

Lunning, Frenchy. *Mechademia 6: User Enhanced*. Paperback First Edition. University of Minnesota Press. 2011. ISBN-10: 0816677344. ISBN-13: 9780816677344.

    eBook. University of Minnesota Press. 2011.

Lunning, Frenchy. *Mechademia 7: Lines of Sight*. Paperback First Edition. University of Minnesota Press. 2012. ISBN-10: 0816680493. ISBN-13: 9780816680498.

    eBook. University of Minnesota Press. 2012.

Lunning, Frenchy. *Mechademia 8: Tezuka's Manga Life*. Paperback First Edition. University of Minnesota Press. 2013. ISBN-10: 0816689555. ISBN-13: 9780816689552.

    eBook. University of Minnesota Press. 2013.

Lunning, Frenchy. *Mechademia 9: Origins*. Paperback First Edition. University of Minnesota Press. 2014. ISBN-10: 0816695350. ISBN-13: 9780816695355.

    eBook. University of Minnesota Press. 2014.

Lunning, Frenchy. *Mechademia 10: World Renewal*. Paperback First Edition. University of Minnesota Press. 2015. ISBN-10: 0816699151. ISBN-13: 9780816699155.

    eBook. University of Minnesota Press. 2015.

Annett, Sandra. Lunning, Frenchy. *Mechademia 11.1: Second Arc*. Paperback First Edition. University Of Minnesota Press. 2019. ISBN-10: 1517906350. ISBN-13: 9781517906351.

Annett, Sandra. Lunning, Frenchy. *Mechademia 12.1: Second Arc*. Paperback First Edition. University of Minnesota. 2020. ISBN-10: 1517908426. ISBN-13: 9781517908423.

Annett, Sandra. Lunning, Frenchy. *Mechademia 12.2: Second Arc*. Paperback First Edition. University of Minnesota. 2020. ISBN-10: 1517908434. ISBN-13: 9781517908430.

Annett, Sandra. Lunning, Frenchy. *Mechademia 13.1: Second Arc*. Paperback First Edition. University of Minnesota. 2020. ISBN-10: 1517911303. ISBN-13: 9781517912048.

Annett, Sandra. Lunning, Frenchy. *Mechademia 13.2: Second Arc*. Paperback First Edition. University of Minnesota. 2021. ISBN-10: 1517912040. ISBN-13: 9781517912048.

Furniss, Maureen. *Animation: An Interdisciplinary Journal*. 45 Issues. 2006-Present. ISSN: 1930-1928.

<u>2020</u>

Institute of Electrical and Electronics Engineers. *Computer Animation*. 1987-Present. ISSN: 1087-4844.

Tringaliz, Billy. *Journal of Anime and Manga Studies*. One Issue. 2020-Present. ISSN: 2689-2596.

<u>2021</u>

Serrazina, Pedro. Woolf, Natalie. *International Journal of Film and Media Arts*. Vol. 6 No. 2, "Animated Space: Engaged animation for the space(s) we live in".

>   Available online at:
>   https://revistas.ulusofona.pt/index.php/ijfma/issue/view/804

Serrazina, Pedro. *The International Journal of Film and Media Arts*. Vol. 6 No. 3, "Ecstatic Truth V, The Age of the Absurd - Documentary animation practices that reimagine our world."

Documentaries

1919

How Animated Cartoons are Made - Produced by Bray Studios and starring animation pioneer Wallace Carlson.

1937

A Trip Through the Walt Disney Studios - Produced as an in-house documentary for RKO Radio Pictures and later recut and re-released in 1939 as *How Walt Disney Cartoons Are Made*. Available on the 2001 DVD release of *Snow White and the Seven Dwarfs* and the 2002 *Walt Disney Treasure: Behind the Scenes at the Walt Disney Studio* DVD.

1941

The Reluctant Dragon - Directed by Walt Disney. Available on the *Walt Disney Treasure: Behind the Scenes at the Walt Disney Studio* DVD as well as on the Blu-ray double feature, *The Adventures of Ichabod* and *Mr. Toad/Fun and Fancy Free*.

1963

A Boy Named Charlie Brown - Directed by Lee Mendelson. Produced by The Coca-Cola Company. Currently Unavailable.

1970

The Art of Lotte Reiniger - Directed by John Isaacs. Available on 16mm Film and Streaming.

1975

Bugs Bunny Superstar - Directed by Larry Jackson. Available through streaming, on DVD as a standalone feature and in the *Looney Tunes Golden Collection: Volume 4*, and as a standalone VHS tape.

Camera Three - Season 21- Episode 2 and 3 - "*The Boys of Termite Terrace*" - Television Docuseries. Originally aired on CBS and PBS. Currently unavailable, though, raw interviews available at request from: http://www.catarchive.com/index.html.

1976

Remembering Winsor McCay - Directed by John Canemaker. Available as a Bonus Feature on the DVD, *Winsor McCay: The Master Edition*.

1977

Otto Messmer and Felix the Cat - Directed and Written by John Canemaker. Available on the 2002 DVD, *John Canemaker: Marching to a Different Toon*.

1978

Claymation: Three Dimensional Clay Animation - Directed by Will Vinton. Currently Unavailable.

1981

Once Upon a Mouse - Directed by Jerry Kramer and Gary Rocklen. Currently Unavailable.

1982

The Animators - Directed by Prescott Wright. PBS documentary. Currently Unavailable.

1984

Disney Family Album (1984-1986) - Twenty episode docuseries directed by Mike Bonifer and Larry Smoot. Currently Unavailable.

1985

The Fantasy Film Worlds of George Pal - Directed by Arnold Leibovit. Available on DVD.

1986

Computer Animation Magic - Directed by Geoffrey de Valois. Available on VHS.

Masters of Animation - Directed by John Halas. Docuseries released on three volumes on VHS.

1988

Animating Art - Directed by Imogen Sutton. Currently Unavailable.

Roger Rabbit and the Secrets of Toontown - Directed by Les Mayfield. Currently Unavailable.

Tex Avery, King of Cartoons - Directed by John Needham. Currently Unavailable.

1989

Cartoons for Big Kids - Directed by Leonard Maltin. Available on VHS.

Hanna-Barbera's 50th: A Yabba Dabba Doo Celebration - Directed by Marshall Flaum. Currently Unavailable.

1990

You Don't Look 40, Charlie Brown - Directed by Lee Mendelson. Currently Unavailable.

1991

Chuck Amuck: The Movie - Directed by Chuck Jones and John Needham. Available as a stand alone feature on VHS and as a Bonus Feature on *The Looney Tunes Golden Collection: Volume Three* (DVD) and *Looney Tunes Platinum Collection: Volume One* (Blu-ray).

Of Moose and Men: The Rocky & Bullwinkle Story - Directed by Marino Amoruso. Currently Unavailable.

1995

Biography - "Betty Boop: The Queen of Cartoons" - Created for A&E. Available on DVD.

Frank and Ollie - Directed by Theodore Thomas. Available on VHS and DVD.

1997

The Harryhausen Chronicles - Directed by Richard Schickle. Available as a standalone title or as a Bonus Feature on the DVD for *Jason and the Argonauts and Mysterious Island*.

1999

The Hand Behind the Mouse: The Ub Iwerks Story - Directed by Leslie Iwerks. Available on VHS and as a Bonus Feature on Disc Two of *The Adventures of Oswald the Lucky Rabbit* DVD, a part of the *Walt Disney Treasures* line.

2000

Cartoons Kick Ass - Directed by Stephen Lennhoff. Currently unavailable.

Chuck Jones Extremes and In-Betweens – A Life in Animation - Directed by Margaret Selby. Available on VHS and DVD.

My Wasted Life - Directed by Selina Mehta. Currently Unavailable.

2001

Disney's 'Snow White and the Seven Dwarfs': Still the Fairest One of All - Directed by Harry Arends. Available on DVD as a Bonus Feature to Platinum Edition of *Snow White and the Seven Dwarfs*.

Lotte Reiniger: Homage to the Inventor of Silhouette Film - Directed by Katja Raganelli. Available on VHS, DVD, and Blu-ray as a Bonus Feature on *The Adventures of Prince Achmed*.

Walt: The Man Behind the Myth - Directed by Jean-Pierre Isbouts. Available on VHS and DVD.

2002

The Sweatbox - Directed by Trudie Styler and John-Paul Davidson. Available on the DVD of *The Emperor's New Groove* as a Bonus Feature.

2003

The Animated Century - Directed by Irina Margolina and Adam Snyder. Available to libraries and schools for rental from Rembrandt Films or The Fremantle Corporation.

Anime - Concept to Reality - Directed by Terrence Walker. Available on DVD.

Imagine - From Pencils To Pixels - BBC Special. Currently Unavailable.

Pink Panther - Behind the Feline: The Cartoon Phenomenon - Directed by John Cork. Available on *The Pink Panther Film Collection* on DVD, T*he Pink Panther Classic Cartoon Collection* on DVD and *The Pink Panther Classic Cartoon Collection* on Blu-ray.

2004

Monster Road - Directed by Brett Ingram. Available on DVD.

2005

An Animated Life: The Phil Roman Story - Directed by Kenny Saylors and Kyle Saylors. Currently Unavailable.

Bambi: Inside Walt's Story Meetings - Available on the Diamond Edition of *Bambi* DVD/Blu-ray as a Bonus feature.

Dream On Silly Dreamer - Directed by Dan Lund. Available on DVD and streaming.

"Once an Ed...Always an Ed... " - Available as an unlockable Bonus Feature on the 2005 video game, *Ed, Edd, N' Eddy: The Mis-Edventures* (GameCube, PS2).

Fine Tooning: Restoring the Warner Bros. Cartoons - Created for and featured as a Bonus Feature on the *Looney Tunes Golden Collection: Volume 3* DVD set.

Taint of Greatness: The Journey of Beavis and Butt-Head - Produced by Jon Mefford. Split into three parts over the three volumes of *Beavis and Butt-Head: The Mike Judge Collection* on DVD and Blu-ray.

2006

Gumby Dharma - Directed by Robina Marchesi for KQED. Available through Streaming.

Modern Marvels - "Walt Disney World" - Written by Bruce Nash. Available on Streaming and DVD.

2007

Anime: Drawing the Revolution - Directed by Karen Somers. Currently unavailable.

Forging the Frame: The Roots of Animation 1900-1920 - Produced by Greg Ford and Mark Nassief. Available on the *Popeye the Sailor: 1933–1938, Volume 1* DVD set.

Hanna-Barbera: From H to B - Available on the *Scooby-Doo, Where Are You! The Complete Third Season* DVD set as well as *The Scooby-Doo, Where Are You! Complete Series* on DVD and Blu-ray.

I Yam What I Yam: The Story of Popeye the Sailor - Directed by Costantine Nasr and Mark Nassief. Available on the *Popeye: Volume One* collection on DVD as a Bonus Feature.

In Search of Moebius: Jean Giraud - Directed by Hasko Baumann. Currently unavailable.

The Pixar Story - Directed by Leslie Iwerks. Available through Streaming and on the *Wall*e* DVD and Blu-ray Releases as a Special Feature.

Quirino Cristiani: The Mystery of the First Animated Movies - Directed by Gabriele Zucchelli. Available on DVD.

2008

Directing the Sailor: The Art of Myron Waldman - Available on the *Popeye the Sailor: 1941–1943, Volume 3* DVD set.

Drawn for Glory: Animation's Triumph at the Oscars - Produced by Constantine Nasr. Available on the *Warner Brothers Home Entertainment Academy Awards Animation Collection* on DVD.

Forging the Frame: The Roots of Animation, 1921-1930 - Produced by Greg Ford and Mark Nassief. Available on the *Popeye the Sailor: 1941–1943, Volume 3* DVD set.

Drawn for Glory: Animation's Triumph at the Oscars - Directed by Constantine Nasr. Available on the DVD, *Warner Brothers Home Entertainment Academy Awards Animation Collection - 15 Winners, 26 Nominees*, as a Bonus Feature.

Mel Blanc: The Man of a Thousand Voices - Directed by Constantine Nasr. Available on Disc Four of the *Looney Tunes Golden Collection: Volume Six* as a Bonus Feature.

Out of the Inkwell: The Fleischer Story - Produced by Constantine Nasr and Mark Nassief. Available on Disc One of the *Popeye The Sailor 1938-1940, Volume Two* DVD set.

Walt and El Grupo - Directed by Theodore Thomas. Available through Streaming.

2009

The Boys: The Sherman Brothers' Story - Directed by Jeffrey Sherman and Gregory Sherman. Available on DVD and Streaming.

Chuck Jones: Memories of a Childhood - Directed by Peggy Stern. Available on *The Looney Tunes Platinum Collection Volume One* Blu-ray collection as a Bonus Feature.

The Great Jonny Quest Documentary - Uncredited. Available through Streaming.

Inside The Wrong Trousers - A Wallace and Gromit Mini Documentary. Produced by Aardman Animations. Available as a special feature on the Wallace & Gromit: The Complete Collection DVD and Blu-ray set.

Square Roots: The Story of SpongeBob SquarePants - Directed by Patrick Creadon. Available on the DVD collection *SpongeBob: The First 100 Episodes* and *SpongeBob: The First 200 Episodes* as a Bonus Feature.

Waking Sleeping Beauty - Directed by Don Hahn. Available on DVD, Blu-ray and Streaming.

2010

Avatar Spirits - Directed by Kurt Mattila. Available on the *Avatar: The Last Airbender Book One Collector's Edition* as a Bonus Feature.

Breaking the Mold: The Re-Making of Mighty Mouse - Directed by Jeffrey Eagle. Currently Unavailable.

Deconstructing Dad - Directed by Stan Warnow. Available on DVD and Streaming.

2011

Adventures of Plymptoons! - Directed by Alexia Anastasio. Available on DVD and through Streaming.

Making 'Em Move - Directed by Steve Stanchfield. Available on DVD.

Six Days to Air - Directed by Arthur Bradford. Available through Streaming.

2012

Blinky & Me - Directed by Tomasz Magierski. Available on DVD.

Leon Schlesinger: The Merrie Cartoon Mogul - Available on *The Looney Tunes Platinum Collection: Volume 2* DVD and Blu-ray.

Persistence of Vision - Directed by Kevin Schreck. Available on DVD.

Seoul Sessions: Tales of a Black Animator in South Korea - Five episode web series directed by LeSean Thomas. Available through Streaming.

2013

I Know That Voice - Directed by Lawrence Sapiro. Available on DVD and through Streaming.

Inside Pixar - Directed by Alex Dean. Available through Streaming.

The Kingdom of Dreams and Madness - Directed by Mami Sunada. Available on DVD, Blu-ray, and Streaming.

2014

Magic Nose Monkeys; The Ren & Stimpy Story - Directed by John Smith. Currently Unavailable.

The Story of Frozen: Making a Disney Animated Classic - Directed by Rudy Bednar. Available through Streaming.

Turtle Power: The Definitive History of the Teenage Mutant Ninja Turtles - Directed by Randall Lobb. Available on DVD and Streaming.

2015

A Grand Night In: The Story of Aardman - Directed by Richard Mears. Available through Streaming.

American Experience - "Walt Disney" - Directed by Sarah Colt. Available on DVD and Streaming.

Where No One Goes: The Making of How to Train Your Dragon 2 - Available on the *How to Train Your Dragon 2* DVD and Blu-ray as a Bonus Feature.

2016

Bricks in Motion - Directed by Philip Heinrich. Available on DVD, Blu-ray, and Streaming.

Floyd Norman: An Animated Life - Directed by Michael Fiore and Erik Shakey. Available on DVD and Blu-ray.

The Giant's Dream - Directed by Anthony Giacchino. Available on the Signature Edition of *The Iron Giant* on Blu-ray as a Bonus Feature.

Imagining Zootopia - Directed by Natalie Osma and Kristopher Rios. Available through Streaming.

<u>2017</u>

American Masters: Tyrus - Season 31, Episode 7. Available on DVD and Streaming.

Hanna-Barbera: The Architects of Saturday Morning - Produced by Jesse Kowalski. Streaming on the Norman Rockwell Museum YouTube channel.

Voice of the Island - Available on the *Moana* Blu-ray as a Bonus Feature.

<u>2018</u>

Carl Bell - A life in Animation – Available through streaming.

Secrets of British Animation - Directed by Sebastion Barfield. Currently Unavailable.

Heart of Batman - Directed by Alexander Gray. Available on the Blu-ray collection of *Batman: The Animated Series* and Streaming.

Howard - Directed by Don Hahn. Available through Streaming.

The Animagic World of Rankin/Bass: Making Rudolph the Red-Nosed Reindeer and other Holiday Classics - Directed by Constantine Nasr. Available on *The Original Christmas Specials Collection* Blu-ray.

<u>2019</u>

Animation Outlaws - Directed by Kat Alioshin. Available on DVD, Blu-ray, and Streaming.

Enter the Anime - Directed by Alex Burunova. Available through Streaming.

Hayao Miyazaki: 10 Years with the Master - Directed by Kaku Arakawa. Available through Streaming.

Never-Ending Man: Hayao Miyazaki - Directed by Kaku Arakawa. Available on Blu-ray.

The Power of Grayskull: The Definitive History of He-Man and the Masters of the Universe - Directed by Randall Lobb and Robert McCallum. Available through Streaming.

<u>2020</u>

Hand Drawn - Directed by Felicity Morland. Available through Streaming and Blu-ray.

Happy, Happy, Joy, Joy: The Ren and Stimpy Story - Directed by Ron Cicero and Kime Easterwood. Available on DVD, Blu-ray and Streaming.

Inside Pixar - Directed by Tony Kaplan and Erica Milsom. Episodic docuseries. Available through Streaming.

Into the Unknown: Making Frozen II - Directed by Megan Harding. Available through Streaming.

The Orange Years: The Nickelodeon Story - Directed by Scott Barber and Adam Sweeney. Available through DVD, Blu-ray and Streaming.

<u>2021</u>

Cartoon Carnival: The Documentary - Produced by Andrew T. Smith. Available on the DVD and Blu-ray.

Le Mystère Méliès - Directed by Eric Lange. Available through streaming.

Who Are You, Charlie Brown? - Directed by Michael Bonfiglio. Available through streaming.

<u>2022</u>

ClayDream - Directed by Marq Evans. Currently showing at festivals.

The American Dream and Other Fairy Tales - Directed by Abigail E. Disney and Kathleen Hughes. Currently showing at festivals.

Sketchbook – Directed by Jason Sterman. Available through streaming.

Index

Aardman Animation

2011 - The Art & Making of Arthur Christmas: An Inside Look at Behind-the-Scenes Artwork with Filmmaker Commentary - Pg. 177 (*Also see Sony Pictures Animation, Inc.*)
2017 - The Art of Aardman: The Makers of Wallace & Gromit, Chicken Run, and More - Pg. 177

Abele, Robert

2013 - The Art of DreamWorks Turbo - Pg. 158

Abraham, Adam.

2012 - When Magoo Flew: The Rise and Fall of Animation Studio UPA - Pg. 92

Adams, T.R.

1991 - Tom & Jerry: Fifty Years of Cat and Mouse - Pg. 92
1994 - The Flintstones: A Modern Stone Age Phenomenon - Pg. 92

Adamson, Joe

1975 - Tex Avery, King of Cartoons - Pg. 79
1985 - The Walter Lantz Story - Pg. 79
1990 - Bugs Bunny: Fifty Years and Only One Grey Hare - Pg. 165

Adler, Arthur C. "Buddy"

2014 - Walt Disney's Garage of Dreams - Pg. 108

Akakce, Haluk

2003 - Animations - Pg. 39 (*Also see Alys, Francis. Bendazzi, Giannalberto. Blake, Jeremy. Canemaker, John. Christov-Bakargiev, Carolyn. Galbraith, David. Gillick, Liam. Harries, Larissa. Klein, Norman. Marks, Melissa. Riegel, Karyn.*)

Alaskey, Joe

2009 - That's Still Not All Folks! - Pg. 79

Alger, Jed

2012 - The Art and Making of ParaNorman - Pg. 179

Allan, Robin

1999 - Walt Disney and Europe: European Influences on the Animated Feature Films of Walt Disney - Pg. 126
2016 - The Walt Disney Film Archives: The Animated Movies 1921-1968 - Pg. 126
(*Also see Ghez, Didier. Kaufman, J. B. Kothenschulte, Daniel. Lasseter, John. Lüthge, Katja. Merritt, Russell. Sibley, Brian. Solomon, Charles.*)

Allen, John

2014 - Anime and Manga (Discovering Art) - Pg. 232

Alley, Maria

2008 - Animation for Russian Conversation - Pg. 220 (*Also see Merrill, Jason. Mikhailova, Julia.*)

Allison, Anne

2006 - Millennial Monsters: Japanese Toys and the Global Imagination - Pg. 185

Aloff, Mindy

2009 - Hippo in a Tutu: Dancing in Disney Animation - Pg. 126

Altman, Rick

1992 - Sound Theory, Sound Practice - Pg. 73

Alys, Francis

2003 - Animations - Pg. 39 (*Also see Akakce, Haluk. Bendazzi, Giannalberto. Blake, Jeremy. Canemaker, John. Christov-Bakargiev, Carolyn. Galbraith, David. Gillick, Liam. Harries, Larissa. Klein, Norman. Marks, Melissa. Riegel, Karyn.*)

Amidi, Amid

2004 - The Art of Robots - Pg. 176
2006 - Cartoon Modern: Style and Design in Fifties Animation - Pg. 56
2009 - The Art of Pixar Short Films - Pg. 154
2011 - The Art of Pixar: 25th Anniversary: The Complete Color Scripts and Select Art from 25 Years of Animation - Pg. 154

Amos, Janine

1989 - Animation- Pg. 222 (*Also see Lane, Kim.*)

Anderson, Paul

2017 - Jack of All Trades: Conversations with Disney Legend Ken Anderson - Pg. 114
2020 - Sharing a House with the Never Ending Man - Pg. 192

Anderson, Ross

2019 - Pulling a Rabbit Out of a Hat: The Making of Roger Rabbit - Pg. 126

Anderson, Wes

2009 - The Making of Fantastic Mr. Fox - Pg. 157

Andersson, Lars Gustaf

2010 - A History of Swedish Experimental Film Culture: From Early Animation to Video Art - Pg. 221 (*Also see Andersson, Lars Gustaf. Sundholm, John. Widding, Astrid Söderbergh.*)

Animallogic

2010 - The Art of Legend of the Guardians: The Owls of Ga'Hoole - Pg. 104

Animation Magazine

2007 - Animation Magazine: 20-Year Collection - Pg. 243

Animation World Network

2010 - On Animation - The Director's Perspective - Pg. 39

Annett, Sandra

2019 - Mechademia 11.1: Second Arc - Pg. 248 (*Also see Lunning, Frenchy.*)
2020 - Mechademia 12.1: Second Arc - Pg. 249 (*Also see Lunning, Frenchy.*)
2020 - Mechademia 12.2: Second Arc - Pg. 249 (*Also see Lunning, Frenchy.*)
2020 - Mechademia 13.1: Second Arc - Pg. 249 (*Also see Lunning, Frenchy.*)
2021 - Mechademia 13.2: Second Arc - Pg. 249 (*Also see Lunning, Frenchy.*)

Aoyama, Takako

2003 - Anime Poster Art: Japan's Movie House Masterpieces - Pg. 206

Apgar, Garry

2014 - A Mickey Mouse Reader - Pg. 126
2015 - Mickey Mouse: Emblem of the American Spirit - Pg. 144
2019 - 2019 Hyperion Historical Society Alliance Annual Report - Pg. 149 (*Also see Bossert, David. Ghez, Didier. Hollifield, Jim. Pierce, Todd James. Seastrom, Lucas.*)

Apodaca, Blanca

2013 - All in a Day's Work: Animator - Pg. 229 (*Also see Serwich, Michael.*)

Arnaldi, Bruno

1999 - Computer Animation and Simulation '98 - Pg. 34 (*Also see Hegron, Gerard.*)

Arnold, Gordon B.

2016 - Animation and the American Imagination: A Brief History - Pg. 66

Arnold, Mark

2009 - Created and Produced by Total TeleVision Productions - Pg. 79
2013 - Frozen in Ice: The Story of Walt Disney Productions, 1966-1985 - Pg. 126
2015 - Think Pink: The Story of DePatie-Freleng - Pg. 79
2019 - Aaaaalllviiinnn!: The Story of Ross Bagdasarian, Sr., Liberty Records, Format Films and the Alvin Show - Pg. 92
2021 - The Total Television Scrapboook – Pg. 92

Artwick, Bruce

1984 - Microcomputer Displays, Graphics and Animation - Pg. 50

Ashley, Michael

2018 - It's Saturday Morning!: Celebrating the Golden Era of Cartoons 1960s-1990s - Pg. 70 (*Also see Garner, Joe.*)

Ashmore, Darren-Jon

2021 - Leiji Matsumoto: Essays on the Manga and Anime Legend - Pg. 199 (*Also see McCarthy, Helen.*)

Axelrod, Mitchell

1999 - BeatleToons, The Real Story Behind The Cartoon Beatles - Pg. 92

Azuma, Hiroki

2009 - Otaku: Japan's Database Animals - Pg. 180
2011 - Beautiful Fighting Girl - Pg. 199 (*Also see Lawson, Dawn. Saitō, Tamaki. Vincent, J. Keith.*)

Bacher, Hans

2007 - Dream Worlds: Production Design for Animation - Pg. 19

Badler, Norman

1993 - Simulating Humans: Computer Graphics Animation and Control - Pg. 50

Baena, Ana Soler

2021 - Anime Studies: Media-Specific Approaches to Neon Genesis Evangelion - Pg. 188 (*Also see Iglesias, José Andrés Santiago.*)

Baer, Brain C.

2017 - How He-Man Mastered the Universe: Toy to Television to the Big Screen - Pg. 93

Bailey, Adrian

1984 - Walt Disney's World of Fantasy - Pg. 136

Baisley, Sarah

1997 - 1997 Animation Industry Directory - Pg. 10
1998 - Animation Industry Directory 1998 - Pg. 10
1999 - Animation Industry Directory 1999 - 2000 - Pg. 10
2001 - Animation Industry Directory 2001 - Pg. 10
2002 - Animation Industry Directory 2002 - Pg. 10

Baker, Christopher

1994 - How Did They Do It?: Computer Illusion in Film & TV - Pg. 19

Baldwin, Gerard

2014 - From Mister Magoo to Papa Smurf - Pg. 93

Ballman, J.

2017 - The Marvel Super Heroes On TV! A Complete Episode Guide to the 1966 Cartoon Series. Book One: Iron Man - Pg. 93
2019 – Spider-Man on TV! A Full-Color Episode Guide to the Grantray-Lawrence Animation Series. Book One: The 1967 Cartoon - Pg. 93
2021 - The Marvel Super Heroes On TV! A Complete Episode Guide To The 1966 Cartoon Series. Book Two: Thor - Pg. 93

Ban, Toshio

2016 - The Osamu Tezuka Story: A Life in Manga and Anime - Pg. 239 (*Also see Tezuka Productions.*)

Bancroft, Tom

2014 - Animator: The Coolest Jobs on the Planet - Pg. 232 (Also see Hunter, Nick.)
2016 - The Art of Disney's Dragons - Pg. 136

Barba, Shelley E.

2017 - The Ascendance of Harley Quinn: Essays on DC's Enigmatic Villain - Pg. 93 (*Also see Barba, Shelley E. Perrin, Joy M.*)

Barbera, Joseph

1994 - My Life in Toons: From Flatbush to Bedrock in Under a Century - Pg. 168

Baricordi, Andrea

2000 - Anime: A Guide to Japanese Animation - Pg. 180 (*Also see De Giovanni, Massimiliano. Pietroni, Andrea. Rossi, Barbara. Tunesi, Sabrina.*)

Barrier, Michael

1978 - Building a Better Mouse: Fifty Years of Animation - Pg. 119
1999 - Hollywood Cartoons: American Animation in Its Golden Age - Pg. 63
2007 - The Animated Man: A Life of Walt Disney - Pg. 108

Bartolotta, Kenneth L.

2017 - Anime: Japanese Animation Comes to America - Pg. 233

Bashara, Dan

2019 - Cartoon Vision: UPA Animation and Postwar Aesthetics - Pg. 56

Bashe, Philip

1988 - That's Not All Folks: My Life in the Golden Age of Cartoons and Radio - Pg. 80 (*Also see Blanc, Mel.*)

Basquin, Kit Smyth

2020 - Mary Ellen Bute: Pioneer Animator - Pg. 80

Baxter, John

2014 - Disney During World War II: How the Walt Disney Studio Contributed to Victory in the War - Pg. 149

Beauchamp, Robin

2005 - Designing Sound for Animation - Pg. 73

Beaudry, Karl

2014 - Disney Destinies: How Passion, Patience, and Determination Can Take Anyone Anywhere - Pg. 114
2015 - Disney Melodies: The Magic of Disney Music - Pg. 147

Beck, Jerry

1981 - The Warner Bros. Cartoons/Looney Tunes and Merrie Melodies: A Complete Illustrated Guide to the Warner Bros. Cartoons - Pg. 10 (*Also see Friedwald, Will.*)
1991 - "I Tawt I Taw a Puddy Tat": Fifty Years of Sylvester and Tweety - Pg. 165
1994 - The 50 Greatest Cartoons: As Selected by 1,000 Animation Professionals - Pg. 10
1997 - Warner Bros. Animation Art: The Characters, the Creators, the Limited Editions - Pg. 165 (*Also see Friedwald, Will.*)
2003 - Outlaw Animation - Pg. 80
2004 - Animation Art: From Pencil to Pixel, the World of Cartoon, Anime, & CGI - Pg. 210
2005 - The Animated Movie Guide - Pg. 10
2005 - Pink Panther: The Ultimate Guide - Pg. 93
2007 - The Art of the Bee Movie - Pg. 158
2007 - The Hanna-Barbera Treasury: Rare Art and Mementos from your Favorite Cartoon Classics - Pg. 168

2007 - Not Just Cartoons: Nicktoons! - Pg. 161
2008 - The Art of DreamWorks Madagascar: Escape 2 Africa - Pg. 158
2008 - The Flintstones: Insight Editions Mini-Classic - Pg. 93
2008 - Scooby-Doo: Insight Editions Mini-Classic - Pg. 94
2008 - Tom and Jerry: Insight Editions Mini-Classic - Pg. 94
2009 - The Flintstones: A Retro Guide to the Hanna-Barbera Classic - Pg. 168
2010 - The 100 Greatest Looney Tunes Cartoons - Pg. 10
2014 - The Art of DreamWorks Mr. Peabody & Sherman - Pg. 158
2015 - You Can't Do That on Television: The Rebellious History of Nickelodeon - Pg. 161
2016 - How to Be a Disney Historian: Tips from the Top Professionals - Pg. 149 (*Also see Ehrbar, Greg. Fanning, Jim. Ghez, Didier. Jurtti, Jeff. Kaufman, J.B. Korkis, Jim. Lowery, Paula Sigman.*)
2016 - Hanna-Barbera: The Architects of Saturday Morning - Pg. 168 (*Also see Kowalski, Jesse. Mallory, Michael.*)
2017 - The Animated Administration of James Norcross a.k.a. Super President - Pg. 93 (*Also see Collier, Kevin Scott. Leonardi, Art.*)

Becker, Bonny

2015 - Cloud Country: Pixar Animation Studios Artist Showcase - Pg. 235 (*Also see Klocek, Noah.*)

Beckerman, Howard

1991 - Krátký Film: The Art of Czechoslovak Animation - Pg. 216 (*Also see Poš, Jan. Wechsler, Jeffrey.*)
2003 - Animation: The Whole Story - Pg. 39

Beecroft, Simon

2021 - Pixar Museum: Stories and Art from the Animation Studio - Pg. 2021 (*Also see Walt Disney Company Ltd.*)

Begin, Mary Jane

2015 - My Little Pony: The Art of Equestria - Pg. 104

Beiman, Nancy

2010 - Animated Performance: Bringing Imaginary Animal, Human and Fantasy Characters to Life - Pg. 39

Bell, Elizabeth

1995 - From Mouse to Mermaid: The Politics of Film, Gender, and Culture - Pg. 144 (*Also see Bell, Elizabeth. Haas, Lynda. Sells, Laura.*)

Bellano, Marco

2021 - Allegro Non Troppo: Bruno Bozzetto's Animated Music - Pg. 219 (*Also see Pallant, Chris.*)

Bendazzi, Giannalberto

1994 - Cartoons: One Hundred Years of Cinema Animation - Pg. 211
2003 - Animations - Pg. 39 (*Also see Alys, Francis. Akakce, Haluk. Blake, Jeremy. Canemaker, John. Christov-Bakargiev, Carolyn. Galbraith, David. Gillick, Liam. Harries, Larissa. Klein, Norman. Marks, Melissa. Riegel, Karyn.*)
2015 - Animation: A World History: Volume 1: Foundations - The Golden Age - Pg. 210
2015 - Animation: A World History: Volume 2: The Birth of Style - The Three Markets - Pg. 210
2015 - Animation: A World History: Volume 3: Contemporary Times - Pg. 210
2017 - Twice the First: Quirino Christiani and the Animated Feature Film - Pg. 212

Bennett, Tara

2013 - The Art of Epic - Pg. 176
2014 - The Art of Rio: Featuring a Carnival of Art From Rio and Rio 2 - Pg. 176
2016 - The Art of Ice Age - Pg. 176
2017 - The Art of Ferdinand - Pg. 176

Berton, Gael

2021 - The Works of Hayao Miyazaki: The Master of Japanese Animation - Pg. 192

Bevilacqua, Joe

2004 - Daws Butler, Characters Actor - Pg. 80 (*Also see Ohmart, Ben.*)

Bierly, Steve R.

2009 - Stronger Than Spinach: The Secret Appeal of the Famous Studios Popeye Cartoons - Pg. 94

Biggers, Buck

2020 - How Underdog Was Born - Pg. 94 (*Also see Stover, Chet.*)

Binski, Paul

1995 - Cartoon, Caricature, Animation - Pg. 39 (*Also see Marcia Pointon.*)

Bissonnette, Sylvie

2019 - Affect and Embodied Meaning in Animation: Becoming-Animated - Pg. 40

Blair, Gavin

2007 - The Art of Reboot - Pg. 104 (*Also see Gibson, Ian. Jackson, Mike. McCarthy, Brendan. Nicholls, Ken. Roberts, David. Su, Jim.*)

Blair, Preston

1947 - Advanced Animation - Pg. 19
1994 - Cartoon Animation - Pg. 40

Blake, Jeremy

2003 - Animations - Pg. 39 (*Also see Alys, Francis. Akakce, Haluk. Bendazzi, Giannalberto. Canemaker, John. Christov-Bakargiev, Carolyn. Galbraith, David. Gillick, Liam. Harries, Larissa. Klein, Norman. Marks, Melissa. Riegel, Karyn.*)

Blattner, Evamarie

2012 - Lotte Reiniger: Born With Enchanting Hands: Three Silhouette Sequels - Pg. 104 (*Also see Reiniger, Lotte. Wiegmann, Karlheinz.*)

Bliss, John

2010 - Art That Moves: Animation Around the World (Culture in Action) - Pg. 229

Bloodsworth-Lugo, Mary K.

2010 - Animating Difference: Race, Gender, and Sexuality in Contemporary Films for Children - Pg. 271 (*Also see King, C. Richard. Lugo-Lugo, Carmen R.*)

Blohm, Craig E.

2019 - Great Cartoonists (Collective Biographies) - Pg. 232
2019 - The Art of Animation - Pg. 233 (*Also see Marcovitz, Hal.*)

Blu, Susan

1987 - Word of Mouth: A Guide to Commercial Voice-Over Excellence - Pg. 73 (*Also see Mullin, Molly Ann.*)

Blue, Jed A.

2015 - The Very Soil: An Unauthorized Critical Study of Puella Magi Madoka Magica - Pg. 188

Bluth, Don

2004 - The Art of Storyboard - Pg. 77
2005 - Art of Animation Drawing - Pg. 19
2022 - Somewhere Out There: My Animated Life - Pg. 80

Bohn, James

2017 - Music in Disney's Animated Features: Snow White and the Seven Dwarfs to the Jungle Book - Pg. 147

Bolton, Christopher

2007 - Robot Ghosts and Wired Dreams: Japanese Science Fiction from Origins to Anime - Pg. 199
2018 - Interpreting Anime - Pg. 199

Booker, M. Keith

2006 - Drawn to Television: Prime-Time Animation from the Flintstones to Family Guy - Pg. 59

Bossert, David A.

2013 - Remembering Roy E. Disney: Memories and Photos of a Storied Life - Pg. 114
2015 - An Animator's Gallery: Eric Goldberg Draws the Disney Characters - Pg. 114
2015 - Dali and Disney: Destino: The Story, Artwork, and Friendship Behind the Legendary Film - Pg. 136
2017 - Oswald the Lucky Rabbit: The Search for the Lost Disney Cartoons - Pg. 126
2017 - The Art of Tennessee Loveless: The Mickey Mouse TEN x TEN x TEN Contemporary Pop Art Series - Pg. 136
2018 - Kem Weber: Mid-Century Furniture Designs for the Disney Studios - Pg. 119
2019 - 2019 Hyperion Historical Society Alliance Annual Report - Pg. 149 (*Also see Apgar, Garry. Ghez, Didier. Hollifield, Jim. Pierce, Todd James. Seastrom, Lucas.*)

Boulic Ph. D., Ronan

1996 - Computer Animation and Simulation '96: Proceedings of the Eurographics Workshop in Poitiers, France, August 31–September 1, 1996 - Pg. 34 (*Also see Hégron Ph. D., Gerard*)

Boy Scouts of America

2015 - Animation Merit Badge Boy Scouts of America - Pg. 19

Bradley, Joff P. N.

2021 - Thinking with Animation - Pg. 211 (*Also see Ju-yu Cheng, Catherine.*)

Brasch, Walter M.

1983 - Cartoon Monickers: An Insight into the Animation Industry - Pg. 59

Brenner, Robin E.

2007 - Understanding Manga and Anime - Pg. 199

Briggs, Paul

2017 - Catch My Breath: Walt Disney Animation Studios Artist Showcase - Pg. 236

Brightman, Homer

2014 - Life in the Mouse House: Memoir of a Disney Story Artist - Pg. 114

Brion, Patrick

1990 - Tom & Jerry: The Definitive Guide to Their Animated Adventures - Pg. 94

Brode, Douglas

2004 - From Walt to Woodstock: How Disney Created the Counterculture - Pg. 144
2006 - Multiculturalism and the Mouse: Race and Sex in Disney Entertainment - Pg. 114
2016 - Debating Disney: Pedagogical Perspectives on Commercial Cinema - Pg. 119 (*Also see Brode, Shea T.*)

Brode, Shea T.

2016 - Debating Disney: Pedagogical Perspectives on Commercial Cinema - Pg. 119 (*Also see Brode, Douglas.*)

Brophy, Philip

2005 - 100 Anime (Screen Guides) - Pg. 180
2010 - Manga Impact: The World of Japanese Animation - Pg. 200 (*Also see Chatfield, Carl. Clements, Jonathan. Costa, Jordi. Della Casa, Luca. Delorme, Stéphane. Di Giorgio, Davide. Dottorini, Daniele. Gariglio, Stefano. Gravett, Paul. Higuinen, Erwan. Liberti, Fabrizio. McCarthy, Helen. Modina, Fabrizio. Nazzaro, Giona A. Paganelli, Grazia. Roberta, Maria. Rondolino, Gianni. Roudevitch, Michel. Rumor, Mario A. Sarrazin, Stephen. Surman, David.*)

Brotherton, Phil

2014 - The Art of The Boxtrolls - Pg. 179

Brown, PhD, Alan

2006 - The Psychology of the Simpsons: D'oh! - Pg. 94 (*Also see Logan, Chris.*)

Brown, Jonatha A.

2005 - Walt Disney (People We Should Know) - Pg. 226

Brown, Noel

2018 - Toy Story: How Pixar Reinvented the Animated Feature (Animation: Key Films/Filmmakers) - Pg. 151 (*Also see Smith, Susan. Summers, Sam.*)

Brown, Steven T.

2006 - Cinema Anime - Pg. 200
2010 - Tokyo Cyberpunk: Posthumanism In Japanese Visual Culture - Pg. 200

Browsh, Jared Bahir

2021 - Hanna-Barbera: A History - Pg. 168

Bruckner, Franziska

2018 - Global Animation Theory: International Perspectives at Animafest Zagreb - Pg. 211 (*Also see Gilic, Nikica. Lang, Holger. Šuljic, Daniel. Turkovic, Hrvoje.*)

Buchan, Suzanne

2007 - Animated Worlds - Pg. 96 (*Also see Hertz, Betti-Sue. Manovich, Lev.*)
2007 - Animated Painting - Pg. 105
2011 - The Quay Brothers: Into a Metaphysical Playroom - Pg. 80
2013 - Pervasive Animation (AFI Film Readers) - Pg. 40

Budd, Mike

2005 - Rethinking Disney: Private Control, Public Dimensions - Pg. 119 (*Also see Kirsch, Max H.*)

Bukatma, Scott

2012 - Poetics of Slumberland: Animated Spirits and the Animating Spirit - Pg. 71

Burchard, Wolf

2021 - Inspiring Walt Disney: The Animation of French Decorative Arts - Pg. 108

Burgess, Clare

2014 - Weta Digital - Pg. 94

Burke, Timothy

1998 - Saturday Morning Fever: Growing up with Cartoon Culture - Pg. 70

Burnes, Brian

2002 - Walt Disney's Missouri: The Roots of a Creative Genius - Pg. 108 (*Also see Butler, Robert W. Viets, Dan.*)

Burr, John

2016 - The Voice Over Actor's Handbook: How to Analyze, Interpret, and Deliver Scripts - Pg. 74

Burton, Bonnie

2019 - The Art of Abominable - Pg. 158

Busack, Richard von

2010 - The Art of DreamWorks Megamind: Bad, Brilliant, Blue - Pg. 159

Butler, Daws

2015 - Scenes for Actors and Voices - Pg. 74

Butler, Robert W.

2002 - Walt Disney's Missouri: The Roots of a Creative Genius - Pg. 108 (*Also see Burnes, Brian. Viets, Dan.*)

Byrne, Eleanor

2000 - Deconstructing Disney - Pg. 127 (*Also see McQuillan, Martin.*)

Cabarga, Leslie

1976 - The Fleischer Story - Pg. 81

Calaitges, Kelsey

2019 - The Art of Bravest Warriors - Pg. 164

Camp, Brian

2007 - Anime Classics Zettai!: 100 Must-See Japanese Animation Masterpieces - Pg. 180 (*Also see Davis, Julie.*)

Canemaker, John

1977 - The Animated Raggedy Ann & Andy: An Intimate Look at the Art of Animation, Its History, Techniques, and Artists - Pg. 95
1987 - The Art of the Animated Image. Vol. 1 - Pg. 40
1987 - Winsor McCay: His Life and Art - Pg. 81
1988 - Storytelling in Animation Vol. 2: The Art of the Animated Image - Pg. 77
1991 - Felix: The Twisted Tale of the World's Most Famous Cat - Pg. 94
1996 - Before the Animation Begins: The Art and Lives of Disney's Inspirational Sketch Artists - Pg. 114
1996 - Tex Avery: The MGM Years, 1942-1955 - Pg. 81
1999 - Paper Dreams: The Art & Artists of Disney Storyboards - Pg. 114
2001 - Walt Disney's Nine Old Men and the Art of Animation - Pg. 115

2003 - Animations - Pg. 39 (*Also see Alys, Francis. Akakce, Haluk. Bendazzi, Giannalberto. Blake, Jeremy. Christov-Bakargiev, Carolyn. Galbraith, David. Gillick, Liam. Harries, Larissa. Klein, Norman. Marks, Melissa. Riegel, Karyn.*)
2003 - The Art And Flair Of Mary Blair: An Appreciation - Pg. 81
2010 - Two Guys Named Joe: Master Animation Storytellers Joe Grant & Joe Ranft - Pg. 81
2014 - The Lost Notebook: Herman Schultheis & the Secrets of Walt Disney's Movie Magic - Pg. 127
2014 - Magic Color Flair: The World of Mary Blair - Pg. 81

Canwell, Bruce

2014 - Genius, Animated: The Cartoon Art of Alex Toth - Pg. 81 (*Also see Canwell, Bruce. Mullaney, Dean. Toth, Alex.*)

Captivating History

2020 - Walt Disney: A Captivating Guide to the Life of an American Entrepreneur and Pioneer of Animated Cartoon Films - Pg. 108
2020 - Walt Disney and Salvador Dali: A Captivating Guide to the Individual Lives of an American Animator and a Spanish Surrealist Painter - Pg. 109

Care, Ross

2016 - Disney Legend Wilfred Jackson: A Life in Animation - Pg. 115

Carlton, Ardith

1986 - Robotech Art I - Pg. 206 (*Also see Reynolds, Kay.*)

Catalano, Frank

2011 - Rand Unwrapped - Confessions of a Robotech Warrior - Pg. 95

Catmull, Ed

2014 - Creativity, Inc. - Pg. 151

Cavalier, Stephen

2011 - The World History of Animation - Pg. 211

Cavallaro, Dani

2006 - The Anime Art of Hayao Miyazaki - Pg. 192
2006 - The Cinema of Mamoru Oshii: Fantasy, Technology and Politics - Pg. 201
2007 - Anime Intersections: Tradition and Innovation in Theme and Technique - Pg. 200
2008 - The Art of Studio Gainax: Experimentation, Style, and Innovation at the Leading Edge of Anime - Pg. 188
2009 - Anime and Memory: Aesthetic, Cultural and Thematic Perspectives - Pg. 200
2009 - Anime and the Visual Novel: Narrative Structure, Design and Play at Crossroads of Animation and Computer Games - Pg. 201
2009 - Magic as Metaphor in Anime: A Critical Study - Pg. 201
2010 - Anime and the Art of Adaptation - Pg. 200
2011 - Art in Anime: The Creative Quest as Theme and Metaphor - Pg. 201
2011 - The Fairy Tale and Anime: Traditional Themes, Images and Symbols at Play on Screen - Pg. 201
2012 - CLAMP in Context - Pg. 201
2012 - Kyoto Animation: A Critical Study and Filmography - Pg. 185
2013 - Japanese Aesthetics and Anime: The Influence of Tradition - Pg. 201
2014 - The Late Works of Hayao Miyazaki: A Critical Study 2004-2013 - Pg. 192
2015 - Hayao Miyazaki's World Picture - Pg. 192

Cawley, John

1991 - The Animated Films of Don Bluth - Pg. 82
1991 - Cartoon Confidential - Pg. 40 (*Also see Korkis, Jim.*)

Cech, John

2009 - Imagination and Innovation: The Story of Weston Woods - Pg. 82

Centore, Michael

2018 - Pixar, Disney, DreamWorks and Digital Animation - Pg. 233

Chang, Jian

2020 - Computer Animation and Social Agents: 33rd International Conference on Computer Animation and Social Agents, CASA 2020, Bournemouth, UK, October 13-15, 2020, Proceedings - Pg. 38 (*Also see Magnenat-Thalmann, Nadia. Thalmann Ph. D., Daniel. Tian, Feng. Xu, Weiwei. Yang, Xiaosong. Zhang, Jian Jun.*)

Charles River Editors

2016 - Walt Disney and Jim Henson: The Lives and Legacies of the Men Behind America's Favorite Cartoons - Pg. 109

Chatfield, Carl

2010 - Manga Impact: The World of Japanese Animation - Pg. 200 (*Also see Brophy, Philip. Clements, Jonathan. Costa, Jordi. Della Casa, Luca. Delorme, Stéphane. Di Giorgio, Davide. Dottorini, Daniele. Gariglio, Stefano. Gravett, Paul. Higuinen, Erwan. Liberti, Fabrizio. McCarthy, Helen. Modina, Fabrizio. Nazzaro, Giona A. Roberta, Maria. Paganelli, Grazia. Rondolino, Gianni. Roudevitch, Michel. Rumor, Mario A. Sarrazin, Stephen. Surman, David.*)

Chen, Shaopeng

2021 - The New Generation in Chinese Animation - Pg. 214

Cheu, Johnson

2013 - Diversity in Disney Films: Critical Essays on Race, Ethnicity, Gender, Sexuality and Disability - Pg. 144

Cholodenko, Alan

1991 - The Illusion of Life: Essays on Animation - Pg. 41
2011 - The Illusion of Life II: More Essays on Animation - Pg. 41

Chong, Andrew

2007 - Basics Animation 02: Digital Animation - Pg. 20

Christiansen, A.A.

2017 - Walt Disney: The Man Behind the Magic - Pg. 109

Christov-Bakargiev, Carolyn

2003 - Animations - Pg. 39 (*Also see Alys, Francis. Akakce, Haluk. Bendazzi, Giannalberto. Blake, Jeremy. Canemaker, John. Galbraith, David. Gillick, Liam. Harries, Larissa. Klein, Norman. Marks, Melissa. Riegel, Karyn.*)

Chunovic, Louis

1996 - The Rocky and Bullwinkle Book - Pg. 95

Citters, Darrell Van

2009 - Mister Magoo's Christmas Carol: The Making of the First Animated Christmas Special - Pg. 95
2013 - The Art of Jay Ward Productions - Pg. 104

Clark, Les

2019 - Glimpses into the Golden Age of Disney Animation - Pg. 127 (*Also see Leslie Clark, Miriam.*)

Clark, Steven

1999 - Disney: The First 100 Years - Pg. 149 (*Also see Smith, David.*)

Clarke, James

2007 - Animated Films - Pg. 154
2013 - The Films of Pixar Animation Studio - Pg. 151

Clements, Jonathan

1998 - The Erotic Anime Movie Guide - Pg. 180 (*Also see McCarthy, Helen.*)
2001 - The Anime Encyclopedia: A Century of Japanese Animation - Pg. 180 (*Also see McCarthy, Helen.*)
2009 - Schoolgirl Milky Crisis: Adventures in the Anime and Manga Trade - Pg. 185

2010 - Manga Impact: The World of Japanese Animation - Pg. 200 (*Also see Brophy, Philip. Chatfield, Carl. Costa, Jordi. Della Casa, Luca. Delorme, Stéphane. Di Giorgio, Davide. Dottorini, Daniele. Gariglio, Stefano. Gravett, Paul. Higuinen, Erwan. Liberti, Fabrizio. McCarthy, Helen. Modina, Fabrizio. Nazzaro, Giona A. Paganelli, Grazia. Roberta, Maria. Rondolino, Gianni. Roudevitch, Michel. Rumor, Mario A. Sarrazin, Stephen. Surman, David.*)
2013 - Anime: A History - Pg. 191

Cline, Rebecca

2019 - Walt Disney Studios: A Lot to Remember - Pg. 119

Clokey, Joe

2017 - Gumby Imagined: The Story of Art Clokey and His Creations - Pg. 82

Coar, Bob

2022 - A Century of American Animation: Act One: Born on the Silver Screen – Pg. 63

Cohen, David S.

2011 - The Ballad of Rango: The Art and Making of an Outlaw Film - Pg. 162

Cohen, Judith Love

2004 - You Can Be A Woman Animator - Pg. 226

Cohen, Karl

1998 - Forbidden Animation: Censored Cartoons and Blacklisted Animators in America - Pg. 59

Cohn, Jessica

2009 - Animator (Cool Careers: Cutting Edge) - Pg. 228

Collier, Kevin Scott

2017 - The Amazing Transformations of Tom Terrific - Pg. 95

2017 - The Animated Administration of James Norcross a.k.a. Super President - Pg. 93 (*Also see Beck, Jerry. Leonardi, Art.*)
2017 - Jay Ward's Animated Cereal Capers - Pg. 96
2017 - Jonny, Sinbad Jr. & Me - Pg. 82 (*Also see Matheson, Tim.*)
2017 - Dreamy Dud: Wallace A. Carlson's Animation Classic - Pg. 96 (*Also see Stathes, Tommy José.*)
2017 - Ralph Bakshi's The Mighty Heroes Declassified - Pg. 96
2017 - Winsor McCay's The Sinking of The Alpena - Pg. 96
2017 - Winsor McCay: Boyhood Dreams: Growing Up In Spring Lake, Michigan 1867-1885 - Pg. 82
2018 - Calvin and the Colonel: The Reincarnation of Amos 'n' Andy - Pg. 95
2018 - Chuck and Jack Luchsinger's Cartoon TeleTales - Pg. 82
2018 - Happy Hooligan: The Animated Cartoons of 1916-1922 - Pg. 96
2018 - Milton the Monster: Horror Hill Epitaph - Pg. 96
2018 - Russia's Winnie-the-Pooh: Fyodor Khitruk's Vinni-Pukh - Pg. 220
2019 - The Chaplin Animated Silent Cartoons - Pg. 282
2018 - The Hare Raising Tales of Crusader Rabbit - Pg. 96
2018 - The Wonderful Animated World of the Wizard of Oz - Pg. 96
2019 - Clutch Cargo's Adventure Log Book - Pg. 96

Computer Graphics Society

1995 - Computer Animation '95: Proceedings: April 19-21, 1995, Geneva, Switzerland- Pg. 36 (*Also see Digimedia, Swiss National Research Foundation*.)

Condry, Ian

2013 - The Soul of Anime: Collaborative Creativity and Japan's Media Success Story - Pg. 185

Connelly, Sherilyn

2017 - Ponyville Confidential: The History and Culture of My Little Pony, 1981-2016 - Pg. 96

Connor, Samuel

2012 - Making it Move: A Short History of Animation - Pg. 230

Cook, Benjamin

2007 - The Animate! Book - Pg. 20 (*Also see Thomas, Gary.*)

Cook, Malcolm

2018 - Early British Animation: From Page to Stage to Cinema Screens - Pg. 217
2020 - Animation and Advertising - Pg. 59 (*Also see Thompson, Kirsten Moana.*)

Cooley, Josh

2019 - The Art of Toy Story 4 - Pg. 154

Cornog, Martha

2011 - Mangatopia: Essays on Manga and Anime in the Modern World - Pg. 202

Cortner, Laura E.

2021 - It's All in the Mind: Inside the Beatles' Yellow Submarine, Vol. 2 - Pg. 97 (*Also see Hieronimus, Robert R.*)

Costa, Jordi

2010 - Manga Impact: The World of Japanese Animation - Pg. 200 (*Also see Brophy, Philip. Chatfield, Carl. Clements, Jonathan. Della Casa, Luca. Delorme, Stéphane. Di Giorgio, Davide. Dottorini, Daniele. Gariglio, Stefano. Gravett, Paul. Higuinen, Erwan. Liberti, Fabrizio. McCarthy, Helen. Modina, Fabrizio. Nazzaro, Giona A. Roberta, Maria. Paganelli, Grazia. Rondolino, Gianni. Roudevitch, Michel. Rumor, Mario A. Sarrazin, Stephen. Surman, David.*)

Cotte, Olivier

2002 - David Ehrlich: Citizen of the World - Pg. 82
2007 - Secrets of Oscar-Winning Animation: Behind the Scenes of 13 Classic Short Animations - Pg. 97

Cotter, Bill

1997 - The Wonderful World of Disney Television: A Complete History - Pg. 119

Coyle, Rebecca

2009 - Drawn to Sound: Animation Film Music and Sonicity - Pg. 74

Crafton, Donald

1982 - Before Mickey: The Animated Film 1898-1928 - Pg. 63
1990 - Emile Cohl, Caricature, and Film - Pg. 82
2012 - Shadow of a Mouse: Performance, Belief, and World-Making in Animation - Pg. 41

Cranfield, Bill

2003 - Flips 7: Animation - Pg. 211

Craven, Thomas

1945 - Cartoon Cavalcade - Pg. 41

Croll, Ben

2021 - The Art of Eric Guillon: From the Making of Despicable Me to Minions, The Secret Life of Pets, and More - Pg. 176

Crump, Rolly

2015 - Great Big Beautiful Tomorrow: Walt Disney and Technology - Pg. 120
(*Also see Gurr, Bob. Moran, Christian.*)

Culhane, John

1983 - Walt Disney's Fantasia - Pg. 127
1992 - Disney's Aladdin: The Making of an Animated Film - Pg. 136
1999 - Fantasia 2000: Visions of Hope - Pg. 136

Culhane, Shamus

1986 - Talking Animals and Other People: The Autobiography of a Legendary Animator - Pg. 83
1990 - Animation: From Script to Screen - Pg. 77

Cullimore, Stan

2002 - Behind the Scenes: Animation - Pg. 225

Curtis, Scott

2019 - Animation (Behind the Silver Screen) - Pg. 41

Da Silva, Raul

1979 - The World of Animation - Pg. 41

Dale, Alan

1943 - Jr's Fun To Draw - Pg. 20

Daliot-Bul, Michal

2017 - The Anime Boom in the United States: Lessons for Global Creative Industries - Pg. 185 (*Also see Otmazgin, Nissim.*)

Dalton, Tony

2006 - The Art of Ray Harryhausen - Pg. 105 (*Also see Harryhausen, Ray.*)
2008 - A Century of Model Animation: From Méliès to Aardman - Pg. 54 (*Also see Harryhausen, Ray.*)

Daly, Steve

1995 - Toy Story The Art and Making of the Animated Film - Pg. 154 (*Also see Lasseter, John.*)

Darley, Andrew

2000 - Visual Digital Culture: Surface Play and Spectacle in New Media Genres - Pg. 50

Dart, Rebecca

2017 - The Art of My Little Pony: The Movie - Pg. 105

Davis, Amy M.

2006 - Good Girls and Wicked Witches: Changing Representations of Women in Disney's Feature Animation, 1937-2001 - Pg. 144
2014 - Handsome Heroes and Vile Villains: Masculinity in Disney's Feature Films - Pg. 127

Davis, Jeffery

1995 - Children's Television, 1947-1990: Over 200 Series, Game and Variety Shows, Cartoons, Educational Programs, and Specials - Pg. 11

Davis, Julie

2007 - Anime Classics Zettai!: 100 Must-See Japanese Animation Masterpieces - Pg. 180 (*Also see Camp, Brian.*)

Davis, Northrop

2015 - Manga and Anime Go to Hollywood - Pg. 186

Davisson, Zack

2015 - The Art of Satoshi Kon - Pg. 206 (*Also see Kon, Satoshi.*)

De Giovanni, Massimiliano

2000 - Anime: A Guide to Japanese Animation - Pg. 180 (*Also see Baricordi, Andrea. Pietroni, Andrea. Rossi, Barbara. Tunesi, Sabrina.*)

de Aguiar, Edilson

2009 - Animation And Performance Capture Using Digitized Models - Pg. 50

De Vries, Tjitte

2010 - "They Thought It Was a Marvel": Arthur Melbourne-Cooper (1874-1961), Pioneer of Puppet Animation - Pg. 83 (*Also see Mul, Ati.*)

de Wit, Alex Dudok

2021 - Grave of the Fireflies (BFI Film Classics) - Pg. 188

Deitch, Gene

1997 - For the Love of Prague - Pg. 83
2013 - How to Succeed in Animation: Don't Let a Little Thing Like Failure Stop You! - Pg. 20
2013 - Nudnik Revealed - Pg. 97

Deja, Andreas

2015 - The Nine Old Men: Lessons, Techniques, and Inspiration from Disney's Great Animators - Pg. 115
2019 - Mickey Mouse: From Walt to the World - Pg. 127
2022 - The Walt Disney's The Jungle Book: Making a Masterpiece – Pg. 127

Della Casa, Luca

2010 - Manga Impact: The World of Japanese Animation - Pg. 200 (*Also see Brophy, Philip. Chatfield, Carl. Clements, Jonathan. Costa, Jordi. Delorme, Stéphane. Di Giorgio, Davide. Dottorini, Daniele. Gariglio, Stefano. Gravett, Paul. Higuinen, Erwan. Liberti, Fabrizio. McCarthy, Helen. Modina, Fabrizio. Nazzaro, Giona A. Paganelli, Grazia. Roberta, Maria. Rondolino, Gianni. Roudevitch, Michel. Rumor, Mario A. Sarrazin, Stephen. Surman, David.*)

Dellaccio, Tanya

2017 - Computer Animation: Telling Stories with Digital Art - Pg. 233

Delisle, Guy

2005 - Pyongyang: A Journey in North Korea - Pg. 237

Delorme, Stéphane

2010 - Manga Impact: The World of Japanese Animation - Pg. 200 (*Also see* Brophy, Philip. Chatfield, Carl. Clements, Jonathan. Costa, Jordi. Della Casa, Luca. Di Giorgio, Davide. Dottorini, Daniele. Gariglio, Stefano. Gravett, Paul. Higuinen, Erwan. Liberti, Fabrizio. McCarthy, Helen. Modina, Fabrizio. Nazzaro, Giona A. Roberta, Maria. Paganelli, Grazia. Rondolino, Gianni. Roudevitch, Michel. Rumor, Mario A. Sarrazin, Stephen. Surman, David.)

Deneroff, Harvey

1997 - The Art of Anastasia: A Twentieth Century Fox Presentation - Pg. 157
2008 - Astro Boy and Anime Come to the Americas: An Insider's View of the Birth of a Pop Culture Phenomenon - Pg. 186 (*Also see Deneroff, Harvey. Ladd, Fred.*)

Denison, Rayna

2015 - Anime: A Critical Introduction - Pg. 202
2018 - Princess Mononoke: Understanding Studio Ghibli's Monster Princess (*Animation: Key Films/Filmmakers*) - Pg. 192

Desroches, Ed

2011 - ASIFA 50th Anniversary by The Association Internationale du Film d'Animation - Pg. 97

Di Giorgio, Davide

2010 - Manga Impact: The World of Japanese Animation - Pg. 200 (*Also see* Brophy, Philip. Chatfield, Carl. Clements, Jonathan. Costa, Jordi. Della Casa, Luca. Delorme, Stéphane. Dottorini, Daniele. Gariglio, Stefano. Gravett, Paul. Higuinen, Erwan. Liberti, Fabrizio. McCarthy, Helen. Modina, Fabrizio. Nazzaro, Giona A. Paganelli, Grazia. Roberta, Maria. Rondolino, Gianni. Roudevitch, Michel. Rumor, Mario A. Sarrazin, Stephen. Surman, David.)

Digimedia

1994 - Computer Animation '94: Proceedings: May 25-28, 1994, Geneva, Switzerland - Pg. 36 (*Also see Swiss National Research Foundation.*)

1995 - Computer Animation '95: Proceedings: April 19-21, 1995, Geneva, Switzerland - Pg. 36 (*Also see Computer Graphics Society, Swiss National Research Foundation.*)

Dilworth, John R.

2019 - The Art of Courage the Cowardly Dog - Pg. 170

DiMartino, Michael Dante

2010 - Avatar: The Last Airbender (The Art of the Animated Series) - Pg. 255 (*Also see Konietzko, Bryan.*)
2013 - Legend of Korra: The Art of the Animated Series Book One: Air - Pg. 162 (*Also see. Konietzko, Bryan. Santos, Joaquim Dos.*)
2014 - Legend of Korra: The Art of the Animated Series Book Two: Spirits - Pg. 162 (*Also see Konietzko, Bryan. Santos, Joaquim Dos.*)
2015 - Legend of Korra: The Art of the Animated Series Book Three: Change - Pg. 163 (*Also see Konietzko, Bryan. Santos, Joaquim Dos.*)
2015 - Legend of Korra: The Art of the Animated Series Book Four: Balance - Pg. 163 (*Also see Konietzko, Bryan. Santos, Joaquim Dos.*)

Dini, Paul

1998 - Batman Animated - Pg. 97 (*Also see Kidd, Chip.*)

Disney

2021 – The Art of Encanto - Pg. 136

Disney Book Group

1997 - Walt Disney's Bambi: The Sketchbook Series - Pg. 137
2008 - Disney's Dogs - Pg. 136
2016 - The Art of Minnie Mouse - Pg. 137
2018 - The Art of Walt Disney's Mickey Mouse and Minnie Mouse - Pg. 137

Disney Editions

2015 - Before Ever After: The Lost Lectures of Walt Disney's Animation Studio - Pg. 121

Disney - Pixar

2000 - Toy Story: The Sketchbook Series - Pg. 154
2015 - Funny!: Twenty-Five Years of Laughter from the Pixar Story Room - Pg. 154
2021 - The Art of Luca - Pg. 154
2022 - The Art of Turning Red – Pg. 154

Dobbs, G. Michael

2007 - Escape: How Animation Broke Into the Mainstream in the 1990s - Pg. 60

Dobson, Nichola

2009 - Historical Dictionary of Animation and Cartoons (Vol 34) - Pg. 11
2010 - A to Z of Animation and Cartoons, The (The A to Z Guide Series) - Pg. 11
2018 - Norman McLaren: Between the Frames (*Animation: Key Films/Filmmakers*) - Pg. 83
2018 - The Animation Studies Reader - Pg. 41 (*Also see Ratelle, Amy. Roe, Annabelle Honess. Ruddell, Caroline.*)

Dobson, Terence

2007 - Film Work of Norman McLaren - Pg. 97

Docter, Pete

2001 - The Art of Monsters, Inc. - Pg. 155 (*Also see Lasseter, John.*)
2015 - The Art Of Inside Out - Pg. 155
2021 - Hayao Miyazaki - Pg. 193 (*Also see Kothenschulte, Daniel. Niebel, Jessica.*)

Dottorini, Daniele

2010 - Manga Impact: The World of Japanese Animation - Pg. 200 (*Also see Brophy, Philip. Chatfield, Carl. Clements, Jonathan. Costa, Jordi. Della Casa, Luca. Delorme, Stéphane. Di Giorgio, Davide. Gariglio, Stefano. Gravett, Paul. Higuinen, Erwan. Liberti, Fabrizio. McCarthy, Helen. Modina, Fabrizio. Nazzaro, Giona A. Roberta, Maria. Paganelli, Grazia. Rondolino, Gianni. Roudevitch, Michel. Rumor, Mario A. Sarrazin, Stephen. Surman, David.*)

Dowen, Elizabeth

2001 - What's it Like to be a... Animator? - Pg. 225

Dowling, Ryan

2019 - The Animated Heart: A Historical and Cultural Insight Into Animation - Pg. 66

Drazen, Patrick

2002 - Anime Explosion!: The What? Why? and Wow! of Japanese Animation - Pg. 181
2007 - A Gathering of Spirits: Japan's Ghost Story Tradition: From Folklore and Kabuki to Anime and Manga - Pg. 202
2017 - Holy Anime!: Japan's View of Christianity - Pg. 202

Du, Daisy Yan

2019 - Animated Encounters: Transnational Movements of Chinese Animation, 1940s-1970s - Pg. 214
2021 - Chinese Animation and Socialism: From Animators Perspectives - Pg. 214

Dunlavey, Ryan

2021 - The Comic Book History of Animation: True Toon Tales of the Most Iconic Characters, Artists and Styles! - Pg. 240 (*Also see Van Lente, Fred*)

Eastman Kodak Company

1983 - The Complete Kodak Animation Book - Pg. 42 (*Also see Solomon, Charles. Stark, Ron.*)

Eatock, James

2016 - He-Man and She-Ra: A Complete Guide to the Classic Animated Adventures - Pg. 11

Ebihara, Isao

2010 - All the World Is Anime - Pg. 181

Edera, Bruno

1984 - Full Length Animated Feature Films - Pg. 11

Edwards, R. Scott

1991 - Cel Magic: The Book on Collecting Animation Art - Pg. 20 (*Also see Stobener, Bob.*)

Edgar, Sean

2017 - The Art of Over the Garden Wall - Pg. 170 (*Also see McHale, Patrick.*)

Ehasz, Aaron

2020 - The Art of the Dragon Prince - Pg. 175 (*Also see Richmond, Justin. Wonderstorm.*)

Ehrbar, Greg

2006 - Mouse Tracks: The Story of Walt Disney Records - Pg. 147 (*Also see Hollis, Tim.*)
2016 - How to Be a Disney Historian: Tips from the Top Professionals - Pg. 149 (*Also see Beck, Jerry. Fanning, Jim. Ghez, Didier. Jurtti, Jeff. Kaufman, J.B. Korkis, Jim. Lowery, Paula Sigman.*)

Ehrlich, Nea

2018 - Drawn from Life: Issues and Themes in Animated Documentary Cinema - Pg. 47 (*Also see Murray, Jonathan.*)
2021 - Animating Truth: Documentary and Visual Culture in the 21st Century - Pg. 47

Eisner, Michael D.

1999 - Work in Progress: Risking Failure, Surviving Success - Pg. 120 (*Also see Schwartz, Tony.*)

Eliot, Marc

1993 - Walt Disney: Hollywood's Dark Prince - Pg. 109

Ellenshaw, Peter

2003 - Ellenshaw Under Glass: Going to the Matte for Disney - Pg. 115

Erickson, Hal

1995 - Television Cartoon Shows: An Illustrated Encyclopedia, 1949 Through 2003 - Pg. 12
2020 - A Van Beuren Production: A History of the 619 Cartoons, 875 Live Action Shorts, Four Feature Films and One Serial of Amedee Van Beuren - Pg. 12

Eury, Michael

2017 - Hero-A-Go-Go: Campy Comic Books, Crimefighters, & Culture of the 1960's - Pg. 66

Faber, Liz

2004 - Animation Unlimited: Innovative Short Films Since 1940 - Pg. 12 (*Also see Walters, Helen.*)

Falk, Nat

1941 - How to Make Animated Cartoons - Pg. 20

Fanning, Jim

2016 - How to Be a Disney Historian: Tips from the Top Professionals - Pg. 149 (*Also see Beck, Jerry. Ehrbar, Greg. Ghez, Didier. Jurtti, Jeff. Kaufman, J.B. Korkis, Jim. Lowery, Paula Sigman.*)

Farago, Andrew

2014 - Teenage Mutant Ninja Turtles: The Ultimate Visual History - Pg. 105
2017 - Totally Awesome: The Greatest Cartoons of the Eighties - Pg. 12

Fay, Matha

2015 - Out of Line: The Art of Jules Feiffer - Pg. 105

Field, Robert D.

1942 - The Art of Walt Disney - Pg. 127

Feinstien, Stephen

2005 - Read About Walt Disney - Pg. 226 (*Also see Feinstein, Stephen.*)

Feltmate, David

2017 - Drawn to the Gods: Religion and Humor in The Simpsons, South Park & Family Guy - Pg. 71

Ferguson Publishing

2010 - Animation (Ferguson's Careers in Focus) - Pg. 71
2010 - What Can I Do Now? Animation - Pg. 229

Ferreira, Cláudio

2012 - Confia: International Conference on Illustration and Animation 2012 - Pg. 34
2013 - Confia: International Conference on Illustration and Animation 2013 - Pg. 34
2015 - Confia: International Conference on Illustration and Animation 2015 - Pg. 35
2016 - Confia: International Conference on Illustration and Animation 2016 - Pg. 35
2017 - Confia: International Conference on Illustration and Animation 2017 - Pg. 35
2018 - Confia: International Conference on Illustration and Animation 2018 - Pg. 35
2019 - Confia: International Conference on Illustration and Animation 2019 - Pg. 35
2020 - Confia: International Conference on Illustration and Animation 2020 - Pg. 35

Feyersinger, Erwin

2015 - Metalepsis in Animation: Paradoxical Transgressions of Ontological Levels - Pg. 42

Finch, Christopher

1973 - The Art of Walt Disney: From Mickey Mouse to the Magic Kingdoms - Pg. 128
1993 - Jim Henson: The Works - The Art, the Magic, the Imagination - Pg. 84
1994 - The Art of The Lion King - Pg. 137
1998 - Sotheby's Guide to Animation Art - Pg. 12 (*Also see Rosenkrantz, Linda. Sotheby's.*)
2013 - The CG Story: Computer-Generated Animation and Special Effects - Pg. 50

Findlay, Kurtis

2011 - Chuck Jones: The Dream that Never Was - Pg. 165 (*Also see Mulaney, Dean.*)

Fink, Moritz

2019 - The Simpsons: A Cultural History - Pg. 66

Fingeroth, Danny

2003 - Backstage at an Animated Series - Pg. 225

Fischer, Stuart

2011 - The Hanna-Barbera Story: The Life And Times Of TV's Greatest Animation Studio - Pg. 168

Fisher, Douglas

2008 - Teaching Visual Literacy: Using Comic Books, Graphic Novels, Anime, Cartoons, and More to Develop Comprehension and Thinking Skills - Pg. 20 (*Also see Frew, Nancy.*)

Fleischer, Richard

2005 - Out of the Inkwell: Max Fleischer and the Animation Revolution - Pg. 84

Fleming, Jeff

2001 - My Reality: Contemporary Art And The Culture Of Japanese Animation - Pg. 188 (*See also Lubowsky Talbott, Susan. Murakami, Takashi.*)

Flower, Joe

1991 - Prince of the Magic Kingdom: Michael Eisner and the Re-Making of Disney - Pg. 120

Foray, June

2009 - Did You Grow Up with Me, Too?: The Autobiography of June Foray - Pg. 84

Forchheimer, Robert

2002 - MPEG-4 Facial Animation: The Standard, Implementation and Applications - Pg. 50 (*Also see Pandzic, Igor.*)

Ford, Barbara

1989 - Walt Disney: A Biography - Pg. 111

Ford, Carin T.

2003 - Walt Disney: Meet the Cartoonist - Pg. 225

Formenti, Christina

2022 - The Classical Animated Documentary and Its Contemporary Evolution – Pg. 47

Fox, David

1984 - Computer Animation Primer - Pg. 50 (*Also see Waite, Mitchell.*)

Francis Parks, Corrie

2015 - Fluid Frames: Experimental Animation with Sand, Clay, Paint, and Pixels - Pg. 56

Frank, Hannah

2019 - Frame by Frame: A Materialist Aesthetics of Animated Cartoons - Pg. 56

Frederator Studios

2021 - Castlevania: The Art of the Animated Series - Pg. 164

Freleng, Friz

1994 - Animation: The Art of Friz Freleng - Pg. 84 (*Also see Weber, David.*)

Frew, Nancy

2008 - Teaching Visual Literacy: Using Comic Books, Graphic Novels, Anime, Cartoons, and More to Develop Comprehension and Thinking Skills - Pg. 20 (*Also see Fisher, Douglas.*)

Friedman, Jake S.

2001 - The Art of Blue Sky Studios - Pg. 176
2021 - The Disney Afternoon: The Making of a Television Renaissance - Pg. 120
2021 - The Disney Revolt: The Great Labor War of Animation's Golden Age - Pg. 120

Friedwald, Will

1981 - The Warner Bros. Cartoons/Looney Tunes and Merrie Melodies: A Complete Illustrated Guide to the Warner Bros. Cartoons - Pg. 10 (*Also see Beck, Jerry.*)
1997 - Warner Bros. Animation Art: The Characters, the Creators, the Limited Editions - Pg. 165 (*Also see Beck, Jerry.*)

Frierson, Michael

1994 - Clay Animation: American Highlights 1908 to Present - Pg. 12

Furniss, Maureen

1998 - Art in Motion: Animation Aesthetics - Pg. 56
2005 - Chuck Jones: Conversations - Pg. 165

2005 - Walt Disney: Conversations - Pg. 110
2009 - Animation: Art and Industry - Pg. 60
2016 - A New History of Animation - Pg. 211
2017 - Animation: The Global History - Pg. 211

Gabler, Neal

2006 - Walt Disney: The Triumph of the American Imagination - Pg. 110
2007 - Walt Disney: The Biography - Pg. 110

Gageldonk, Maarten van

2020 - Animation and Memory - Pg. 42 (*Also see Munteán, László. Shobeiri, Ali.*)

GAINAX

2019 - The FLCL Archives - Pg. 206

Gainer, Darius S.

2021 - Black Representation in the World of Animation - Pg. 66

Galbraith, David

2003 - Animations - Pg. 39 (*Also see Alys, Francis. Akakce, Haluk. Bendazzi, Giannalberto. Blake, Jeremy. Canemaker, John. Christov-Bakargiev, Carolyn. Gillick, Liam. Harries, Larissa. Klein, Norman. Marks, Melissa. Riegel, Karyn.*)

Galbraith, Patrick

2009 - The Otaku Encyclopedia: An Insider's Guide to the Subculture of Cool Japan - Pg. 181
2017 - The Moe Manifesto: An Insider's Look at the Worlds of Manga, Anime, and Gaming - Pg. 181

Gallery 1988

2019 - Rick and Morty: Show Me What You Got - The Gallery 1988 Artwork - Pg. 172

Gandinetti, Fred

1994 - Popeye: An Illustrated Cultural History - Pg. 66

Garcia, Hector

2011 - A Geek in Japan: Discovering the Land of Manga, Anime, Zen, and the Tea Ceremony - Pg. 181

Garcia, Roger

1994 - Frank Tashlin - Pg. 84

Gardner, Ph. D., Garth

2001 - Computer Graphics and Animation: History, Careers, Expert Advice - Pg. 51
2001 - Gardner's Guide to Internships at Multimedia and Animation Studios - Pg. 20
2001 - Gardner's Guide to Multimedia & Animation Studios: The Industry Directory - Pg. 12

Gariglio, Stefano

2010 - Manga Impact: The World of Japanese Animation - Pg. 200 (*Also see Brophy, Philip. Chatfield, Carl. Clements, Jonathan. Costa, Jordi. Della Casa, Luca. Delorme, Stéphane. Di Giorgio, Davide. Dottorini, Daniele. Gravett, Paul. Higuinen, Erwan. Liberti, Fabrizio. McCarthy, Helen. Modina, Fabrizio. Nazzaro, Giona A. Paganelli, Grazia. Roberta, Maria. Rondolino, Gianni. Roudevitch, Michel. Rumor, Mario A. Sarrazin, Stephen. Surman, David.*)

Garner, Joe

2018 - It's Saturday Morning!: Celebrating the Golden Era of Cartoons 1960s-1990s - Pg. 70 (*Also see Ashley, Michael.*)

Gehman, Chris

2005 - The Sharpest Point: Animation at the End of Cinema - Pg. 42 (*Also see Reinke, Steve.*)

Gerstein, David

2018 - Walt Disney's Mickey Mouse: The Ultimate History - Pg. 128 (*Also see Kaufman, J.B.*)

Ghazala, Mohamed

2011 - Animation in The Arab World: A Glance on the Arabian Animated Films Since 1936 - Pg. 212

Ghez, Didier

2005 - Walt's People: Volume 1: Talking Disney With The Artists Who Knew Him - Pg. 27
2005 - Walt's People: Volume 2: Talking Disney With The Artists Who Knew Him - Pg. 27
2006 - Walt's People: Volume 3: Talking Disney With The Artists Who Knew Him - Pg. 28
2007 - Walt's People: Volume 4: Talking Disney With The Artists Who Knew Him - Pg. 28
2007 - Walt's People: Volume 5: Talking Disney With The Artists Who Knew Him - Pg. 28
2008 - Walt's People: Volume 6: Talking Disney With The Artists Who Knew Him - Pg. 28
2008 - Walt's People: Volume 7: Talking Disney With The Artists Who Knew Him - Pg. 28
2009 - Walt's People: Volume 8: Talking Disney With The Artists Who Knew Him - Pg. 29
2010 - Walt's People: Volume 9: Talking Disney With The Artists Who Knew Him - Pg. 29
2011 - Walt's People: Volume 10: Talking Disney With The Artists Who Knew Him - Pg. 29
2011 - Walt's People: Volume 11: Talking Disney With The Artists Who Knew Him - Pg. 29
2012 - Walt's People: Volume 12: Talking Disney With The Artists Who Knew Him - Pg. 29
2013 - Walt's People: Volume 13: Talking Disney With The Artists Who Knew Him - Pg. 29
2013 - Disney's Grand Tour: Walt and Roy's European Summer Vacation, Summer 1935 - Pg. 110
2014 - Walt's People: Volume 14: Talking Disney With The Artists Who Knew

Him - Pg. 29
2014 - Walt's People: Volume 15: Talking Disney With The Artists Who Knew Him - Pg. 29
2015 - Walt's People: Volume 16: Talking Disney With The Artists Who Knew Him - Pg. 30
2015 - Walt's People: Volume 17: Talking Disney With The Artists Who Knew Him - Pg. 30
2015 - They Drew as They Pleased: The Hidden Art of Disney's Golden Age (The 1930s) - Pg. 27
2016 - They Drew As they Pleased: The Hidden Art of Disney's Musical Years (The 1940s - Part One) - Pg. 27
2016 - Walt's People: Volume 18: Talking Disney With The Artists Who Knew Him - Pg. 30
2016 - The Walt Disney Film Archives: The Animated Movies 1921-1968 - Pg. 126 (*Also see Allan, Robin. Kaufman, J. B. Kothenschulte, Daniel. Lasseter, John. Lüthge, Katja. Merritt, Russell. Sibley, Brian. Solomon, Charles.*)
2016 - How to Be a Disney Historian: Tips from the Top Professionals - Pg. 149 (*Also see Beck, Jerry. Ehrbar, Greg. Fanning, Jim. Jurtti, Jeff. Kaufman, J.B. Korkis, Jim. Lowery, Paula Sigman.*)
2017 - Walt's People: Volume 19: Talking Disney With The Artists Who Knew Him - Pg. 30
2017 - Walt's People: Volume 20: Talking Disney With The Artists Who Knew Him - Pg. 30
2017 - They Drew as They Pleased Vol. 3: The Hidden Art of Disney's Late Golden Age (The 1940s - Part Two) - Pg. 27
2018 - Walt's People: Volume 21: Talking Disney With The Artists Who Knew Him - Pg. 30
2018 - They Drew As They Pleased Vol 4: The Hidden Art of Disney's Mid-Century Era - Pg. 27
2019 - Walt's People: Volume 22: Talking Disney With The Artists Who Knew Him - Pg. 31
2019 - Walt's People: Volume 23: Talking Disney With The Artists Who Knew Him - Pg. 31
2019 - 2019 Hyperion Historical Society Alliance Annual Report - Pg. 149 (*Also see Apgar, Garry. Bossert, David. Hollifield, Jim. Pierce, Todd James. Seastrom, Lucas.*)
2019 - They Drew as They Pleased Vol 5: The Hidden Art of Disney's Early Renaissance: The 1970s and 1980s - Pg. 27
2020 - Walt's People: Volume 24: Talking Disney With The Artists Who Knew Him - Pg. 31

2020 - 2020 Hyperion Historical Society Alliance Annual Report - Pg. 149 (*Also see Johnson, Mindy. Kaufman, J.B. Kern, Kevin M. Moryc, Matt.*)
2020 - They Drew As They Pleased Volume 6: The Hidden Art of Disney's New Golden Age - Pg. 27
2021 - Walt's People: Volume 25: Talking Disney With The Artists Who Knew Him - Pg. 31

Gibson, Ian

2007 - The Art of Reboot - Pg. 104 (*Also see Blair, Gavin. Jackson, Mike. McCarthy, Brendan. Nicholls, Ken. Roberts, David. Su, Jim.*)

Gibson, Jon M.

2008 - Unfiltered: The Complete Ralph Bakshi - Pg. 97 (*Also see McDonnell, Chris.*)

Giesen, Rolf

2012 - Animation Under the Swastika: A History of Trickfilm in Nazi Germany, 1933-1945 - Pg. 217
2014 - Chinese Animation: A History and Filmography, 1922-2012 - Pg. 214
2017 - Acting and Character Animation: The Art of Animated Films, Acting and Visualizing - Pg. 42 (*Also see Khan, Anna.*)

Gifford, Denis

1979 - The Great Cartoon Stars: A Who's Who - Pg. 13
1987 - British Animated Films, 1895-1985: A Filmography - Pg. 217
1990 - American Animated Films: The Silent Era, 1897-1929 - Pg. 13

Gilfor, Jeremy

2021 - The Art of Rick and Morty Volume 2 - Pg. 172

Gillam, Ken

2014 - Pixar's Boy Stories: Masculinity in a Postmodern Age - Pg. 151 (*Also see Wooden, Shannon R.*)

Gilliam, Terry

1978 - Animations of Mortality - Pg. 20

Gilic, Nikica

2018 - Global Animation Theory: International Perspectives at Animafest Zagreb - Pg. 211 (*Also see Bruckner, Franziska. Lang, Holger. Šuljic, Daniel. Turkovic, Hrvoje.*)

Gillick, Liam

2003 - Animations - Pg. 39 (*Also see Alys, Francis. Akakce, Haluk. Bendazzi, Giannalberto. Blake, Jeremy. Canemaker, John. Christov-Bakargiev, Carolyn. Galbraith, David. Harries, Larissa. Klein, Norman. Marks, Melissa. Riegel, Karyn.*)

Gilman, John

2003 - Mickey Mouse: The Evolution, The Legend, The Phenomenon! - Pg. 225 (*Also see Heide, Robert.*)

Giroux, Henry A.

1999 - The Mouse that Roared: Disney and the End of Innocence - Pg. 145

Girveau, Bruno

2007 - Once Upon a Time: Walt Disney: The Sources of Inspiration for the Disney Studios - Pg. 120

Gitlin, Martin "Marty"

2018 - A Celebration of Animation: The 100 Greatest Cartoon Characters in Television History - Pg. 13

Glass, Sherri

2006 - Cool Careers Without College for People Who Love Manga, Comics, and Animation - Pg. 225 (*Also see Wentzel, Jim.*)

Godfrey, Bob

1974 - The Do-It-Yourself Film Animation Book - Pg. 21 (*Also see Jackson, Anna.*)

Goldberg, Aaron

2016 - The Disney Story: Chronicling The Man, The Mouse & The Parks - Pg. 110

Goldberg, Eric

2008 - Character Animation Crash Course! - Pg. 21

Goldman, Michael

2010 - Original Cartoons, Volume 2 : The Frederator Studios Postcards 2006-2010 - Pg. 164 (*Also see Goldman, Michael. Homan, Eric. Seibert, Fred.*)
2019 - The Art and Making of the Lion King - Pg. 137

Goldmark, Daniel

2002 – The Cartoon Music Book - Pg. 74 (*Also see Granata, Charles L.*)
2005 - Tunes for 'Toons: Music and the Hollywood Cartoon - Pg. 74
2011 - Funny Pictures: Animation and Comedy in Studio-Era Hollywood - Pg. 60 (*Also see Keil, Charlie.*)

Goldschmidt, Rick

1997 - The Enchanted World of Rankin/Bass - Pg. 98
2001 - Rudolph The Red-Nosed Reindeer: The Making Of The Rankin/Bass Holiday Classic - Pg. 98
2011 - Rankin/Bass' Mad Monster Party - Pg. 98
2014 - The Arthur Rankin, Jr. Scrapbook: The Birth of Animagic - Pg. 98
2018 - The Making of Santa Claus Is Comin' To Town and The Daydreamer - Pg. 84
2019 - Rankin/Bass' Frosty the Snowman's 50th Anniversary Scrapbook - Pg. 98

Gordon, Bruce

2000 - A Brush with Disney: An Artist's Journey, Told through the words and works of Herbert Dickens Ryman - Pg. 115 (*Also see Mumford, David.*)

Graber, Sheila

2011 - Animation: A Handy Guide - Pg. 21

Grace, Whitney

2017 - Lotte Reiniger: Pioneer of Film Animation - Pg. 85

Graham, Jefferson

1998 - Ultimate Rugrats Fan Book - Pg. 224

Graham, Miyako

1986 - A Viewer's Guide to Japanese Animation - Pg. 181 (*Also see Smith, Toren.*)

Granata, Charles L.

2002 – The Cartoon Music Book - Pg. 74 (*Also see Goldmark, Daniel.*)

Grandinetti, Fred M.

1990 - Popeye, the Collectible: Dolls, Coloring Books, Games, Toys, Comic Books, Animation - Pg. 21
2007 - He Am What He Am! Jack Mercer, the Voice of Popeye. - Pg. 85
2022 – Popeye the Sailor: The 1960s TV Cartoons – Pg. 99

Grant, John

1987 - Encyclopedia of Walt Disney's Animated Characters: From Mickey Mouse to Hercules - Pg. 129
2001 - Masters of Animation - Pg. 85

Gravett, Paul

2010 - Manga Impact: The World of Japanese Animation - Pg. 200 (*Also see Brophy, Philip. Chatfield, Carl. Clements, Jonathan. Costa, Jordi. Della Casa, Luca. Delorme, Stéphane. Di Giorgio, Davide. Dottorini, Daniele. Gariglio, Stefano. Higuinen, Erwan. Liberti, Fabrizio. McCarthy, Helen. Modina, Fabrizio. Nazzaro, Giona A. Roberta, Maria. Paganelli, Grazia. Rondolino, Gianni. Roudevitch, Michel. Rumor, Mario A. Sarrazin, Stephen. Surman, David.*)

Graydon, Danny

2009 - The Art of Planet 51 - Pg. 105

Green, Amy Boothe

1999 - Remembering Walt: Favorite Memories of Walt Disney - Pg. 111 (*Also see Green, Howard E.*)

Green, Howard E.

1999 - Tarzan Chronicles - Pg. 137
1999 - Remembering Walt: Favorite Memories of Walt Disney - Pg. 111 (*Also see Green, Amy Boothe*)

Green, Sara

2019 - Animation - Pg. 233

Greenberg, Raz

2018 - Hayao Miyazaki: Exploring the Early Work of Japan's Greatest Animator (Animation: Key Films/Filmmakers) - Pg. 193

Greene, Katherine

1998 - The Man Behind the Magic: The Story of Walt Disney - Pg. 223 (*Also see Greene, Richard.*)
2001 - Inside the Dream - Pg. 111 (*Also see Greene, Richard.*)

Greene, Richard

1998 - The Man Behind the Magic: The Story of Walt Disney - Pg. 223 (*Also see Greene, Katherine.*)
2001 - Inside the Dream - Pg. 111 (*Also see Greene, Katherine.*)

Gregory, Josh

2014 - Animation: From Concept to Consumer - Pg. 232

Grenville, Bruce

2008 - KRAZY!: The Delirious World of Anime + Comics + Video Games + Art - Pg. 99

Gresh, Lois H.

2005 - The Science of Anime: Mecha-Noids and AI-Super-Bots - Pg. 226 (*Also see Weinberg, Robert.*)

Gross, Yoram

2014 - My Animated Life - Pg. 85

Grover, Ron

1991 - The Disney Touch: How a Daring Management Team Revived an Entertainment Empire - Pg. 121

Guglielmo, Amy

2017 - Pocket Full of Colors: The Magical World of Mary Blair, Disney Artist Extraordinaire - Pg. 236 (*Also see Tourville, Jacqueline.*)

Gurr, Bob

2015 - Great Big Beautiful Tomorrow: Walt Disney and Technology - Pg. 120 (*Also see Crump, Rolly. Moran, Christian.*)

Gutierrez, Jorge

2014 - The Art of the Book of Life - Pg. 157
2021 - The Art of Maya and the Three - Pg. 175

Haas, Lynda

1995 - From Mouse to Mermaid: The Politics of Film, Gender, and Culture - Pg. 144 (*Also see Bell, Elizabeth. Sells, Laura.*)

Hahn, Don

2008 - The Alchemy of Animation: Making an Animated Film in the Modern Age - Pg. 121
2017 - Yesterday's Tomorrow: Disney's Magical Mid-Century - Pg. 149

Hahn, Matthew

2017 - The Animated Marx Brothers - Pg. 99
2020 - The Animated Peter Lorre - Pg. 99

Halas, John

1958 - How to Cartoon for Amateur Films - Pg. 21 (*Also see Privett, Bob.*)
1959 - The Technique of Film Animation - Pg. 21 (*Also see Manvell, Roger.*)
1974 - Computer Animation - Pg. 51
1981 - Timing for Animation - Pg. 77 (*Also see Whitaker, Harold.*)
1987 - Masters of Animation - Pg. 85
1990 - The Contemporary Animator - Pg. 42

Halas, Vivien

2007 - Halas & Batchelor Cartoons - Pg. 217 (*Also see Wells, Paul.*)

Hamalainen, Karina

2017 - Animation - Pg. 233

Hamlyn, Nicky

2018 - Experimental and Expanded Animation: New Perspectives and Practices (Experimental Film and Artists' Moving Image) 2018 Edition - Pg. 57 (*Also see Smith, Vicky.*)

Hamm, Gene

2006 - How To Get A Job In Animation (and Keep It) - Pg. 21

Hammelef, Danielle S.

2015 - Eye-Popping CGI: Computer-Generated Special Effects - Pg. 232

Hammer, Doc

2018 - Go Team Venture!: The Art and Making of The Venture Bros. - Pg. 172 (*Also see Hammer, Doc. Plume, Ken. Publick, Jackson.*)

Hammontree, Marie

1997 - Walt Disney: Young Movie Maker - Pg. 224

Hamonic, Gerald

2018 - Terrytoons: The Story of Paul Terry and His Classic Cartoon Factory - Pg. 85

Hand, David Dodd

1991 - Memoirs - Pg. 86
2018 - Animation Pioneer: David Dodd Hand - Pg. 85 (*Also see Hand, David Hale.*)

Hand, David Hale

2018 - Animation Pioneer: David Dodd Hand - Pg. 85 (*Also see Hand, David Dodd.*)

Handke, Daniel

2012 - Poster Art of the Disney Parks (A Disney Parks Souvenir Book) - Pg. 137 (*Also see Hunt, Vanessa.*)

Hankin, Mike

2008 - Ray Harryhausen - Master of the Majicks Volume 2 - Pg. 31
2010 - Ray Harryhausen - Master of the Majicks: The British Films Volume 3 - Pg. 31
2013 - Ray Harryhausen - Master of Majicks Volume 1 - Pg. 31

Hanna, Jack

2017 - From Donald Duck's Daddy to Disney Legend - Pg. 115

Hanna, William

1996 - A Cast of Friends - Pg. 168

Hansen, Grace

2015 - Walt Disney: Animator & Founder - Pg. 232

Hara, Kunio

2020 - Joe Hisaishi's Soundtrack for My Neighbor Totoro (33 1/3 Japan) - Pg. 188

Harmony Gold

2017 - Robotech Visual Archive: The Macross Saga - Pg. 206

Harries, Larissa

2003 - Animations - Pg. 39 (*Also see Alys, Francis. Akakce, Haluk. Bendazzi, Giannalberto. Blake, Jeremy. Canemaker, John. Christov-Bakargiev, Carolyn. Galbraith, David. Gillick, Liam. Klein, Norman. Marks, Melissa. Riegel, Karyn.*)

Harrington, Seán J.

2015 - The Disney Fetish - Pg. 145

Harris, Miriam

2019 - Experimental Animation: From Analogue to Digital - Pg. 57 (*Also see Husbands, Lilly. Taberham, Paul.*)

Harryhausen, Ray

2003 - Ray Harryhausen: An Animated Life - Pg. 83
2006 - The Art of Ray Harryhausen - Pg. 105 (*Also see Dalton, Tony.*)
2008 - A Century of Stop-Motion Animation: From Melies to Aardman - Pg. 54
2008 - A Century of Model Animation: From Méliès to Aardman - Pg. 54 (*Also see Dalton, Tony.*)

Hartline, Aaron

2018 - Box Meets Circle: Pixar Animation Studios Artist Showcase - Pg. 236

Hauser, Tim

2008 - The Art of WALL-E - Pg. 155
2009 - The Art of Up - Pg. 155

Hayashibara, Megumi

2021 - The Characters Taught Me Everything: Living Life One Episode at a Time - Pg. 189

Haynes, Emily

2016 - The Art of Kubo and the Two Strings - Pg. 179

Hégron Ph. D., Gerard

1996 - Computer Animation and Simulation '96: Proceedings of the Eurographics Workshop in Poitiers, France, August 31–September 1, 1996 - Pg. 34 (*Also see Ronan Boulic Ph. D.*)
1999 - Computer Animation and Simulation '98 - Pg. 34 (*Also see Hegron, Gerard.*)

Heide, Robert

2003 - Mickey Mouse: The Evolution, The Legend, The Phenomenon! - Pg. 225 (*Also see Gilman, John.*)

Hellige, Hendrik

2001 - Anime! - Pg. 206 (*Also see Hillmen, Jan-Rikus. Klanten, Robert. Meyer, Birga. Tielgekamp, Vicky.*)

Hendershot, Heather

1999 - Saturday Morning Censors: Television Regulation before the V-Chip - Pg. 70

2004 - Nickelodeon Nation: The History, Politics, and Economics of America's Only TV Channel for Kids - Pg. 161

Heraldson, Donald

1975 - Creators of Life: A History of Animation - Pg. 63

Herdeg, Walter

1976 - Film and TV Graphics, 2 - Pg. 60

Herhuth, Eric

2017 - Pixar and the Aesthetic Imagination: Animation, Storytelling, and Digital Culture - Pg. 152

Hernández-Pérez, Manuel

2019 - Japanese Media Cultures in Japan and Abroad: Transnational Consumption of Manga, Anime, and Media-Mixes - Pg. 186

Hershenson, Bruce

1994 - Cartoon Movie Posters - Pg. 105
1999 - Vintage Hollywood Posters II - Pg. 105

Hertz, Betti-Sue

2007 - Animated Worlds - Pg. 77 (*Also see Buchan, Suzanne. Manovich, Lev.*)

Hiaasen, Carl

1998 - Team Rodent: How Disney Devours the World - Pg. 145

Hickner, Steve

2013 - Animating Your Career - Pg. 22

Hieronimus, Robert

2002 - Inside the Yellow Submarine: The Making of the Beatles' Animated Classic - Pg. 99

Higgins, Steven

2006 - Pixar: At the Museum of Modern Art - Pg. 155 (*Also see Magliozzi, Ronald S.*)

Higuinen, Erwan

2010 - Manga Impact: The World of Japanese Animation - Pg. 200 (*Also see Brophy, Philip. Chatfield, Carl. Clements, Jonathan. Costa, Jordi. Della Casa, Luca. Delorme, Stéphane. Di Giorgio, Davide. Dottorini, Daniele. Gariglio, Stefano. Gravett, Paul. Liberti, Fabrizio. McCarthy, Helen. Modina, Fabrizio. Nazzaro, Giona A. Paganelli, Grazia. Roberta, Maria. Rondolino, Gianni. Roudevitch, Michel. Rumor, Mario A. Sarrazin, Stephen. Surman, David.*)

Hillmen, Jan-Rikus

2001 - Anime! - Pg. 206 (*Also see Hellige, Hendrik. Klanten, Robert. Meyer, Birga. Tielgekamp, Vicky.*)

Hinote Lanier, Wendy

2020 - Making an Animated Movie (How It's Done) - Pg. 234

Hischak, Thomas S.

2009 - The Disney Song Encyclopedia - Pg. 147
2011 - Disney Voice Actors: A Biographical Dictionary - Pg. 115
2018 - 100 Greatest American and British Animated Films - Pg. 13

Hobby Book Editorial Department

2022 – Overlord: The Complete Anime Artbook II III - Pg. 206

Hodge, James

2019 - Sensations of History: Animation and New Media Art - Pg. 43

Hodge, Matthew

2020 - Cool Cats and a Hot Mouse: A History of Jazz and Disney - Pg. 147

Hoena, Blake

2019 - A Stop-Motion Animation Mission - Pg. 240 (*Also see McClintock Miller, Shannon.*)

Hoffer, Thomas W.

1981 - Animation: A Reference Guide - Pg. 22

Holliday, Christopher

2020 - Fantasy/Animation: Connections Between Media, Mediums and Genres - Pg. 47 (*Also see Holliday, Christopher. Sergeant, Alexander.*)
2021 - Snow White and the Seven Dwarfs: New Perspectives on Production, Reception, Legacy - Pg. 129 (*Also see Holliday, Christopher. Sergeant, Alexander.*)

Hollifield, Jim

2019 - 2019 Hyperion Historical Society Alliance Annual Report - Pg. 149 (*Also see Apgar, Garry. Bossert, David. Ghez, Didier. Pierce, Todd James. Seastrom, Lucas.*)

Hollis, Tim

2006 - Mouse Tracks: The Story of Walt Disney Records - Pg. 147 (*Also see Ehrbar, Greg.*)
2015 - Toys in Toyland: The Story of Cartoon Character Merchandise - Pg. 60

Holliss, Richard

1987 - Walt Disney's Snow White and the Seven Dwarfs & the Making of the Classic Film - Pg. 129
1988 - The Disney Studio Story - Pg. 121
2018 - Harryhausen - The Movie Posters - Pg. 105

Holloway, Ronald

1972 - Z is for Zagreb - Pg. 217

Holman, L. Bruce

1975 - Puppet Animation In The Cinema: History And Technique - Pg. 54

Holt, Nathalia

2019 - The Queens of Animation: The Untold Story of the Women Who Transformed the World of Disney and Made Cinematic History - Pg. 86

Holz, Jo

2017 - Kids' TV Grows Up: The Path from Howdy Doody to SpongeBob - Pg. 60

Homan, Eric

2005 - Original Cartoons: The Frederator Studio Postcards 1998-2005 - Pg. 163 (*Also see Seibert, Fred.*)
2010 - Original Cartoon Posters: From Frederator Studios - Pg. 163
2010 - Original Cartoons, Volume 2 : The Frederator Studios Postcards 2006-2010 - Pg. 163 (*Also see Goldman, Michael. Seibert, Fred.*)

Honess Roe, Annabelle

2013 - Animated Documentary - Pg. 47
2018 - The Animation Studies Reader - Pg. 41 (*Also see Dobson, Nichola. Ratelle, Amy. Ruddell, Caroline.*)
2020 - Aardman Animations: Beyond Stop-Motion - Pg. 55

Hooks, Ed

2001 - Acting for Animators - Pg. 22
2005 - Acting in Animation: A Look at 12 Films - Pg. 99

Hopkins, John

2004 - Shrek: From the Swamp to the Screen - Pg. 158

Horn, Geoffrey M.

2006 - Movie Animation (The Magic of Movies) - Pg. 227

Horn, Maurice

1979 - The World Encyclopedia of Cartoons - Pg. 13

Horrocks, Roger

2001 - Len Lye: A Biography - Pg. 219

Horvath, Gyongyi

2020 - Animating the Spirited: Journeys and Transformations - Pg. 71 (*Also see Hu, Tze-yue. Yokota, Masao.*)

Hosoda, Mamoru

2021 - Summer Wars: Material Book - Pg. 206

Hosei University

2010 - Anime and Its Roots in Early Japanese Monster Art - Pg. 191 (*Also see Papp, Tokyo Zilia.*)

Hristova, Svetla

2015 - The Animation World of Ivan Vesselinov - Pg. 213 (*Also see Minaeva, Oksana.*)

Hu, Tze-yue

2010 - Frames of Anime: Culture and Image-Building - Pg. 202
2020 - Animating the Spirited: Journeys and Transformations - Pg. 71 (*Also see Horvath, Gyongyi. Yokota, Masao.*)

Hueso, Noela

2013 - The Art of DreamWorks The Croods - Pg. 158

Hulett, Scott

2014 - Mouse in Transition: An Insider's Look at Disney Feature Animation - Pg. 129
2018 - Mouse in Orbit: An Inside Look at How the Walt Disney Company Took a Neglected, Moribund Art Form and Turned It into a Mainstream Movie Powerhouse - Pg. 121

Hunt, Vanessa

2012 - Poster Art of the Disney Parks (A Disney Parks Souvenir Book) - Pg. 137 (*Also see Handke, Daniel.*)

Hunter, Nick

2014 - Animator: The Coolest Jobs on the Planet - Pg. 232 (*Also see Bancroft, Tom.*)

Husbands, Lilly

2019 - Experimental Animation: From Analogue to Digital - Pg. 57 (*Also see Harris, Miriam. Taberham, Paul.*)

Hyperion

1993 - The Disney Poster: The Animated Film Classics from Mickey Mouse to Aladdin - Pg. 136

IEEE Computer Society

1998 - Computer Animation '98: Proceedings Philadelphia, University Of Pennsylvania June 8-10, 1998 - Pg. 37 (*Also see Institute of Electrical and Electronics Engineers.*)
2002 - Proceedings Of Computer Animation 2002: 19-21 June 2002 Geneva, Switzerland - Pg. 36
2003 - 16th International Conference on Computer Animation and Social Agents: 8-9 May 2003, New Brunswick, New Jersey - Pg. 38

Iger, Robert

2019 - The Ride of a Lifetime: Lessons Learned from 15 Years as CEO of the Walt Disney Company - Pg. 121

Iglesias, José Andrés Santiago

2021 - Anime Studies: Media-Specific Approaches to Neon Genesis Evangelion - Pg. 188 (*Also see Baena, Ana Soler.*)

Institute of Electrical and Electronics Engineers

1996 - Computer Animation Conference 1996: June 3, 1996 to June 4, 1996, Geneva, Switzerland - Pg. 37
1997 - Computer Animation '97: June 5-6, 1997, Geneva, Switzerland - Pg. 37
1998 - Computer Animation '98: Proceedings Philadelphia, University Of Pennsylvania June 8-10, 1998 - Pg. 37 (*Also see IEEE Computer Society.*)
1999 - Computer Animation '99: May 26-29, 1999 Geneva, Switzerland - Pg. 38
2001 - Computer Animation 2000: May 3, 2000 to May 5, 2000, Philadelphia, Pennsylvania - Pg. 38
2001 - Computer Animation 2001: The Fourteenth Conference on Computer Animation Seoul, Korea November 7-8, 2001 - Pg. 38

Isbouts, Jean-Pierre

2001 - Discovering Walt: The Magical Life of Walt Disney - Pg. 225

Ison, Stephen H.

1994 - Walt Disney's Snow White and the Seven Dwarfs: An Art in Its Making - Pg. 137 (*Also see Krause, Martin. Witowski, Linda.*)

Itou, Naoyuki

2020 - Overlord: The Complete Anime Artbook - Pg. 206

Iwerks, Don

2019 - Walt Disney's Ultimate Inventor: The Genius of Ub Iwerks - Pg. 116

Iwerks, Leslie

2001 - The Hand Behind the Mouse: An Intimate Biography of Ub Iwerks - Pg. 116 (*Also see Kenworthy, John.*)

Jackson, Anna

1974 - The Do-It-Yourself Film Animation Book - Pg. 21 (*Also see Godfrey, Bob.*)

Jackson, Kathy Merlock

1993 - Walt Disney: A Bio-Bibliography - Pg. 111
2005 - Walt Disney: Conversations - Pg. 111
2014 - Walt Disney, from Reader to Storyteller: Essays on the Literary Inspirations - Pg. 129 (*Also see West, Mark I.*)

Jackson, Mike

2007 - The Art of Reboot - Pg. 104 (*Also see Blair, Gavin. Gibson, Ian. McCarthy, Brendan. Nicholls, Ken. Roberts, David. Su, Jim.*)

Jacobs, Brendan

2020 - Explanatory Animations in the Classroom: Student-Authored Animations as Digital Pedagogy - Pg. 234

Jacobs, Chip

2016 - Strange as it Seems: The Impossible Life of Gordon Zahler - Pg. 86

Jeffery, S. B.

2011 - The History of Walt Disney Animation - Pg. 130

Jenkins, Eric

2014 - Special Affects: Cinema, Animation and the Translation of Consumer Culture - Pg. 61

Jeup, Dan

2015 - 50 Years in the Mouse House: The Lost Memoir of One of Disney's Nine Old Men - Pg. 116 (*Also see Kaufman, J.B. Larson, Eric.*)

Johnson, David

2017 - Snow White's People: An Oral History of the Disney Film Snow White and the Seven Dwarfs (Volume 1) - Pg. 130
2018 - Snow White's People: An Oral History of the Disney Film Snow White and the Seven Dwarfs (Volume 2) - Pg. 130

Johnson, Jimmy

2014 - Inside the Whimsy Works: My Life with Walt Disney Productions - Pg. 116

Johnson, Mindy

2013 - Tinker Bell: An Evolution - Pg. 130
2017 - Ink & Paint: The Women of Walt Disney's Animation - Pg. 116
2019 - Pencils, Pens & Brushes: A Great Girls' Guide to Disney Animation - Pg. 237
2020 - 2020 Hyperion Historical Society Alliance Annual Report - Pg. 146 (*Also see Ghez, Didier. Kaufman, J.B. Kern, Kevin M. Moryc, Matt.*)

Johnston, Andrew R.

2021 - Pulses of Abstraction: Episodes from a History of Animation - Pg. 57

Johnston, Jacob

2020 - The Art of Baobab: The Beginning - Pg. 177

Johnston, Ollie

1987 - Too Funny for Words: Disney's Greatest Sight Gags - Pg. 130 (*Also see Thomas, Frank.*)
1990 - Walt Disney's Bambi: The Story and the Film - Pg. 138 (*Also see Thomas, Frank.*)
1998 - Disney's Lady and the Tramp: The Sketchbook Series - Pg. 137 (*Also see Thomas, Frank.*)
1998 - Disney's Peter Pan: The Sketchbook Series - Pg. 138 (*Also see Thomas, Frank.*)

Jones, Angie

2006 - Thinking Animation: Bridging the Gap Between 2D and CG - Pg. 51 (*Also see Oliff, Jamie.*)

Jones, Chuck

1989 - Chuck Amuck: The Life and Times of an Animated Cartoonist - Pg. 165
1996 - Chuck Reducks: Drawing from the Fun Side of Life - Pg. 166
2019 - The Animated Art Of Chuck Jones, Volume 1 - Pg. 105
2020 - The Animated Art Of Chuck Jones, Volume 2 - Pg. 106
2022 - The Animated Art Of Chuck Jones, Volume 3 - Pg. 106

Jones, Kathleen

2007 - Shrek: The Art of the Quest - Pg. 158

Jones, Stephen

2009 - Coraline: A Visual Companion - Pg. 179

Josephson, Judith Pinkerton

2006 - Walt Disney: Genius of Entertainment - Pg. 227

Ju-yu Cheng, Catherine

2021 - Thinking with Animation - Pg. 209 (*Also see Bradley, Joff P. N.*)

Julius, Jessica

2014 - The Art of Big Hero 6 – Pg. 138
2016 - The Art of Zootopia - Pg. 138
2016 - The Art of Moana - Pg. 138 (*Also see Malone, Maggie.*)
2018 - The Art of Wreck-It Ralph 2 - Pg. 138
2019 - The Art of Frozen 2 - Pg. 138

Jurtti, Jeff

2016 - How to Be a Disney Historian: Tips from the Top Professionals - Pg. 149 (*Also see Beck, Jerry. Ehrbar, Greg. Fanning, Jim. Ghez, Didier. Kaufman, J.B. Korkis, Jim. Lowery, Paula Sigman.*)

Justice, Bill

1992 - Justice for Disney - Pg. 116

K, Suresh

2008 - Animation Industry (Industry Analysis Series) - Pg. 61 (*Also see Rao, Krishna.*)

Kaiser, Lisbeth

2021 - Who Was Walt Disney?: A Who Was? Board Book - Pg. 238

Kalen, Elizabeth

2012 - Mostly Manga: A Genre Guide to Popular Manga, Manhwa, Manhua, and Anime - Pg. 182

Kallay, William

2011- The Making of Tron: How Tron Changed Visual Effects and Disney Forever - Pg. 130

Kanfer, Stefan

1997 - Serious Business: The Art And Commerce Of Animation In America From Betty Boop To Toy Story - Pg. 61

Karahashi, Takayuki

1997 - Anime Interviews: The First Five Years of Animerica, Anime & Manga Monthly - Pg. 245

Katsaridou, Maria

2022 - Sylvain Chomet's Distinctive Animation: From The Triplets of Belleville to The Illusionist - Pg. 86

Katz, Maya Balakirsky

2016 - Drawing the Iron Curtain: Jews and the Golden Age of Soviet Animation - Pg. 220

Kaufman, J.B.

2006 - Walt Disney's Silly Symphonies: A Companion to the Classic Cartoon Series - Pg. 131 (*Also see Merritt, Russell.*)
2009 - South of the Border with Disney - Pg. 122
2012 - The Fairest One of All: The Making of Snow White and the Seven Dwarfs - Pg. 131
2012 - Snow White and the Seven Dwarfs: The Art and Creation of Walt Disney's Classic Animated Film - Pg. 138
2015 - Pinocchio - The Making of an Epic - Pg. 130
2015 - 50 Years in the Mouse House: The Lost Memoir of One of Disney's Nine Old Men - Pg. 116 (*Also see Jeup, Dan. Larson, Eric.*)
2016 - The Walt Disney Film Archives: The Animated Movies 1921-1968 - Pg. 126 (*Also see Allan, Robin. Ghez, Didier. Kothenschulte, Daniel. Lasseter, John. Lüthge, Katja. Merritt, Russell. Sibley, Brian. Solomon, Charles.*)
2016 - How to Be a Disney Historian: Tips from the Top Professionals - Pg. 149 (*Also see Beck, Jerry. Ehrbar, Greg. Fanning, Jim. Ghez, Didier. Jurtti, Jeff. Korkis, Jim. Lowery, Paula Sigman.*)
2018 - Walt Disney's Mickey Mouse: The Ultimate History - Pg. 128 (*Also see Gerstein, David.*)
2019 - The Making of Walt Disney's Fun and Fancy Free - Pg. 131
2020 - 2020 Hyperion Historical Society Alliance Annual Report - Pg. 149 (*Also see Ghez, Didier. Johnson, Mindy. Kern, Kevin M. Moryc, Matt.*)

Keefer, Cindy

2013 - Oskar Fischinger (1900-1967): Experiments in Cinematic Abstraction - Pg. 86

Keenan, Sheila

1995 - The History of Moviemaking: Animation and Live-Action, from Silent to Sound, Black-And-White to Color - Pg. 223

Keil, Charlie

2011 - Funny Pictures: Animation and Comedy in Studio-Era Hollywood - Pg. 60 (*Also see Goldmark, Daniel.*)

Kelland, Matt

2005 - Machinima - Pg. 51 (*Also see Lloyd, Dave. Morris, Dave.*)

Keller, James R.

2009 - The Deep End of South Park: Critical Essays on Television's Shocking Cartoon Series - Pg. 99 (*Also see Stratyner, Leslie.*)

Kelts, Roland

2007 - Japanamerica: How Japanese Pop Culture Has Invaded the U.S. - Pg. 186
2022 - The Art of Blade Runner: Black Lotus - Pg. 106

Kemper, Tom

2015 - Toy Story: A Critical Reading (BFI Film Classics) - Pg. 152

Kenner, Hugh

1994 - Chuck Jones: A Flurry of Drawings (Portraits of American Genius #3) - Pg. 166

Kenworthy, John

2001 - The Hand Behind the Mouse: An Intimate Biography of Ub Iwerks - Pg. 116 (*Also see Iwerks, Leslie.*)

Kerlow, Isaac Victor

1996 - The Art of 3-D Computer: Animation and Imaging – Pg. 51

Keslowitz, Steven

2006 - The World According to The Simpsons: What Our Favorite TV Family Says about Life, Love, and the Pursuit of the Perfect Donut - Pg. 100

Kern, Kevin M.

2020 - 2020 Hyperion Historical Society Alliance Annual Report - Pg. 149 (*Also see Ghez, Didier. Johnson, Mindy. Kaufman, J.B. Moryc, Matt.*)

Khan, Anna

2017 - Acting and Character Animation: The Art of Animated Films, Acting and Visualizing - Pg. 42 (*Also see Giesen, Rolf.*)

khara, Inc.

2019 - Evangelion Illustrations 2007-2017 - Pg. 207

Kidd, Chip

1998 - Batman Animated - Pg. 97 (*Also see Dini, Paul.*)

Kilmer, David

1998 - The Animated Film Collector's Guide: Worldwide Sources for Cartoons on Videotape and Laserdisc - Pg. 14

Kinder, Bill

2022 - Making the Cut at Pixar: The Art of Editing Animation – Pg. 152 (*Also see O'Steen, Bobbie.*)

King, C. Richard

2010 - Animating Difference: Race, Gender, and Sexuality in Contemporary Films for Children - Pg 40 (*Also see Bloodsworth-Lugo, Mary K. and Lugo-Lugo, Carmen R.*)

Kinney, Jack

1988 - Walt Disney and Other Assorted Characters: An Unauthorized Account of the Early Years at Disney's - Pg. 122

Kirsch, Max H.

2005 - Rethinking Disney: Private Control, Public Dimensions - Pg. 119 (*Also see Budd, Mike.*)

Kitson, Clare

2005 - Yuri Norstein and Tale of Tales: An Animator's Journey - Pg. 220
2009 - British Animation: The Channel 4 Factor - Pg. 218

Klanten, Robert

2001 – Anime! - Pg. 206 (*Also see Hellige, Hendrik. Hillmen, Jan-Rikus. Meyer, Birga. Tielgekamp, Vicky.*)

Klein, Norman

1993 - 7 Minutes: The Life and Death of the American Animated Cartoon - Pg. 67
2003 - Animations - Pg. 39 (*Also see Alys, Francis. Akakce, Haluk. Bendazzi, Giannalberto. Blake, Jeremy. Canemaker, John. Christov-Bakargiev, Carolyn. Galbraith, David. Gillick, Liam. Harries, Larissa. Marks, Melissa. Riegel, Karyn.*)

Klocek, Noah

2015 - Cloud Country: Pixar Animation Studios Artist Showcase - Pg. 235 (*Also see Becker, Bonny.*)

Ko, Hyeong-Seok

2001 - Computer Animation 2001: The Fourteenth Conference on Computer Animation Seoul, Korea November 7-8, 2001: Proceedings - Pg. 38

Koenig, David

1997 - Mouse Under Glass: Secrets of Disney Animation and Theme Parks - Pg. 131

Kolk, Melinda

2006 - Teaching with Clay Animation - Pg. 227

Komorowski, Thad

2013 - Sick Little Monkeys: The Unauthorized Ren & Stimpy Story - Pg. 161

Kon, Satoshi

2015 - The Art of Satoshi Kon - Pg. 206 (*Also see Davisson, Zack.*)

Konietzko, Bryan

2010 - Avatar: The Last Airbender (The Art of the Animated Series) - Pg. 162 (*Also see DiMartino, Michael Dante.*)
2013 - Legend of Korra: The Art of the Animated Series Book One: Air - Pg. 162 (*Also see DiMartino, Michael Dante. Santos, Joaquim Dos.*)
2014 - Legend of Korra: The Art of the Animated Series Book Two: Spirits - Pg. 162 (*Also see DiMartino, Michael Dante. Santos, Joaquim Dos.*)
2015 - Legend of Korra: The Art of the Animated Series Book Four: Balance - Pg. 163 (*Also see DiMartino, Michael Dante. Santos, Joaquim Dos.*)
2015 - Legend of Korra: The Art of the Animated Series Book Three: Change - Pg. 163 (*Also see DiMartino, Michael Dante. Santos, Joaquim Dos.*)

Korkis, Jim

1991 - Cartoon Confidential - Pg. 40 (*Also see Cawley, John.*)
2010 - The Vault of Walt - Pg. 31
2012 - Who's Afraid of the Song of the South? and Other Forbidden Disney Stories - Pg. 122
2012 - The Revised Vault of Walt: Unofficial Disney Stories Never Told - Pg. 31
2013 - The Vault of Walt: Volume 2: Unofficial, Unauthorized, Uncensored Disney Stories Never Told - Pg. 32
2013 - The Book of Mouse: A Celebration of Walt Disney's Mickey Mouse - Pg. 132 (*Also see Williams, Don.*)

2014 - Animation Anecdotes: The Hidden History of Classic American Animation - Pg. 63

2014 - Who's the Leader of the Club? Walt Disney's Leadership Lessons - Pg. 122

2014 - The Vault of Walt: Volume 3: Even More Unofficial Disney Stories Never Told - Pg. 32

2015 – Everything I Know I Learned from Disney Animated Feature Films: Advice for Living Happily After - Pg. 131

2015 - The Vault of Walt: Volume 4: Still More Unofficial Disney Stories Never Told - Pg. 32

2016 - Walt's Words - Pg. 111

2016 - The Vault of Walt: Volume 5: Additional Unofficial Disney Stories Never Told - Pg. 32

2016 - How to Be a Disney Historian: Tips from the Top Professionals - Pg. 149 (*Also see Beck, Jerry. Ehrbar, Greg. Fanning, Jim. Ghez, Didier. Jurtti, Jeff. Kaufman, J.B. Lowery, Paula Sigman.*)

2017 - Gremlin Trouble! The Cursed Roald Dahl Film Disney Never Made - Pg. 132

2017 - The Vault of Walt: Volume 6: Other Unofficial Disney Stories Never Told - Pg. 32

2017 - Call Me Walt: Everything You Never Knew About Walt Disney - Pg. 111

2018 - The Vault of Walt Volume 7: Christmas Edition: Yuletide Tales of Walt Disney, Disney Theme Parks, Cartoons & More - Pg. 32

2018 - Secret Stories of Mickey Mouse - Pg. 132

2019 - The Vault of Walt Volume 8: Outer Space Edition: Out-of-This-World Stories of Walt Disney, Disney Theme Parks, Films & More - Pg. 32

2020 - Vault of Walt 9: Halloween Edition: Spooky Stories of Disney Films, Theme Parks, and Things That Go Bump In the Night - Pg. 33

2021 - The Vault of Walt: Volume 10: Final Edition - Pg. 33

Kornhaber, Donna

2019 - Nightmares in the Dream Sanctuary: War and the Animated Film - Pg. 64

Kothenschulte, Daniel

2016 - The Walt Disney Film Archives: The Animated Movies 1921-1968 - Pg. 126 (*Also see Allan, Robin. Ghez, Didier. Kaufman, J. B. Lasseter, John. Lüthge, Katja. Merritt, Russell. Sibley, Brian. Solomon, Charles.*)

2021 - Hayao Miyazaki - Pg. 193 (*Also see Docter, Pete. Niebel, Jessica.*)

Kowalski, Jesse

2016 - Hanna-Barbera: The Architects of Saturday Morning - Pg. 168 (*Also see Beck, Jerry. Kowalski, Jesse. Mallory, Michael.*)

Koyama-Richard, Brigitte

2010 - Japanese Animation: From Painted Scrolls to Pokémon - Pg. 191

Kramer, Barbara

2017 - National Geographic Readers: Walt Disney - Pg. 233

Kraniewicz, Louise

2010 - Walt Disney: A Biography - Pg. 222

Kratter, Tia

2017 - The Color of Pixar - Pg. 155

Krause, Martin

1994 - Walt Disney's Snow White and the Seven Dwarfs: An Art in Its Making - Pg. 137 (*Also see Ison, Stephen H.. Witowski, Linda.*)

Kriger, Judith

2011 - Animated Realism: A Behind The Scenes Look at the Animated Documentary Genre - Pg. 47

Kroyer, Bill

2019 - On Animation: The Directors Perspective Vol. One - Pg. 77 (*Also see Sito, Tom.*)
2019 - On Animation - The Directors Perspective Vol. Two - Pg. 78 (*Also see Sito, Tom.*)

Kurata, Hideyuki

2013 - Read or Die: R.O.D. Official Archive - Pg. 207 (*Also see Masunari, Koji.*)

Kurtti, Jeff

2008 - Walt Disney's Sleeping Beauty: The Storybook and the Making of a Masterpiece - Pg. 132
1997 - The Art of the Little Mermaid - Pg. 139
1998 - The Art of Mulan - Pg. 138
1998 - A Bug's Life: The Art and Making of an Epic of Miniature Proportions - Pg. 155
2000 - Dinosaur: The Evolution of an Animated Feature - Pg. 138
2001 - Atlantis: The Lost Empire: The Illustrated Script - Pg. 138
2001 - Treasure Planet: A Voyage of Discovery - Pg. 139
2009 - The Art of The Princess and the Frog - Pg. 139
2010 - The Art of Tangled - Pg. 139
2018 - From All of Us to All of You The Disney Christmas Card - Pg. 138

Kuznets, Lois Rostow

1994 - When Toys Come Alive: Narratives of Animation, Metamorphosis, and Development - Pg. 54

Ladd, Fred

2008 - Astro Boy and Anime Come to the Americas: An Insider's View of the Birth of a Pop Culture Phenomenon - Pg. 186 (*Also see Deneroff, Harvey.*)

Lallo, M.J.

2009 - Voice-Over for Animation - Pg. 75 (*Also see Wright, Jean Ann.*)

Lamarre, Thomas

2009 - The Anime Machine: A Media Theory of Animation - Pg. 202
2018 - The Anime Ecology: A Genealogy of Television, Animation, and Game Media - Pg. 182

Lambert, Pierre

1997 - Pinocchio - Pg. 132
1998 - Mickey Mouse - Pg. 132
2013 – La Belle au Bois Domant – Pg. 139
2017 – Bambi – Pg. 139

Lane, Andy

2004 - The World of Wallace and Gromit - Pg. 100
2005 - The Art of Wallace & Gromit: The Curse of the Were-Rabbit - Pg. 177 (*Also see Simpson, Paul.*)

Lane, Kim

1989 - Animation - Pg. 222 (*Also see Amos, Janine.*)

Lang, Holger

2018 - Global Animation Theory: International Perspectives at Animafest Zagreb - Pg. 211 (*Also see Bruckner, Franziska. Gilic, Nikica. Šuljic, Daniel. Turkovic, Hrvoje.*)

Lanpher, Dorse A.

2010 - Flyin' Chunks and Other Things to Duck: Memoirs of a Life Spent Doodling for Dollars - Pg. 86

Larson, Eric

2015 - 50 Years in the Mouse House: The Lost Memoir of One of Disney's Nine Old Men - Pg. 116 (*Also see Jeup, Dan. Kaufman, J.B.*)

LaReau, Kara

2014 - No Slurping, No Burping! A Tale of Table Manners: Walt Disney Animation Studios Artist Showcase Book - Pg. 235

Lasseter, John

1995 - Toy Story The Art and Making of the Animated Film - Pg. 154 (*Also see Daly, Steve.*)
2001 - The Art of Monsters, Inc. - Pg. 155 (*Also see Docter, Pete.*)
2016 - The Art of Finding Dory - Pg. 155
2016 - The Walt Disney Film Archives: The Animated Movies 1921-1968 - Pg. 126 (*Also see Allan, Robin. Ghez, Didier. Kaufman, J. B. Kothenschulte, Daniel. Lüthge, Katja. Merritt, Russell. Sibley, Brian. Solomon, Charles.*)
2017 - The Art of Cars 3 - Pg. 155
2017 - The Art of Coco - Pg. 155

Lawson, Dawn

2011 - Beautiful Fighting Girl - Pg. 199 (*Also see Azuma, Hiroki. Saitō, Tamaki. Vincent, J. Keith.*)

Lawson, Tim

2004 - The Magic Behind the Voices: A Who's Who of Cartoon Voice Actors - Pg. 75

Laybourne, Kit

1979 - The Animation Book: A Complete Guide to Animated Filmmaking from Flip-Books to Sound Cartoons - Pg. 22

Le Blanc, Michelle

2009 - Studio Ghibli: The Films of Hayao Miyazaki and Isao Takahata - Pg. 194 (*Also see Odell, Colin.*)
2014 - Akira (BFI Film Classics) - Pg. 188
2014 - Anime - Pg. 182 (*Also see Odell, Colin.*)

Leab, Daniel

2007 - Orwell Subverted: The CIA and the Filming of Animal Farm - Pg. 67

Leasher, Ryan

2009 - Wilderness of the Mind: The Art of Joseph Mugnaini - Pg. 106

Ledoux, Trish

1996 - The Complete Anime Guide: Japanese Animation Film Directory & Resource Guide - Pg. 182 (*Also see Ranney, Doug.*)

Lee, Jennifer

2012 - The Art of Wreck-It Ralph - Pg. 139 (*Also see Malone, Maggie.*)

Lee, Newton

2012 - Disney Stories: Getting to Digital - Pg. 122 (*Also see Madej, Krystina.*)

Lehman, Christopher P.

2006 - American Animated Cartoons of the Vietnam Era: A Study of Social Commentary in Films And Television Programs, 1961-1973 - Pg. 67
2007 - The Colored Cartoon: Black Representation in American Animated Short Films, 1907-1954 - Pg. 67

Leigh, Michele

2020 - She Animates: Gendered Soviet and Russian Animation - Pg. 220 (*Also see Mjolsness, Lora.*)

Lemieux Wilson, Suzanne

2012 - Rowland B. Wilson's Trade Secrets: Notes on Cartooning and Animation - Pg. 91 (*Also see Wilson, Rowland B.*)

Lenburg, Jeff

1981 - The Encyclopedia of Animated Cartoon Series - Pg. 14
1983 - The Great Cartoon Directors - Pg. 86
2004 - How to Make a Million Dollars With Your Voice (Or Lose Your Tonsils Trying) - Pg. 75 (*Also see Owens, Gary.*)
2006 - Who's Who in Animated Cartoons: An International Guide to Film and Television's Award-Winning and Legendary Animators - Pg. 15
2011 - Career Opportunities in Animation - Pg. 22
2011 - Matt Groening: From Spitballs to Springfield - Pg. 229
2011 - Tex Avery: Hollywood's Master of Screwball Cartoons - Pg. 229
2011 - Walt Disney: The Mouse That Roared - Pg. 230
2011 - William Hanna and Joseph Barbera: The Sultans of Saturday Morning - Pg. 230
2012 - John Lasseter: The Whiz Who Made Pixar King - Pg. 230
2012 - Genndy Tartakovsky: From Russia to Coming-of-Age Animator - Pg. 230
2012 - Hayao Miyazaki: Japan's Premier Anime Storyteller - Pg. 230
2012 - Walter Lantz: Made Famous by a Woodpecker - Pg. 231

Lent, John

1994 - Animation, Caricature, and Gag and Political Cartoons in the United States and Canada: An International Bibliography - Pg. 15
2000 - Animation in Asian and the Pacific - Pg. 212

Leonardi, Art

2017 - The Animated Administration of James Norcross a.k.a. Super President - Pg. 93 (*Also see Beck, Jerry. Collier, Kevin Scott.*)

Lerew, Jenny

2012 - The Art of Brave - Pg. 156

Lescher, Mary E.

2022 - The Disney Animation Renaissance: Behind the Glass at the Florida Studio - Pg. 123

Lesjak, David

2014 - Service with Character: The Disney Studio & World War II - Pg. 149
2015 - In the Service of the Red Cross: Walt Disney's Early Adventures: 1918-1919 - Pg. 112

Leslie, Esther

2002 - Hollywood Flatlands: Animation, Critical Theory and the Avant-garde - Pg. 43

Leslie Clark, Miriam

2019 - Glimpses into the Golden Age of Disney Animation - Pg. 127 (*Also see Clark, Les.*)

Levete, Sarah

2013 - Make an Animation! - Pg. 231

Levi, Antonia

1998 - Samurai from Outer Space: Understanding Japanese Animation - Pg. 203

Levitan, Eli L.

1960 - Animation Art in the Commercial Film - Pg. 61
1962 - Animation Techniques and Commercial Film Production - Pg. 15
1977 - Electronic Imaging Techniques: A Handbook Of Conventional And Computer-Controlled Animation, Optical, And Editing Processes - Pg. 15
1979 - Handbook of Animation Techniques - Pg. 15

Levitt, Deborah

2018 - The Animatic Apparatus: Animation, Vitality, and the Futures of the Image - Pg. 43

Levy, David B.

2006 - Your Career in Animation: How to Survive and Thrive - Pg. 23
2010 - Directing Animation - Pg. 43
2011 - Independently Animated: Bill Plympton: The Life and Art of the King of Indie Animation - Pg. 87

Lewald, Eric

2017 - Previously on X-Men: The Making of an Animated Series - Pg. 100
2020 - X-Men: The Art and Making of The Animated Series - Pg. 106 (*Also see Lewald, Julia.*)

Liberti, Fabrizio

2010 - Manga Impact: The World of Japanese Animation - Pg. 200 (*Also see Brophy, Philip. Chatfield, Carl. Clements, Jonathan. Costa, Jordi. Della Casa, Luca. Delorme, Stéphane. Di Giorgio, Davide. Dottorini, Daniele. Gariglio, Stefano. Gravett, Paul. Higuinen, Erwan. McCarthy, Helen. Modina, Fabrizio. Nazzaro, Giona A. Roberta, Maria. Paganelli, Grazia. Rondolino, Gianni. Roudevitch, Michel. Rumor, Mario A. Sarrazin, Stephen. Surman, David.*)

Litten, Frederick

2017 - Animated Film in Japan Until 1919: Western Animation and the Beginnings of Anime - Pg. 191

Lloyd, Dave

2005 - Machinima - Pg. 51 (*Also see Kelland, Matt. Morris, Dave.*)

Lockman, Darcy

2000 - Computer Animation - Pg. 224

Logan, Chris

2006 - The Psychology of the Simpsons: D'oh! - Pg. 94 (*Also see Brown, PhD, Alan.*)

Lollar, Phil

1997 - The Complete Guide To Adventures in Odyssey - Pg. 100

Lord, Peter

1998 - Cracking Animation: The Aardman Book of 3-D Animation - Pg. 54 (*Also see Sibley, Brian.*)
2018 - Aardman: An Epic Journey: Taken One Frame At A Time - Pg. 54 (*Also see Sproxton, David.*)
2019 - A Grand Success!: The People and Characters Who Created Aardman - Pg. 54 (*Also see Park, Nick. Sproxton, David.*)

Lotman, Jeff

1995 - Animation Art: The Early Years, 1911-1954 - Pg. 15 (*See also Smith, Jonathan.*)
1996 - Animation Art: The Later Years, 1954-1993 - Pg. 15 (*See also Smith, Jonathan.*)
1998 - Animation Art at Auction: Recent Years - Pg. 15

Lowe, Richard

2007 - Learning with Animation: Research Implications for Design - Pg. 43 (*See also Schnotz, Wolfgang.*)

Lowenthal, Yuri

2010 - Voice-Over Voice Actor: What It's Like Behind the Mic - Pg. 75 (*Also see Platt, Tara.*)

Lowery, Paula Sigman

2016 - How to Be a Disney Historian: Tips from the Top Professionals - Pg. 149 (*Also see Beck, Jerry. Ehrbar, Greg. Fanning, Jim. Ghez, Didier. Jurtti, Jeff. Kaufman, J.B. Korkis, Jim.*)

Lubowsky Talbott, Susan

2001 - My Reality: Contemporary Art And The Culture Of Japanese Animation - Pg. 188 (*See also Fleming, Jeff. Murakami, Takashi.*)

Lugo-Lugo, Carmen R.

2010 - Animating Difference: Race, Gender, and Sexuality in Contemporary Films for Children - Pg. 40 (*Also see Bloodsworth-Lugo, Mary K. King, C. Richard.*)

Lunning, Frenchy

2006 - Mechademia 1: Emerging Worlds of Anime and Manga - Pg. 247
2007 - Mechademia 2: Networks of Desire - Pg. 247
2008 - Mechademia 3: Limits of the Human - Pg. 247
2009 - Mechademia 4: War/Time - Pg. 247
2010 - Mechademia 5: Fanthropologies - Pg. 248
2011 - Mechademia 6: User Enhanced - Pg. 248
2012 - Mechademia 7: Lines of Sight - Pg. 248
2013 - Mechademia 8: Tezuka's Manga Life - Pg. 248
2014 - Mechademia 9: Origins - Pg. 248
2015 - Mechademia 10: World Renewal - Pg. 248
2019 - Mechademia 11.1: Second Arc - Pg. 248 (*Also see Annett, Sandra.*)
2020 - Mechademia 12.1: Second Arc - Pg. 249 (*Also see Annett, Sandra.*)
2020 - Mechademia 12.2: Second Arc - Pg. 249 (*Also see Annett, Sandra.*)

2020 - Mechademia 13.1: Second Arc - Pg. 249 (*Also see Annett, Sandra.*)
2021 - Mechademia 13.2: Second Arc - Pg. 249 (*Also see Annett, Sandra.*)

Lüthge, Katja

2016 - The Walt Disney Film Archives: The Animated Movies 1921-1968 - Pg. 126 (*Also see Allan, Robin. Ghez, Didier. Kaufman, J. B. Kothenschulte, Daniel. Lasseter, John. Merritt, Russell. Sibley, Brian. Solomon, Charles.*)

Lutz, Edwin George

1920 - Animated Cartoons: How They Are Made, Their Origin and Development - Pg. 64

Lyons, Jonathan

2015 - Comedy for Animators - Pg. 48

Lyons, Michael

2022 - Drawn to Greatness: Disney's Animation Renaissance - Pg. 132

Macdonald, Sean

2017 - Animation in China: History, Aesthetics, Media - Pg. 214

Macek, Carl

1981 - The Art of Heavy Metal, the Movie: Animation for the Eighties - Pg. 106
1988 - Robotech Art 3: The Sentinels - Pg. 207

MacFadyen, David

2005 - Yellow Crocodiles and Blue Oranges: Russian Animated Film since World War II - Pg. 220

Macias, Patrick

2022 - Crunchyroll Essential Anime: Fan Favorites, Memorable Masterpieces, and Cult Classics - Pg. 182 (*Also see Macias, Patrick.*)

MacLean, Fraser

2011 - Setting the Scene: The Art & Evolution of Animation Layout - Pg. 78

MacWilliams, Mark W.

2008 - Japanese Visual Culture: Explorations in the World of Manga and Anime - Pg. 203

Madden, Scott M.

2018 - The Mouse and the Mallet: The Story of Walt Disney's Hectic Half-Decade in the Saddle - Pg. 112

Madej, Krystina

2012 - Disney Stories: Getting to Digital - Pg. 122 (*Also see Lee, Newton.*)

Madsen, Roy P.

1969 - Animated Film: Concepts, Methods, Uses - Pg. 43

Magliozzi, Ronald S.

2006 - Pixar: At the Museum of Modern Art - Pg. 155 (*Also see Higgins, Steven.*)

Magnenat-Thalmann, Nadia

1985 - Computer Animation: Theory and Practice - Pg. 52 (*Also see Thalmann Ph. D., Daniel.*)
1989 - State-of-the-Art in Computer Animation: Proceedings of Computer Animation '89 - Pg. 36 (*Also see Thalmann Ph. D., Daniel.*)
1990 - Computer Animation '90 - Pg. 36 (*Also see Thalmann Ph. D., Daniel.*)
1990 - Synthetic Actors in Computer-Generated 3D Films - Pg. 52 (*Also see Thalmann Ph. D., Daniel.*)
1991 - Computer Animation '91 - Pg. 36 (*Also see Thalmann Ph. D., Daniel.*)
1991 - New Trends in Animation and Visualization - Pg. 44 (*Also see Thalmann Ph. D., Daniel.*)
1992 - Creating and Animating the Virtual World - Pg. 52
1993 - Communicating With Virtual Worlds - Pg. 52

1999 - Computer Animation and Simulation '99: Proceedings of the Eurographics Workshop in Milano, Italy, September 7–8, 1999 - Pg. 37 (*Also see Thalmann Ph. D., Daniel.*)
2020 - Computer Animation and Social Agents: 33rd International Conference on Computer Animation and Social Agents, CASA 2020, Bournemouth, UK, October 13-15, 2020, Proceedings - Pg. 38 (*Also see Chang, Jian. Thalmann Ph. D., Daniel. Tian, Feng. Xu, Weiwei. Yang, Xiaosong. Zhang, Jian Jun.*)

Mallory, Michael

1998 - Hanna-Barbera Cartoons - Pg. 168
2016 - Hanna-Barbera: The Architects of Saturday Morning - Pg. 168 (*Also see Beck, Jerry. Kowalski, Jesse.*)

Malone, Maggie

2012 - The Art of Wreck-It Ralph - Pg. 139 (*Also see Lee, Jennifer.*)
2016 - The Art of Moana - Pg. 138 (*Also see Julius, Jessica.*)

Maltin, Leonard

1973 - The Disney Films - Pg. 132
1980 - Of Mice and Magic: A History of American Animated Cartoons - Pg. 64
2008 - Leonard Maltin's Movie Crazy - Pg. 44
2020 - Over the Moon: Illuminating the Journey - Pg. 175

Mangels, Andy

2003 - Animation on DVD: The Ultimate Guide - Pg. 15
2012 - Lou Scheimer: Creating the Filmation Generation - Pg. 87 (*Also see Scheimer, Lou.*)

Manovich, Lev

2007 - Animated Worlds - Pg. 77 (*Also see Buchan, Suzanne. Hertz, Betti-Sue.*)

Manvell, Roger

1959 - The Technique of Film Animation - Pg. 21 (Also see Halas, John.)
1980 - Art and Animation: The Story of the Halas and Batchelor Animation Studio - Pg. 218

Marcovitz, Hal

2007 - Computer Animation (Eye on Art) - Pg. 227
2019 - The Art of Animation - Pg. 233 (*Also see Blohm, Craig E.*)

Mark, Harrison

2003 - Prime Time Animation: Television Animation and American Culture - Pg. 67 (*Also see Stabile, Carol.*)

Marks, Melissa

2003 - Animations - Pg. 39 (*Also see Alys, Francis. Akakce, Haluk. Bendazzi, Giannalberto. Blake, Jeremy. Canemaker, John. Christov-Bakargiev, Carolyn. Galbraith, David. Gillick, Liam. Harries, Larissa. Klein, Norman. Riegel, Karyn.*)

Mariotti, Brian

2007 - Classic Hanna-Barbera Collectibles: An Authorized Guide – Pg. 168

Marshall, Dallas

2020 - Anime Adrenaline! - Pg. 182

Martin, Pete

1957 - Walt Disney: An Intimate Biography by His Daughter Diane Disney Miller As Told to Pete Martin - Pg. 112 (*Also see Miller, Diane Disney.*)

Masamune, Shirow

2017 - Ghost in the Shell README: 1995-2017 - Pg. 189

Mason, Fergus

2014 - Disney's Nine Old Men: A History of the Animators Who Defined Disney Animation - Pg. 116

Masters, Kim

2000 - The Keys to the Kingdom: How Michael Eisner Lost His Grip - Pg. 123

Masunari, Koji

2013 - Read or Die: R.O.D. Official Archive - Pg. 207 (*Also see Kurata, Hideyuki.*)

Matheson, Tim

2017 - Jonny, Sinbad Jr. & Me - Pg. 82 (*Also see Collier, Kevin Scott.*)

Mattel

2022 - The Art of Masters of the Universe Revelation - Pg. 106

Maverick, Cody

2007 - Surf's Up: The Art and Making of a True Story - Pg. 173

Mazurkewich, Karen

1999 - Cartoon Capers: The History of Canadian Animators - Pg. 213

McCall, Douglas

1998 - Film Cartoons: A Guide to 20th Century American Animated Features and Shorts - Pg. 16

McCarthy, Brendan

2007 - The Art of Reboot - Pg. 104 (*Also see Blair, Gavin. Gibson, Ian. Jackson, Mike. Nicholls, Ken. Roberts, David. Su, Jim.*)

McCarthy, Helen

1993 - Anime! A Beginner's Guide to Japanese Animation - Pg. 183
1997 - The Anime Movie Guide: Movie-by-Movie Guide to Japanese Animation since 1983 - Pg. 183
1998 - The Erotic Anime Movie Guide - Pg. 180 (*Also see Clements, Jonathan.*)
1999 - Hayao Miyazaki: Master of Japanese Animation - Pg. 193
2001 - The Anime Encyclopedia: A Century of Japanese Animation - Pg. 180 (*Also see Clements, Jonathan.*)
2009 - 500 Essential Anime Movies: The Ultimate Guide - Pg. 182

2010 - Manga Impact: The World of Japanese Animation - Pg. 200 (*Also see Brophy, Philip. Chatfield, Carl. Clements, Jonathan. Costa, Jordi. Della Casa, Luca. Delorme, Stéphane. Di Giorgio, Davide. Dottorini, Daniele. Gariglio, Stefano. Gravett, Paul. Higuinen, Erwan. Liberti, Fabrizio. Modina, Fabrizio. Nazzaro, Giona A. Paganelli, Grazia. Roberta, Maria. Rondolino, Gianni. Roudevitch, Michel. Rumor, Mario A. Sarrazin, Stephen. Surman, David.*)
2021 - Leiji Matsumoto: Essays on the Manga and Anime Legend - Pg. 199 (*Also see Ashmore, Darren-Jon.*)

McClintock Miller, Shannon

2019 - A Stop-Motion Animation Mission - Pg. 240 (*Also see Hoena, Blake.*)

McConville, Yasmin

2006 - The Animation Producer's Handbook - Pg. 23 (*Also see Milic, Lea.*)

McCray, Mark

2015 - The Best Saturdays of Our Lives - Pg. 70

McDonnell, Chris

2008 - Unfiltered: The Complete Ralph Bakshi - Pg. 97 (*Also see Gibson, Jon M.*)
2017 - Steven Universe: Art & Origins - Pg. 170
2018 - BoJack Horseman: The Art Before the Horse - Pg. 175
2020 - Steven Universe: End of an Era - Pg. 170
2020 - The Art of Invader Zim - Pg. 163

McGowan, David

2019 - Animated Personalities: Cartoon Characters and Stardom in American Theatrical Shorts - Pg. 67

McHale, Patrick

2017 - The Art of Over the Garden Wall - Pg. 170 (*Also see Edgar, Sean.*)

McKibben, Charles H.

2017 - Mel Blanc, the Voice of Bugs Bunny...and Me: Inside the Studio with Hollywood's "Man of 1,000 Voices" - Pg. 87

McKinnon, Robert

2008 - Stepping in the Picture: Cartoon Designer Maurice Noble - Pg. 88

McKimson Jr., Robert

2012 - "I Say, I Say . . . Son!": A Tribute to Legendary Animators Bob, Chuck, and Tom McKimson - Pg. 166

McLaughlin Jr., Dan F.

2017 - Animation Rules!: Book One: Words - Pg. 23
2017 - Animation Rules!: Book Two: Art - Pg. 23

McMahan, Alison

2005 - The Films of Tim Burton: Animating Live Action in Contemporary Hollywood - Pg. 100

McQuillan, Martin

2000 - Deconstructing Disney - Pg. 127 (*Also see Byrne, Eleanor.*)

McSorley, Tom

2014 - Dark Mirror: The Films of Theodore Ushev - Pg. 88

Meehan, Eileen R.

2001 - Dazzled by Disney? The Global Disney Audiences Project - Pg. 123 (*Also see Phillips, Mark and Wasko, Janet.*)

Meinel, Dietmar

2018 - Pixar's America: The Re-Animation of American Myths and Symbols - Pg. 152

Melnyk, George

2004 - One Hundred Years of Canadian Cinema - Pg. 213

Menache, Alberto

1999 - Understanding Motion Capture for Computer Animation - Pg. 52

Merkl, Ulrich

2007 - Dreams of the Rarebit Fiend - Pg. 240

Merrill, Jason

2008 - Animation for Russian Conversation - Pg. 220 (*Also see Alley, Maria. Mikhailova, Julia.*)

Merritt, Russell

1993 - Walt in Wonderland: The Silent Films of Walt Disney - Pg. 131
2006 - Walt Disney's Silly Symphonies: A Companion to the Classic Cartoon Series - Pg. 131 (*Also see Kaufman, J. B.*)
2016 - The Walt Disney Film Archives: The Animated Movies 1921-1968 - Pg. 126 (*Also see Allan, Robin. Ghez, Didier. Kaufman, J. B. Kothenschulte, Daniel. Lasseter, John. Lüthge, Katja. Sibley, Brian. Solomon, Charles.*)

Meyer, Birga

2001 – Anime! - Pg. 206 (*Also see Hellige, Hendrik. Hillmen, Jan-Rikus. Klanten, Robert. Tielgekamp, Vicky.*)

Mihailova, Mihaela

2021 - Coraline: A Closer Look at Studio LAIKA's Stop-Motion Witchcraft - Pg. 55

Mikhailova, Julia

2008 - Animation for Russian Conversation - Pg. 220 (*Also see Alley, Maria. Merrill, Jason.*)

Milic, Lea

2006 - The Animation Producer's Handbook - Pg. 23 (*Also see McConville, Yasmin.*)

Miller, Diane Disney

1957 - Walt Disney: An Intimate Biography by His Daughter Diane Disney Miller As Told to Pete Martin - Pg. 112 (*Also see Martin, Pete.*)

Miller-Zarneke, Tracey

2007 - The Art of Meet the Robinsons - Pg. 139
2007 - Surf's Up: The Art and Making of a True Story – Pg. 173
2008 - The Art of DreamWorks Kung Fu Panda - Pg. 158
2009 - The Art and Making of Cloudy with a Chance of Meatballs - Pg. 173
2010 - The Art of How to Train Your Dragon - Pg. 158
2011 - The Art of Kung Fu Panda 2 - Pg. 158
2012 - The Art and Making of Hotel Transylvania - Pg. 173
2013 - The Art of Cloudy with a Chance of Meatballs 2: Revenge of the Leftovers - Pg. 173
2014 - The Art of Planes - Pg. 139
2015 - Before Ever After: The Lost Lectures of Walt Disney's Animation Studio – Pg. 121
2015 - The Art of Kung Fu Panda 3 - Pg. 158
2017 - The LEGO® Batman Movie: The Making of the Movie - Pg. 167
2021 - The Art of Baba Yaga - Pg. 177

Miller, W.R.

2018 - The Animated Voice Volume One - Pg. 75
2019 - The Animated Voice Volume Two - Pg. 75

Minaeva, Oksana

2015 - The Animation World of Ivan Vesselinov - Pg. 213 (*Also see Hristova, Svetla.*)

Miramax

1999 - Princess Mononoke: The Art and Making of Japan's Most Popular Film of All Time - Pg. 197

Mitchell, Ben

2017 - Independent Animation: Developing, Producing and Distributing Your Animated Films - Pg. 23

Mitenbuler, Reid

2020 - Wild Minds: The Artists and Rivalries That Inspired the Golden Age of Animation - Pg. 64

Mittell, Jason

2004 - Genre and Television: From Cop Shows to Cartoons in American Culture - Pg. 48

Miyazaki, Hayao

1997 - The Art of Princess Mononoke - Pg. 197
2002 - The Art of Spirited Away - Pg. 197
2005 - The Art of My Neighbor Totoro - Pg. 197
2005 - The Art of Howl's Moving Castle - Pg. 197
2005 - The Art of Porco Rosso - Pg. 197
2006 - The Art of Kiki's Delivery Service - Pg. 197
2007 - Nausicaä of the Valley of the Wind: Watercolor Impressions - Pg. 197
2009 - The Art of Ponyo - Pg. 197
2009 - Starting Point: 1979-1996 - Pg. 194
2014 - The Art of the Wind Rises - Pg. 198
2014 - Princess Mononoke: The First Story - Pg. 197
2014 - Turning Point: 1997-2008 - Pg. 194
2016 - The Art of Castle in the Sky - Pg. 197

Mjolsness, Lora

2020 - She Animates: Gendered Soviet and Russian Animation - Pg. 220 (*Also see Leigh, Michele.*)

Moana Thompson, Kirsten

2020 - Animation and Advertising - Pg. 59 (*Also see Cook, Malcolm.*)

Modina, Fabrizio

2010 - Manga Impact: The World of Japanese Animation - Pg. 200 (*Also see Brophy, Philip. Chatfield, Carl. Clements, Jonathan. Costa, Jordi. Della Casa, Luca. Delorme, Stéphane. Di Giorgio, Davide. Dottorini, Daniele. Gariglio, Stefano. Gravett, Paul. Higuinen, Erwan. Liberti, Fabrizio. McCarthy, Helen. Nazzaro, Giona A. Roberta, Maria. Paganelli, Grazia. Rondolino, Gianni. Roudevitch, Michel. Rumor, Mario A. Sarrazin, Stephen. Surman, David.*)

Moen, Kristian

2019 - New York's Animation Culture: Advertising, Art, Design and Film, 1939-1940 - Pg. 68

Mollet, Tracey

2017 - Cartoons in Hard Times: The Animated Shorts of Disney and Warner Brothers in Depression and War 1932-1945 - Pg. 149
2020 - A Cultural History of the Disney Fairy Tale: Once Upon an American Dream - Pg. 145

Monnin, Katie

2013 - Get Animated! Teaching 21st Century Early Readers and Young Adult Cartoons in Language Arts - Pg. 231

Montini, Barbara

2022 - Disney The Lion King: The Full Film Script – Pg. 133 (*Also see Scollon, Bill.*)
2022 - Disney The Little Mermaid: The Full Film Script – Pg. 133 (*Also see Scollon, Bill.*)

Moody, Juniko

2020 - Filming the Fantastic with Virtual Technology: Filmmaking on the Digital Backlot - Pg. 52 (*See also Sawicki, Mark.*)

Moore, Frazier

2019 - Inside Family Guy: An Illustrated History - Pg. 157

Moore, Samantha

2016 - The Fundamentals of Animation - Pg. 25 (*Also see Wells, Paul.*)

Moore, Tomm

2015 - Song of the Sea Artbook - Pg. 178
2021 - Designing the Secret of Kells - Pg. 178 (*Also see Stewart, Ross.*)

Moran, Christian

2015 - Great Big Beautiful Tomorrow: Walt Disney and Technology - Pg. 120 (*Also see Crump, Rolly. Gurr, Bob.*)

Mori, Haruji

2015 - Osamu Tezuka: Anime Character Illustrations - Pg. 207

Moritz, William

2004 - Optical Poetry: The Life and Work of Oskar Fischinger - Pg. 88

Morris, Dave

2005 - Machinima - Pg. 51 (*Also see Kelland, Matt. Lloyd, Dave.*)

Moryc, Matt

2020 - 2020 Hyperion Historical Society Alliance Annual Report - Pg. 149 (*Also see Ghez, Didier. Johnson, Mindy. Kaufman, J.B. Kern, Kevin M.*)

Moseley, Rachel

2015 - Hand-Made Television: Stop-Frame Animation for Children in Britain, 1961-1974 – Pg. 218

Mosley, Leonard

1985 - Disney's World: A Biography - Pg. 112

Mul, Ati

2010 - "They Thought It Was a Marvel": Arthur Melbourne-Cooper (1874-1961), Pioneer of Puppet Animation - Pg. 83 (*Also see De Vries, Tjitte.*)

Mulaney, Dean

2011 - Chuck Jones: The Dream that Never Was - Pg. 165 (*Also see Findlay, Kurtis.*)

Muller, Jacques

2018 - 40 Years of Animated Cartoons - Pg. 65

Mullin, Molly Ann

1987 - Word of Mouth: A Guide to Commercial Voice-Over Excellence - Pg. 73 (*Also see Blu, Susan.*)

Mullins, Matt

2010 - Multimedia Artist and Animator (Cool Careers) - Pg. 229

Mumford, Britt

2017 - 40 Years of Ottawa: Collected Essays on Award-Winning Animation - Pg. 34 (*Also see Robinson, Chris.*)

Mumford, David

2000 - A Brush with Disney: An Artist's Journey, Told through the words and works of Herbert Dickens Ryman - Pg. 115 (*Also see Gordon, Bruce.*)

Munteán, László

2020 - Animation and Memory - Pg. 42 (*Also see Gageldonk, Maarten van. Shobeiri, Ali.*)

Murakami, Takashi

2001 - My Reality: Contemporary Art And The Culture Of Japanese Animation - Pg. 188 (*See also Fleming, Jeff. Lubowsky Talbott, Susan.*)

Murase, Shūkō

2001 - Art of Gundam Wing - Pg. 207

Murray, Joe

2010 - Creating Animated Cartoons with Character: A Guide to Developing and Producing Your Own Series for TV, the Web, and Short Film - Pg. 23

Murray, Jonathan

2018 - Drawn from Life: Issues and Themes in Animated Documentary Cinema - Pg. 47 (*Also see Ehrlich, Nea.*)

Murray, Robin L.

2011 - That's All Folks?: Ecocritical Readings of American Animated Features - Pg. 72

Murry, Matt

2011 - The World of Smurfs: A Celebration of Tiny Blue Proportions - Pg. 100

Musburger Ph.D., Robert B.

2017 - Animation Production: Documentation and Organization - Pg. 78

Musker, John

2008 - Walt Disney Animation Studios: Studio Caricatures 1989-2006 - Pg. 139

Muthalib, Hassan Abdul

2016 - From Mouse Deer To Mouse – 70 Years of Malaysian Animation - Pg. 219

Myers, Dale K.

1999 - Computer Animation: Expert Advice on Breaking Into the Business - Pg. 53

N/A

1997 – Disney's The Little Mermaid: The Sketchbook Series – Pg. 139
2012 - Cartoon Network: 20th Anniversary Book - Pg. 170
2018 - The Art of Hotel Transylvania 3 - Pg. 173
2019 - Neon Genesis Evangelion: TV Animation Production Art Collection - Pg. 207
2020 - My Neighbor Hayao: Art Inspired by the Films of Miyazaki - Pg. 198

Napier, Susan J.

2001 - Anime: From Akira to Princess Mononoke, Experiencing Contemporary Japanese Animation - Pg. 183
2008 - From Impressionism to Anime: Japan as Fantasy and Fan Cult in the Mind of the West - Pg. 203
2018 - Miyazakiworld: A Life in Art - Pg. 193

Nardo, Don

1992 - Animation: Drawings Spring to Life - Pg. 223

National Geographic School Publishing

2000 - I Make Pictures Move: Inside Theme Book - Pg. 224

Nazzaro, Giona A.

2010 - Manga Impact: The World of Japanese Animation - Pg. 200 (*Also see Brophy, Philip. Chatfield, Carl. Clements, Jonathan. Costa, Jordi. Della Casa, Luca. Delorme, Stéphane. Di Giorgio, Davide. Dottorini, Daniele. Gariglio, Stefano. Gravett, Paul. Higuinen, Erwan. Liberti, Fabrizio. McCarthy, Helen. Modina, Fabrizio. Paganelli, Grazia. Roberta, Maria. Rondolino, Gianni. Roudevitch, Michel. Rumor, Mario A. Sarrazin, Stephen. Surman, David.*)

Nelson, Reed

2022 - 50 Animated Years of LUPIN THE 3rd - Pg. 189

Neupert, Richard

2011 - French Animation History - Pg. 217
2016 - John Lasseter (Contemporary Film Directors) - Pg. 88

Neuwirth, Allan

2002 - Makin' Toons: Inside the Most Popular Animated TV Shows and Movies - Pg. 61

Ng, Andrew Hock Soon

2008 - Asian Gothic: Essays on Literature, Film and Anime - Pg. 203

Nicholls, Ken

2007 - The Art of Reboot - Pg. 104 (*Also see Blair, Gavin. Gibson, Ian. Jackson, Mike. McCarthy, Brendan. Roberts, David. Su, Jim.*)

Niebel, Jessica

2021 - Hayao Miyazaki - Pg. 193 (*Also see Docter, Pete. Kothenschulte, Daniel.*)

Noake, Roger

1988 - Animation: The Guide to Animated Film Techniques - Pg. 24

Norman, Floyd

1992 - Faster! Cheaper!: The Flip Side to the Art of Animation - Pg. 241
2004 - Son Of Faster Cheaper A Sharp Look Inside The Animation Business - Pg. 140
2005 - How The Grinch Stole Disney - Pg. 241
2010 - Disk Drive: Animated Humor in the Digital Age - Pg. 240
2012 - Suspended Animation: The Art Form That Refuses To Die - Pg. 241
2013 - Animated Life: A Lifetime of Tips, Tricks, Techniques and Stories from an Animation Legend - Pg. 116

Norris, Van

2014 - British Television Animation 1997-2010: Drawing Comic Tradition - Pg. 218

Nourigat, Natalie

2018 - I Moved to Los Angeles to Work in Animation - Pg. 241

Novesky, Amy

2019 - Mary Blair's Unique Flair: The Girl Who Became One of the Disney Legends - Pg. 237

Novielli, Maria Roberta

2018 - Floating Worlds: A Short History of Japanese Animation - Pg. 191

O'Leary, Shannon

2015 - The Art of Regular Show - Pg. 170

O'Steen, Bobbie

2022 - Making the Cut at Pixar: The Art of Editing Animation – Pg. 152 (*Also see Kinder, Bill.*)

Odell, Colin

2009 - Studio Ghibli: The Films of Hayao Miyazaki and Isao Takahata - Pg. 194 (*Also see Le Blanc, Michelle.*)
2014 - Anime - Pg. 182 (*Also see Le Blanc, Michelle.*)

Ogihara-Schuck, Eriko

2014 - Miyazaki's Animism Abroad: The Reception of Japanese Religious Themes by American and German Audiences - Pg. 195

Ohmart, Ben

2004 - Daws Butler, Characters Actor - Pg. 80 (*Also see Bevilacqua, Joe.*)

2004 - Welcome Foolish Mortals...The Life and Voices of Paul Frees - Pg. 117
2012 - Mel Blanc: The Man of a Thousand Voices - Pg. 89
2016 - Buddy Baker: Big Band Arranger, Disney Legend & Musical Genius - Pg. 148
2015 - Yabba Dabba Doo or, Never a Star: The Alan Reed Story - Pg. 89 (*Also see Reed, Alan.*)

Okada, Mari

2018 - From Truant to Anime Screenwriter: My Path to "Anohana" and "The Anthem of the Heart" - Pg. 189

Okuyama, Yoshiko

2015 - Japanese Mythology in Film: A Semiotic Approach to Reading Japanese Film and Anime - Pg. 203

Oliff, Jamie

2006 - Thinking Animation: Bridging the Gap Between 2D and CG - Pg. 51 (*Also see Jones, Angie.*)

Oriolo, Don

2014 - Felix the Cat Paintings - Pg. 104
2015 - Another Book of Felix the Cat Paintings: A Second Collection of Paintings from the Prolific Imagination of the Felix the Cat Guy - Pg. 106

Ortved, John

2009 - The Simpsons: An Uncensored, Unauthorized History - Pg. 101

Osmond, Andrew

2011 - 100 Animated Feature Films - Pg. 16

Otfinoski, Steven

2001 - Book Treks: Clay Magic: The Art of Clay Animation - Pg. 225
2021 - Tim Burton - Pg. 234

Otmazgin, Nissim

2008 - The BFI Film Classics Study of Spirited Away - Pg. 194
2017 - The Anime Boom in the United States: Lessons for Global Creative Industries - Pg. 185 (*Also see Daliot-Bul, Michal.*)

Otomo, Katsuhiro

2017 - OTOMO: A Global Tribute to the Mind Behind Akira - Pg. 207

Owada, Hideki

2021 - The Men Who Created Gundam - Pg. 189

Owen, Ruth

2020 - CGI Artists - Pg. 234 (*Also see Willis, John.*)

Owens, Gary

2004 - How to Make a Million Dollars With Your Voice (Or Lose Your Tonsils Trying) - Pg. 75 (*Also see Lenburg, Jeff.*)

Paganelli, Grazia

2010 - Manga Impact: The World of Japanese Animation - Pg. 200 (*Also see Brophy, Philip. Chatfield, Carl. Clements, Jonathan. Costa, Jordi. Della Casa, Luca. Delorme, Stéphane. Di Giorgio, Davide. Dottorini, Daniele. Gariglio, Stefano. Gravett, Paul. Higuinen, Erwan. Liberti, Fabrizio. McCarthy, Helen. Modina, Fabrizio. Nazzaro, Giona A. Roberta, Maria. Rondolino, Gianni. Roudevitch, Michel. Rumor, Mario A. Sarrazin, Stephen. Surman, David.*)

Paik, Karen M.

2007 - Art of Ratatouille - Pg. 156
2007 - To Infinity and Beyond!: The Story of Pixar Animation Studios - Pg. 152
2013 - The Art of Monsters University - Pg. 156
2018 - The Art of Incredibles 2 - Pg. 156

Pallant, Chris

2015 - Animated Landscapes: History, Form and Function - Pg. 57
2011 - Demystifying Disney: A History of Disney Feature Animation - Pg. 133
2015 - Storyboarding: A Critical History - Pg. 78 (*Also see Price, Steven.*)
2021 - Animation: Critical and Primary Sources - Pg. 16
2021 - Allegro Non Troppo: Bruno Bozzetto's Animated Music - Pg. 219 (*Also see Bellano, Marco.*)

Panne Ph. D., Michiel van de

1997 - Computer Animation and Simulation '97: Proceedings of the Eurographics Workshop in Budapest, Hungary, September 2–3, 1997 – Pg. 37 (*Also see Thalmann Ph. D., Daniel.*)

Pandzic, Igor

2002 - MPEG-4 Facial Animation: The Standard, Implementation and Applications - Pg. 50 (*Also see Forchheimer, Robert.*)

Papapetros, Spyros

2012 - On the Animation of the Inorganic: Art, Architecture, and the Extension of Life - Pg. 58

Papp, Zilia

2010 - Anime and Its Roots in Early Japanese Monster Art - Pg. 191

Park, Nick

2019 - A Grand Success!: The People and Characters Who Created Aardman - Pg. 54 (*Also see Lord, Peter. Sproxton, David.*)

Patel, Sanjay

2015 - The Art of Sanjay's Super Team - Pg. 156

Patten, Fred

2004 - Watching Anime, Reading Manga: 25 Years of Essays and Reviews - Pg. 203
2014 - Funny Animals and More: From Anime to Zoomorphics - Pg. 183
2019 - Furry Tales: A Review of Essential Anthropomorphic Fiction - Pg. 48

Paulsen, Rob

2019 - Voice Lessons: How a Couple of Ninja Turtles, Pinky, and an Animaniac Saved My Life – Pg. 76

Pearson, Joe

2020 - Pearl Jam: Art of Do The Evolution - Pg. 106

Peary, Danny

1980 - The American Animated Cartoon: A Critical Anthology - Pg. 44 (*Also see Peary, Gerald.*)

Peary, Gerald

1980 - The American Animated Cartoon: A Critical Anthology - Pg. 44 (*Also see Peary, Danny.*)

Peet, Bill

1994 – Bill Peet: An Autobiography – Pg. 235

Pellitteri, Marco

2021 - Japanese Animation in Asia: Transnational Industry, Audiences, and Success - Pg. 186 (*Also see Wong, Heung-wah.*)

Peri, Don

2011 - Working with Disney: Interviews with Animators, Producers, and Artists - Pg. 117

Perimutter, David

2014 - America Toons in: A History of Television Animation - Pg. 65
2018 - The Encyclopedia of American Animated Television Shows - Pg. 16

Perisic, Zoran

1978 - The Focal Guide to Shooting Animation – Pg. 24

Perrin, Joy M.

2017 - The Ascendance of Harley Quinn: Essays on DC's Enigmatic Villain - Pg. 93 (*Also see Barba, Shelley E.*)

Peterson, Monique

2004 - Home on the Range: The Adventures of a Bovine Goddess - Pg. 140 (*Also see Revenson, Jody.*)

Pettigrew, Neil

1999 - The Stop-Motion Filmography: A Critical Guide to 297 Features Using Puppet Animation - Pg. 16

Phillips, Mark

2001 - Dazzled by Disney? The Global Disney Audiences Project - Pg. 123 (*Also see Meehan, Eileen R. and Wasko, Janet.*)

PIE International

2018 - Everyday Scenes from a Parallel World – Pg. 207

Pierce, Todd James

2019 - The Life and Times of Ward Kimball: Maverick of Disney Animation - Pg. 117
2019 - 2019 Hyperion Historical Society Alliance Annual Report - Pg. 149 (*Also see Apgar, Garry. Bossert, David. Ghez, Didier. Hollifield, Jim. Seastrom, Lucas.*)

Pietroni, Andrea

2000 - Anime: A Guide to Japanese Animation - Pg. 180 (*Also see Baricordi, Andrea. De Giovanni, Massimiliano. Rossi, Barbara. Tunesi, Sabrina.*)

Pike, Deidre

2012 - Enviro-Toons: Green Themes in Animated Cinema and Television - Pg. 72

Pilcher, Steve

2014 - Over There: Pixar Animation Studios Artist Showcase Book - Pg. 235

Pilling, Jayne

1992 - Women and Animation: A Compendium - Pg. 89
1998 - A Reader In Animation Studies - Pg. 44
2001 - Animation: 2D & Beyond - Pg. 44
2007 - The Book of BAA Art - Artists, Animators & Sheep - Pg. 89
2012 - Animating the Unconscious: Desire, Sexuality, and Animation - Pg. 44

Pinsky, Mark I.

2004 - The Gospel According to Disney: Faith, Trust, and Pixie Dust - Pg. 146

Pintoff, Ernest

1999 - Animation 101 - Pg. 24

Pixar

2020 - Art of Soul - Pg. 156

Place-Verghnes, Floriane

2006 - Tex Avery: A Unique Legacy - Pg. 89

Platt, Tara

2010 - Voice-Over Voice Actor: What It's Like Behind the Mic - Pg. 75 (*Also see Lowenthal, Yuri.*)

Pointer, Ray

2017 - (The Art and Inventions of) Max Fleischer: American Animation Pioneer - Pg. 89

Plume, Ken

2018 - Go Team Venture!: The Art and Making of The Venture Bros. - Pg. 172 (*Also see Hammer, Doc. Publick, Jackson.*)

Plympton, Bill

2012 - Making 'Toons That Sell Without Selling Out: The Bill Plympton Guide to Independent Animation Success - Pg. 24

Pointon, Marcia

1995 - Cartoon, Caricature, Animation - Pg. 39 (*Also see Binski, Paul.*)

Poitras, Gilles

1999 - The Anime Companion: What's Japanese in Japanese Animation - Pg. 183
2000 - Anime Essentials: Every Thing a Fan Needs to Know - Pg. 183
2005 - The Anime Companion 2: More What's Japanese in Japanese Animation - Pg. 183

Polson, Tod

2013 - The Noble Approach: Maurice Noble and the Zen of Animation Design - Pg. 89

Pontieri, Laura

2012 - Soviet Animation and the Thaw of The 1960s: Not Only for Children - Pg. 221

Poš, Jan

1991 - Krátký Film: The Art of Czechoslovak Animation - Pg. 216 (*Also see Beckerman, Howard. Wechsler, Jeffrey.*)

Preston, Greg

2007 - The Artist Within - Pg. 90
2017 - The Artist Within: Book 2 - Pg. 90

Preszler, June

2003 - Walt Disney: A Photo-Illustrated Biography - Pg. 226

Price, David A.

2008 - The Pixar Touch: The Making of a Company - Pg. 153

Price, Kathryn M.

2018 - Walt Disney's Melody Makers: A Biography of the Sherman Brothers - Pg. 148

Price, Steven

2015 - Storyboarding: A Critical History - Pg. 78 (*Also see Pallant, Chris.*)

Priebe, Ken A.

2006 - The Art of Stop-Motion Animation - Pg. 55
2010 - The Advanced Art of Stop-Motion Animation - Pg. 55

Publick, Jackson

2018 - Go Team Venture!: The Art and Making of The Venture Bros. - Pg. 172 (*Also see Hammer, Doc. Plume, Ken.*)

Purves, Barry J.C.

2010 - Basics Animation 04: Stop-Motion Animation: Frame by Frame Film-Making with Puppets and Models - Pg. 24

Queen, Ben

2011 - The Art of Cars 2 - Pg. 156

Radivoeva, Svetla

2020 - Malina's Jam: Walt Disney Animation Studios Artist Showcase - Pg. 237

Rall, Hannes

2017 - Animation: From Concept to Production - Pg. 78
2019 - Adaptation for Animation: Transforming Literature Frame by Frame - Pg. 48

Rall, Hans-Martin

2012 - Tradigital Mythmaking: Singaporean Animation for the 21st Century - Pg. 221

Ranney, Doug

1996 - The Complete Anime Guide: Japanese Animation Film Directory & Resource Guide - Pg. 182 (*Also see Ledoux, Trish.*)

Ratelle, Amy

2018 - The Animation Studies Reader - Pg. 41 (*Also see Dobson, Nichola. Roe, Annabelle Honess. Ruddell, Caroline.*)

Rao, Krishna

2008 - Animation Industry (Industry Analysis Series) - Pg. 61 (*Also see K, Suresh.*)

Rauf, Don

2008 - Virtual Apprentice: Cartoon Animator - Pg. 228 (*Also see Vescia, Monique.*)

Raugust, Karen

2004 - The Animation Business Handbook - Pg. 24

Rawls, Walton H.

2004 - Disney Dons Dogtags: The Best of Disney Military Insignia from World War II - Pg. 150

Rebello, Stephen

1995 - The Art of Pocahontas - Pg. 140
1996 - The Art of The Hunchback of Notre Dame - Pg. 140
1997 - The Art of Hercules: The Chaos of Creation - Pg. 140

Rector, Brett

2015 - The Art and Making of Hotel Transylvania 2 - Pg. 173

Redrobe Beckman, Karen

2014 - Animating Film Theory - Pg. 39

Reed, Alan

2015 - Yabba Dabba Doo or, Never a Star: The Alan Reed Story - Pg. 89 (*Also see Ohmart, Ben.*)

Reiniger, Lotte

2012 - Lotte Reiniger: Born With Enchanting Hands: Three Silhouette Sequels - Pg. 104 (*Also see Blattner, Evamarie. Wiegmann, Karlheinz.*)

Reinke, Steve

2005 - The Sharpest Point: Animation at the End of Cinema - Pg. 42 (*Also see Gehman, Chris.*)

Renaut, Christian

2020 - The Best of Disney's Animated Features: Volume One - Pg. 133

Ressel, Steve

2010 - Animation: The Inner Workings - Pg. 24

Revenson, Jody

2004 - Home on the Range: The Adventures of a Bovine Goddess - Pg. 140 (*Also see Peterson, Monique.*)

Reynolds, Kay

1986 - Robotech Art I - Pg. 206 (*Also see Carlton, Ardith.*)
1987 - Robotech Art 2: New Illustrations & Original Art from The Robotech Universe - Pg. 207

Riegel, Karyn

2003 - Animations - Pg. 39 (*Also see Alys, Francis. Akakce, Haluk. Bendazzi, Giannalberto. Blake, Jeremy. Canemaker, John. Christov-Bakargiev, Carolyn. Galbraith, David. Gillick, Liam. Harries, Larissa. Klein, Norman. Marks, Melissa.*)

Riekeles, Stefan

2012 - Proto Anime Cut: Archive - Pg. 208
2020 - Anime Architecture: Imagined Worlds and Endless Megacities - Pg. 208

Richmond, Justin

2020 - The Art of the Dragon Prince - Pg. 175 (*Also see Ehasz, Aaron. Wonderstorm.*)

Richmond, Simon

2009 - The Rough Guide to Anime - Pg. 184

Robb, Brian J.

2014 - A Brief History of Walt Disney - Pg. 112

Roberta, Maria

2010 - Manga Impact: The World of Japanese Animation - Pg. 200 (*Also see Brophy, Philip. Chatfield, Carl. Clements, Jonathan. Costa, Jordi. Della Casa, Luca. Delorme, Stéphane. Di Giorgio, Davide. Dottorini, Daniele. Gariglio, Stefano. Gravett, Paul. Higuinen, Erwan. Liberti, Fabrizio. McCarthy, Helen. Modina, Fabrizio. Nazzaro, Giona A. Paganelli, Grazia. Roberta, Maria. Rondolino, Gianni. Roudevitch, Michel. Rumor, Mario A. Sarrazin, Stephen. Surman, David.*)

Roberts, David

2007 - The Art of Reboot - Pg. 104 (*Also see Blair, Gavin. Gibson, Ian. Jackson, Mike. McCarthy, Brendan. Nicholls, Ken. Su, Jim.*)

Robertson, Barbara

2012 - The Art of DreamWorks Madagascar 3 - Pg. 159
2014 - The Art of DreamWorks Penguins of Madagascar - Pg. 159

Robinson, Chris

2006 - Unsung Heroes of Animation - Pg. 90
2007 - The Animation Pimp - Pg. 61
2007 - Estonian Animation: Between Genius and Utter Illiteracy - Pg. 216
2008 - Canadian Animation: Looking for a Place to Happen - Pg. 213
2008 - The Ballad of a Thin Man: In Search of Ryan Larkin - Pg. 90
2010 - Animators Unearthed: A Guide to the Best of Contemporary Animation - Pg. 16
2010 - Japanese Animation: Time Out of Mind - Pg. 204
2017 - 40 Years of Ottawa: Collected Essays on Award-Winning Animation - Pg. 34 (*Also see Mumford, Britt.*)

Robinson, Fiona

2022 - Out of the Shadows: How Lotte Reiniger Made the First Animated Fairytale Movie - Pg. 238

Robinson, Jeremy Mark

2011 - The Cinema of Hayao Miyazaki - Pg. 195
2012 - Princess Mononoke: Pocket Movie Guide - Pg. 195
2012 - Spirited Away: Hayao Miyazaki: Pocket Movie Guide - Pg. 196
2016 - Cowboy Bebop: The Anime TV Series and Movie - Pg. 190
2016 - The Art of Katsuhiro Otomo - Pg. 208
2017 - The Akira Book: Katsuhiro Otomo: The Movie and the Manga - Pg. 189
2021 - The Art of Masamune Shirow: Volume 2: Anime - Pg. 189
2021 - Berserk: Kentaro Miura: The Manga and the Anime - Pg. 189

Rockport Publishers

1998 – Animation – Pg. 44

Rodosthenous, George

2017 - The Disney Musical on Stage and Screen: Critical Approaches from 'Snow White' to 'Frozen' - Pg. 148

Roeder, Katherine

2014 - Wide Awake in Slumberland: Fantasy, Mass Culture, and Modernism in the Art of Winsor McCay - Pg. 68

Roncarelli, Robi

1989 - The Computer Animation Dictionary: Including Related Terms Used in Computer Graphics, Film and Video, Production, and Desktop Publishing - Pg. 17

Rondolino, Gianni

2010 - Manga Impact: The World of Japanese Animation - Pg. 200 (*Also see Brophy, Philip. Chatfield, Carl. Clements, Jonathan. Costa, Jordi. Della Casa, Luca. Delorme, Stéphane. Di Giorgio, Davide. Dottorini, Daniele. Gariglio, Stefano. Gravett, Paul. Higuinen, Erwan. Liberti, Fabrizio. McCarthy, Helen. Modina, Fabrizio. Nazzaro, Giona A. Paganelli, Grazia. Roberta, Maria. Roudevitch, Michel. Rumor, Mario A. Sarrazin, Stephen. Surman, David.*)

Rosenkrantz, Linda

1998 - Sotheby's Guide to Animation Art - Pg. 12 (*Also see Finch, Christopher. Sotheby's.*)

Rösing, Lilian Munk

2015 - Pixar with Lacan: The Hysteric's Guide to Animation - Pg. 153

Rossi, Barbara

2000 - Anime: A Guide to Japanese Animation - Pg. 180 (*Also see Baricordi, Andrea. De Giovanni, Massimiliano. Pietroni, Andrea. Tunesi, Sabrina.*)

Rothrock, Richard

2017 - Sunday Nights With Walt: Everything I Know I Learned From The Wonderful World of Disney - Pg. 146

Roudevitch, Michel

2010 - Manga Impact: The World of Japanese Animation - Pg. 200 (*Also see Brophy, Philip. Chatfield, Carl. Clements, Jonathan. Costa, Jordi. Della Casa, Luca. Delorme, Stéphane. Di Giorgio, Davide. Dottorini, Daniele. Gariglio, Stefano. Gravett, Paul. Higuinen, Erwan. Liberti, Fabrizio. McCarthy, Helen. Modina, Fabrizio. Nazzaro, Giona A. Paganelli, Grazia. Roberta, Maria. Rondolino, Gianni. Rumor, Mario A. Sarrazin, Stephen. Surman, David.*)

Rovin, Jeff

2010 - Illustrated Encyclopedia of Cartoon Animals - Pg. 17

Rubiano, Brittany

2017 - A Kiss Goodnight - Pg. 236 (*Also see Sherman, Richard.*)

Rubin, Susan

1984 - Animation: The Art and the Industry – Pg. 62

Ruddell, Caroline

2018 - The Animation Studies Reader - Pg. 41 (*Also see Dobson, Nichola. Ratelle, Amy. Roe, Annabelle Honess.*)
2019 - The Crafty Animator: Handmade, Craft-based Animation and Cultural Value - Pg. 25 (*Also see Ward, Paul.*)

Ruh, Brian

2004 - Stray Dog of Anime: The Films of Mamoru Oshii - Pg. 190

Rumor, Mario A.

2010 - Manga Impact: The World of Japanese Animation - Pg. 200 (*Also see Brophy, Philip. Chatfield, Carl. Clements, Jonathan. Costa, Jordi. Della Casa, Luca. Delorme, Stéphane. Di Giorgio, Davide. Dottorini, Daniele. Gariglio, Stefano. Gravett, Paul. Higuinen, Erwan. Liberti, Fabrizio. McCarthy, Helen. Modina, Fabrizio. Nazzaro, Giona A. Paganelli, Grazia. Roberta, Maria. Rondolino, Gianni. Roudevitch, Michel. Sarrazin, Stephen. Surman, David.*)

Russet, Robert

1976 - Experimental Animation: Origins of a New Art - Pg. 58 (*Also see Starr, Cecile.*)
2009 - Hyperanimation: Digital Images and Virtual Worlds - Pg. 53

Russo, Ron

2005 - Adult Swim and Comedy - Pg. 49

Ruzic, Andrijana

2020 - Michael Dudok de Wit: A Life in Animation - Pg. 90

Ryan, Jeff

2018 - A Mouse Divided: How Ub Iwerks Became Forgotten, and Walt Disney Became Uncle Walt - Pg. 117

Ryder, David

1976 – The Great Movie Cartoon Parade - Pg. 106

Sacks, Terence J.

2000 – Opportunities in Animation and Cartooning Careers - Pg. 224

Sadamoto, Yoshiyuki

2006 - Der Mond: The Art of Neon Genesis Evangelion - Pg. 208

Saddleback Educational Publishing

2008 - Walt Disney, Graphic Biography - Pg. 228

Saitō, Tamaki

2011 - Beautiful Fighting Girl - Pg. 199 (*Also see Azuma, Hiroki. Lawson, Dawn. Vincent, J. Keith.*)

Salda, Michael

2013 - Arthurian Animation: A Study of Cartoon Camelots on Film and Television - Pg. 101

Salisbury, Mark

2005 - Tim Burton's Corpse Bride: An Invitation to the Wedding - Pg. 179
2013 - Frankenweenie: The Visual Companion - Pg. 140

Sammond, Nicholas

2005 - Babes in Tomorrowland: Walt Disney and the Making of the American Child, 1930-1960 - Pg. 146
2015 - Birth of an Industry: Blackface Minstrelsy and the Rise of American Animation - Pg. 62

Sampson, Henry T.

1998 - That's Enough Folks: Black Images in Animated Cartoons, 1900-1960 - Pg. 65

Sandler, Kevin S.

1998 - Reading the Rabbit: Explorations in Warner Bros. Animation - Pg. 166

Sands, Ryan

2019 - The Art of Steven Universe: The Movie - Pg. 170 (*Also see Sugar, Rebecca.*)

Santoli, Lorraine

2015 - Inside The Disney Marketing Machine: In The Era Of Michael Eisner And Frank Wells - Pg. 123

Santos, Joaquim Dos

2013 - Legend of Korra: The Art of the Animated Series Book One: Air - Pg. 162 (*Also see DiMartino, Michael Dante. Konietzko, Bryan.*)
2014 - Legend of Korra: The Art of the Animated Series Book Two: Spirits - Pg. 162 (*Also see DiMartino, Michael Dante. Konietzko, Bryan.*)
2015 - Legend of Korra: The Art of the Animated Series Book Three: Change - Pg. 163 (*Also see DiMartino, Michael Dante. Konietzko, Bryan.*)
2015 - Legend of Korra: The Art of the Animated Series Book Four: Balance - Pg. 163 (*Also see DiMartino, Michael Dante. Konietzko, Bryan.*)

Sarrazin, Stephen

2010 - Manga Impact: The World of Japanese Animation - Pg. 200 (*Also see Brophy, Philip. Chatfield, Carl. Clements, Jonathan. Costa, Jordi. Della Casa, Luca. Delorme, Stéphane. Di Giorgio, Davide. Dottorini, Daniele. Gariglio, Stefano. Gravett, Paul. Higuinen, Erwan. Liberti, Fabrizio. McCarthy, Helen. Modina, Fabrizio. Nazzaro, Giona A. Paganelli, Grazia. Roberta, Maria. Rondolino, Gianni. Roudevitch, Michel. Rumor, Mario A. Surman, David.*)

Sastrawinata-Lemay, Griselda

2019 - Blue Spot: Walt Disney Animation Studios Artist Showcase - Pg. 237

Sattin, Samuel

2022 - Crunchyroll Essential Anime: Fan Favorites, Memorable Masterpieces, and Cult Classics - Pg. 182 (*Also see Macias, Patrick.*)

Sava, Scott Christian

2021 - The Art of Animal Crackers - Pg. 175

Sawicki, Mark

2020 - Filming the Fantastic with Virtual Technology: Filmmaking on the Digital Backlot - Pg. 52 (*See also Moody, Juniko.*)

Saygo, Omar

2021 - Arab Animation: Images of Identity - Pg. 212

Scheimer, Lou

2012 - Lou Scheimer: Creating the Filmation Generation - Pg. 87 (*Also see Mangels, Andy.*)

Schelly, Bill

2017 - John Stanley: Giving Life to Little Lulu - Pg. 90

Schickel, Richard

1968 - The Disney Version: The Life, Times, Art and Commerce of Walt Disney - Pg. 123

Schmitt, Bertrand

2013 - Jan Švankmajer: Dimensions of Dialogue: Between Film and Fine Art - Pg. 216

Schmitz, Jerry

2010 - The Art of Shrek Forever After - Pg. 159
2015 - The Art and Making of The Peanuts Movie - Pg. 176
2016 - The Art of Trolls - Pg. 159

Schneider, Steve

1988 - That's All Folks!: Art of Warner Bros. Animation - Pg. 166

Schnotz, Wolfgang

2007 - Learning with Animation: Research Implications for Design - Pg. 43 (*Also see Lowe, Richard.*)

Schodt, Frederik L.

2007 - The Astro Boy Essays: Osamu Tezuka, Mighty Atom, and the Manga/Anime Revolution - Pg. 190

Schroeder, Russell

1996 - Walt Disney: His Life in Pictures - Pg. 112
1997 - Mickey Mouse: My Life in Pictures - Pg. 235
2007 - Disney's Lost Chords - Pg. 148
2008 - Disney's Lost Chords: Volume Two - Pg. 148

Schultz, Ron

1992 - Looking Inside Cartoon Animation - Pg. 223

Schwartz, Tony

1999 - Work in Progress: Risking Failure, Surviving Success - Pg. 120 (*Also see Eisner, Michael D.*)

Scoggin, Lisa

2016 - The Music of Animaniacs: Postmodern Nostalgia in a Cartoon World - Pg. 76

Scollon, Bill

2004 - Walt Disney: Drawn from Imagination - Pg. 232
2022 - Disney The Lion King: The Full Film Script - Pg. 133 (*Also see Montini, Barbara.*)
2022 - Disney The Little Mermaid: The Full Film Script - Pg. 133 (*Also see Montini, Barbara.*)

Scott, Jameson

1999 - Cartoon Figural Toys – Pg. 25

Scott, Keith

2000 - The Moose That Roared: The Story of Jay Ward, Bill Scott, a Flying Squirrel, and a Talking Moose - Pg. 101

Scott, Orrin

2022 - The Animation History Bibliography - Pg. 17

Seastrom, Lucas

2019 - 2019 Hyperion Historical Society Alliance Annual Report - Pg. 149 (*Also see Apgar, Garry. Bossert, David. Ghez, Didier. Hollifield, Jim. Pierce, Todd James.*)

Seibert, Fred

2005 - Original Cartoons: The Frederator Studio Postcards 1998-2005 - Pg. 164 (*Also see Homan, Eric.*)
2010 - Original Cartoons, Volume 2 : The Frederator Studios Postcards 2006-2010 - Pg. 164 (*Also see Goldman, Michael. Homan, Eric.*)

Seitz, Matt Zoller

2013 - The Wes Anderson Collection - Pg. 101

Selby, Andrew

2009 - Animation in Process - Pg. 45
2013 - Animation - Pg. 231

Selden, Bernice

1989 - The Story of Walt Disney: Maker of Magical Worlds - Pg. 222

Sells, Laura

1995 - From Mouse to Mermaid: The Politics of Film, Gender, and Culture - Pg. 144 (*Also see Bell, Elizabeth. Haas, Lynda.*)

Sennett, Ted

1989 - The Art of Hanna-Barbera: Fifty Years of Creativity - Pg. 169

Sergeant, Alexander

2020 - Fantasy/Animation: Connections Between Media, Mediums and Genres - Pg. 47 (*Also see Holliday, Christopher.*)
2021 - Snow White and the Seven Dwarfs: New Perspectives on Production, Reception, Legacy - Pg. 129 (*Also see Holliday, Christopher.*)

Serwich, Michael

2013 - All in a Day's Work: Animator - Pg. 231 (*Also see Apodaca, Blanca.*)

Shale, Richard

1982 - Donald Duck Joins Up: The Walt Disney Studio During World War II - Pg. 150

Shapurjee, Shanaz

2009 - South African Animation: A Historical Enquiry into the South African Broadcasting Corporation's Animation Unit: 1976-88 - Pg. 221

Shaw, Mel

2016 - Animator on Horseback: The Autobiography of Disney Artist Mel Shaw - Pg. 118

Sherman, Richard

2017 - A Kiss Goodnight - Pg. 236 (*Also see Rubiano, Brittany.*)

Sherman, Richard M.

1998 - Walt's Time - From Before to Beyond - Pg. 113 (*Also see Sherman, Robert B.*)

Sherman, Robert B.

1998 - Walt's Time - From Before to Beyond - Pg. 113 (*Also see Sherman, Richard M.*)

Shinkai, Makoto

2022 - your name. The Official Visual Guide - Pg. 208

Shows, Charles

1980 - Walt: Backstage Adventures With Walt Disney - Pg. 113

Shobeiri, Ali

2020 - Animation and Memory - Pg. 42 (*Also see Gageldonk, Maarten van. Munteán, László.*)

Shue, Ken

2012 - A Disney Sketchbook - Pg. 140

Shull, Michael S.

1987 - Doing Their Bit: Wartime American Animated Short Films, 1939-1945 - Pg. 65 (*Also see Wilt, David E.*)

Shum, Benson

2017 - Holly's Day at the Pool: Walt Disney Animation Studios Artist Showcase - Pg. 236

Sibley, Brian

1998 - Cracking Animation: The Aardman Book of 3-D Animation - Pg. 54 (*Also see Lord, Peter.*)

1998 - Wallace and Gromit - "The Wrong Trousers": Storyboard Collection – Pg. 177
2000 - Chicken Run: Hatching the Movie - Pg. 177
2014 - Weta Digital - Pg. 94
2016 - The Walt Disney Film Archives: The Animated Movies 1921-1968 - Pg. 126 (*Also see Allan, Robin. Ghez, Didier. Kaufman, J. B. Kothenschulte, Daniel. Lasseter, John. Lüthge, Katja. Merritt, Russell. Solomon, Charles.*)

Siciliano, James

2017 - The Art of Rick and Morty - Pg. 172

Sigall, Martha.

2005 - Living Life Inside the Lines: Tales from the Golden Age of Animation - Pg. 90

Silvester, William

2014 - The Adventures of Young Walt Disney - Pg. 113
2015 - Saving Disney: The Story of Roy E. Disney - Pg. 118

Simon, Charnan

1999 - Walt Disney: Creator of Magical Worlds - Pg. 224

Simpson, Paul

2005 - The Art of Wallace & Gromit: The Curse of the Were-Rabbit - Pg. 177 (*Also see Lane, Andy.*)

Sito, Tom

2006 - Drawing the Line: The Untold Story of the Animation Unions from Bosko to Bart Simpson - Pg. 62
2013 - Moving Innovation: A History of Computer Animation - Pg. 53
2019 - On Animation: The Directors Perspective Vol. One - Pg. 77 (*Also see Kroyer, Bill.*)
2019 - On Animation: The Directors Perspective Vol. Two - Pg. 78 (*Also see Kroyer, Bill.*)
2019 - Eat, Drink, Animate: An Animators Cookbook - Pg. 45

Smith, David

1996 - Disney A to Z: The Official Encyclopedia - Pg. 133
1999 - Disney: The First 100 Years - Pg. 149 (*Also see Clark, Steven.*)
2001 - Quotable Walt Disney - Pg. 11.

Smith, Jonathan

1995 - Animation Art: The Early Years, 1911-1954 - Pg. 15 (*See also Lotman, Jeff.*)
1996 - Animation Art: The Later Years, 1954-1993 - Pg. 15 (*See also Lotman, Jeff.*)

Smith, Lella F.

2009 - New Orleans Museum of Art: Dreams Come True - Pg. 141

Smith, Susan

2018 - Toy Story: How Pixar Reinvented the Animated Feature (Animation: Key Films/Filmmakers) - Pg. 151 (*Also see Brown, Noel. Summers, Sam.*)

Smith, Toren

1986 - A Viewer's Guide to Japanese Animation - Pg. 181 (*Also see Graham, Miyako.*)

Smith, Vicky

2018 - Experimental and Expanded Animation: New Perspectives and Practices (Experimental Film and Artists' Moving Image) 2018 Edition - Pg. 57 (*Also see Hamlyn, Nicky.*)

Smoodin, Eric

1993 - Animating Culture: Hollywood Cartoons from the Sound Era - Pg. 68
1994 - Disney Discourse: Producing the Magic Kingdom - Pg. 124
2012 - Snow White and the Seven Dwarfs (BFI Film Classics) - Pg. 133

Sohn, Peter

2015 - The Art of The Good Dinosaur - Pg. 156

Solomon, Charles

1983 - The Complete Kodak Animation Book - Pg. 42 (*Also see Eastman Kodak Company. Stark, Ron.*)
1989 - The History of Animation: Enchanted Drawings - Pg. 65
1995 - The Disney That Never Was: The Stories and Art from Five Decades of Unproduced Animation - Pg. 141
1998 - The Prince of Egypt: A New Vision in Animation - Pg. 159
2008 - Disney Lost and Found: Exploring the Hidden Artwork from Never-Produced Animation - Pg. 141
2010 - Tale as Old as Time: The Art and Making of Beauty and the Beast - Pg. 141
2010 - The Art of Toy Story 3 - Pg. 154
2012 - The Art and Making of Peanuts Animation: Celebrating Fifty Years of Television Specials - Pg. 107
2012 - The Toy Story Films: An Animated Journey - Pg. 153
2013 - The Art of Frozen - Pg. 138
2014 - Once Upon a Dream: From Perrault's Sleeping Beauty to Disney's Maleficent - Pg. 134
2016 - The Walt Disney Film Archives: The Animated Movies 1921-1968 - Pg. 126 (*Also see Allan, Robin. Ghez, Didier. Kaufman, J. B. Kothenschulte, Daniel. Lasseter, John. Lüthge, Katja. Merritt, Russell. Sibley, Brian.*)
2020 - The Art of Wolfwalkers - Pg. 178
2020 - The Disney Princess: A Celebration of Art and Creativity - Pg. 142
2022 - The Man Who Leapt Through Film: The Art of Mamoru Hosoda - Pg. 208

Sony Pictures Animation, Inc.

2011 - The Art & Making of Arthur Christmas: An Inside Look at Behind-the-Scenes Artwork with Filmmaker Commentary - Pg. 177 (*Also see Aardman Animation*)

Sorenson, Jim

2016 - The Art of the Angry Birds Movie - Pg. 175
2019 - Transformers: A Visual History - Pg. 208

Sotheby's

1998 - Sotheby's Guide to Animation Art - Pg. 12 (*Also see Finch, Christopher. Rosenkrantz, Linda.*)

Spain, Steve

2016 - The Art of Disney's 'Golden Age' Films and the Animation Process That Brought The to Life: The Steve Spain Disney Art Collection - Pg. 134

Sperb, Jason

2012 - Disney's Most Notorious Film: Race, Convergence, and the Hidden Histories of Song of the South - Pg. 134

Spiegel, Josh

2015 - Yesterday is Forever: Nostalgia and Pixar Animation Studios - Pg. 153
2018 - Pixar and the Infinite Past: Nostalgia and Pixar Animation - Pg. 153
2018 - Walt's Original Sins: Disney and Racism - Pg. 146

Spilsbury, Richard

2008 - Cartoons and Animation (Art Off the Wall) - Pg. 227

Springer, Justin

2010 - The Art of Tron: Legacy - Pg. 141

Sproxton, David

2018 - Aardman: An Epic Journey: Taken One Frame At A Time - Pg. 54 (*Also see Sproxton, David.*)
2019 - A Grand Success!: The People and Characters Who Created Aardman - Pg. 54 (*Also see Lord, Peter. Park, Nick.*)

Stabile, Carol

2003 - Prime Time Animation: Television Animation and American Culture - Pg. 67 (*Also see Mark, Harrison.*)

Stanchfield, Walt

2009 - Drawn to Life: 20 Golden Years of Disney Master Classes: Volume 1: The Walt Stanchfield Lectures - Pg. 118

2009 - Drawn to Life: 20 Golden Years of Disney Master Classes: Volume 2: The Walt Stanchfield Lectures - Pg. 118

Stanley Kiste, Andrew

2021 - The Early Life of Walt Disney - Pg. 111

Stark, Ron

1983 - The Complete Kodak Animation Book - Pg. 42 (Also see Eastman Kodak Company. Solomon, Charles.)

Starr, Cecile

1976 - Experimental Animation: Origins of a New Art - Pg. 58 (*Also see Russet, Robert.*)

Stathes, Tommy José

2017 - Dreamy Dud: Wallace A. Carlson's Animation Classic - Pg. 96 (*Also see Collier, Kevin Scott.*)

Steiff, Josef

2010 - Anime and Philosophy: Wide Eyed Wonder - Pg. 204 (*Also see Tamplin, Tristan.*)

Steinberg, Marc

2012 - Anime's Media Mix: Franchising Toys and Characters in Japan - Pg. 186

Stephenson, Ralph

1967 - The Animated Film (The International Film Guide Series) - Pg. 17
1967 - Animation in the Cinema - Pg. 54

Stern, Leslie

2012 - Living with a Legend: A Personal Look at Animation Legend Iwao Takamoto, Designer of Scooby-Doo - Pg. 169

Stevenson, Ryan

2018 - The Wes Anderson Collection: Isle of Dogs - Pg. 102

Stewart, James B.

2005 - Disney War - Pg. 124

Stewart, Jez

2021 - The Story of British Animation - Pg. 218

Stewart, Ross

2021 - Designing the Secret of Kells - Pg. 178 (*Also see Moore, Tomm.*)

Stewart, Whitney

2009 - Who Was Walt Disney? - Pg. 228

Stoffman, Daniel

2001 - The Nelvana Story: Thirty Animated Years - Pg. 102

Stover, Chet

2020 - How Underdog Was Born - Pg. 94 (*See also Biggers, Buck.*)

Stratyner, Leslie

2009 - The Deep End of South Park: Critical Essays on Television's Shocking Cartoon Series - Pg. 99 (*Also see Keller, James R.*)

Stobener, Bob

1991 - Cel Magic: The Book on Collecting Animation Art - Pg. 20 (*See also Edwards, R. Scott.*)

Street, Rita

1996 - The Best New Animation Design - Pg. 45

1997 - The Best of New Animation Design 2 - Pg. 45

Struskova, Eva

2014 - The Dodals: Pioneers of Czech Animated Film - Pg. 216

Stuckmann, Chris

2018 - Anime Impact: The Movies and Shows that Changed the World of Japanese Animation - Pg. 184

Studio Colorido

2020 - Penguin Highway Book Set - Pg. 107

Studio Ghibli

2021 - Hayao Miyazaki and the Ghibli Museum - Pg. 198

Stumpf, Charles

2016 - Walter Tetley: For Corn's Sake - Pg. 90 (*Also see Stumpf, Ohart.*)

Stumpf, Ohart

2016 - Walter Tetley: For Corn's Sake - Pg. 90 (*Also see Stumpf, Charles.*)

Su, Jim

2007 - The Art of Reboot - Pg. 104 (*Also see Blair, Gavin. Gibson, Ian. Jackson, Mike. McCarthy, Brendan. Nicholls, Ken. Roberts, David.*)

Suan, Stevie

2013 - The Anime Paradox: Patterns and Practices Through the Lens of Traditional Japanese Theatre - Pg. 203
2021 - Anime's Identity: Performativity and Form Beyond Japan - Pg. 204

Sugar, Rebecca

2019 - The Art of Steven Universe: The Movie - Pg. 170 (*Also see Sands, Ryan.*)

Šuljic, Daniel

2018 - Global Animation Theory: International Perspectives at Animafest Zagreb - Pg. 211 (*Also see Bruckner, Franziska. Gilic, Nikica. Lang, Holger. Turkovic, Hrvoje.*)

Sullivan, Rosana

2019 - Mommy Sayang: Pixar Animation Studios Artist Showcase - Pg. 237

Summers, Sam

2018 - Toy Story: How Pixar Reinvented the Animated Feature (Animation: Key Films/Filmmakers*)* - Pg. 151 (*Also see Brown, Noel. Smith, Susan.*)
2020 - DreamWorks Animation: Intertextuality and Aesthetics in Shrek and Beyond - Pg. 58

Sun, Lijun

2020 - The History of Chinese Animation Volume I - Pg. 215
2020 - The History of Chinese Animation Volume II - Pg. 215

Sundholm, John

2010 - A History of Swedish Experimental Film Culture: From Early Animation to Video Art - Pg. 221 (*Also see Andersson, Lars Gustaf. Widding, Astrid Söderbergh.*)

Sunshine, Linda

2006 - The Art of Open Season - Pg. 173
2009 - The Art of Monsters vs. Aliens - Pg. 159
2011 - The Art and Making of Arthur Christmas - Pg. 177
2014 - The Art of DreamWorks How to Train Your Dragon 2 - Pg. 159
2019 - The Art of How to Train Your Dragon: The Hidden World - Pg. 159

Surman, David

2010 - Manga Impact: The World of Japanese Animation - Pg. 200 (*Also see Brophy, Philip. Chatfield, Carl. Clements, Jonathan. Costa, Jordi. Della Casa, Luca. Delorme, Stéphane. Di Giorgio, Davide. Dottorini, Daniele. Gariglio, Stefano. Gravett, Paul. Higuinen, Erwan. Liberti, Fabrizio. McCarthy, Helen. Modina, Fabrizio. Nazzaro, Giona A. Paganelli, Grazia. Roberta, Maria. Rondolino, Gianni. Roudevitch, Michel. Rumor, Mario A. Sarrazin, Stephen.*)

Susanin, Timothy S.

2011 - Walt Before Mickey: Disney's Early Years, 1919-1928 - Pg. 150

Sussman, Elissa

2021 - Drawn That Way - Pg. 237

Svitil, Torene

2007 - So You Want to Work in Animation & Special Effects? - Pg. 227

Swale, Alistair

2015 - Anime Aesthetics: Japanese Animation and the 'Post-Cinematic' Imagination - Pg. 204

Swanigan, Michael

2014 - Animation by Filmation - Pg. 102

Sweet, Derek R.

2015 - Star Wars in the Public Square: The Clone Wars as Political Dialogue - Pg. 102

Swiss National Research Foundation

1994 - Computer Animation '94: Proceedings: May 25-28, 1994, Geneva, Switzerland - Pg. 36 (*Also see Swiss National Research Foundation.*)
1995 - Computer Animation '95: Proceedings: April 19-21, 1995, Geneva, Switzerland- Pg. 36 (*Also see Computer Graphics Society, Digimedia.*)

Szasz, Ioan

2017 - Awaking Beauty: The Art of Eyvind Earle - Pg. 118

Taberham, Paul

2019 - Experimental Animation: From Analogue to Digital - Pg. 57 (*Also see Harris, Miriam. Husbands, Lilly.*)

Takahata, Isao

2022 - The Art of the Tale of the Princess Kaguya - Pg. 198

Takamoto, Iwao

2009 - Iwao Takamoto: My Life with a Thousand Characters - Pg. 87

Takeda, Yasuhiro

2005 - The Notenki Memoirs: Studio Gainax and the Men Who Created Evangelion - Pg. 190

Tamplin, Tristan

2010 - Anime and Philosophy: Wide Eyed Wonder - Pg. 204 (*Also see Steiff, Josef.*)

Tatsunoko Production

2019 - Samurai Pizza Cats: Official Fan Book - Pg. 208

Tao, Dacheng

2013 - Modern Machine Learning Techniques and Their Applications in Cartoon Animation Research - Pg. 53 (*Also see Yu, Jun.*)

Taylor, Drew

2020 - The Art of Onward - Pg. 156

Taylor, John

1987 - Storming the Magic Kingdom: Wall Street, The Raiders and the Battle for Disney - Pg. 124

Taylor, Richard

1996 - Encyclopedia of Animation Techniques: A Comprehensive, Step-by-Step Directory of Techniques - Pg. 17

Tell, Darcy

2007 - Times Square Spectacular: Lighting Up Broadway - Pg. 62

Telotte, J.P.

2004 - Disney TV – Pg. 125
2008 - The Mouse Machine: Disney and Technology – Pg. 125
2010 - Animating Space: From Mickey to WALL-E - Pg. 134
2017 - Animating the Science Fiction Imagination - Pg. 49

Tembo, Kwasu David

2021 - Genndy Tartakovsky: Sincerity in Animation - Pg. 91

Terzopoulos, Demetri

1995 - Computer Animation and Simulation '95: Proceedings of the Eurographics Workshop in Maastricht, The Netherlands, September 2–3, 1995 - Pg. 37 (*Also see Thalmann Ph. D., Daniel.*)

Tezuka Productions

2003 - Tezuka School of Animation Vol. 1: Learning the Basics - Pg. 184
2003 - Tezuka School of Animation Vol. 2: Animals in Motion - Pg. 184
2016 - The Osamu Tezuka Story: A Life in Manga and Anime - Pg. 239 (*Also see Ban, Toshio.*)

Thalmann Ph. D., Daniel

1985 - Computer Animation: Theory and Practice - Pg. 52 (*Also see Magnenat-Thalmann, Nadia.*)
1989 - State-of-the-Art in Computer Animation: Proceedings of Computer Animation '89 - Pg. 36 (*Also see Magnenat-Thalmann, Nadia.*)
1990 - Computer Animation '90 - Pg. 36 (*Also see Magnenat-Thalmann, Nadia.*)
1990 - Synthetic Actors in Computer-Generated 3D Films - Pg. 38 (*Also see Magnenat-Thalmann, Nadia.*)
1991 - New Trends in Animation and Visualization - Pg. 44 (*Also see Magnenat-Thalmann, Nadia.*)
1991 - Computer Animation '91 - Pg. 36 (*Also see Magnenat-Thalmann, Nadia.*)
1995 - Computer Animation and Simulation '95: Proceedings of the Eurographics Workshop in Maastricht, The Netherlands, September 2–3, 1995 - Pg. 37 (*Also see Terzopoulos, Demetri*)
1997 - Computer Animation and Simulation '97: Proceedings of the Eurographics Workshop in Budapest, Hungary, September 2–3, 1997 - Pg. 37 (*Also see Panne Ph. D., Michiel van de.*)
1999 - Computer Animation and Simulation '99: Proceedings of the Eurographics Workshop in Milano, Italy, September 7–8, 1999 - Pg. 37 (*Also see Magnenat-Thalmann, Nadia.*)
2020 - Computer Animation and Social Agents: 33rd International Conference on Computer Animation and Social Agents, CASA 2020, Bournemouth, UK, October 13-15, 2020, Proceedings - Pg. 38 (*Also see Chang, Jian. Magnenat-Thalmann, Nadia. Tian, Feng. Xu, Weiwei. Yang, Xiaosong. Zhang, Jian Jun.*)

The Museum of Television & Radio

1995 - The World of Hanna-Barbera Cartoons - Pg. 168

Theme Ament, Vanessa

2009 - The Foley Grail: The Art of Performing Sound for Film, Games, and Animation - Pg. 73

Thomas, Bob

1958 - The Art of Animation: The Story of the Disney Studio Contribution to a New Art – Pg. 141
1958 - Walt Disney: The Art of Animation - Pg. 141
1966 - Walt Disney: Magician of the Movies - Pg. 222
1977 - Walt Disney Biography - Pg. 113

1994 - Walt Disney: An American Original (Disney Editions Deluxe) - Pg. 113
1998 - Building a Company: Roy O. Disney and the Creation of an Entertainment Empires - Pg. 125

Thomas, Frank

1981 - The Illusion of Life: Disney Animation - Pg. 130
1987 - Too Funny for Words: Disney's Greatest Sight Gags - Pg. 130 (*Also see Johnston, Ollie.*)
1990 - Walt Disney's Bambi: The Story and the Film - Pg. 138 (*Also see Johnston, Ollie.*)
1993 - The Disney Villain - Pg. 130
1998 - Disney's Lady and the Tramp: The Sketchbook Series - Pg. 137 (*Also see Johnston, Ollie.*)
1998 - Disney's Peter Pan: The Sketchbook Series - Pg. 138 (*Also see Johnston, Ollie.*)

Thomas, Gary

2007 - The Animate! Book - Pg. 20 (*Also see Cook, Benjamin.*)

Thomas, Jolyon Baraka

2012 - Drawing on Tradition: Manga, Anime, and Religion in Contemporary Japan - Pg. 204

Thompson, Frank

1993 - Tim Burton's Nightmare Before Christmas: The Film - The Art - The Vision - Pg. 142

Tian, Feng

2020 - Computer Animation and Social Agents: 33rd International Conference on Computer Animation and Social Agents, CASA 2020, Bournemouth, UK, October 13-15, 2020, Proceedings - Pg. 38 (*Also see Chang, Jian. Magnenat-Thalmann, Nadia. Thalmann Ph. D., Daniel. Xu, Weiwei. Yang, Xiaosong. Zhang, Jian Jun.*)

Tielgekamp, Vicky

2001 – Anime! - Pg. 206 (*Also see Hellige, Hendrik. Hillmen, Jan-Rikus. Klanten, Robert. Meyer, Birga.*)

Tieman, Robert

2003 - The Disney Treasures - Pg. 226

Tobin, Joseph

2004 - Pikachu's Global Adventure: The Rise and Fall of Pokémon - Pg. 212

Torre, Dan

2017 - Animation – Process, Cognition and Actuality - Pg. 45
2018 - Australian Animation: An International History - Pg. 213 (*Also see Torre, Lienors.*)
2021 - Grendel, Grendel, Grendel: Animating Beowulf - Pg. 102 (*Also see Torre, Lienors.*)

Torre, Lienors

2018 - Australian Animation: An International History - Pg. 213 (*Also see Torre, Dan.*)
2021 - Grendel, Grendel, Grendel: Animating Beowulf - Pg. 102 (*Also see Torre, Dan.*)

Tourville, Jacqueline

2017 - Pocket Full of Colors: The Magical World of Mary Blair, Disney Artist Extraordinaire - Pg. 236 (*Also see Guglielmo, Amy.*)

Treeheart, Eric

2020 - The Medium-Sized Book of Zem Scripts Vol. 1: Pigs 'n' Waffles: The Stories and the Stories Behind the Stories of Your Favorite Invader - Pg. 161

Tumbusch, Thomas E.

1998 - Tomart's Value Guide to Disney Animation Art: An Easy-to-use Compilation of Over 40 Animation Art Auctions Organized by Film, Character and Art Type - Pg. 181 (*Also see Welbaum, Bob.*)

Tunesi, Sabrina

2000 - Anime: A Guide to Japanese Animation - Pg. 180 (*Also see Baricordi, Andrea. De Giovanni, Massimiliano. Pietroni, Andrea. Rossi, Barbara.*)

Turner, Chris

2004 - Planet Simpson: How a Cartoon Masterpiece Documented an Era and Defined a Generation – Pg. 102

Turner, Pamela Taylor

2019 - Infinite Animation: The Life and Work of Adam Beckett - Pg. 91

Turney, Harold Merrill

1940 - Film Guide's Handbook: Cartoon Production - Pg. 205

Turkovic, Hrvoje

2018 - Global Animation Theory: International Perspectives at Animafest Zagreb - Pg. 211 (*Also see Bruckner, Franziska. Gilic, Nikica. Lang, Holger. Šuljic, Daniel.*)

Tytle, Harry

1997 - One of "Walt's Boys": An Insider's Account of Disney's Golden Years - Pg. 118

UDON

2021 - Robotech Visual Archive: The Southern Cross - Pg. 209
2021 - Robotech Visual Archive: Genesis Climber MOSPEADA - Pg. 208

Uhrig, Meike

2018 - Emotion in Animated Films - Pg. 45

Valinoti, Jr., Raymond

2020 - Hanna-Barbera's Prime Time Cartoons - Pg. 169

Valliere, Richard Auzenne

1994 - The Visualization Quest: A History Of Computer Animation - Pg. 53

Van de Peer, Stefanie

2017 - Animation in the Middle East: Practice and Aesthetics from Baghdad to Casablanca - Pg. 219

Van Lente, Fred

2021 - The Comic Book History of Animation: True Toon Tales of the Most Iconic Characters, Artists and Styles! - Pg. 240 (*Also see Dunlavey, Ryan.*)

Van Riper, A. Bowdoin

2011 - Learning from Mickey, Donald and Walt: Essays on Disney's Edutainment Films - Pg. 134

Vaz, Mark Cotta

2003 - The Art of Finding Nemo - Pg. 156
2004 - The Art of The Incredibles - Pg. 156
2008 - The Art of Bolt - Pg. 142

Vescia, Monique

2008 - Virtual Apprentice: Cartoon Animator - Pg. 228 (*Also see Rauf, Don.*)

Vince, John

2000 - Essential Computer Animation Fast: How to Understand the Techniques and Potential of Computer Animation - Pg. 53

Vincent, J. Keith

2002 - Walt Disney's Missouri: The Roots of a Creative Genius - Pg. 108 (Also see Burnes, Brian; Butler, Robert W.)
2011 - Beautiful Fighting Girl - Pg. 199 (*Also see Azuma, Hiroki. Lawson, Dawn. Saitō, Tamaki.*)

Vischer, Phil

2007 - Me, Myself & Bob: A True Story About God, Dreams, and Talking Vegetables - Pg. 91

Viska, Peter

1993 - The Animation Book - Pg. 223

VIZ Media

2003 - The Best Of Animerica: 2003 Edition - Pg. 245

Waguespack, Jason

2017 - Rise and Fall of the 80's Toon Empire: A Behind the Scenes Look at When He-Man, G.I. Joe and Transformers Ruled the Airwaves - Pg. 62

Waite, Mitchell

1984 - Computer Animation Primer - Pg. 50 (*Also see Fox, David.*)

Wakabayashi, Hiro Clark

2002 - Lilo & Stitch: Collected Stories from the Film's Creators - Pg. 134
2003 - Brother Bear: A Transformation Tale - Pg. 142

Wallace, Daniel

2019 - The World of RWBY - Pg. 103
2020 - The Art of Star Wars Rebels - Pg. 142
2021 - The Art of gen:Lock - Pg. 107

Wallis, Michael

2006 - The Art of Cars - Pg. 155 (*Also see Fitgerald Wallis, Suzanne.*)

Wallis, Suzanne Fitgerald

2006 - The Art of Cars - Pg. 156 (*Also see Wallis, Michael.*)

Walsh, John

2019 - Harryhausen: The Lost Movies - Pg. 103

Walt Disney Animation Research Library

2008 – The Archive Series: Story - Pg. 143
2009 - The Archive Series: Animation - Pg. 142
2010 - The Archive Series: Design - Pg. 143
2011 - The Archive Series: Layout & Background - Pg. 142

Walt Disney Company Ltd.

2009 - Disney's Neglected Prince: The Art of Disney's Knights in Shining Armor (and Loincloth) - Pg. 143
2005 - Read About Walt Disney - Pg. 224 (*Also see Feinstein, Stephen.*)
2010 - Pixar: 25 Years Of Animation - Pg. 153
2014 - Marc Davis: Walt Disney's Renaissance Man - Pg. 118
2021 - Pixar Museum: Stories and Art from the Animation Studio - Pg. 154 (*Also see Beecroft, Simon.*)

The Walt Disney Family Museum

2016 - Disney & Dali: Architects of the Imagination - Pg. 113
2021 - The Walt Disney Studios and WWII - Pg. 150

Walters, Helen

2004 - Animation Unlimited: Innovative Short Films Since 1940 - Pg. 12 (*Also see Faber, Liz.*)

Walz, Gene

2001 - Cartoon Charlie: The Life and Art of Animation Pioneer Charles Thorson - Pg. 91

Ward, Annalee

2002 - Mouse Morality: The Rhetoric of Disney Animated Films - Pg. 134

Ward, Jessica

2018 - The Art of Walt Disney's Mickey Mouse - Pg. 137

Ward, Paul

2019 - The Crafty Animator: Handmade, Craft-based Animation and Cultural Value – Pg. 25 (*See also Ruddell, Caroline.*)

Ward, Pendleton

2014 - Adventure Time: The Art of Ooo - Pg. 170
2014 - Adventure Time: The Original Title Cards (Vol 1) The Original Cartoon Title Cards Season 1 & 2 - Pg. 170
2014 - Adventure Time: The Original Title Cards (Vol 2) The Original Cartoon Title Cards Season 3 & 4 - Pg. 171

Wasko, Janet

2001 - Dazzled by Disney? The Global Disney Audiences Project - Pg. 123 (*Also see Meehan, Eileen R. and Phillips, Mark.*)
2001 - Understanding Disney: The Manufacture of Fantasy - Pg. 125

Watts, Steven

1998 - The Magic Kingdom: Walt Disney and the American Way of Life - Pg. 146

Webb, Graham

2000 - The Animated Film Encyclopedia: A Complete Guide to American Shorts, Features and Sequences, 1900-1999 - Pg. 18

Webber, Marilyn

2000 - Gardner's Guide to Animation Scriptwriting: The Writer's Road Map - Pg. 25

Webber, Roy

2004 - The Dinosaur Films of Ray Harryhausen: Features, Early 16mm Experiments and Unrealized Projects - Pg. 103

Weber, David

1994 - Animation: The Art of Friz Freleng - Pg. 84 (*Also see Freleng, Friz.*)

Weinberg, Robert

2005 - The Science of Anime: Mecha-Noids and AI-Super-Bots - Pg. 224 (*Also see Gresh, Lois H.*)

Weinman, Jaime

2021 - Anvils, Mallets & Dynamite: The Unauthorized Biography of Looney Tunes - Pg. 167

Weinstock, Neal

1986 – Computer Animation – Pg. 53

Weishar, Peter

2002 - Blue Sky: The Art of Computer Animation - Pg. 176

Welbaum, Bob

1998 - Tomart's Value Guide to Disney Animation Art: An Easy-to-use Compilation of Over 40 Animation Art Auctions Organized by Film, Character and Art Type - Pg. 18 (*See also Tumbusch, Thomas E.*)

Wells, Paul

1997 - Art and Animation - Pg. 87
1998 - Understanding Animation - Pg. 46

2002 - Animation and America - Pg. 67
2002 - Animation: Genre and Authorship - Pg. 49
2006 - Fundamentals of Animation - Pg. 25
2007 - Halas & Batchelor Cartoons - Pg. 217 (*Also see Halas, Vivien.*)
2007 - Basics Animation 01: Scriptwriting - Pg. 25
2008 - Basics Animation 03: Drawing for Animation - Pg. 25
2008 - The Animated Bestiary: Animals, Cartoons, and Culture - Pg. 68
2008 - Re-imagining Animation: The Changing Face of the Moving Image - Pg. 41
2014 - Animation, Sport and Culture - Pg. 69
2016 - The Fundamentals of Animation - Pg. 25 (*Also see Moore, Samantha.*)
2022 - Screenwriting For Animation - Pg. 26

Wentzel, Jim

2006 - Cool Careers Without College for People Who Love Manga, Comics, and Animation - Pg. 225 (*Also see Glass, Sherri.*)

Wechsler, Jeffrey

1991 - Krátký Film: The Art of Czechoslovak Animation - Pg. 216 (*Also see Beckerman, Howard. Poš, Jan.*)

West, Mark I.

2008 - The Japanification of Children's Popular Culture: From Godzilla to Miyazaki - Pg. 205
2014 - Walt Disney, from Reader to Storyteller: Essays on the Literary Inspirations - Pg. 129 (*Also see Jackson, Kathy Merlock.*)

Weta Workshop

2011 - The Art of the Adventures of Tintin - Pg. 107

Whaley, Deborah Elizabeth

2015 - Black Women in Sequence: Re-Inking Comics, Graphic Novels, and Anime - Pg. 187

Whitaker, Harold

1981 - Timing for Animation - Pg. 77 (*Also see Halas, John.*)

White, Mark Andrew

2011 - A Century Of Magic: The Animation Of The Walt Disney Studio – Pg. 143

White, Tony

2009 - How to Make Animated Films: Tony White's Complete Masterclass on the Traditional Principles of Animation - Pg. 26

Whitehead, Mark

2004 - Animation - Pg. 46

Whitley, David

2008 - The Idea of Nature in Disney Animation (Studies in Childhood, 1700 to the Present) - Pg. 135

Whybray, Adam

2020 - The Art of Czech Animation: A History of Political Dissent and Allegory - Pg. 216

Widding, Astrid Söderbergh

2010 - A History of Swedish Experimental Film Culture: From Early Animation to Video Art - Pg. 221 (*Also see Andersson, Lars Gustaf. Sundholm, John.*)

Wiedemann, Julius

2007 - Animation Now! - Pg. 212

Wiegmann, Karlheinz

2012 - Lotte Reiniger: Born With Enchanting Hands: Three Silhouette Sequels - Pg. 104 (*Also see Blattner, Evamarie. Reiniger, Lotte.*)

Wilcox, Janet

2007 - Voiceovers: Techniques and Tactics for Success - Pg. 76

Williams, Don

2013 - The Book of Mouse: A Celebration of Walt Disney's Mickey Mouse - Pg. 132 (*Also see Korkis, Jim.*)

Williams, Richard

2000 - The Animator's Survival Kit - Pg. 26

Willis, John

2020 - CGI Artists - Pg. 234 (*Also see Owen, Ruth.*)

Wilson, Rowland B.

2012 - Rowland B. Wilson's Trade Secrets: Notes on Cartooning and Animation - Pg. 91 (*Also see Lemieux Wilson, Suzanne.*)

Wilson, S. S.

1980 - Puppets and People: Dimensional Animation Combined with Live Action in the Cinema - Pg. 55

Wilt, David E.

1987 - Doing Their Bit: Wartime American Animated Short Films, 1939-1945 - Pg. 65 (*Also see Shull, Michael S.*)

Witowski, Linda

1994 - Walt Disney's Snow White and the Seven Dwarfs: An Art in Its Making - Pg. 129 (*Also see Ison, Stephen H.. Krause, Martin.*)

Wizig, Enid Denbo

2018 - I Never Asked, Why Me? - Pg. 91

Wolfgram Evans, Noell K.

2011 - Animators of Film and Television: Nineteen Artists, Writers, Producers and Others - Pg. 84

Wonderstorm

2020 - The Art of the Dragon Prince - Pg. 175 (*Also see Ehasz, Aaron. Richmond, Justin.*)

Wong, Heung-wah

2021 - Japanese Animation in Asia: Transnational Industry, Audiences, and Success - Pg. 186 (*Also see Pellitteri, Marco.*)

Wooden, Shannon R.

2014 - Pixar's Boy Stories: Masculinity in a Postmodern Age - Pg. 151 (*Also see Gillam, Ken.*)

Woods, Samuel G.

2000 - Made in the USA - Computer Animation - Pg. 225

Woog, Adam

2008 - John Lasseter: Pixar Animator - Pg. 228

Wrightson, Bernie

2017 - Bernie Wrightson: Art And Designs For The Gang Of Seven Animation Studio - Pg. 107

Wright, Jean Ann

2009 - Voice-Over for Animation - Pg. 75 (*Also see Lallo, M.J.*)

Wu, Mike

2018 - Henri's Hats: Pixar Animation Studios Artist Showcase - Pg. 236

Wu, Weihua

2017 - Chinese Animation, Creative Industries and Digital Culture - Pg. 215

Xu, Weiwei

2020 - Computer Animation and Social Agents: 33rd International Conference on Computer Animation and Social Agents, CASA 2020, Bournemouth, UK, October 13-15, 2020, Proceedings - Pg. 38 (*Also see Chang, Jian. Magnenat-Thalmann, Nadia. Thalmann Ph. D., Daniel. Tian, Feng. Yang, Xiaosong. Zhang, Jian Jun.*)

Yang, Xiaosong

2020 - Computer Animation and Social Agents: 33rd International Conference on Computer Animation and Social Agents, CASA 2020, Bournemouth, UK, October 13-15, 2020, Proceedings - Pg. 38 (*Also see Chang, Jian. Magnenat-Thalmann, Nadia. Thalmann Ph. D., Daniel. Tian, Feng. Xu, Weiwei. Zhang, Jian Jun.*)

Yokota, Masao

2013 - Japanese Animation: East Asian Perspectives - Pg. 205
2020 - Animating the Spirited: Journeys and Transformations - Pg. 71 (*Also see Horvath, Gyongyi. Hu, Tze-yue.*)

Yonebayashi, Hiromasa

2012 - The Art of The Secret World of Arrietty - Pg. 198

Young Filmakers Foundation

1973 - Young Animators And Their Discoveries: A Report From Young Filmakers Foundation - Pg. 222

Yu, Jun

2013 - Modern Machine Learning Techniques and Their Applications in Cartoon Animation Research - Pg. 53 (*Also see Tao, Dacheng.*)

Yune, Tommy

2007 - The Art of Robotech: The Shadow Chronicles - Pg. 209

Zahed, Ramin

2011 - The Art of DreamWorks Puss in Boots - Pg. 160
2012 - The Art of DreamWorks Rise of the Guardians - Pg. 160
2014 - The Art of DreamWorks Animation: Celebrating 20 Years of Art - Pg. 160
2015 - The Art of Home - Pg. 160
2016 - The Art of The Iron Giant - Pg. 167
2016 - The Little Prince: The Art of the Movie - Pg. 107
2017 - The Art of The Boss Baby - Pg. 159
2017 - The Art of Captain Underpants: The First Epic Movie - Pg. 159
2018 - Spider-Man: Into the Spider-Verse - The Art of the Movie - Pg. 173
2019 - Klaus: Art of the Movie - Pg. 175
2019 - The Art of Missing Link - Pg. 179
2019 - The Art of The Addams Family - Pg. 175
2021 - The Art of The Mitchells vs. The Machines - Pg. 173
2021 - The Art of VIVO - Pg. 174

Zhang, Jian Jun

2020 - Computer Animation and Social Agents: 33rd International Conference on Computer Animation and Social Agents, CASA 2020, Bournemouth, UK, October 13-15, 2020, Proceedings - Pg. 279 (*Also see Chang, Jian. Magnenat-Thalmann, Nadia. Thalmann Ph. D., Daniel. Tian, Feng. Xu, Weiwei. Yang, Xiaosong.*)

Zhou, Wenhai

2020 - Chinese Independent Animation: Renegotiating Identity in Modern China - Pg. 215

Zipes, Jack

2010 - The Enchanted Screen: The Unknown History of Fairy-Tale Films - Pg. 103